PLAYS AND PLAYWRIGHTS

2011

edited and with an introduction by

Martin Denton

This collection copyright © 2011 by The New York Theatre Experience, Inc.

Introduction copyright © 2011 by Martin Denton

All rights reserved. Except for brief passages quoted in newspaper, magazine, radio, or television reviews, no part of this book may be reproduced in any form or by any means, electronic or mechanical, including photocopying or recording, or by any information storage and retrieval system, without permission in writing from the publisher.

CAUTION: These plays are fully protected, in whole, in part, or in any form, under the copyright laws of the United States of America and of all countries covered by the International Copyright Union (including the Dominion of Canada and the rest of the British Commonwealth), and of all countries covered by the Pan-American Copyright Convention and the Universal Copyright Convention, and of all countries with which the United States has reciprocal copyright relations, and are subject to royalty. All performance rights, including professional, amateur, stock, motion picture, radio, television, recitation, and public reading are strictly reserved. Please refer to Permissions, beginning on page i, for information concerning such inquiries.

Published by The New York Theatre Experience, Inc.
P.O. Box 1606, Murray Hill Station, New York, NY 10156
www.nyte.org
email: info@nyte.org

ISBN-13: 978-0-9794852-5-1
ISSN 1546-1319

 *Plays and Playwrights 2011* is made possible, in part, with public funds from the New York State Council on the Arts, a state agency.

Plays and Playwrights 2011 is made possible, in part, with public funds from the New York City Department of Cultural Affairs.

Book and cover designed by Nita Congress

PERMISSIONS

Fault Lines copyright © 2009 by Rebecca Louise Miller. Amateurs and professionals are hereby warned that *Fault Lines* is fully protected by copyright law and is subject to royalty. All rights in all current and future media are strictly reserved. No part of this work may be used for any purpose without the written consent of the author. All inquiries concerning production, publication, reprinting, or use of this work in any form should be addressed to the author in care of The New York Theatre Experience, Inc., P.O. Box 1606, Murray Hill Station, New York, NY 10156; by email: rebeccalou@gmail.com.

Post Modern Living copyright © 2011 by Richard Sheinmel and Clay Zambo. Amateurs and professionals are hereby warned that *Post Modern Living* is fully protected by copyright law and is subject to royalty. All rights in all current and future media are strictly reserved. No part of this work may be used for any purpose without the written consent of the author. All inquiries concerning production, publication, reprinting, or use of this work in any form should be addressed to the author in care of The New York Theatre Experience, Inc., P.O. Box 1606, Murray Hill Station, New York, NY 10156; or by email: info.sheinmel@gmail.com.

G.I. Joe Jared, Based on One Really Bad Date copyright © 2010 by Amy E. Witting. Amateurs and professionals are hereby warned that *G.I. Joe Jared, Based on One Really Bad Date* is fully protected by copyright law and is subject to royalty. All rights in all current and future media are strictly reserved. No part of this work may be used for any purpose without the written consent of the author. All inquiries concerning production, publication, reprinting, or use of this work in any form should be addressed to the author in care of The New York Theatre Experience, Inc., P.O. Box 1606, Murray Hill Station, New York, NY 10156; by email: info@nyte.org.

Love Me copyright © 2009 by Jason S. Grossman. Amateurs and professionals are hereby warned that *Love Me* is fully protected by copyright law and is subject to royalty. All rights in all current and future media are strictly reserved. No part of this work may be used for any purpose without the written consent of the author. All inquiries concerning production, publication, reprinting, or use of this work in any form should be addressed to the author in care of The New York Theatre Experience, Inc., P.O. Box 1606, Murray Hill Station, New York, NY 10156; by email: info@nyte.org; or contact the writer directly at funnysheesh@verizon.net.

Hassan and Sylvia copyright © 2010 by Manuel Igrejas. Amateurs and professionals are hereby warned that *Hassan and Sylvia* is fully protected by copyright law and is subject to royalty. All rights in all current and future media are strictly reserved. No part of this work may be used for any purpose without the written consent of the author. All inquiries concerning production, publication, reprinting, or use of this work in any form should be addressed to the author in care of The New York Theatre Experience, Inc., P.O. Box 1606, Murray Hill Station, New York, NY 10156; by email: info@nyte.org.

FLORIDITA, my Love copyright © 2010 by Javierantonio González. Amateurs and professionals are hereby warned that *FLORIDITA, my Love* is fully protected by copyright law and is subject to royalty. All rights in all current and future media are strictly reserved. No part of this work may be used for any purpose without the written consent of the author. All inquiries concerning production, publication, reprinting, or use of this work in any form should be addressed to the author in care of The New York Theatre Experience, Inc., P.O. Box 1606, Murray Hill Station, New York, NY 10156; by email: info@nyte.org.

West Lethargy copyright © 2010 by Stephen Kaliski. Amateurs and professionals are hereby warned that *West Lethargy* is fully protected by copyright law and is subject to royalty. All rights in all current and future media are strictly reserved. No part of this work may be used for any purpose without the written consent of the author. All inquiries concerning production, publication, reprinting, or use of this work in any form should be addressed to the author in care of The New York Theatre Experience, Inc., P.O. Box 1606, Murray Hill Station, New York, NY 10156; by email: info@nyte.org.

Endless Summer Nights copyright © 2010 by Tim Errickson. Amateurs and professionals are hereby warned that *Endless Summer Nights* is fully protected by copyright law and is subject to royalty.

All rights in all current and future media are strictly reserved. No part of this work may be used for any purpose without the written consent of the author. All inquiries concerning production, publication, reprinting, or use of this work in any form should be addressed to the author in care of The New York Theatre Experience, Inc., P.O. Box 1606, Murray Hill Station, New York, NY 10156; by email: info@nyte.org.

TABLE OF CONTENTS

PERMISSIONS i

FOREWORD vii
    Kelly McAllister

ACKNOWLEDGMENTS ix

INTRODUCTION 1
    Martin Denton

FAULT LINES 7
    Rebecca Louise Miller

POST MODERN LIVING 37
    Book by Richard Sheinmel
    Music and Lyrics by Clay Zambo

G.I. JOE JARED, BASED ON ONE REALLY
BAD DATE 69
    Amy E. Witting

LOVE ME 95
    Jason S. Grossman

HASSAN AND SYLVIA 149
    Manuel Igrejas

FLORIDITA, MY LOVE.. 179
    Javierantonio González

WEST LETHARGY 215
    Stephen Kaliski

ENDLESS SUMMER NIGHTS 247
    Tim Errickson

FOREWORD

Kelly McAllister

You have in your hand something rare and wonderful—an intensely magic book of theatrical spells; a collection of recipes for meals of the mind; an unfinished poem on the possibilities of art. You are holding a year's worth of searching the very best indie theater that New York City has to offer, put together by one of the most stalwart and amazing advocates of theatre there has ever been.

You are holding *Plays and Playwrights 2011*, and I guarantee it kicks ass.

Let me put it this way—the Theatre is dead! Long live the Theatre! The wicked stage is constantly pronounced dead, and always being reborn. One of its main resuscitators is Martin Denton. For over a decade, he's championed indie theater in New York City with his indispensable website, nytheatre.com, and with the yearly anthology *Plays and Playwrights*. It is impossible to figure how many careers he's helped—the number is in the tens of thousands, at a bare minimum.

New York is one of the few places in the world where you can see a different play every day of the year, with no repeats, and in as many different styles and spaces as you can imagine. Want to see Shakespeare in a parking lot? No problem. A multimedia event about the life of a flower? Got it. And new plays? Oh yes indeedy. New York has those in abundance. Gotham is a mecca for aspiring theatre artists from around the world. It is the playwrights' great laboratory. Sure, there are plenty of stinkers. But there are also moments of genius, flashes of brilliance that dazzle the mind, shake the soul, and stay with the audience for the rest of their lives.

How does one find these diamonds in the ruff, these as yet undiscovered masters of the stage? Simple—nytheatre.com, the website founded and run by Martin. Every week, he and his staff see twenty or more shows, most of them indie theater presented by groups like the Boomerang Theatre Company, La MaMa E.T.C., Horse Trade Theatre Group, and more, at such venues as Metropolitan Playhouse, Manhattan Repertory Theatre, and The Brick. He posts reviews that are thoughtful, well written, and widely read by the theatre-going public. His efforts are perhaps best exemplified by nytheatre.com's yearly coverage of the New York International Fringe Festival, in which he and his intrepid staff review around two hundred shows in about two weeks—a truly Herculean feat. These reviews can be vital to the life of a show in the indie theater world. I know this from first-hand experience.

My first play, *Last Call*, was selected for FringeNYC in the summer of 2002, and Martin reviewed its first performance. When the review (thankfully positive) came out, the reaction was instantaneous and life changing. The shows began to sell out. We added a performance. People I had never met contacted me, and my life as a playwright took a huge step forward. Then, while I was still floating on air from that experience, he asked me if my play could be included in the 2003 edition of *Plays and Playwrights*. And my head exploded.

Each year, Martin takes several of the best new plays he's seen, and publishes them in an anthology—that's right, like the one you are holding right now. These writers are among the best the indie theater scene has to offer; most will go on to have long, exciting careers. Many writers in past editions have been produced all over the world and featured online, on television, and on screen. You could very well be holding the first publication of a future Pulitzer winner. I do not exaggerate.

So, here's my advice to you, fellow traveler and lover of theatre. Read nytheatre.com on a daily basis. Go to as many plays as you can. Read the playwrights contained in this anthology. Remember their names. And lastly, thank the Theatre Gods for Martin and Rochelle Denton.

Enjoy.

> *Kelly McAllister is a playwright/actor/director. His plays include* Last Call *(2002 Excellence in Playwriting FringeNYC),* Burning the Old Man *(2005 Outstanding Full Length Script NYIT),* Hela and Troy *(Finalist 2011 Heideman Award),* Fenway: Last of the Bohemians, Some Unfortunate Hour, The Morons, *and* Muse of Fire. *In 2003, he was named Graduate of the Last Decade by San Jose State University. You can read his blog at rkmcallister.blogspot.com.*

ACKNOWLEDGMENTS

One of my favorite tasks in creating the *Plays and Playwrights* anthology each year is to reflect back on the many generous people who have played a role in making it possible. I am so grateful to them for their contributions to NYTE Small Press and to the world of indie theater.

Nita Congress, who copy edits and designs our books every year, ensures that we present our plays beautifully and accurately. She's the best editor I know and makes everything about this project easy and pleasurable.

Rochelle Denton, NYTE's Managing Director, does all the behind-the-scenes stuff that makes publication of these volumes possible. During the past year, she has taken the lead in moving NYTE Small Press into the world of electronic publishing, which is a significant and exciting new venture that will bring the plays we've collected over the years to a broader audience than ever before.

Our major government funders, the New York State Council on the Arts and the New York City Department of Cultural Affairs, provide necessary support for our work in recognizing and promoting the remarkable foundational art that we highlight in these anthologies. We are very grateful to them for that. And the software grants we have received from Microsoft Corporation have been invaluable to our development of the technological infrastructure we need to bring our books online.

A very warm thank you to the friends and colleagues who helped me find the plays in this book and introduced me to the playwrights: David Epstein, Ron Lasko, Jason Jacobs, Michael Baron, Bev Petty and all our friends at La MaMa E.T.C., Ken Wolf and Jennifer Pierro at Manhattan Repertory Theatre, Chris Harcum, Amber Gallery, Glory Kadigan and the Planet Connections Theatre

Festivity staff, Sharon Fogarty, David Hilder, Carol Polcovar and the folks at the Fresh Fruit Festival, Winston Estevez and Teatro IATI, Elena K. Holy of the New York International Fringe Festival, Michael Criscuolo, Joe Trentacosta, and Kelly McAllister.

And of course there would be no book at all without the plays themselves. I am indebted to all nine of the 2011 playwrights for entrusting their work to me: Rebecca Louise Miller, Richard Sheinmel, Clay Zambo, Amy E. Witting, Jason S. Grossman, Manuel Igrejas, Javierantonio González, Stephen Kaliski, and Tim Errickson.

Finally, a brief but heartfelt thanks to years of comradeship and support from Daniel Talbott, Addie Johnson, Denis Butkus, Sam Soule, and Julie Kline, who together comprise the core of Rising Phoenix Repertory Theatre. Whether it was Sam setting out snacks at one of our book launch events or Denis and Daniel doing some impromptu lighting and stage direction, these dedicated colleagues never shrink from doing whatever it takes to help NYTE and the indie theater community. This book is dedicated to them. (Thanks, D, A and da B!)

Martin Denton
March 2011

INTRODUCTION

Martin Denton

When NYTE's first anthology, *Plays and Playwrights for the New Millennium*, was published back in 2000, few collections of new American plays were available. *The Best Plays of 1999–2000* lists only four: fewer than twenty-five full-length plays anthologized out of the hundreds written and produced that season!

Plays and Playwrights for the New Millennium featured eight plays by nine playwrights, none of whom had ever been published before, and none of whom had ever had any significant success beyond the NYC indie theater world. The purpose of the book was to introduce new work and new artists to the greater theatre community outside New York; to broaden the canon by exposing new audiences to new drama, and vice versa. I'm very proud of the fact that we achieved this goal—that within a few years, works published in our first anthology had been produced in London, Edinburgh, Australia, San Francisco, Boston, and other cities and countries; that the book was used as a text for a number of college courses at U.S. universities; and that many of the playwrights involved received, for the very first time in their careers, payments and royalties for their artistic output.

Because *Plays and Playwrights for the New Millennium* was a success, we've followed it up with a new anthology every year since. The one you are reading right now is Number Twelve in a series that has become, if I may be permitted a moment of boastfulness, one of the standard sources for contemporary American drama. There are more than 150 *Plays and Playwrights* alumni now, almost all of them still active contributors to the theatrical community. Two of them turned their plays into successful indie films, and one of them (Josh Fox, *Plays and Playwrights 2006*) was an Academy Award nominee this past year for a documentary he wrote and directed. Many of them have made careers as professors at colleges and universities while continuing to write new plays. Our playwrights' works—either the ones included in our books, or others—have won prizes, received productions at regional theatres, toured to countries on six continents, and served as sources for new monologues and scenes used by countless actors at competitions and auditions. We have, in short, shared with the world scores of emerging playwrights whose work we discovered and admired, and the world has embraced them. Most gratifying.

Our mission is to find the playwrights who have the courage and talent to develop their own individual artistic voices and use them to tell stories loaded with insight, intelligence, compassion, and humanity. I think you will find evidence of all of this as you read the eight plays collected here.

✒ ✒ ✒ ✒ ✒

Fault Lines, by Rebecca Louise Miller, is a very wise and mature play about a reunion of three women who, many years before, shared a painful experience that irrevocably changed all of their lives. One of the themes running through this drama is the very modern problem of appropriation of a personal incident by some larger cause or political movement, or by the media; the question becomes, whose story is this to tell? But an even larger idea in *Fault Lines*, I think, is whether there can ever be a correct answer to such a question. Each of us sees the moments in our lives, big or small, in our own way, and we have to resolve the problems and crises that we face in our own hearts and minds.

Post Modern Living is a program of two linked plays by Richard Sheinmel, with songs by Clay Zambo. They focus on a downtown performance artist named Mitch who writes shows about his life; the two that comprise *Post Modern Living* depict an after-Christmas celebration with friends and Mitch's mom's recent discovery that she has breast cancer. They're witty, impressionistic, jaunty vignettes that are humane and, above all, life affirming. Zambo's songs add to the joyfulness of the show, bringing zest and rhythm and creating a form that, as I said in my original review of the show, stands in stark and happy contrast to the formulaic bombast of too many mainstream musicals.

Amy E. Witting's comedy *G.I. Joe Jared, Based on One Really Bad Date*, is about friendship and trust, in particular the relationship between two young women who have known each other forever but have, in some ways, let their individual relationships with men pull them apart. They meet in a Manhattan pub and together encounter the Jared of the play's title, whom one of them has befriended online. In ways he neither expects or probably understands, Jared brings the two back together. This is, by the way, a very funny comedy. Tarot cards are involved.

Love Me is Jason S. Grossman's sweet and utterly heartfelt tale of a guy in search of a soul mate. Grossman, who is a talented improv performer as well as a playwright, gives us characters and vignettes here that are laugh-out-loud hilarious, but he never sacrifices the reality of his plot or the integrity of his themes. Instead, he gives us the kind of touching and tender romantic comedy we long for but seldom actually get to see. I sense a movie sale in *Love Me*'s future.

Manuel Igrejas's *Hassan and Sylvia* starts out with its gay thirty-something hero despondent over his eviction from the home he shared with his now-deceased lover; we assume right away that this is going to be a political play about the fight for gay civil rights. But then Igrejas switches gears, and suddenly his protagonist finds himself involved with a mysterious, glamorous pair (the play's title characters), who feel like characters from a Douglas Carter Beane play or a Patrick Dennis novel. But wait: the author has one more surprise for us. *Hassan and Sylvia* uncovers uncomfortable truths about the ways that all of us bargain for the things we think we need.

Javierantonio González, author of *FLORIDITA, my Love*, told me that he doesn't like to use the term "magic realism" to describe his work. But it is indeed very magical and very real at the same time: this play, an exploration of the life of one of America's invisible people (a possibly illegal immigrant from Latin America working as a waitress in a diner), unfolds in a world where coffee makers materialize out of subway trash cans and the lady at the next table might just possibly be the spirit of a sainted poet who died more than three hundred years ago. Everything in this play is at once visceral and vague, in the same way that our experiences with each other ultimately must be.

Stephen Kaliski's *West Lethargy* is similarly surreal, playing fast and loose with time by juxtaposing two very different couples—one a pair of pioneers heading toward California in what appears to be the nineteenth century, the other a contemporary husband and wife in search of her brother and, not at all incidentally, a place to settle down, also in some mythic "West"—in a pair of neighboring cabins in the middle of the American Heartland. Rich and carefully crafted, and full of incisive details and delightful conceits, *West*

Lethargy challenges conventional dramaturgical ideas with poetic and brave imagination.

Completing this collection is *Endless Summer Nights*, by Tim Errickson. Set in a beach town in southern New Jersey, this very adult romantic dramedy tells the story of Sam and Tracy. Twenty years ago, they were young and in love on this very beach. They haven't seen each other again…until now, when, on the very day that Sam is planning to finally leave town forever, Tracy stumbles upon him during a rare visit home. The play makes us wonder whether it's possible to pick up the pieces and start again. Errickson constantly surprises us, giving us characters who behave like real people rather than an author's playthings.

❧ ❧ ❧ ❧ ❧

And now, I want to introduce you to the playwrights, and tell you something about how I got to know each of them.

I've been a fan of Invisible City Theatre Company since it started up operations more than a decade ago. David Epstein, its artistic director, has unerring good taste, and so when he invited me to review their production of Rebecca Louise Miller's first play, *Fault Lines*, I was eager to check it out. I had seen Rebecca's work as an actress in ICTC shows like *Arcadia*; as you have gathered, her talent as a playwright impressed me greatly.

Richard Sheinmel has been part of the indie theater scene for at least two decades, and he's collaborated with a host of artists for whom I have enormous respect—La MaMa E.T.C., Theatre Askew, and Peculiar Works Project among them. His collaborator, songwriter Clay Zambo, has equally solid credits. *Post Modern Living* debuted at The Club at La MaMa, where it fit like a glove and made for one of the most pleasurable evenings of musical theatre I'd had in quite some time.

I knew Amy E. Witting by reputation (through various colleagues), and so when I saw that Manhattan Repertory Theatre's Ken Wolf and Jennifer Pierro were presenting her play *G.I. Joe Jared, Based on One Really Bad Date* as part of their Winterfest in 2010, I jumped at the chance to sample her work. Ken and Jennifer are real champions of new playwrights, hosting dozens of them every year at their Times Square space. Amy of course proved to be a true find, and I am pleased that she has brought us this play.

Jason S. Grossman is another indie theater hyphenate, with a substantial list of credits as actor, producer, improv performer and teacher, and comedy writer in many media. I first got to know him as an actor in some of the audacious anti-musicals of Sharon Fogarty, and then virtuosically playing all of the roles in his own one-man adaptation of the classic holiday film *It's a Wonderful Life*. He's a gifted theatre artist and I am proud that *Love Me*, which premiered at the Planet Connections Festivity, is in this book.

Manny Igrejas has spent most of his career as a publicist, notably for Blue Man Group and Richard Foreman. But he's also been writing plays for several years now, and when I saw *Hassan and Sylvia* at last year's Fresh Fruit Festival, with its great heart and humor and its sly take on some of humankind's baser instincts, I was thrilled to ask him to be part of this volume.

I first heard about Javierantonio González when he participated in the 2006 FringeNYC with his early play *Uneventful Deaths for Agathon* (which got a rave review on nytheatre.com). A few years later, another of our reviewers praised his Spanish-language play *Barceloneta, de noche*. My interest was piqued, and so I made a point of checking out *FLORIDITA, my Love* at Teatro IATI, and I am glad I did. González is one of a growing number of playwrights moving fluidly between Spanish and English, often within individual plays; his work is reflective of the changing face of America in the twenty-first century.

Stephen Kaliski is the youngest playwright in this book, with *West Lethargy* his first theatre credit. I got to know him when he volunteered to join nytheatre.com's reviewing staff, and his astute theatre criticism and articulate writing style made me eager to sample his work. I am happy to have done so, catching *West Lethargy* at FringeNYC 2010.

Tim Errickson has appeared in previous *Plays and Playwrights* books a couple of times, as producer of *The Monster Tales* (2004) and both producer and director of *Burning the Old Man* (2006). Tim is mostly known as a director, and as the artistic director of Boomerang Theatre Company, which he founded in 1999, and for which he won a Caffe Cino Award (from the New York Innovative Theatre Foundation) in 2008. *Endless Summer Nights* is his first produced play as author, and I am delighted it is here.

✦ ✦ ✦ ✦ ✦

It occurs to me as I write this that, for the first time in the history of these volumes, I won't know whether you are reading these words in a traditional book made of paper and ink, or in an ebook on a Kindle, Nook, iPhone, or PC. I guess it doesn't matter, but it helps put into perspective how much our world has changed since the *Plays and Playwrights* series began in 2000. I think that the plays in this book reflect the way our world is right now, in 2011. Certainly, by publishing an ebook version of *Plays and Playwrights 2011* simultaneously with the trade paperback edition, we're reflecting the realities of the book industry in America today.

We've created both editions with care and love, and with the sole purpose of helping the playwrights responsible for the work included here to continue and grow as theatre artists. They've worked very hard to get to the place where they are in their careers, and so I hope you will support them by reading their plays and producing them. Thank you for buying this book or ebook so that they can begin to be paid for their creative work and make a living following their calling.

FAULT LINES

Rebecca Louise Miller

REBECCA LOUISE MILLER was born in Santa Rosa, California, in 1981. She is a graduate of Brown University and spent a semester at the O'Neill National Theater Institute, where she was lucky enough to study playwriting with Rachel Sheinkin. Rebecca has worked in the theatre primarily as an actor. She originated the role of Gina in Dennis Lehane's first play, *Coronado,* at Invisible City Theater Company, as well as the role of Jessica in *Fault Lines*. She has also appeared on television, notably starring as Jeanette in the Emmy-nominated *Prayers for Bobby*, opposite Sigourney Weaver (Lifetime TV, 2009). Rebecca resides in Clinton Hill, Brooklyn, with her husband, David Epstein, and their cat, Raja. *Fault Lines* is her first play.

Fault Lines was first presented by Invisible City Theater Company (David Epstein, Artistic Director) on December 9, 2009, at the Abingdon Theatre Arts Complex, New York City, with the following cast and credits:

Bethany .... Jenna Doolittle
Kat .... Anaïs Alexandra
Jessica .... Rebecca Louise Miller
Grayson .... Tobin Ludwig
Fourth Figure .... Jocelyn Kuritsky

Directed by: David Epstein
Lighting Design: Joe W. Novak
Set Design: Ira Haskell
Sound Design: David Epstein
Stage Manager: Alexander Cape
Producer: Cecelia Frontero

Fault Lines was a semifinalist for the O'Neill National Playwrights Conference and a finalist for Playwrights Week at the Lark Play Development Center.

The playwright would like to thank the members of Invisible City Theater Company for their tireless enthusiasm and hard work on behalf of *Fault Lines*.

For David: midwife, dramaturg, director, taskmaster, partner. Thank you for holding my feet to the fire.

A NOTE TO THE ACTORS

During our run, the original cast learned that this play works best when comedic moments are mined for all they're worth, and actors resist the urge to lean into the drama. These characters are determined to show one another how well they are coping with the past; when they finally reveal their battle scars, a twisted pleasure comes from the disclosure. The moment the play sinks into the maudlin is the moment it loses effectiveness.

CHARACTERS

BETHANY: A happily married stay-at-home mom, Bethany leads a values-centered life. She works hard to maintain her cheerful demeanor and tries to see the best in people.

KAT: The charred remains of a former idealist, Kat hides her sensitivity behind a ferocious tongue. Her life has begun to unravel, and she has lost the ability to keep up appearances.

JESSICA: A tightly wound superachiever; only comfortable when she is in charge. Jessica lives in New York City and proudly devotes her entire life to her nonprofit organization.

GRAYSON: An on-camera reporter struggling to climb the ranks at a cable news channel. Accustomed to getting what he wants by meaning what he says.

The characters can range in age from late twenties to late thirties, though all four should appear to be approximately the same age.

ACT I
Scene 1

In the darkness, the sound of five dead bolts unlocking, then the beeps of an alarm system being deactivated. Lights up on the living room of a lovingly restored Victorian farmhouse, conveniently located five minutes from the nearest Ultra Premium Shopping Outlets. It is Sunday afternoon, a hot late-summer day. BETHANY is dressed thoughtfully but practically. Keys in hand, she buzzes into the room, leading KAT. The kind of woman often described as "earthy," KAT dresses as though she works from home; she carries a large duffel bag. Both women are in their early thirties, extremely nervous and tentative, working hard to approximate normal behavior.

BETHANY: ... it was a working farm till the '80s, Steve took almost two years to finish renovating. Would've taken even longer, but when the twins arrived we decided to simplify.

KAT: *(Looking around.)* It's beautiful.

BETHANY: And green! He's found his calling doing eco-friendly renovations on antique properties. He's done a few new buildings, but rehabs are his passion—I call him the Betty Ford of Sonoma County. Speaking of which—our toilets are dual flush.

(Off KAT's blank look.)

BETHANY: There's a yellow button... *(Quickly breezing through the rest.)* and a brown one. Little flush, big flush, I'll leave it to your imagination.

KAT: Wow.

BETHANY: Yep! Josh and Sam usually give a demonstration, but you can probably figure it out yourself. I just wish there was some way to solar power a hot tub, because that's the only way we'll ever buy one! Very hard to justify, from an environmental point of view. We talked about hooking a generator up to the boys and running them on treadmills in the backyard, but we figure the neighbors probably won't get it.

KAT: It's a lovely home, Bethany.

BETHANY: Thanks—we do love it. It's taken such good care of the four of us. Um. Have a seat.

KAT: Thanks.

(They sit. BETHANY suddenly produces a large set of keys, attached to a Jesus fish keychain.)

BETHANY: I'll just give you your own set so you can come and go while you're here. They're arranged in color groups starting from the top lock down—red ones will get you in the front door, yellow are for coming in through the garage. The blue ones are for the back way... but it's complicated, I wouldn't bother. Our backyard's up against an empty field, so maybe we went a little nuts with security. There's no alligator moat or anything... but we're looking into it. *(In a whisper.)* Oh, and the code for the alarm is 4675 *(Back to normal.)* and you know, our house is your house this week. I can make space for your car in the garage if you want, I just need to move the toys and stuff. I'm really sorry, sort of ran out of guest-prep time—life with twins!

KAT: *(A little firmer than necessary.)* Stop it. *(Catching herself.)* Thank you for putting me up.

BETHANY: No—I'm so glad you're here—I'm sure it's tough to leave your baby for this long, but I'm relieved we'll have a chance to catch up before things get going.

KAT: My mom's watching Sarah, it was an easy sell.

BETHANY: I bet.

KAT: Mom is actually living with us. For right now.

BETHANY: Oh, well, that's... nice.

KAT: It has been, shockingly. Are your boys around?

BETHANY: Steve took them camping in the redwoods. They're out with the neighborhood dads and their kids—it's been a weirdly fertile couple years on the cul de sac—we always tell our friends to stick to bottled water unless they wanna wind up pregnant! So. Consider yourself warned.

KAT: I'm not at risk for that disease at the moment.

BETHANY: Oh?

KAT: Mike and I have separated. In our fashion.

BETHANY: Oh. No need to—I'm glad you're here. I wondered if you'd think I was crazy for sending that letter—

KAT: *(Keeping it light.)* No! I have no idea what I'd be doing if I wasn't down here for this thing. My plan was to bundle up Sarah and make a run for the Canadian border—least I could talk to a shrink for free—but. When I got your letter I realized that I do need to be back here for all of it. I'm just glad this will be finished before she's old enough to hear about it at school.

BETHANY: Yeah. Steve and I have talked a lot about how to handle things, what to tell the boys.

KAT: If anything.

BETHANY: Right—honestly it's something we can be more open about later. And you know…the six o'clock news is not the way we want to start this conversation.

KAT: *(Mostly joking.)* You let your kids watch TV?

BETHANY: We keep one in our bedroom. There's a lock for that too.

(They share a smile. Maybe this won't be so difficult?)

BETHANY: Jessica should be here any time. Her flight got in at two. I made a blackberry crumble, we serve it with ice cream, it's really yummy. Boys picked 'em this morning—we all washed our hands—I just think it'd be best to break the ice with something low stress.

KAT: You've thought this through.

BETHANY: I'm just happy to have people over who won't try to stick their fingers in the sockets every time I turn around.

KAT: I hope you're joking.

BETHANY: You'll see!

KAT: Is Jessica staying here too?

BETHANY: She'll be with her mom in Cotati. Have you two been in touch at all?

KAT: I've seen her on TV. I went to the Foundation's website. Once.

BETHANY: *(Nodding enthusiastically.)* She's done so much for awareness…

KAT: Yep, every six months another photogenic white kid goes missing and Jessica Cohn shows up on cable news. She's an Expert Victim. I guess I should be grateful anyone puts that much energy into it.

BETHANY: Lord knows I wouldn't be able to. *Dental hygiene* was too dark and stressful for me. But I'm probably gonna have to go back real soon. Sam and Josh are going into first grade next month, we can't keep squeezing by on one income.

KAT: Nobody can.

BETHANY: The cost of living here—

KAT: It's crazy, I know.

BETHANY: I'm spoiled to dread going back to work as much as I do—but, I just really enjoy…hanging out with them.

KAT: I know exactly what you mean.

(A sudden burst of emotion takes hold of BETHANY and she is fighting back tears. She moves to KAT and hugs her tightly. KAT awkwardly returns the embrace. BETHANY steps back and takes a long look at her, gripping both of her shoulders.)

BETHANY: It is very good to see you again.

(The closeness immediately becomes uncomfortable and they break apart. BETHANY buzzes into the kitchen.)

BETHANY: How would you feel about a glass of Chardonnay right now?

KAT: Perfect.

KAT: *(Calling to her.)* Hey—do you remember my eleventh birthday party? We made those ridiculous sundaes…

BETHANY: *(Offstage.)* Wait—was that the one when / Julia

KAT: / Yes! Julia Peterson cracked her head open!

(BETHANY enters with wine, opens the bottle, and pours two generous glasses.)

BETHANY: Oh, I remember! We were laughing so hard, and then *boom*—Julia's head smacked back against that windowsill. What were we all cracking up about?

KAT: Who knows? Remember how Julia just smiled up at us and said "ow." No tears, total calm—

BETHANY: Till she looked down and saw the blood in her hand. We all started crying.

KAT: Except / Nina

BETHANY: / Except Nina, who was so level-headed about it. Remember? She just cupped her little hand on Julia's head and led her up the stairs. All business. I was sure she was gonna grow up to be a doctor. Your mom was thrilled we didn't drip any blood on the carpet.

KAT: At least she waited till they'd gone to the emergency room to inspect the floor. And Julia made it back in time for cake!

BETHANY: *(Wistful.)* I never got to have stitches as a kid.

KAT: Wasn't as fun as it looked.

BETHANY: She got eight of 'em. Remember? We kept counting them. Every kid with something sewn up could tell you exactly how many little knots had been tied onto their body.

KAT: After Julia's mom took her to the ER that night I kept saying over and over that I'd never have another slumber party again.

BETHANY: I remember that. I don't think there was another one until…

KAT: Until Nina's twelfth.

(A pause.)

BETHANY: My parents hated letting me sleep over, they said I was always so cranky for church the next day. They were right. But Nina was my best friend, so.

KAT: Do you ever think about what it would've been like if you hadn't been there?

BETHANY: I've thought about it, sure. Probably would've led to a different kind of grief: wondering if I could have stopped it, instead of knowing it was out of my control.

KAT: You believe that? There was nothing we could've done?

BETHANY: Kat—he walked in in the middle of Truth or Dare.

KAT: We were right next to her mom's room.

BETHANY: Are you—

KAT: No. I haven't spent all these years—

BETHANY: No, it's okay, this is why—

KAT: I'm sorry. I've been thinking about it a lot lately.

BETHANY: Of course you have! You've got a baby at home. I went through a rough patch too, after the boys were born.

KAT: You did?

BETHANY: Oh yeah. When we moved into this place, Steve can tell you, I freaked out pretty much entirely. Everyone assumed it was postpartum, and I don't know—that could've been part of it. I couldn't leave the house. He had to stop working for a while—stay home and take care of the three of us. I had been so thrilled to just be nesting, piecing together our little doubled-up nursery, but as soon as they arrived I was gripped by this *panic*, all the time.

KAT: What changed? How'd you get past it?

BETHANY: It's a…tough thing to explain.

KAT: Please. Try.

(Beat.)

KAT: Bethany.

BETHANY: I had a revelation.

(The doorbell rings, and BETHANY rushes to answer it. From offstage we hear the high-pitched greeting calls unique to uncomfortable women. BETHANY reenters leading JESSICA, who wears a wrinkle-free button-up and slacks. She is friendly, but not familiar.)

BETHANY: Come in, come in! How was your flight?

JESSICA: Uneventful, so I won't complain. *(To KAT.)* Hi!

(JESSICA moves toward KAT, they hug tentatively.)

KAT: Good to see you.

JESSICA: You too. It's been way too long.

BETHANY: You must be starving. Can I get you—

JESSICA: I'm okay—stopped for In-N-Out on the way. I feel so dirty. But satisfied—still can't get it in New York.

(JESSICA's BlackBerry chirps.)

JESSICA: Crap. Just a sec. Sorry!

(She types a quick text while BETHANY pours and hands her a glass of wine, then refills the other two glasses.)

KAT: Work calling?

JESSICA: No, thankfully. They've let me out on the long leash this week—more personal than business this time. I'm meeting an old friend tomorrow.

BETHANY: Anyone we know?

JESSICA: *(Shaking her head.)* College. Is there a breakfast place near the DoubleTree?

KAT: I hate that DoubleTree.

(Off their perplexed looks.)

KAT: They built it on top of my summer camp.

JESSICA: That land was worth millions, it's amazing the place lasted as long as it did.

KAT: God bless America. And the goddamn tech boom.

BETHANY: You sound glad to be back!

KAT: I feel like one of those guys who goes back to visit 'Nam.

BETHANY: We were just talking about Julia Peterson's stitches—

JESSICA: Oh, those were cool!

KAT: What is with you two?

JESSICA: What? She looked like a pirate!

BETHANY: Her dad told her to say she got 'em in a bar fight.

JESSICA: *(Laughing.)* She said that to the principal!

BETHANY: He was the funniest dad in the neighborhood. *(Beat.)* Didn't he leave her family junior year?

KAT: Oh yeah. Had an affair with his chiropractor, moved down to Laguna. She was like twenty-six, Julia had to be their bridesmaid.

JESSICA: I remember now. God, how depressing.

KAT: 'Tis the season.

BETHANY: *(To JESSICA.)* How are things at the Foundation?

JESSICA: You guys don't want to hear about this stuff now.

BETHANY: I do.

KAT: *(Looking through her bag.)* Tell us everything.

JESSICA: Well. Ten endangered children returned to their families in the last year and a half. In September we got the mandatory sex offender registry passed in five more states, which was huge. I never thought we'd see another victory on par with Three Strikes—

KAT: —Oh yeah, Three Strikes is the gift that keeps on giving. Twenty-five to life for stealing a car or dealing weed?

(Producing a prescription bottle, she takes out a few pills and downs them with her wine. JESSICA watches her and proceeds with some caution.)

JESSICA: It's not that hard to avoid committing a felony, Kat. And Prop 36 ensured that people busted for possession wind up in treatment instead of—

KAT: How rude of me—anybody else for Xanax? It's really the *only* proper accompaniment to a… *(Checking the bottle.)* 2001 Sonoma Coastal Chardonnay. It was a good year. *(Beat.)* Not really.

(She pops a pill and quickly downs it with a gulp of wine. She holds the pillbox out to the other women, shakes it seductively.)

KAT: Sure I can't tempt you? Takes a couple minutes to really get working, but it's *dynamite* with Chardonnay.

JESSICA: *(A cold smile.)* Can't. Not sure about the Zoloft interaction.

KAT: Wise decision. You always were the shrewd one, Jessica. Bethany? Can you possibly abstain?

BETHANY: *(Uncomfortable.)* We've been all organic for going on three years now—except the occasional bottle of Sonoma Coastal, of course. Steve did a rehab on their tasting room, we buy it by the case now—wholesale. I figure Jesus drank wine, we're in good company!

(They sit with that a moment. KAT and JESSICA share a glance.)

BETHANY: How long since you've been back?

JESSICA: I fly in a couple times a year. *(To KAT.)* What about you?

KAT: It's been at least a decade. Been up in Humboldt for six years now, Ukiah before that.

JESSICA: You're only a couple hours away.

KAT: Yup.

JESSICA: I'm always shocked to see how quickly it changes—all the new developments.

BETHANY: For years the city councils just sold us out to the worst kind of contractors. No one's building with the landscape in mind, they just throw up these cookie-cutter monstrosities, cover the hillsides.

KAT: It's turning into Orange County down here.

BETHANY: Bite your tongue!

JESSICA: It's still beautiful, though, great area to raise kids...you can't stop people from moving in. *(Towards KAT.)* Building on top of our summer camps.

(KAT takes this in, then raises her glass in somber tribute—JESSICA and BETHANY follow suit.)

KAT: To Cloverleaf Ranch: with the DoubleTree on top of her stables and the Walmart over girls' camp, she lives on in the hearts and minds of the now-grown children of privilege who loved her.

JESSICA and BETHANY: To Cloverleaf Ranch.

(They drink, then fall into silence.)

KAT: *(Looking out the window.)* They drained the lake and put a biotech firm there. I had my first kiss on that lake. Smelled like horse sweat and bay trees, romantic as hell. I think there's a reporter parked in front of the house. I noticed him on the way in, he gave me that "don't mind me, just thinking about buying in the neighborhood" look.

(KAT moves away from the window as JESSICA and BETHANY look to each other, rush to peer outside.)

KAT: Brings back great memories, don't it? *(Moves back to the table, pours herself more wine, drinks it with some urgency.)*

BETHANY: *(Quietly.)* Well if they're here, maybe they're leaving her family alone.

KAT: I wouldn't count on it. Fucking vultures.

(She looks pointedly in JESSICA's direction. JESSICA takes a step towards her and a deep breath, prepared for battle. At the last possible moment, she recovers her composure and speaks instead to BETHANY.)

JESSICA: You know, it was such a surprise to get that letter from you, Bethany. I couldn't even remember the last time I'd gotten a handwritten note like that. Through the mail and everything? It's like a little gift. *(Beat. A glance towards KAT.)* I'm sorry we fell out of touch.

BETHANY: I'm just glad you both decided to be here. I really felt that it would be best for the three of us to experience this week together.

JESSICA: *(Carefully, to BETHANY.)* You ever see Nina's mother around?

BETHANY: Not on any regular basis, but sure...from time to time we run into each other at the grocery store or something. We do the brief-polite-update-and-move-along.

KAT: How is Ellen?

BETHANY: *(Shrugging.)* It's been such a long time.

KAT: I can't believe she's stayed here.

BETHANY: Well, I do think—obviously things changed a lot after Nina was taken, but I think it was more a coming of age than a permanent scar on the town as a whole. I'm trying to see it that way in terms of my own life too.

JESSICA: I think that's healthy. He doesn't have the right to define our existence, he's not worthy of it.

KAT: *(To JESSICA.)* I'm sorry, but...you don't think you've let it define who you are? You go to work every day at a company named after her—*Nina Foundation.*

(BETHANY looks on uncomfortably. JESSICA takes a moment, proceeds carefully. She speaks like an offended politician, all control and careful choice of language.)

JESSICA: My work is just my way of dealing with what happened. It wasn't in the cards for me to try to have a normal life after we all experienced what we did. You know—in a roundabout sort of way, he is responsible for so much progress in the field of victims' rights.

BETHANY: I'm glad you've done all you have.

JESSICA: Thank you.

KAT: And, you know, just out of curiosity—how well does it pay you?

JESSICA: Excuse me?

BETHANY: Whoa, hold on—

KAT: *(Polite, but insistent.)* It's a fair question: if Smith is paying your bills, *in a roundabout sort of way*, I'd like to know what I've been missing out on. Because other than some heinous recurring nightmares, he really hasn't done shit for me. All three of us were there that night. I would like to know how well it pays to be a Spokesperson for Senseless Tragedy. That seem fair to you?

JESSICA: Like I said, the Foundation is doing really well. We're up to a nine million dollar operating budget for next year.

KAT: No, Jess. What about you? What do you take home at the end of your long, hard days in Ninaland?

BETHANY: Kat, please stop.

KAT: *(To JESSICA.)* Oh—I'm not trying to make you uncomfortable, we don't have to—

JESSICA: It's fine. I work seventy hours a week for thirty-five grand. Ralph Lauren donates six new outfits a year that I use for television appearances and fundraisers, so we can call it an even thirty-eight. If you're more comfortable with that. *(JESSICA's BlackBerry emits a chirp, she reads the message, her tone switching to a forced politeness.)* I have to take this, is there somewhere I can...

BETHANY: The office is down the hall.

JESSICA: *(Trotting out of the room, dialing as she goes.)* Thanks.

(BETHANY refills the wineglasses; KAT heads back to stare out the window.)

KAT: Endangered children.

SCENE 2

Monday morning. JESSICA and GRAYSON are walking through a park. He is also in his early thirties, absolutely earnest, with the casual authority of a newsman.

JESSICA: *(Barely controlled fury.)* Did it occur to you how Bethany might respond to a strange man lurking outside her house?

GRAYSON: I was just—

JESSICA: I know what you were doing.

GRAYSON: We're running out of time, Jess.

JESSICA: You're gonna have to wait—why did you follow me here?

GRAYSON: I followed the story.

JESSICA: I said I'd bring them to you, after the execution. Remember? Now is not the right time—

GRAYSON: I understand how sensitive things are—

JESSICA: I don't think you do.

GRAYSON: —but I cannot stress enough the importance of an exclusive with all three of the girls who witnessed the kidnapping—here, where it all took place.

JESSICA: It has to happen this week? Emotions are too high, and frankly those two have spent the last twenty years dodging reporters who look and sound exactly like you.

GRAYSON: How do I look and sound?

JESSICA: Shallow, but commanding.

GRAYSON: I'll take "commanding."

(He watches JESSICA stifle a smile.)

GRAYSON: The network isn't going to run the story without all three interviews. Your POV is powerful, but it's been out there. The public demands it, too. The Nina case was wakeup call for families across the country. It taught us...

(There is a pause as he realizes that he has no idea what to say. She does not swoop in to save him.)

JESSICA: What?

GRAYSON: It taught us no community is immune. That to release violent predators back into society is to stand complicit in whatever unforgivable actions they go on to commit—that criminal justice is at its core a *human rights* issue—children are being put at risk every time one of these psychos is allowed to walk free.

JESSICA: That's a start.

GRAYSON: Sorry to—it's something I'm passionate about.

JESSICA: What happened? You were never an issues guy.

GRAYSON: Well it's been a while. You look good, by the way.

(Off her look.)

GRAYSON: You know, considering the circumstances. When you skipped out on the reunion I figured you'd probably gained fifty pounds, adopted sixteen cats.

JESSICA: I had a conference.

GRAYSON: I'm just saying: you've held up all right.

JESSICA: Well thank you so much. You still talk like a frat boy.

GRAYSON: *(This old argument.)* It wasn't a fraternity, it was a *literary society*. We drank a lot and passionately discussed the Great Books.

JESSICA: Lord Byron and beer pong.

GRAYSON: If I recall, you never made it to our parties.

JESSICA: I had to study, I was—

GRAYSON: —on scholarship! Convenient excuse.

JESSICA: It was the best I could think of at the time.

GRAYSON: You were a very serious person. Still are. I promise you—I will be absolutely sensitive. In fact, I'd like for you to stick around while the other two interviews are planned out and taped—*you* can let us know if we're crossing the line. Believe me, it is not my intention to further traumatize Bethany or Kat. Or you. What made you decide to talk about it?

JESSICA: I never didn't. I gave her eulogy.

GRAYSON: In front of that huge choir.

(She is startled.)

GRAYSON: My family watched the memorial on TV.

JESSICA: You never told me that.

GRAYSON: You never mentioned Nina in college, I wasn't gonna bring her up.

(Beat.)

GRAYSON: I don't remember much, just that you were so tiny you had to stand on a box behind the podium. And even after you started to cry, I could understand every word you said. You seemed like a sweet kid.

JESSICA: They kept asking me to talk about it. Once the Foundation got going, I was needed all the time. We went to the White House on the first anniversary—on her birthday. Mom and me had tea with the First Lady.

GRAYSON: What do you think you'd be doing with your life if Nina was never taken?

JESSICA: Are you interviewing me?

GRAYSON: Not without your express consent, on terms mutually agreed upon by our respective legal teams.

JESSICA: Damn straight. *(She takes a deep breath.)* I'll float the idea of a meeting.

GRAYSON: Today?

JESSICA: Relax.

GRAYSON: I appreciate the show of faith. All of this will be done with total sensitivity and respect.

JESSICA: I'll let you know.

(She nearly jogs off, dialing the BlackBerry as she goes. He watches her.)

Scene 3

Tuesday, dusk. Back in BETHANY's living room. JESSICA and BETHANY are chatting—they are well into their second bottle of red wine.

BETHANY: ...and I saw him bend over and pick something up so *carefully*...and there was this tiny baby bird. Fell out of the nest, I guess. And his calloused, woodworking palms, cradling the little creature with such...it almost looked like love, you know? Blew me apart. I drove him to the Bird Rescue Center, and that was it. Oh, it sounds bizarre, I know. Steve makes fun of me for it—calls me his Bird of Prey. Says I swooped in when he was vulnerable. *(She makes their special Bird of Prey "caw" and gesture.)* Anyway. It's not like we ran off to Vegas or anything—just shacked up as quickly as possible and waited a reasonable amount of time to get married. We said we'd release that bird at our wedding, but we were too afraid to call the lady at the Rescue Center and find out what happened to the poor little thing. Didn't look very good.

JESSICA: You moved right in together?

BETHANY: Oh yeah. It made us *insane* to be apart in the beginning.

JESSICA: Oh. Well I don't mean to—aren't you religious?

BETHANY: Well I wasn't. I mean, I am *now*, for sure.

(She looks up at a crucifix somewhere in the room, habitually crosses herself. JESSICA looks at her hands.)

BETHANY: And I was! When we were kids. Well. It was my parents' church—I was compelled to attend Sunday School, you know. But actually—I decided to stop going…well. After they found Nina.

JESSICA: How did your parents react?

BETHANY: How could they ask me to believe in an all-powerful God after that? They left the church a couple months after I did.

JESSICA: Oh.

BETHANY: Yeah. Not something I feel great about. But I have to accept that they had their experience of the kidnapping, and it's as valid as my own. I keep encouraging Mom and Dad to look beyond the Catholic Church. I think they'd be really happy with a nice Unitarian congregation. Or Quakers, they're fantastic. If you like quiet.

(A commotion in the yard catches JESSICA's attention; she rushes to the window and quickly closes the blinds.)

JESSICA: There are six news vans parked in front of your house. How did they know to find us here?

BETHANY: We're listed in the phonebook. I thought since I'd taken Steve's name…

JESSICA: Kat's gonna be livid.

BETHANY: She just took off after lunch, said she had errands to run, left her phone in the guest room. Maybe they'll get whatever they need and leave before she comes back?

JESSICA: I don't think these guys are going anywhere until Friday night. I can't have them trailing me to Mom's!

BETHANY: So stay here.

JESSICA: Oh look, Bethany—

BETHANY: I mean it. The twins' room is clean, for once. Steve stocked up the fridge, we'll just have a girls' night! Or four.

JESSICA: Thanks, but things with Kat are tense enough.

BETHANY: She'll come around.

(She grabs and holds both of JESSICA's hands. JESSICA looks helplessly out towards the window.)

BETHANY: Please. Stay.

JESSICA: Okay.

(BETHANY squeals, wraps JESSICA in a tight hug, which is stiffly received. Then she sits and refills the wineglasses.)

BETHANY: Anyway. What about you? Are you religious? Or "spiritual"? So many people make that distinction.

JESSICA: Oh—I'm your typical yoga-practicing secular Manhattan Jew. In times of trouble I whisper prayers to Saint Einstein. I thought about visiting an ashram this summer, to try to get connected to…something. But I thought "Ech, all that meditation, it might get me centered but no way can it work my abs like Power Vinyasa Flow," so what's the point?

BETHANY: I see.

JESSICA: I guess I'm pretty Old Testament about a few things though.

BETHANY: Like what?

JESSICA: Punishment.

(Before there is time to respond, we hear the labored unlocking of the locks on the front door. BETHANY jumps up and begins unlocking from the inside as KAT is unlocking from outside. As is inevitable in these situations, they relock one or two by accident. Finally, BETHANY unlocks the final lock and swings the door open. The light and din of press gathered outside fills the house for an instant, and the alarm starts to go off. They slam the door, and BETHANY shuts down the alarm as KAT marches in, visibly shaken.)

KAT: What the fuck is going on out there?!

BETHANY: They tracked us down.

KAT: *(To BETHANY.)* I told you we should've confiscated her BlackBerry. *(To JESSICA.)* Do you mind calling off the dogs?

BETHANY: It's my fault, I'm listed in the phonebook.

JESSICA: They can't come further than the sidewalk without permission.

KAT: Well by all means, Jessica, call them in!

BETHANY: Are you okay?

KAT: Gonna have to be. Well, let's get comfy—I just spent two hours stuck in traffic listening to the eco-freaks on local radio. You guys hear about the spent hens?

(Interrupting before they can respond.)

KAT: That's *spent*, as in…no longer able to lay eggs. So the local egg farmers can't use them…and they're too tough to eat. So they gas them, I think, and bury them. Yeah, and it gets worse—not all of them are being completely *destroyed*, see, and some of the neighbors have been finding very confused, muddy old birds walking around their yards. Zombie Chickens! And here comes the kicker—a group of concerned senior citizens are *organizing on behalf of the hens*. I shit you not! Only in Northern California, where old liberals come to die! So I'm sitting on the highway, listening to this crone from Greenpeace pitch a retirement home for poultry, and suddenly it occurs to me that my car is sitting not twenty feet away from the Rodgers Creek Fault. And I think: our major roadway stretches over land that every expert predicts will *liquefy without warning* at some point in the next few years, and the people on the radio are screaming about the rights of menopausal chickens?

BETHANY: The fault cuts through Memorial Hospital too. And Burbank Elementary.

KAT: We've known about Rodgers Creek since we were kids, why haven't they done anything?!

BETHANY: Who?

KAT: I don't know! Doesn't it seem like everybody's job? Where are the grown-ups in this place?

JESSICA: Somehow I don't think we're talking about chickens anymore.

(She raises her wineglass to her lips and makes a soft clucking sound. KAT snaps towards her, but BETHANY interrupts before she can explode.)

BETHANY: Where've you been all day, Kat?

(Pause.)

KAT: I went to the house.

JESSICA: What house?

BETHANY: Kat, what house?

KAT: Nina's house! You'd said her mom was still there, I just needed—I have spent so many years imagining some tear-soaked catharsis on Ellen's doorstep. I feel like an asshole. I'm standing on the stoop, wondering will she recognize my face or do I have to introduce myself, and how in the hell do I go about doing that? And then I start to think, you know, "What right do I have to encroach on her like this? What kind of person just shows up this way?" So I'm turning to go back to my car and the door opens, and this horrifically cute blonde girl is standing there, staring up at me. And I can't speak. The mom comes out, obviously thinks I'm a Jehovah's Witness or something. And then she steps in between us. Like she's afraid I'm going to grab her.

BETHANY: What did you say?

KAT: Nothing—I puked on her geraniums.

BETHANY and JESSICA: NO!

(BETHANY and JESSICA are unable to stifle their amusement. They start to giggle and KAT joins them.)

KAT: Oh yes.

BETHANY: You poor thing!

JESSICA: What did she do?

KAT: What can you do? She ran inside. Maybe she was gonna come back with a glass of ginger ale and a breath mint, but I kind of doubt it. When you buy a house like that, does the realtor have to tell you what happened there?

JESSICA: Are you gonna be okay?

KAT: Eventually.

(BETHANY hands KAT a glass of wine.)

BETHANY: Here's to that.

JESSICA: I have had more to drink in the last two days…

BETHANY: Wine country living, my dear.

KAT: Where the weather is mellow and the disasters epic. But hey, when in Pompeii… *(Turns sharply to JESSICA.)* How long till we can leave the house?

JESSICA: Those people are out there because the public is curious, Kat. You're just feeding the fire by refusing to deal with it. I know you don't want to hear this from me, but if you want to be left alone, one interview would go a very long way. *(She takes a deep breath.)* I have a friend—*colleague*—someone I've known for quite a while. His name is Grayson Daniels, he did a TV news story on the Foundation about a year ago. I told him on no uncertain terms he'd have to wait until after this week to approach the two of you, but I found out yesterday he's here anyway. It was a shitty thing to do, I'm not defending it, but he's passionate about our story, and he's honest. You can set out all the parameters of the interview. You'll tell him what's off limits, there will be no surprises.

BETHANY: I don't think I want to—

JESSICA: Look. I'm not asking you to talk to him on camera. Just hear him out.

KAT: We agreed on this years ago—if you want to wallow in tragedy for cable news or your Foundation or anybody else, that is your business.

JESSICA: This is okay, I understand why you're—

KAT: No, I don't think you do. I think you've built your life around the fact that you survived a brutal attack from a sociopath at your friend's birthday party. You seem to forget, Jessica, that you haven't survived shit. He didn't touch you, he took *Nina* out the door that night and it is the best thing that ever happened to you.

BETHANY: I don't / think that's fair—

JESSICA: / Just let her go.

KAT: / While you're weeping for dollars in the Hamptons, you ever notice that in spite of all this "work" you're doing, the world isn't getting any safer? Does it ever make you sick? That you're working the room in your fab Ralph Lauren because our friend was tortured for three days and left to rot a few miles down the road from your house?

JESSICA: Wouldn't it be great if I could fund the Foundation by *not* talking about Nina? Like you?

KAT: It's not your story to tell.

JESSICA: It's the only thing worth talking about! What have you contributed? What have you even been doing for the last twenty years?

KAT: I've lived a good life!

JESSICA: And I've been living this every single day so that other people won't have to. You can judge me however you want for that, but I sleep well.

KAT: *(Calmly.)* No, you don't.

(It's the truth, and JESSICA is shaken by it. She takes a moment to compose herself.)

JESSICA: If you want this to go away, all you have to do is go on record and put it to rest. I'm not asking you to do the interview, I'm just asking you to meet him—whatever happens afterwards will be on your terms. I trust this guy.

Scene 4

Late Tuesday night. BETHANY enters, bone tired. She begins to clear away the bottles and glasses that have proliferated throughout her living room. Suddenly she is startled by something out of the corner of her eye, snaps to attention, then relaxes and smiles. Her tone is casual, calm.

BETHANY: I was starting to wonder if you were gonna come by. Glad you did. *(Gesturing to the empty wine bottles.)* It's been a...weird week so far. I can understand why you'd keep your distance—there's been a good deal of yelling. I figure just let 'em go to town, wear themselves out like Josh and Sam do—they're fast asleep now. One thing about motherhood, it makes you a lot smarter about people. You would love it, Nina. *(Beat.)* Thank you for bringing them here. I don't mean to complain. They aren't as angry as they think, they just really miss you. You know this would all be a lot easier if you could just speak to them yourself? *(Beat.)* I will. I know what I have to do, please give me the strength. Can you stay a little bit longer?

ACT II
Scene 1

Wednesday. BETHANY's living room. GRAYSON has settled into an easy chair, JESSICA is sitting near him, BETHANY is serving tea. No one really knows what to say. The light and noise from outside the house continue throughout the scene.

KAT: Haven't I seen you before? On television, reporting on a rainstorm?

GRAYSON: Hurricane Joanne, probably. The network has me covering extreme weather. I figure it's a growth market...

(Silence—none of them smile at his joke.)

KAT: Do you need a meteorology degree for that? Or just a windbreaker and stiff hair?

GRAYSON: I'm not a meteorologist, I'm a journalist. Stiff hair runs on my father's side.

(BETHANY giggles, buoying his confidence.)

GRAYSON: I've been with the network for two years now, and in that time I've been working towards reporting on more substantive issues. With a particular focus on child welfare.

KAT: Oh, he's into kids—always promising. And how did you hook up with our Jessica?

GRAYSON: We were classmates at Cornell, bumped into each other at a fundraiser for the Nina Foundation a few years ago. I tipped off the network about her, wound up doing a little story, and they fell in love.

JESSICA: *(Shrugging it off.)* They started having me consult on abduction cases—

GRAYSON: —and put her on the air as quickly as humanly possible. I've never seen anything like it. A few weeks ago, I sent Jessica a letter requesting an interview with the three of you—which she politely rebuffed—then followed up with a series of phone calls that she ignored outright. So I decided to come and speak with you myself.

KAT: The police reports are public record, what can we tell you that people can't just figure out for themselves?

GRAYSON: People around the country really cared—still care—about the case, and there are still a lot of unanswered questions. About what happened that night, between the five of you.

KAT: "The five of us." Well, that's a new low. Are you going to interview him, too?

GRAYSON: Smith? Of course not. There's nothing to learn there, he's already gotten more coverage than he deserves. I want to know why the three of you sat in silence for ten minutes after your friend was carried out the door.

(The women are all taken aback. He continues before they can protest.)

GRAYSON: I'm sorry to put it so bluntly, but there *is* a story that needs to be told. Nina was not the only victim of this crime. The public deserves to know what happened to her three friends that night.

(Silence.)

BETHANY: There is this…*obsession* with her suffering. People want us to work through those events over and over like a rosary. And you know what? I'm glad we don't know everything. That so much time passed before they found her. I think it was—I feel now it was God's way of shielding her from all the curiosity. How would she ever be able to rest? Think of all the kids they've reported on, every agonizing moment reenacted and televised. Your network aired footage of her bloodstained pajamas. Do you remember that? I try not to follow the news too closely anymore, but my God, you all have crossed more lines than any mother could forgive.

GRAYSON: The interview will consist of questions you'll have approved in advance. I'm not looking to exploit Nina's story, I'm trying to uncover yours.

BETHANY: We were kids. How were we supposed to react? Believe me, there aren't any secrets left. He held a knife to her throat, he said he'd kill her if we screamed—

KAT: Apparently none of us had watched that much *America's Most Wanted* at that point, so we didn't make a sound.

BETHANY: He didn't sit us down and explain his intentions.

KAT: All this is public knowledge! Look at Jessica's website! If I could have the memory of that night surgically removed from me, I would. It's a tumor. It doesn't belong to me, it isn't *of* me, and I can't begin to justify feeding my daughter by selling another victim back to America.

JESSICA: You would *not* be selling her out! You'd be choosing to speak for the first time about an event that has shaped your community and your life.

KAT: It doesn't belong to the community, it never did! It took me twenty years and several moves to finally stop being "one of the girls at the party"; my friends don't know, only my husband has heard the story and he knows me well enough to just leave it alone.

GRAYSON: *(Sympathetically.)* You must really miss him.

(KAT stiffens.)

GRAYSON: I discussed his case with a friend of mine at the ACLU. He's kind of a celebrity in drug law reform circles. I was told he could be eligible for parole in five years?

(He glances over to JESSICA. She stares back, confused.)

KAT: I hadn't shared that yet, thanks.

GRAYSON: Oh Jesus, I didn't mean to bring it up this way. I thought you all—

BETHANY: *(Quickly to KAT.)* Never mind, we don't need to talk about it. *(To GRAYSON.)* I think we may have had it for today. Thanks for coming, it was really…nice to meet you—

KAT: Our tactful friend from the TV was talking about Mike's jail sentence. He was arrested for a field of pot he'd been growing a couple miles from the house. He'd had two busts for dealing after high school, and it was his third strike.

JESSICA: Oh my God.

KAT: He—very stupidly and without my knowledge—started growing it after I had told him I wanted to have a baby. *(To JESSICA.)* That was a great law you got passed. It's a real shame, too, Mike always sent the Nina Foundation twenty bucks during your big fund drive. After he got busted I decided we'd better stop donating, since clearly the Foundation is doing better than we are. He got a great job at the prison laundromat—not quite as lucrative as dealing to college kids, but y'know, thank God they got him off the street. Humboldt State is now one hundred percent drug free and the children of California sleep soundly in their beds. Another monster behind bars, thanks to Three Strikes You're Out.

JESSICA: Kat, I had no idea—

KAT: Of course not! You never thought to follow up on the families destroyed by the ludicrous fucking law you helped pass. Ironic, right? That the Nina Foundation is the reason my child is growing up without a father?

BETHANY: You don't need to talk about it!

KAT: Thanks, it's really okay. *(Making no attempt to camouflage the fact that she's popping two more Xanax.)* I've come to terms with the fact that I married a dealer. It's actually pretty sexy—we get conjugal visits and all—you don't know desire until you've fucked a felon. Plus I get a strip search on my way in to see him, so...I'm just glad he was gone before Sarah was old enough to develop any memory of him. So I'm the one who gets to do all the missing. Well—me and the dog. He's been looking at me with the most *accusatory* expression since Mike went away. I'm kidding! We get along great without him. I bought a vibrator and a goat so I don't have to mow the lawn, no sweat.

GRAYSON: I think you should tell your story. The Three Strikes angle—

KAT: *(Fiercely.)* This is an angle, now? My life is a fucking angle to you?

GRAYSON: I'm sorry, I didn't mean—

KAT: Of course you didn't. I'm a touch sensitive about my husband's prison time. He's awful pretty for jail.

GRAYSON: Coming from someone who was so personally affected by the Nina kidnapping, it's a powerful story about the unforeseen consequences of Three Strikes. I know that an increase in public awareness surrounding your husband's...situation would be a powerful tool towards securing an early release.

KAT: *(Caught off guard; stands absolutely still.)* You manipulative piece of shit.

GRAYSON: Well. I think I've done enough damage for one night. Please, consider me on call. Any questions, concerns, whatever. The network understands what a huge leap of faith we're asking you to take. I promise—we can make this a positive experience for everyone.

(JESSICA ushers him towards the door.)

JESSICA: Goodnight, Grayson. I'll be in touch.

KAT: Like a moth to a fucking flame.

(He looks at the three of them and exits quietly.)

Scene 2

BETHANY's house. It is very late Wednesday night. Faint blue light glows through the windows into the dark room. We hear giggling, whispered secrets, bare feet scampering across the floor as THREE BARELY DISCERNIBLE SILHOUETTES appear. Then a FOURTH. They scamper across the room, hiding and seeking in the dark, jumping out to surprise each other from behind furniture, enjoying free reign while doing their best to not wake the grown-ups who undoubtedly sleep nearby. White light comes up outside the house, building in intensity as the FIGURES' frenetic movement slows, becomes meditative, connected. One by one, BETHANY, KAT, and JESSICA become visible. The FOURTH FIGURE is gone. They are spread throughout the living room, surrounded by blankets and half-empty snack food containers. They are eating ice cream from a shared carton. Bright light now streams in through the shutters. The three are in a state of loopy late-night euphoria. For the first few moments, it should be unclear whether we are seeing them as children or adults.

KAT: Can anyone name *one* time in the history of the world that game has ever worked?!

BETHANY: You're supposed to play it with more people!

JESSICA: Now she tells us.

BETHANY: *(Ultra serious.)* I went to a party where it worked one time, you have to really focus your energy—

KAT: Oh, please!

BETHANY: It worked! We lifted John Franco with our pinkies. I think there were seven of us?

KAT: I keep wondering if I'll ever host a slumber party for Sarah. *(To BETHANY.)* You're lucky you've got boys.

BETHANY: We used to say we'd try for a girl, but after going through everything with the twins…I think I've got post-traumatic stress from the nursing alone.

KAT: How in the hell did you deal with two?

BETHANY: The first few months were brutal, you can imagine. We said we'd give it six months, I was able to keep going for a year and a half. Basically just learned to live with cracked nipples.

JESSICA: They crack?!

KAT: And bleeeeeed. And occasionally get infected, in which case you have to stop breastfeeding because your milk turns—

JESSICA: *(Putting down her spoon in disgust.)* I get it. What happens to moms that makes them think it's okay to share this stuff?

KAT: Oh, just wait…

BETHANY: After you have a baby it all becomes public domain.

KAT: No—as soon you start showing! Please. If I liked being groped by strangers, I'd have become a stripper. I carried pepper spray in my last trimester.

BETHANY: And once that kid's out, forget it!

KAT: We shouldn't talk like this, we're scaring Jessica.

BETHANY: *(Reassuringly, to JESSICA.)* Believe me, it's all worth it in the end. The first moment their little faces look up at you—

JESSICA: I'm not having kids.

KAT: That sounds definitive.

JESSICA: *(Grabbing the ice cream.)* Couple years back I found myself ogling babies on the subway instead of cute men—

BETHANY: Ooooh, the tick-tock.

JESSICA: —so I dismantled the timer.

KAT: How'd you do that?

JESSICA: *(Digging in her spoon.)* I got my tubes tied. *(She takes a big bite and grins widely.)*

KAT: Wow.

JESSICA: Took a few tries to find a doctor who'd do it—I was twenty-five. They all told me to just get the shot or an IUD, something reversible in case I changed my mind, but they were missing the point. Probably would have made more sense if I was actually getting laid, but I figured best to hedge my bets.

BETHANY: I guess you can always adopt if you ever decide—

(JESSICA quickly looks away. The party mood has evaporated.)

KAT: Do you know the rules of…who's going to be in there with him on Friday night?

JESSICA: Family members if they want to watch, probably a lot of press. He gets to invite five witnesses, two clergy.

KAT: Are her parents going?

JESSICA: Haven't heard. Bethany?

(BETHANY shakes her head no.)

KAT: Would you want to watch it? I would.

JESSICA: Me too. In a heartbeat.

BETHANY: Really?

KAT: Absolutely. Just to experience some semblance of justice—

BETHANY: *Not* justice, it won't bring her back.

JESSICA: Bethany, he derailed our lives.

KAT: He took away any chance we had of making it through with a shred of normalcy. And we still haven't gotten any explanation beyond meth and a twelve-pack. In the absence of reason, I can be satisfied with blood.

JESSICA: To know beyond any doubt that he is gone, to *see it*, it'd be satisfying to be there.

KAT: What do you think he looks like now? Smith.

BETHANY: *(Very quietly.)* I've seen him.

(KAT and JESSICA stare at her.)

JESSICA: What?

BETHANY: I went to visit. He asked me to.

JESSICA: How did Smith get in touch with you?

BETHANY: I…I started writing him letters a few years ago.

KAT: What?

BETHANY: I found his mailing address online. I wanted to see if I could forgive him. I had come out of a long depression, reconfirmed my faith, and…something wouldn't let me rest until I'd made the attempt to…

JESSICA: To what?!

BETHANY: I'm not sure. I wrote him a letter, just saying that I was still angry, but I know he is a human being and deserves love and compassion. Just like Nina did.

KAT: No.

BETHANY: I needed to see him as he is—not a monster, just a man with his own history and pain. I wrote a letter, he didn't respond. After a few months I wrote another one. After the third I got a reply.

JESSICA: What did he say?

(BETHANY goes to a drawer, gets several letters, which she tries to show other two, who refuse to look at them.)

BETHANY: Um…you know, he thanked me for writing, he sort of described his daily life at San Quentin.

JESSICA: Did he say anything about Nina?

BETHANY: Not in the first one. I'm sure it was kind of overwhelming. To hear from me. Eventually he did apologize. He said he couldn't explain why it had happened, but he was sorry that it did. He said it was a good thing he'd been locked up. He said he hopes he can ask forgiveness of both of you.

(They look at her in silence. She is terrified but goes on.)

BETHANY: I promised to help him try.

JESSICA: Which is why you invited us here this week.

KAT: Oh my God. I don't want to hear this.

BETHANY: Let me finish. Smith invited me to witness on Friday night. He invited all of us. I'm gonna go, and I think you should come with me.

KAT: Why?

BETHANY: So he won't have to go through it alone. He doesn't have anyone. The arrangements have all been made with the prison if you want to. I know it would mean a great deal to him have you there.

(KAT and JESSICA are unified in their shock.)

KAT: *(Chuckling.)* …it would mean a great deal to him…

JESSICA: This is insane. How can you even ask?

BETHANY: I'm not asking. He is. You both just said you wanted to see it.

KAT: Not like that. Not for him.

BETHANY: Whether we like it or not, we are bound to one another. The five of us. You can't just wake up and get over…this *thing* that has possessed our lives since we were little girls—believe me, you can't let it go until you can forgive him.

KAT: It's not up to me to forgive anything, that would be Nina's privilege, and since she's not around to cast a vote I'm going to go ahead and say Fuck. Smith.

JESSICA: He's sent you on this sick errand, can't you see what's going on here?

KAT: What's going on is Bethany gets a gold star from God if we find love and forgiveness in our hearts. Nina stays a martyr, Bethany's guaranteed entrance into heaven's VIP lounge, and you and I find a lifetime's worth of solace in the lunatic scribblings of dead men.

JESSICA: He laughed in her parents' faces in court, do you remember that?

BETHANY: I remember.

KAT: The man is a walking nightmare. The last thing I want is to provide him any comfort in his final moments.

BETHANY: I was in court that day too.

KAT: And what did you see that was worthy of forgiveness? If I had the chance to kill him myself, tonight, I would give anything to take a shot.

BETHANY: Listen to me! It's not just for his sake. Listen: I am finally free of it. No more nightmares, no more phobias or panic attacks. No more prescriptions.

KAT: Just fifteen locks on your front door. And I'm guessing a handgun locked away with the TV set?

BETHANY: *(Quietly.)* Steve has his license.

KAT: Yeah, well I bet *Steve* didn't buy it. I'm not judging you, Bethany, God knows I've got a small arsenal at my place too, but since we're on the topic of forgiveness, wouldn't the Christian thing be to just let someone like Smith break in here and carry out your boys? Turn the other cheek and pray the police respond a helluva lot faster than they used to?

JESSICA: Stop it, Kat. She can forgive him if she wants.

(KAT turns away from them both. JESSICA crosses to BETHANY, reaches out to her old friend.)

JESSICA: I can't do it Bethany. It *has* me, you know? Smith was the only person who ever had any power in this situation, he has no right to ask anything from us.

BETHANY: That's not true anymore.

KAT: He made every parent in the country explain to their children why on earth a grown man might want three days alone with a twelve-year-old girl.

JESSICA: Remember when her mom and dad had to go on camera and beg him to bring her back? Do you think he watched it on the news? It doesn't matter to me how sorry he is now.

KAT: I had been dreading this week, but now I'm just desperate for Friday to come. He's had twenty years of his goddamn process. On Friday, it ends. No appeals, no final word from the defense team, just a quick, sterile exorcism with the blessing of the State of California. Thank God we live in a civilized country where we still kill criminals. *(Stops short as her own words register and begins to cry.)*

BETHANY: I am not asking you to speak to him, it's too late for that. Just be there. Be there for her sake, so she can finally rest. I know it's what Nina would want.

(Off their looks.)

BETHANY: I have it on good authority.

Scene 3

The Interview: KAT, JESSICA, and BETHANY are seated on stools. They each speak to an INTERVIEWER in front of them and do not hear or respond to one another.

KAT: I once read that when the first European explorers landed in America, the native people living here physically *could not see* their ships. These giant floating cities were so foreign to the universe as they understood it, there was just no frame of reference. No way to contextualize the new reality that had descended upon them—so it didn't compute. And the boats were rendered invisible; impossible to confront. That book is trying to prove the existence of aliens, which is not my point. What happened to Nina was my introduction to the large-scale Scary. I mean, we all had been warned to not go around taking unwrapped candy at Halloween. Our generation was raised to fear razor blades in apples, cyanide pills masquerading as Tylenol—but this was different. It took me a really long time to wrap my head around it. And I was there. I was a witness.

JESSICA: This place was never supposed to be your average suburbia—we were the babies of the Enlightened Class. Our parents were the ones who could pick out a good bottle of wine to go with any meal for under ten bucks, the ones who still insist on telling their children they are just middle class. When we got old enough to snoop around, almost every kid I knew found a copy of *The Joy of Sex* on a high shelf, alongside a stash of weed—for weekends only, of course. Well, it couldn't have been easy for the flower children to grow up. They'd already seen their movements die, their bank accounts expand. And then this.

BETHANY: I met Nina in the third grade. She was new in school and everybody just wanted to be close to her, immediately. She was always smiling. Had that sparkle, you know? I remember the Slip 'n Slide in the backyard, sore ribs after long burnt summer days. She'd always get that pink freckle line across her nose in the summer—you know the one I mean? It sounds trite to say it now, but she was a special girl. We all knew that. I remember the posters. Every single window of every single building in town. Thousands of tiny Ninas everywhere you looked, alongside this police sketch the three of us had worked on at the station.

KAT: We argued for hours over the width of his face

BETHANY: the thickness of his eyebrows.

KAT: Green eyes

BETHANY: Brown eyes

KAT: and a bushy gray beard. Eventually they released two different images, but the poster was more or less the same:

JESSICA: Her seventh grade school portrait shining and blissfully oblivious to the black and white bogeyman on her right.

BETHANY: I always wished they would make those posters separate, so she wouldn't be next to him like that.

JESSICA: The search spread across the state in two days, by the end of the week it had gone national.

KAT: They canceled soccer season 'cause all the parents were spending their weekends searching through parks,

JESSICA: alongside freeways.

BETHANY: I couldn't just sit there and not help, you know? They had an orientation where they gave us whistles and said we should look for—pieces of her pajamas. I didn't go on another search after that.

JESSICA: *People* magazine called her

ALL THREE: "America's Child."

KAT: And just like that:

BETHANY: a tent city mushroomed out of our lawn.

JESSICA: Overnight. Our mailman gave up after three days of fighting his way through the press—he started leaving our letters with a neighbor, who'd sneak through the backyards after dark and hand them off to Dad.

BETHANY: All of the sudden Nina belonged to the masses, the TV crews, shining out from those thousands of Missing Person posters.

KAT: In high school, my friends told me they would take down the posters and use 'em to roll joints. Good a use as any, when you think about it.

BETHANY: Right up until the day they found her, there was such hope. But as soon as word went out that we'd spent all those months searching and she'd been dead since day three…

JESSICA: All the kids in town were suddenly trying to work out what it meant—

BETHANY: What did he want with her?

KAT: Did he know it was her birthday?

JESSICA: Why did he just leave us?

ALL THREE: Sitting there.

BETHANY: Why didn't anyone lock the door? / Why didn't I do it myself?

KAT: / Why didn't I lock the door?

JESSICA: / Why wasn't that door locked?

KAT: I had only just stopped believing there were monsters living under my bed, and I'm sorry, but what a messed-up thing to do to your children, to convince them to not be afraid of the dark.

JESSICA: The four of us were sitting in a circle. I remember wondering if he knew he was in the wrong house.

BETHANY: It was Jessica's turn at Truth or Dare,

JESSICA: and he walked right into the middle of the room.

BETHANY: I think I laughed. Just because it was such a surprise, and obviously he had to be a relative or something.

KAT: A birthday visitor.

JESSICA: He smelled awful.

KAT: He stood there…I don't know…

JESSICA: a couple seconds?

BETHANY: Several minutes. Maybe five?

KAT: Breathing hard, looking at the four of us.

BETHANY: I remember thinking

ALL THREE: *(Whispering, overlapped—this continues over the next several lines.)* Please don't hurt me please don't hurt me please don't hurt me.

KAT: just turn around and go.

BETHANY: But he didn't.

JESSICA: But he didn't. He kneeled down next to her,

KAT: he pulled her in close and lifted her up like an infant.

(ALL THREE look up toward the ceiling, caught in the memory.)

BETHANY: His head almost reached the ceiling. That can't be right.

KAT: He told us that he'd be listening outside, and if we made a sound we were all dead. Then he carried her out the front door.

(The whispering stops.)

JESSICA: When they were gone I just kept thinking "oh thank goodness, she didn't have her shoes on. He can't take her too far in bare feet."

KAT: I know now that I should have screamed my head off as soon as the guy walked in,

BETHANY: but when you're a child in that situation, and he chooses to take your friend,

KAT: maybe part of you is just relieved that it wasn't you.

JESSICA: So you stay quiet.

BETHANY: I don't know.

JESSICA: I can see her pale little face, the way she looked as she was being carried away. She was whispering to him—

KAT: *(In a whisper.)* Please don't hurt my friends.

JESSICA: —please don't hurt my friends.

BETHANY: Police report says the three of us were there for ten minutes before we were able to get free. It was such a relief to hear that, because I really thought we'd been in there for hours.

KAT: Before we could wake her mom. Bethany was crying too hard, Jessica was in shock I guess. She couldn't stand.

JESSICA: My legs just stopped working.

KAT: So I was the one who had to go into Ellen's room.

BETHANY: Everyone kept saying over and over, "Well, you never *needed* to lock your doors here."

JESSICA: Maybe no one wanted to admit to themselves that there are horrible things that can happen—

KAT: —in this world, which is random and ferocious. And don't you think Nina's mother sees it that way? Don't you think she thinks about that damn lock every second of the day? That it gnaws her awake every night?

JESSICA: These days I feel most at home in New York City—where we're all prepared for the brutality of strangers. On every level. We keep our distance, our doors are deadbolted. This community, on the other hand, has been built on the tremendous faith—and maybe foolishness—of a population that prefers to focus on living the good life.

KAT: Everyone knows the Big One is coming. It's coming. It could be tomorrow, it could be twenty years down the line. But it will happen. This is a mathematical certainty. But the weather's nice, for now. Everybody's comfortable and some even have a couple granola bars stowed away in the name of Readiness.

BETHANY: We can't know what we're supposed to be bracing ourselves for until it comes. And each season that goes by without incident lulls everyone into believing that the threat somehow isn't real—just a parable invented to scare naughty children. People talk about it too, spend their lives in the shadow of something terrible and unnameable.

KAT: Mount Vesuvius continues to smolder, and we take in the view over sunset and a good bottle of wine.

SCENE 4

Late Friday night. BETHANY enters, sits down in a folding chair. She has been led into the execution witness room. She holds her hands in her lap, doesn't know where to look. After a few long moments, we see light rise on her as the curtain in front of the witnesses is lifted. Lights up on KAT in BETHANY's bedroom. The light of the television flickers on her face, and we hear the sounds of a news broadcast. After a moment, she turns the volume all the way down, continues to stare. JESSICA enters with a half-drunk bottle of wine, watches the silenced TV. Both are keyed up and antsy—like children in the midst of late-night mischief. Every part of them struggles against giving into the painful reality of this moment.

KAT: Look!

JESSICA: What?

KAT: These anchors are working so hard to keep from smiling.

(JESSICA looks at the TV.)

KAT: You can see it better with the sound off, this woman's been licking her chops for ten minutes.

JESSICA: Aren't you?

(They snicker uncomfortably.)

KAT: Are they gonna do it exactly at midnight?

JESSICA: They'll try. He's probably getting last rites now, it takes a little while. There will be some paperwork for him to sign.

KAT: You're kidding.

JESSICA: Afraid not.

KAT: Can Bethany…will she be able to see him?

(JESSICA passes KAT the bottle.)

JESSICA: They lift a curtain before it starts. The witnesses are on the other side of a window. He'll see her as well. They usually bring in some freaked-out nurse who has to hook the IV up to both arms, which I guess is hard enough without an audience. They'll make another announcement when it's done.

(Both stare blankly at the screen.)

KAT: Are they just going to keep talking until he's dead?

JESSICA: That's the news, Kat.

KAT: I can turn the sound back up.

JESSICA: Don't.

(Beat.)

KAT: Think we'll feel any different afterwards?

JESSICA: I keep hoping. Maybe in the morning we can call our shrinks, declare ourselves cured.

KAT: Donate our leftover prescriptions to a more worthy cause.

(A light comes up on BETHANY as the curtain is lifted. She makes eye contact with SMITH, weakly raises a hand, then sits very still.)

KAT: How long have you been on meds?

JESSICA: *(Oddly proud.)* I had a meltdown sophomore year of college, took a leave of absence for a couple semesters. A therapist told me I'd have to give up the Foundation in order to have a normal life. Guess I gave up on normal.

KAT: Any idea what set you off?

JESSICA: First love, I guess? First *relationship*. I had to come to terms with the fact that I can't get involved with people. Romantically.

KAT: Not...at all?

JESSICA: Don't look at me like that, it's less weird than it sounds. There are all these people out there who are totally unfit to be dating, / who just go out and do it anyway.

KAT: / And you just know your limits.

JESSICA: Yeah.

KAT: So you just. When was the last time...?

(This question. JESSICA looks at KAT, smiles, and shakes her head. This is her trump card.)

KAT: You've never been with anyone?

JESSICA: My shrink calls it emotional scar tissue.

KAT: Jack Smith ruined your fucking life.

(JESSICA shrugs, nods.)

KAT: I spent a lot of years thinking that he had ruined mine too.

JESSICA: Didn't he?

KAT: No. *(Beat.)* You did.

(JESSICA takes this in, not knowing what to do with her hands, where to focus her vision. BETHANY puts her head down.)

KAT: Well...that does make me feel better.

JESSICA: *(Suddenly looks up at the screen, and realizes:)* It's over.

(Something begins to bubble over in her, her knees give way, and she sits in front of the television, starts humming a faint melody. It is the tune of the hatzi kaddish. She is trying to remember the words. KAT sits and watches her.)

JESSICA: *(Closes her eyes and begins to speak. Shakily.)* Yitgadal v'yit-kadash sh'mei rabba, *(She starts over, singing this time.)* Yitgadal v'yit-kadash sh'mei rabba b'almah dee-v'ra chiru-teh v'yamlich malchuteh

(KAT moves towards JESSICA, who looks at her, takes a breath, and continues. KAT reaches for her hand and begins her own prayer.)

KAT: Our Father, who art in heaven hallowed be thy Name, thy kingdom come, thy will be done, on earth as it is in heaven. Give us this day our daily bread and forgive us our trespasses, as we forgive those who trespass against us. And lead us not into temptation, but deliver us from evil. For thine is the kingdom, and the power, and the glory, for ever and ever. Amen.

JESSICA: b'chay-yechon uv'yo-meychon uv'chay-yey de-chol beit Yisra-el, ba-agalah ba-aga-lah uvizman kareev, v'imru: Amen. Y'hey sh'mey rab-bah m'varach l'olam ul'olmey almah-yah. Yitbarach. Yitbarach v'yishtabach, v'yitpa-ar v'yitromam v'yisnasseh v'yit-haddar v'yit-alleh v'yit-hallal sh'mey de kud-shah, b'reech hu, l'eylah min kol birchatah v'shiratah tush-b'chatah v'nechematah daa-amiran b'almah v'imru: Amen.

(They lean on each other for a moment, then KAT turns to JESSICA.)

KAT: What did that mean?

(Beat.)

JESSICA: I have no idea.

(They laugh hard.)

Scene 5

The following morning. KAT is asleep on a couch upstage. JESSICA is zipping up her suitcase, hears a tap on the window. It is GRAYSON. She lets him inside, does not look at him.

JESSICA: What did I tell you about coming here?

GRAYSON: You're not answering your phone.

JESSICA: Shocking, I know.

GRAYSON: I was worried. You heading back to New York today?

JESSICA: Got a dinner in Oakland.

GRAYSON: Tonight? No rest for the weary. How'd you end up making it through the week?

JESSICA: What do you mean?

GRAYSON: How are you doing?

JESSICA: *(Turning to him and beaming.)* My demons are exorcised and I'm free to move on with my life.

GRAYSON: Really?

JESSICA: No. Sound okay though? I'm thinking about releasing it as a state-ment. What'd the network say about the interview?

GRAYSON: Big meeting this week. Things are looking promising, ratings were solid.

JESSICA: I'm glad to hear it.

GRAYSON: Thank you for your help.

JESSICA: I'm sorry to have been so hard to reach.

GRAYSON: You've been hard to reach since I've known you. Why don't we grab dinner in the city after you settle in? I at least owe you a meal. It's been good to see you again.

(She steps toward him, finally looking into his face. Very tentatively, she touches his shoulders, moves her hands down his arms. She stops abruptly, moves back and looks away again.)

JESSICA: I can't. I'm sorry.

GRAYSON: Guess I'll see you after the next one.

JESSICA: Have a safe flight.

(He exits. JESSICA tries to pull herself together and heads for the front door, where BETHANY is entering and blocks her escape.)

BETHANY: Glad I caught you. You were going to leave without saying goodbye?

JESSICA: I'm sorry. I didn't know when you'd be back.

BETHANY: Oh.

JESSICA: I have to drive to the East Bay this morning—I'm sorry.

(KAT speaks, startling them, from the couch.)

KAT: You said that already. *(To BETHANY.)* You saw it?

BETHANY: Yeah. I can make breakfast. Steve called, he's on his way home with Josh and Sam. I know they'd like to meet you both.

JESSICA: I have to go. *(She moves toward KAT.)* I'm going to do everything I can for Mike's case.

KAT: Send him a cake with a file inside.

(JESSICA grabs KAT's hands.)

JESSICA: I mean it.

KAT: So do I.

(JESSICA lets go of KAT, looks to BETHANY. They do not embrace or touch.)

BETHANY: Take good care.

(JESSICA exits.)

KAT: *(Gathering her things.)* I think Mom's ready to give Sarah back for a while—we've hit the Grandma wall.

BETHANY: Oh. Well. Thank you for coming.

KAT: I'm sorry I wasn't able to go with you last night.

BETHANY: Don't be.

(KAT starts to move toward the door, but BETHANY quickly positions herself between her guest and the exit. They stand looking at one another.)

BETHANY: You will always be in my prayers.

(They hug, then KAT exits. BETHANY is left alone in her living room. She walks to the couch, curls up in the fetal position. After a few beats, she abruptly rises, trots to the door, and turns all the locks. She goes to her couch, curls up again, and waits for her family to come home.)

(END OF PLAY)

POST MODERN LIVING

Book by Richard Sheinmel
Music and Lyrics by Clay Zambo

RICHARD SHEINMEL was born on May 24, 1967, on Coney Island. He grew up on Staten Island and attended the New York City High School of Performing Arts (his was the first class to graduate from the school's current home at Lincoln Center). Richard holds a BFA from NYU's Tisch School of the Arts, Experimental Theater Wing. During his time at NYU he studied in Paris, and after college he worked with many seminal artists from the early days of American indie theater, including Reza Abdoh, Penny Arcade, John Jesurun, Everett Quinton and the Ridiculous Theatrical Company, Jean-Claude van Itallie, Ridge Theater, and MCC Theater (where he was a core member during its formative years). As an actor, he is probably best known for performing for more than ten years in Jeff Weiss and Richard Martinez's *Hot Keys* serial at Naked Angels, MCC Theater, and P.S. 122. He frequently collaborates with the indie company Peculiar Works Project and most recently with Theatre Askew. Richard's produced plays include *Downtown Dysfunctionals* (librettist; Zipper Theater, 2001), *Jitter* (Arclight Theatre, 2006), and *Modern Living* (La MaMa E.T.C., 2006; directed by *Plays and Playwrights 2006* author Michael Baron). Among other projects, Richard is currently at work on parts 5 and 6 of the *Modern Living* series. He lives in Hell's Kitchen, Manhattan, with his companion of twenty-plus years, Christopher Frommer.

CLAY ZAMBO is a composer, lyricist, and sometime book writer. He was born in 1961 in western Pennsylvania, and grew up in McKeesport, a small former steelmaking city near Pittsburgh.

He was graduated from Ohio University in 1983 with a degree in theatre. His diverse theatre credits include *Greenbrier Ghost* (Susan Murray, book; Spirit of Broadway Theatre, Connecticut, 2010), *Modern Living* (Richard Sheinmel, book; La MaMa E.T.C., 2006), *I Am Star Trek* (Scott Ethier, music; Rick Vorndran, book; Edinburgh Fringe and Greenwich Theatre, London, 2005), and *Downtown Dysfunctionals* (Richard Sheinmel, book; Zipper Theatre, 2001). He has also composed/cowritten more than a dozen musicals for young audiences for New York's Poppyseed Players and Merkin Hall, among them *Yo, Jonah!* (Steve Brennan, book) and *Latkes and Applesauce*. Clay teaches and musically directs classes for adults and children at the Lucy Moses School in Manhattan, and is also director of music for a parish in suburban Connecticut. He lives in Norwalk, Connecticut, with his wife, Caran-marie, a writer, artist, and educator. Clay is a proud member of the BMI–Lehman Engel Musical Theatre Workshop.

Post Modern Living was first presented by La MaMa E.T.C. (Ellen Stewart, Founder and Artistic Director) on April 16, 2010, at The Club at La MaMa with the following cast and credits:

The Twelfth Day

Mitch	Richard Sheinmel
Chester	Mick Hilgers
Cousin Louie/Taxi Driver/College Advisor	Chris Orbach
Dr. Zappi	Frank Blocker
Meg	Catherine Porter
Gerrie	Briana Davis
Joy	Wendy Merritt

Über Mom

Joy	Wendy Merritt
Mitch	Richard Sheinmel
Robby	Frank Blocker
Cousin Louie	Chris Orbach
Grace	Catherine Porter
Gertrude	Briana Davis

Featuring the All-Star Spirit Guides:
   Scott Ethier, piano
   Gabriel Luce, bass
   Dan Acquisto, drums
   Gian Stone, drum alternate

Director: Jason Jacobs
Music Director: Scott Ethier
Production Stage Manager: Heather Olmstead
Associate Producer: Jenny Seaquist
Costume Design: Jennifer Caprio
Set Design: John McDermott
Sound Design: Tim Schellenbaum
Light Design: Timothy M. Walsh
Hair Design: Monica Minoui
Publicity: Ron Lasko, Spin Cycle
Poster Art: Christopher Frommer
Production Assistance: Moira Cutler, Dan Shaked

La MaMa E.T.C.:
    Founder and Artistic Director: Ellen Stewart
    Co-Artistic Director: Mia Yoo
    Managing Director: Mary Fulham
    Associate Director: Beverly Petty
    Director of Programming, The Club: Nicky Paraiso
    Special Projects: Denise Greber
    Marketing: Kiku Sakai
    Development: Kaori Fujiyabu
    Production Manager: Mark Tambella
    Production Coordinator: Sarah Murphy
    House Manager: Anna Hendricks
    Box Office: Michael David Arian, Tracy Francis, Michal Gamily, Craig Mungavin

Special thanks—Christopher Frommer and Caran-marie Zambo, Meg Anderson, Michael Baron, Christopher Borg, Rome Brown, Tim Cusack, David Derbyshrie, Will Lang, Ralph Lewis, Stephen Mosher, Barry Rowell, Nomi Tichman, Mike Wade, Atlantic Theater Company, BMI-Lehman Engel Musical Theater Workshop, and MCC Theater

The Twelfth Day and *Über Mom* were developed through the Naked Angels' Tuesdays at Nine series, Joe Danisi and Stephanie Cannon curators.

CHARACTERS

MITCH, a performance artist who writes plays about his life
CHESTER, his companion who paints
JOY, Mitch's mother
COUSIN LOUIE, Mitch's spirit guide who sings
ROBBY, Mitch's brother
MEG, an actress; Mitch and Chester's friend
GERRIE, a singer; also a friend of Mitch and Chester
DR. ZAPPI, a dermatologist
TAXI DRIVER
COLLEGE ADVISOR
GRACE, a lab technician
GERTRUDE, Grace's spirit guide

MUSICAL NUMBERS

"Modern Living 2.0" – Cousin Louie and Company
"How Christmas Ends" – Cousin Louie and Gerrie
"You Know" – Cousin Louie and Gerrie
"The Bear" – Cousin Louie
"Modern Living" (reprise) – Company

NOTES

Post Modern Living is part of a growing series of plays and songs about the life and work of fictional performance artist Mitch Mitchell. The series began with *Modern Living*, at La MaMa E.T.C. in 2006. Although it is preferable to present each installment as written, the one-act plays and songs can be performed individually with special permission from the authors. To find out more about the *Modern Living* series, go to www.sheinmel.com.

To hear samples of the music or license it for production, visit www.clayzambo.com.

The alternative spelling of Gxd used in this script is a reflection of the author's conservative Jewish beliefs, and does not affect the pronunciation or meaning.

MODERN LIVING 2.0

As the audience enters, there is the casual and welcoming feel of a downtown theatre. THE BAND is onstage—keyboard, bass, drums. After they finish a set of preshow music, the guitarist—COUSIN LOUIE—enters, along with GERRIE, a young woman who will sing backup and play percussion. COUSIN LOUIE counts off the opening and sings.

COUSIN LOUIE: THERE'S A HUNKY YOUNG CRO-MAGNON IN A CAVE.
THERE A HANDSOME WALL STREET LAWYER
WITH A HUNDRED-DOLLAR SHAVE.
THE TWO HAVE MORE IN COMMON
THAN THEY EVER WOULD SUSPECT.
THE ONE'S A HUNTER-GATHERER,
ONE ORDERS FRESH DIRECT.
BUT BOTH OF THEM NEED SOMETHING
AND IT'S SO HARD TO CONNECT.

THERE IS NOISE
AND THERE IS MUSIC,
THERE ARE GRUNTS
AND THERE IS MASS COMMUNICATION.
WE HAVE RICH IMAGINATION
BUT NO TIME FOR CONTEMPLATION.

CAN YOU HEAR ME?
DO YOU KNOW WHAT I AM SAYING?
IS THE SIGNAL
ALL-TOO-RAPIDLY DECAYING?
AM I GARBLED IN THE STATIC?
DO I SOUND DISTORTION-FREE?
THEY CALL IT MODERN LIVING
BUT IT DOESN'T SEEM LIKE ALL THAT MUCH HAS CHANGED
TO ME.

SAY YOUR PROBLEMS COULDN'T BE, BEFORE TODAY.
I'VE GOT HASSLES THAT I SEE AND SAY,
"IT'S ALWAYS BEEN THAT WAY."
WE THINK THE PROPER TOOL
WOULD SIMPLIFY THE WHOLE ORDEAL.
AN IPHONE AND A SHARPENED STICK,
THEY BOTH HAVE THEIR APPEAL.
WE SAY WE'RE MAKING PROGRESS
AS WE REINVENT THE WHEEL.

CAN YOU HEAR ME?
DO YOU KNOW WHAT I AM SAYING?
IS THE MESSAGE
LIKE AN ENDLESS LOOP REPLAYING?
IT'S AN ECHO IN THE CANYON,
IT'S A SILENT FALLING TREE.
THEY CALL IT MODERN LIVING,
BUT IT DOESN'T SEEM LIKE ALL THAT MUCH HAS CHANGED
FOR YOU AND ME.

WE HAVE PARENTS IN THE HOSPICE,
WE HAVE HEROES IN THE REHAB,
WE HAVE LOVERS IN THE BACKGROUND
WE HAVE JOBS—WELL, IF WE'RE LUCKY.
WE CAN TRY TO STAY IN BALANCE
AS WE STRETCH TO ALMOST BREAKING
OR JUST PULL OUR PELTS AROUND OURSELVES
AND SHIVER...

(Music continues under.)

COUSIN LOUIE: Welcome to Modern Living, here in The Club at La MaMa. Scott Ethier back here with the All-Star Spirit Guides: Gabriel Luce on bass, Dan Acquisto—drums, that's Gerrie—ain't she sexy? And me—You can call me Cousin Louie. And now I'd like to welcome to the stage, the reason we're all here—Mitch Mitchell—Mitch Mitchell everybody.

MITCH: We're back!!! Back where it all began, back in The Club here at La MaMa. *Modern Living—Post Modern* edition—we got some new stories to tell—and some great new songs by Clay Zambo.

What you need to know? It's morning in Hell's Kitchen—I slip from the bed, get the paper, start the coffee, slip back into bed with...Chester: my companion; my LTR; my husband, no we're not legally married; he's still sleeping (I love to watch him sleep). Our friends Gerrie and Meg, both just back into town (no, they're not girlfriends—everyone thinks they are). Gerrie sings with the band, and Meg acts in all my shows. There's my brother Robby, it's seven a.m. and he's already on the phone with...—Mom, our mom Joy, that's her on the other end of the modern umbilical chord. And me? I'm Mitch Mitchell and I act in plays I write about my life. You're here—I'm here; we're here...the band's here. Let's do it.

COUSIN LOUIE: HERE IN LIFE-OR-SOMETHING-LIKE-IT 2.0,
THERE'S NO EASY WAY TO FIND SOMEONE
WE'D LIKE TO GET TO KNOW.
TECHNOLOGY BRINGS MIRACLES

THAT NEVER LEAVE OUR CLUTCH.
THE UPGRADE PATH IS COSTLY,
BUT IT PROMISES SO MUCH.
WHAT ONCE WAS UNIMAGINED
CAN SO FAST BECOME A CRUTCH.
I HAVE SO MANY WAYS TO REACH YOU,

ALL: BUT WE NEVER REALLY TOUCH.
CAN YOU HEAR ME?

COUSIN LOUIE AND GERRIE: WE HAVE SOMETHING HERE WORTH TRYING TO SAVE.
WOULD YOU LIKE TO COME AND JOIN ME
IN MY CAVE?

(NOTE: The opening monologue can be amended to reflect the name of the theatre where the show is being performed, and the names of the actual performers involved, with the exceptions of MITCH, COUSIN LOUIE, and the ALL-STAR SPIRIT GUIDES.)

THE TWELFTH DAY

The play begins with the sound of electronic beeping. It's early morning as MITCH rises from bed, leaving CHESTER who pulls the covers toward himself. MITCH approaches an automatic drip coffee maker; when he touches it, the beeping stops. MITCH steps up to a microphone.

MITCH: How Christmas ends? Some holidays linger; others flash by in a puff of smoke and are gone. Like birthdays: now you're twenty, flash, now you're thirty, flash, now you're forty, flash. Now what year were you born? Some play dress-up, go to big fancy affairs with strings of balloons and fireworks. Some tiptoe by in darkness, sneak around corners, go unnoticed, lay forgotten. And some, they outstay their welcome. Like this one: unwrapped presents under the tree, our wreath has lost its fresh scent, brittle, she drops pine needles. They gather and wait by the door. The last day of Christmas is slowly passing, leaving a new scar.

(MITCH arrives bedside with two cups of coffee and the Times. *CHESTER rises. COUSIN LOUIE, a large man with a guitar, holds the pillows.)*

MITCH: Newspaper delivery service—what's that smell?

CHESTER: It wasn't me.

MITCH: No it's like sweet, like cinnamon. You don't smell that?

CHESTER: No.

(CHESTER pulls MITCH into the bed.)

MITCH: Hey watch my stitches.

CHESTER: Sorry.

MITCH: Today's the day.

CHESTER: Goodbye stitches.

MITCH: Hello scar.

CHESTER: No more Lumpy?

MITCH: I'm still Lumpy, just with one lump less.

CHESTER: I don't want to look, I don't want to look at the paper anymore.

MITCH: Just politics as usual.

CHESTER: Please, the left had one minute of power and what do they do? Nothing—their radical change is more of the same—and they have missed it, they have missed the boat. Health care is never going to pass.

MITCH: It's not that bad.

CHESTER: It won't be long before the conservatives are running the whole show again—and then, forget about gay marriage—they'll want us all to pack up and leave.

MITCH: I wish Manhattan could secede.

CHESTER: Don't know how being our own state would help things.

MITCH: Wait.

CHESTER: What?

MITCH: The Jews have Israel.

CHESTER: Yes?

MITCH: Start our own country.

CHESTER: Where?

MITCH: Buy an island.

CHESTER: Think you could get a loan?

MITCH: "Gaytopia."

CHESTER: Sounds like a fruity drink.

MITCH: Fruity—yes—mmmm—delicious Gaytopia.

CHESTER: How 'bout "Gayville"?

MITCH: Gaytopia is a promise—Gaytopia is a dream. Gayville could be the capital of Gaytopia.

CHESTER: A haven for the homosexual.

MITCH: Give us your bulldykes, trannys, twinks, and bears yearning for…? A good time on a Saturday night.

CHESTER: We'll name provinces after famous people: like the Oscar Wilde

MITCH: and Whitman after Walt.

CHESTER: Where Whitman Samplers come from.

MITCH: —and the resort town of Lesbos

CHESTER: located deep within the heart of the Ruby Fruit Jungle.

MITCH: Who needs Israel?

CHESTER: Seriously, if you had to leave—where would we go?

MITCH: I think Italy.

CHESTER: Oh Italy definitely.

MITCH: If you're going to live in exile you might as well drink good wine.

CHESTER: What are you doing?

MITCH: Sorting.

CHESTER: I hate when you start the laundry before I get out of bed, it makes me feel so ineffectual.

MITCH: Stay in bed, enjoy your coffee. I just feel motivated. Got to get things done. Got to clean the place up. We're having company tonight. Laundry first, then I do my yoga then I'm going swimming, and then I have my stitches out. There's that smell again.

CHESTER: Not guilty I swear.

MITCH: No—sweet like roses; you don't smell like that. Maybe it's the laundry—old cologne?

(MITCH steps out of the action and up to a microphone as he would in his show. Using abstract but everyday movements, he walks through the tasks as he performs them. COUSIN LOUIE accompanies on guitar.)

MITCH: Towels, whites, colors, jeans; there's that smell. Sorted now—dump in the machine. Five quarters twice—one, two, three, four, five—

COUSIN LOUIE: ka-ching,

MITCH: …detergent—softener, close to start—the water flows, check. Set the timer. Done. And there's that smell again—a fragrance kind of sweet-like?

COUSIN LOUIE: Molasses?

MITCH: I can taste it? I can taste it? I can almost taste it in my mouth. Chester will make the move from washer to dryer. Me? I go swim. Goggles, flip flops, towel, locker, lock it, shower first—remove your shoes. Toes on tile; find my spot. Warm sunlight streams across my side as I reach up, stretch forward, press down, pull back, press forward, twist up—feet under swing out and up toward the sun I'm a flower. Growing, twisting, raising, opening, my bloom unfolding; without me, within me—a flower it surrounds me, restrains me, contains me and then…

COUSIN LOUIE: It's gone.

MITCH: I dive into the water—cold gives way to cool gives way to warmth—sunlight, shattered splinters into hues of blue, sparkling on the white tile bottom each wave unfolding, washing over the other; flip turn, push off…

COUSIN LOUIE: Kick deeper

MITCH: …into the waves that surround me. My petals, my wings, outstretched descending deeper into this sweet blue flower. What are you? Azalea? Petunia? Begonia?

COUSIN LOUIE: Gardenia?

MITCH: I see white folds—smells so sweet like clove now. I'm the bee lost in the flower.

(Music ends. Shift in light back to apartment. The laundry is now in piles.)

CHESTER: How was your swim?

MITCH: Strange—it was good, but I felt kind of disjointed, like I was outside myself.

CHESTER: Will you put these away? You are so much better at it than I am.

MITCH: Flatterer.

CHESTER: You are.

MITCH: And I am—I'd rather put stuff away myself; that way I know where it is. Knowing where things are isn't one of my special skills. I just can't seem to find anything ever. Especially when I'm running late—like I am now. Chester, in contrast, is brilliant at it. Chester I can't find my keys.

CHESTER: Hallway bookshelf.

MITCH: Chester, have you seen my wallet?

CHESTER: Next to your keys.

MITCH: Where?

CHESTER: Right in front of you.

MITCH: Great thanks—Chester?

CHESTER: Your blue mittens?

MITCH: Please.

CHESTER: Right or left?

MITCH: I'm late.

CHESTER: The right one is in your pocket.

MITCH: Oh?

CHESTER: The left one is under the chair.

MITCH: I don't see it.

CHESTER: Here you go.

MITCH: Okay—wallet, cell phone, keys—kiss the boyfriend.

(They kiss.)

CHESTER: Bye lovee.

MITCH: See ya later. And with that I'm out the door off to Dr. Zappi. Late now, hand up—hail a cab not far, not too far to the doctor district—Park Avenue and 63rd. My doctor, Dr. Zappi—dermatologist—there's a joke in that, a dermatologist who wields a laser called Dr. Zappi. "Zap zap zap—zappie!" "Zap happy Zappi." "Buzzzzzzz—Zap—Buzzzzzzz—Zap, Buzzzzzzz—Zapie!"

TAXI DRIVER (COUSIN LOUIE): Everything okay back there?

MITCH: Swipe the debit card—get a receipt from the driver. Through the lobby, pass reception and into Dr. Zappi's.

(Shift in light, we are now in DR. ZAPPI's examining room.)

DR. ZAPPI: So let's take a look at those stitches—you want to roll up your sleeve.

MITCH: Sure.

DR. ZAPPI: There are two ways to do this—I pull away slowly and cut the hairs.

MITCH: Or?

DR. ZAPPI: Or quickly on a count of "one two three." Just—one, two.

(DR. ZAPPI pulls off the bandage.)

MITCH: Yowie!

DR. ZAPPI: Three. Oh nicey nice—this is doing well. You know usually I take the stitches out after two weeks so these have had a little extra time to heal.

MITCH: What did it turn out to be?

DR. ZAPPI: Calcium, I could tell pretty much right away, but it's best to run a lab report. You had one of the most healthiest fibromas I've ever seen, all pink and white. This may pinch a little.

MITCH: Is it going to bleed?

DR. ZAPPI: Unlikely—want to take off your shirt?

MITCH: Maybe I better. *(Takes off his shirt.)* So how was your vacation?

DR. ZAPPI: Fantastic, thanks for asking, you know you were the last patient I had before I left and here you are on my first day back. You're my continuity. *(Notices something.)* Hello? What's this?

MITCH: A pimple—I think.

DR. ZAPPI: I'm not so sure about that—let's take a closer look.

MITCH: Ow.

DR. ZAPPI: And it hurts?

MITCH: A little—I can feel it like a pulling.

DR. ZAPPI: That's got to come off Mitch.

MITCH: What?

DR. ZAPPI: I think we should take that off right now.

MITCH: Now?

DR. ZAPPI: I want a pathology. It's not a good color; it's not a good shape—and it's certainly not a pimple. You never noticed this before?

MITCH: Well I think I've seen it—it's like a birthmark.

DR. ZAPPI: That you don't remember?

MITCH: Yeah—um I don't know—um?

DR. ZAPPI: Can we do this—have you got time?

MITCH: If you think it's necessary.

DR. ZAPPI: I'll be right back—I have to go check in with the front desk and push back my schedule. This won't take long, okay?

(Exit DR. ZAPPI. MITCH calls CHESTER, he dials but hangs up—as he puts the phone back into his pocket, it rings.)

MITCH: Hey

CHESTER: Did you call me?

MITCH: I dialed but I hung up.

CHESTER: How's it going?

MITCH: Good.

CHESTER: Stitches out?

MITCH: Yeah—

CHESTER: You're on your way home?

MITCH: No, I'm still here—there, you know at Zappi's.

CHESTER: What?

MITCH: Something else, he found something else.

CHESTER: Under your arm?

MITCH: On my side—of my chest.

CHESTER: I knew it, that spot has been weird.

MITCH: He wants to take it off.

CHESTER: Well then let him.

MITCH: I'm just getting over the last set of stitches.

(Music sneaks in, like the last Christmas carol played on the radio.)

CHESTER: Don't wait a minute.

MITCH: Maybe it's nothing.

CHESTER: Maybe's not good enough.

MITCH: But—

(MITCH and CHESTER freeze—COUSIN LOUIE sings "How Christmas Ends.")

COUSIN LOUIE: THE STING IS SHARP AND SUDDEN.
IT HURTS A LOT AT FIRST,
BUT THEN IT'S PAST.

LIKE PULLING OFF A BANDAGE,
IT'S BEST TO DO IT FAST.
THE TRUTH I LEARNED OF SANTA CLAUS,
THE GROWN ME COMPREHENDS.
THIS IS HOW CHRISTMAS ENDS.

(Music continues under. DR. ZAPPI returns.)

MITCH: He's back.

CHESTER: Do it.

(MITCH hangs up his cell phone.)

DR. ZAPPI: Okay let's do this.

COUSIN LOUIE: THE SNOWY STREETS
  AND SIDEWALKS
I REALLY USED TO LOVE,
I SWEAR I DID.
BUT NOW, DON'T MENTION SNOW DAYS
UNLESS YOU'LL TAKE THE KID.
I'VE READ MY FILL OF BRAGGING LETTERS
ALL MY FAMILY SENDS.
THIS IS HOW CHRISTMAS ENDS.

DR. ZAPPI: Okay—it's laser time.

COUSIN LOUIE: WHEN I WAS A CHILD,
I THOUGHT AS A CHILD
I SPOKE AS A CHILD.
BUT I'VE ABANDONED CHILDISH WAYS,
I WORRY NOW OF SHOPPING DAYS.

(First music sting—representing the laser.)

MITCH: Wow.

(Second sting—MITCH shudders.)

MITCH: Ooooh—

(Third music sting.)

MITCH: I feel like it's going through my heart.

DR. ZAPPI: That's it we're done.

COUSIN LOUIE: THE DRUMMER BOY'S
  STILL DRUMMING.
THE LEAPING LORDS STILL LEAP,

JUST NOT SO HIGH.
THE GOLD RINGS HAVE SOME TARNISH,
BUT THAT'S NO CAUSE TO CRY,
A NOT-SO-TRUE LOVE BROKE MY HEART
AND SHE WANTS TO STILL BE FRIENDS.
THIS IS HOW CHRISTMAS ENDS.

(GERRIE sings backup as the song concludes.)

COUSIN LOUIE: THIS IS HOW
NEXT YEAR I MAY CHANGE MY MIND
IF DISBELIEF SUSPENDS,
BUT FOR NOW,
THIS IS HOW CHRISTMAS ENDS.
THIS IS HOW CHRISTMAS ENDS.
THIS IS HOW...

(Music changes—much later in the evening a small party winds down in MITCH's living room. There are Christmas presents. GERRIE, MEG, MITCH, and CHESTER all drink bright red cocktails. They sing.)

ALL: ...DANNY PARTRIDGE ON MY BARE
  KNEE.

CHESTER: A toast.

MITCH: A toast?

MEG: To the holiday.

GERRIE: For Christ sake it's almost Easter.

CHESTER: Arbor Day.

MITCH: There are twelve days of Christmas.

MEG: Is this lords a'leaping, or geese a'laying?

CHESTER: I think Martin Luther King Day is next up.

MITCH: We are mere minutes away from the end of Yuletime but we are still in the zone.

GERRIE: Well: to Christmas.

ALL: To Christmas.

GERRIE: Merry Christmas, this is the holiday I've been waiting for—back in New York, I can finally breathe.

(GERRIE swoons.)

MEG: You okay love?

GERRIE: I stood up way too fast—the room just started swimming, spinning round like…

CHESTER: Oh boy—here we go.

GERRIE: No I'm fine—I'm fine

MITCH: You look a little pale.

GERRIE: Maybe I better sit down. *(Sits on the floor.)* Oh that's much better.

MEG: You want to move to the sofa.

GERRIE: Oh no—I'm perfectly fine right here. *(Lies down.)*

MITCH: Well—it's official—it's a party.

MEG: Gerrie's turn to pass out.

GERRIE: I'm just resting my eyes.

MEG: You do that honey.

CHESTER: You glad to be back in New York?

MEG: I don't miss the city when I'm away—but I am glad to get a little Internet private time.

MITCH: I didn't know girls did that—

MEG: Did what?

MITCH: Never mind.

MEG: I'm talking about eHarmony.

CHESTER: You go girl.

MITCH: What's that like?

MEG: Well it has turned out to be in fact what I knew it would, a part-time unpaid job.

MITCH: Isn't it better to meet in person?

CHESTER: Why not go to a bar or something?

MEG: Oh please—bars are for girls who giggle. No, I finally concluded after years of wondering the desert in virtual celibacy, which was fine, in one sense very much needed, certainly the first five years, but then the second half was? It was like "Okay—dating has gone away," it's gone somewhere else. I have to go where it lives now.

CHESTER: So you go there.

MEG: It's simply the way dating is now. This is the medium for people these days—my age especially. It's the medium and past a certain point you have no choice but to catch up with it. Dive in there and swim.

MITCH: Digitally.

MEG: And while they don't seem to have an agenda, it pisses the fuck out of me that my gay friends aren't welcome there.

MITCH: Boys move much faster than that—I mean we can pick up a guy on my iPhone.

MEG: There's an app for that?

MITCH: Yeah—there is.

CHESTER: Gay men aren't interested in relationships.

MEG: Oh so you say.

MITCH: Well—we're the exception that makes the rule.

MEG: How'd you two meet again?

CHESTER: I saw him in this play—you tell it.

MITCH: No you—

CHESTER: You're the real storyteller.

MITCH: You haven't heard this before?

MEG: I'll let you know. Is it romantic or purely physical?

MITCH: Both actually.

CHESTER: It is a pretty good story.

MITCH: Very romantic and sexy; it involves a golden swing and an angel.

MEG: Go on…

CHESTER: I met Mitch backstage.

MITCH: He had come to see my show.

CHESTER: It was his senior year at college.

MITCH: *The Balcony* by Jean Genet.

CHESTER: You know it?

MEG: Know it and love it.

MITCH: Most people don't.

CHESTER: It takes place in a brothel.

MITCH: And first scene, curtain up—you see this priest getting his sex on with a nun.

CHESTER: Scandal right?

MEG: Like that never happens.

MITCH: But in our production—it was an altar boy.

CHESTER: Scandal, scandal.

MEG: Like that never happens.

CHESTER: How do you get a nun pregnant?

GERRIE: Dress her like an altar boy.

MITCH: Right—glad you're still with us.

GERRIE: I'm listing—listening. Listening and listing a little to the left, whoa.

MEG: Oh, sweetheart.

MITCH: I was an altar boy in the workshop—but by the time we got to production—things changed. They put me in wings.

CHESTER: These huge, pre-Raphaelite white feathered things.

MITCH: And nothing but a…a…—

CHESTER: swaddling cloth.

MITCH: Just enough to cover up my manhood.

CHESTER: And little else.

MITCH: I entered flying.

CHESTER: The first time I saw him.

MITCH: I came flying in on a golden swing my wings outstretched.

CHESTER: When I looked up, I gasped. I lost my breath.

MEG: Talk about an entrance.

CHESTER: And his hair hung down.

MITCH: Right—I had hair down to here.

CHESTER: In ringlets.

MITCH: Ringlets—did I mention that this was the eighties?

MEG: My Gxd you two have been together a long time.

MITCH: 1988.

GERRIE: Ronald Reagan was president.

MITCH: This was my senior production.

MEG: How did you end up there?

CHESTER: My cousin brought me; I was new in town.

MITCH: Which made him perfect—that and he had the cutest black hornrim glasses.

MEG: What do you mean perfect?

MITCH: Actually this story begins in Paris.

CHESTER: *(Refreshes the glasses.)* Another round of "Run Run Rudolphs"?

MITCH: Yes please.

MEG: I wouldn't say no to one more.

MITCH: Just a splash, I'm serious.

GERRIE: Don't forget the dormouse.

MEG: Honey? Maybe you should have some water instead?

GERRIE: Yes—yes, can I have a glass of water?

CHESTER: Sure love.

MITCH: I had been studying abroad in a program with the Experimental Theater Wing, I was nineteen and on my own.

CHESTER: A recipe for trouble.

MITCH: Absolutely—It's true—I was a recipe for trouble. In fact trouble was how I got there in the first place.

MEG: Why am I not surprised?

MITCH: To make a long story longer—going back just a little further—at the end of my freshman year at NYU, I found myself in the middle of this scandal. I was in trouble: basically I had been sleeping with everyone in my movement class.

MEG: Isn't that why you go to college?

MITCH: That's what I thought. I mean the class was called Contact Improvisation and I've always had a problem telling where the improv begins and ends; but it wasn't long before no one wanted to talk to me, forget about work with me—and so the teacher asked me to stay after in his office for a chat. Well chatting wasn't what he had in mind—and when I refused, he kicked me out of our production—and was going to fail me—but worse than that—everyone was talking. So, I went to my advisor...who gave me some of the best advice ever:

COLLEGE ADVISOR (COUSIN LOUIE): Have you ever considered going to Paris?

CHESTER: Just get out of Dodge boy.

COLLEGE ADVISOR (COUSIN LOUIE): We have a fantastic program there. You'll act with a theater company and get credit for it. I see you've taken French.

MEG: Of course you took French—I bet you did.

MITCH: Oui, oui.

COLLEGE ADVISOR (COUSIN LOUIE): These things loom large now but if you go and take a year abroad—by the time you get back, the school will be up to their eyeballs in some new scandal and no one will remember a thing.

MITCH: And it was absolutely true. So I went to Paris; but my problems didn't end there. No—I wasn't in Paris some three months before no one in my class wanted to talk with me, forget about work with me—and the director asked me if I could come back to his place for a private discussion on how I was performing or wasn't performing or should be performing if you get what I mean. The French have a word for "No" but me? I never learned it. And oddly enough here I am three months later and three thousand miles away and I'm the one who's up to his eyeballs in this remarkably similar scandal to the one I had run away from and left behind me in New York City. How could this be? Why do these things always happen to me? I mean the only thing in common between New York and Paris was—New York and Paris? New York and Paris—was me. Hmmm? Hmmmm? Me—yeah.

GERRIE: Epiphany!

MITCH: Me. Maybe, just maybe—I am causing my own problems. So right then and there, I swore off everything: all my vices, drinking, smoking, and my favorite distraction—

CHESTER: Sex.

MITCH: I was going to learn something Gxd damn it, even if I had to get blue balls to do it. And that is how I became celibate. And it was amazing; I actually started to learn something in college. I dedicated myself to study. I was a priest.

MEG: Without the altar boy.

MITCH: A monk.

CHESTER: That doesn't work either.

MITCH: Franciscan Friar? Whatever. Flash forward a few years later, to the now twenty-one-year-old Mitchie, who is playing a whore in a Genet play with a rehearsal process that involves a lot of choreographed sexual stimulation, I mean simulation of sex—I mean I was ready to climb the walls. So I decided enough was enough and so much for being celibate—I've got to do something.

MEG: You mean some*one*.

MITCH: Yeah do someone soon—those rehearsals were brutal, with all this rubbing and touching and I was twenty-one; but it couldn't be someone from school, and certainly not anyone in the cast…and in walked Chester, cousin to a classmate, new in town—perfect. So we got together.

MEG: What'd you boys do on your first date?

MITCH: Gay men don't date.

CHESTER: That's not true. Our first date we went to see this foreign film.

MITCH: *Wings of Desire.*

CHESTER: About an angel.

MITCH: Who wanders into a Big Top and falls in love with a trapeze artist.

CHESTER: Who dresses like an angel.

MITCH: She flies in on a golden swing

CHESTER: Her white-feathered wings fluttered.

MITCH: With her arms outstretched.

CHESTER: I should have known then.

MITCH: Before Chester—things wouldn't work out. Oh I tried, and I tried hard—but my relationships were these intense things that lasted one, two, three days at the most.

GERRIE: Run run Rudolph—run, run!

MEG: Hey—that's mine kitty.

MITCH: With Chester—one, two, three weeks go by and we're still seeing each other regularly; mostly we meet for sex—hot sweaty fun between class sex…you know—you made a good fuck buddy.

CHESTER: I may have been your fuck buddy—but you were always special to me.

MITCH: A month becomes a year, a little more, and we are living together in separate apartments. I can't think of a place I'd rather be then by his side; and I've been a one-dog man ever since.

CHESTER: So you say.

(MITCH's house phone rings.)

MITCH: It's Joy.

CHESTER: Kind of late for her; aren't you going to answer it?

MITCH: Of course. *(Answers.)* Hey Mom what's up?

JOY: Where are you?

MITCH: Where am I? You called me.

JOY: Oh boy.

MITCH: What's going on?

JOY: I didn't want to leave it on your machine; I've been calling all day.

MITCH: Is it Robby? Did he do something?

JOY: I wish it was—I wish it was Robby; he's useless you know, no help at all and I'm going to need help.

MITCH: What?

JOY: Are you home now?

MITCH: Mom?

JOY: It's cancer.

MITCH: And in my mind—I'm back in the doctor's office with the smell of burning flesh—and the sting as he zaps me with his laser ripping out a small piece of my heart…and the smell.

CHESTER: Mitchie? What is it?

JOY: Just the smallest, the tiniest dot.

MITCH: Mom?

JOY: I have cancer.

MITCH: I think, Mom, the Über Mom; the Mom from which all Moms come. The Mom without which there could be no other Mom. My Mom.

JOY: It sounds like you're having a party.

MITCH: It's just a little Christmas thing. Gerrie and Meg came over, back from the Holidays. *(Pause.)* Mom?

JOY: I know, I know Mitchie. It's in me.

(Music and COUSIN LOUIE return: "You Know.")

COUSIN LOUIE: FOUR CALLING BIRDS,
THREE FRENCH HENS,
TWO TURTLE DOVES…
AND A LUMP IN THE THROAT…
AND A PUNCH TO THE GUT…
AND THE TEST MAY BE NEGATIVE…
BUT…

MITCH: And that's how Christmas ends.

YOU KNOW

GERRIE: EVER KNOW THE PHONE WAS ABOUT TO RING?
EVER KNOW WHO WAS GOING TO CALL?
EVEN BEFORE YOU HEARD A KNOCK ON THE DOOR,
EVER KNOW WHO WAS OUT IN THE HALL?

COUSIN LOUIE: EVER WONDER HOW IT HAPPENS,
WHAT PSYCHIC PRINCIPLE IS APROPOS?

BOTH: *(Alternating.)* YOU KNOW,
YOU KNOW YOU KNOW,
YOU KNOW YOU KNOW YOU KNOW,
YOU KNOW YOU KNOW YOU KNOW YOU KNOW,
YOU KNOW?

(Instrumental break during which the set begins to change.)

GERRIE: EVER TAKE A RIGHT WHEN YOU SHOULD GO LEFT,
JUST TO STOP FOR SOME CHIPS AND A TAB?

COUSIN LOUIE: WHAT LITTLE SPARK, WHAT LITTLE VOICE IN THE DARK
KEPT YOU SAFE FROM A RUNAWAY CAB?

GERRIE: IS IT LUCK OR INTUITION,

COUSIN LOUIE: A WARNING SIGNAL FROM A U.F.O?

BOTH: *(Alternating.)* YOU KNOW,
YOU KNOW YOU KNOW,
YOU KNOW YOU KNOW YOU KNOW,
YOU KNOW YOU KNOW YOU KNOW YOU KNOW
YOU KNOW.

COUSIN LOUIE: IS IT SPIRIT GUIDE OR ANGEL
WHO SENDS THE MAGIC MENTAL CLUE?

GERRIE: YOU CAN CHOOSE NOT TO BELIEVE IT…

COUSIN LOUIE: TRY TO IGNORE IT…

BOTH: BUT HAVE I GOT NEWS FOR YOU:
YOU KNOW,
YOU KNOW YOU KNOW,
YOU KNOW YOU KNOW YOU KNOW,
YOU KNOW YOU KNOW YOU KNOW YOU KNOW.

YOU KNOW,
YOU KNOW YOU KNOW,
YOU KNOW YOU KNOW YOU KNOW,
YOU KNOW YOU KNOW YOU KNOW YOU KNOW,
YOU KN—

(A phone rings.)

COUSIN LOUIE: I *knew* that was going to happen!

ÜBER MOM

The play begins with the ringing of a telephone. We are in JOY's kitchen. MITCH sets the table for lunch.

JOY: It's your brother.

MITCH: You know without looking.

JOY: Please, he's having one of his fits—he calls me every fifteen minutes.

MITCH: Why don't you just let the machine get it?

JOY: He knows I'm home. *(Picks up the phone—puts ROBBY on speaker phone.)* Yes Robby.

ROBBY: I think he's trying to aggravate me personally, that doctor. How can I not think that? You got to agree.

JOY: No Robby I don't.

ROBBY: But he purposely put off filing that form just because he knows I'm waiting.

JOY: You told me that already.

ROBBY: He's a psycho.

JOY: I do not think your doctor's a psycho. He's a professional.

ROBBY: Yeah—Dr. Professional Psycho.

(JOY and MITCH laugh a little.)

ROBBY: You know it.

JOY: I'll try to straighten it out on Monday. I have got to go—your brother is here.

ROBBY: You won't—you're just trying to get me off the phone.

JOY: No I will—I'll straighten it out on Monday. Hello—Robby it's Sunday morning there is nothing I can do now. I'm going. I'll call him—I promise.

ROBBY: You'll call him?

JOY: I will—I'll call him.

ROBBY: You promise?

JOY: Now I'm going okay?

ROBBY: If he delays past Monday, I'll miss the deadline.

JOY: Okay I'm hanging up now—

ROBBY: Dr. Psycho—head of the idiot patrol.

JOY: Goodbye.

(JOY hangs up the phone and joins MITCH at the table; together, they prepare a salad for lunch.)

MITCH: How long has he been like this?

JOY: I know he sounds crazy—and he half is—but the other side is his doctor who really does torment him. He's not making that up. His doctor knows he gets upset about these things—and I think he enjoys agitating him—sort of in turn for all the grief Robby gives him. Every now and then this doctor sticks it to him. *(Makes a stabbing gesture.)*

MITCH: He's probably calling his doctor too.

JOY: Oh—I know he's calling his doctor. It's always about Robby, twenty-four-seven; every day's a nonstop flight to Robby Robby Robby. The world can be going to hell in a hand basket; his problem is always bigger. He takes precedent. He's first in line.

MITCH: He's not even in the room and he's dominating the conversation.

JOY: What were we talking about before Hurricane Robby blew in?

MITCH: How you found out about, you know, about the cancer.

JOY: The first time I had a lump

MITCH: Lump one.

JOY: it turned out to be nothing.

MITCH: Nothing—not cancer.

JOY: Right, I found it demonstrating one of those exams—because a good health educator teaches everyone to do those breast exams.

MITCH: Right and you were doing that.

JOY: The "how to" part.

MITCH: Just like you tell people to.

JOY: I don't do—"do as I say not as I do."

MITCH: Um hmm?

JOY: I do. And so I do; and I am *(Demonstrates the movement one does when doing a self-exam.)* and of course I find this damn little thing: the spot.

MITCH: Lump one.

JOY: My lump one.

MITCH: Like two years ago.

JOY: I had to take it out. It was a no brainer.

MITCH: Sure.

JOY: So I went through the pre-op and the post-op; the surgery; the anesthesia. It was awful. It was an awful experience I don't know why it was such an awful experience.

MITCH: Of course it was awful.

JOY: Yeah, it was awful; but all through all that I knew—I knew—I did not have cancer. Because I know my body. I KNOW my body. And I can shut my eyes and I can scan my body and when something goes wrong generally I'm the first person to know.

MITCH: Yeah.

JOY: Do you like sunflower seeds in your salad?

MITCH: Oh I love them—I do.

JOY: You are so my son—I'm crazy about nuts. They're in the Ziploc.

MITCH: This one?

JOY: That's it. Now onto lump two.

MITCH: The cancer.

JOY: That was a whole 'nother story. No one could find it—but I knew—I knew exactly where it was. It was saying "Here, here—here!"

MITCH: So what do you do?

JOY: I go in for a mammogram—anyway, I was overdue by three months.

(A TECHNICIAN, a woman in a lab coat with a clipboard, appears. Music starts. COUSIN LOUIE, watching the scene, sings "The Bear.")

COUSIN LOUIE: SOMETIMES YOU GET THE BEAR...

GRACE: Joy Wendell?

COUSIN LOUIE: SOMETIMES THE BEAR GETS YOU.

GRACE: Dr. Joy Wendell?

COUSIN LOUIE: SOMETIMES YOU GET AWAY.

JOY: That's me.

COUSIN LOUIE: SOMETIMES THAT'S THE BEST THAT YOU CAN DO.

GRACE: I'm Grace, I'll be your Mammo Tech. Follow me, we're back here in Lab Three.

COUSIN LOUIE: SOMETIMES A LUCKY BREAK,
SOMETIMES YOU END UP BROKE.
SOMETIMES YOU'RE JUST ON FIRE,
SOMETIMES YOU GO UP IN SMOKE.
AND YOU NEVER KNOW
WHICH WAY IT'S GONNA GO.
MY ADVICE IS TAKE A BREATH.
I MEAN, IT'S ONLY LIFE OR DEATH.
IT DOESN'T QUITE SEEM FAIR,
BUT WHO SAID IT WOULD BE?
SOMETIMES YOU GET THE BEAR.
SOMETIMES...WAIT AND SEE.

(Music out.)

GRACE: *(Reading the chart.)* Dr. Wendell?

JOY: Most people just call me Joy.

GRACE: Joy?

JOY: *(To MITCH.)* Definitely a member of the sisterhood.

MITCH: No.

JOY: Trust me, we Older Wiser Lesbian OWLs—we know these things.

GRACE: Do you mind if I ask you a professional question?

JOY: Not at all.

GRACE: Oh that's great because I have this problem—with my balance—the room will start spinning.

JOY: I'm not that kind of doctor...

GRACE: Oh—It's just I'm worried—I'm thinking maybe lupus.

JOY: I'm a therapist—a psychotherapist.

GRACE: Do you know anything about lupus?

JOY: I'm a doctor of sexology.

GRACE: Oh.

JOY: But if you ask me—it could be something simple, like a sinus infection. That can mess with your balance.

GRACE: I was thinking R.A.

JOY: Arthritis?

GRACE: Yeah rheumatoid—one of our doctors in radiology, she has R.A., and she gets these dizzy spells all the time.

JOY: *(To MITCH.)* So I shut my eyes and I look at her to see if I could see anything, because I can scan people when I shut my eyes. I can see if there is something hurting someone inside—sometimes. *(Shuts her eyes.)* And so when I shut my eyes—like right now on you—I'm getting a funny kind of line here.

MITCH: Really.

JOY: It seems like you have a slight headache or something going on?

MITCH: Up here?

JOY: Yeah—I'm getting a light spot. You're going to get an allergy attack from the cat!

MITCH: Sweet as she is I am seriously allergic to Sappho.

JOY: It's starting.

MITCH: And the little bits of herself she leaves on everything.

JOY: Bottom line is.

MITCH: How do you do that?

JOY: I can see it.

MITCH: Like an aura.

JOY: Auras are different—they're like a glow around you. This is more in you—can be a dark patch or area.

MITCH: These are delicious.

JOY: I get them at the Costco—they come in this je-gunda bag. Most of it goes to Robby.

MITCH: So could you see anything on the Mammo Tech?

JOY: Grace? No. But something else—actually she was impossible to miss—she was in my face from the moment I walked in the door.

MITCH: I don't understand—the Mammo Tech was in your face?

JOY: No—Gertrude.

MITCH: I thought her name was Grace.

JOY: No—not the Mammo Tech—her spirit guide. Now some people don't want to know about spirit guides—it creeps them out—they pretend they just do not exist—but other people find comfort in the idea that we are not alone.

MITCH: Do I have one?

JOY: Sure you do.

MITCH: Really—what's she like?

JOY: Actually—I'm pretty sure he's a guy, kind of big—sometimes he has a guitar.

MITCH: Is he here now?

JOY: I don't think so—usually when he's around—I see flowers, gardenias all white.

MITCH: Cool. What do spirit guides do?

JOY: I really don't know, I just know that they're often there and—I've learned it's best not to just blurt these things out. So I say to her "You ever wonder if you have anything like a guardian angel?'

GRACE: Well not really.

JOY: Do you believe in that stuff?

GRACE: Well, yeah—I've always thought so.

JOY: If you had one, would you want to know?

GRACE: I think I would—yes.

JOY: Okay. Yes you do. And she's very young and I think she's like an aunt.

GRACE: I'm sorry I only have one aunt and she's really getting along, in her eighties—and I can tell you she's very much alive.

JOY: G—R something. She's got a very long name.

GRACE: I've never lost any...

JOY: I'm getting a G and an R—a long name.

GRACE: It can't be a relative.

JOY: Maybe her first name begins with a G and her second begins with the R?

GRACE: Well my name begins with a G and an R: Grace.

JOY: Ask your dad about it.

GRACE: It can't be.

(A music sting as GERTRUDE is revealed—a twelve-year-old girl who looks like she is from another time.)

GERTRUDE: Go home and ask your dad.

JOY: No, she says "Go home and ask your dad."

GRACE: Who does?

JOY: Your spirit guide.

GRACE: Okay then.

JOY: Look I'm just telling you what I'm picking up.

GRACE: Now I know this is going to be a bit uncomfortable.

JOY: *(To MITCH.)* Meantime she's doing my mammogram and she's squeezing my breast between these two plates. Men would never put up with that—I mean can you imagine if you had to have your balls squeezed between two plates of glass? No man would do it. My breast was like this. *(Demonstrates.)*

MITCH: That's why there's no "Manogram" test for ball cancer.

JOY: Testicular.

MITCH: Instead, a doctor gently cups you and gives them like a mini-massage.

JOY: You're kidding me?

MITCH: It's what they do.

JOY: You know how they tell you to prepare for a mammogram? There's a website I swear. Google "How to prepare for a mammogram"—they say lie down in the street, take your breast out, and gently place it between two bricks—then rest a long board down on top of it—and have a truck drive back and forth over it again and again.

(They both laugh.)

MITCH: Yowie!

JOY: You're not kidding—it hurts.

MITCH: I'll take these to the kitchen.

JOY: Sit, I'll do it later.

(The telephone rings again.)

JOY: Right on schedule. *(Answers.)* Yes Robby.

ROBBY: Now his service has stopped taking my calls.

JOY: That makes sense.

ROBBY: Can they do that? Just hang up on me? Hello, click, Hello click. I don't think they can do that—legally. What if this was an emergency?

JOY: Exactly Robby.

ROBBY: It's their job to answer the phone.

JOY: What if it was an emergency Robby—someone else is having a heart attack and needs to get through to the doctor—and they're busy with you.

ROBBY: He'll miss the deadline, I'll lose my benefits, the program already hates me—they all hate me, all they need is an excuse and I'm out—and Dr. Psycho knows it.

JOY: I know. We've been over this—you are being abusive by calling me constantly.

ROBBY: I am not calling you constantly.

JOY: Think about it Robby—Goodbye. *(Hangs up.)*

MITCH: Oh dear.

JOY: I'm starting to think there's something wrong with his meds. We'll see if he calms down in an hour or two. Back to the story at hand...

MITCH: The mammogram...

JOY: I never expected anything to show up on it.

MITCH: But you said you had a sense about it—that's why you went in the first place.

JOY: I had a sense yes—but denial is not just a river in Egypt. I kept thinking—I had done everything, everything I could.

MITCH: You exercise every day.

JOY: I mean I really have followed a very healthy kind of lifestyle.

MITCH: You eat right.

JOY: Like not eating trans—I mean I worked at the Food Co-op so I could get away from trans fatty acids long before anyone had ever heard of what those darn things were. But nobody: not Grandma, nobody had—nobody in my family, not my sister, none of my aunts or cousins, I mean not a one has ever had—breast cancer and so I really wasn't very concerned. Of course as a good health educator I know that it does happen to one out of every seven women and you don't have to have a relative. I know that. But still—

(The telephone rings. Music starts: "The Bear, Part 2.")

JOY: Three days later...

(It rings again, she answers it.)

JOY: Hello.

COUSIN LOUIE: SOMETIMES YOU GET THE LAUGHS.

GRACE: Hello Dr. Joy? This is Grace from Columbia Services Imaging.

COUSIN LOUIE: SOMETIMES THE LAUGH'S ON YOU.

JOY: How are you?

GRACE: Oh me I'm fine—thanks for asking—

COUSIN LOUIE: SOMETIMES YOUR TIMING'S BAD,

GRACE: We got the results back from your test

COUSIN LOUIE: SOMETIMES YOU ARE PERFECTLY ON CUE.

GRACE: Not that you should worry but we do see some clusters of calcium.

JOY: Calcium?

GRACE: Spots.

JOY: I don't understand.

GRACE: It's just a precaution—Calcium spots like these are a known precursor.

COUSIN LOUIE: SOMETIMES IT'S GO TO JAIL, GO TO JAIL, GO DIRECTLY TO JAIL,

GRACE: We should do a sonogram to take a closer look-see.

COUSIN LOUIE: SOMETIMES YOU'RE ON PARK PLACE.

GRACE: Our first opening is Thursday next—how's that for you?

COUSIN LOUIE: SOMETIMES IT'S EASY AS PIE, SOMETIMES A PIE IN YOUR FACE.

JOY: So Thursday next I'm back there. I immediately want to ask her if she talked to her father about her spirit guide; but silently we walked to the room.

COUSIN LOUIE: AND YOU'RE NEVER CLEAR WHICH WAY YOU'RE GONNA VEER.

GRACE: Okay, sit up here and lean back.

COUSIN LOUIE: MY ADVICE IS MOVE AHEAD.
THE NEWS IS BETTER LEFT…SAID.

JOY: I'm nervous.

GRACE: There's nothing to be nervous about, this doesn't hurt—it just tingles.

(GRACE turns on the sonogram machine, dabs some oil on the head of a paddle, and starts to move it in a circular motion.)

COUSIN LOUIE: SOMETIMES YOU'RE IN THE SQUARE,

JOY: I see what you mean.

COUSIN LOUIE: SOMETIMES YOU'RE OUT OF TOUCH.

GRACE: I'm just going to concentrate on the calcium spots.

COUSIN LOUIE: SOMETIMES YOU GET THE BEAR,
SOMETIMES, NOT SO MUCH.

(Music out.)

JOY: I got to ask you—Did you talk with your dad about your spirit or…?

GRACE: I wanted to call you but it felt awkward, somehow inappropriate calling a patient.

JOY: I'm not like that—it would have been fine with me.

GRACE: Anyway I knew I was going to see you—I scheduled you into my room.

JOY: So—what happened?

GRACE: When I got home, my father was sitting at the table drinking. He had a scotch, which he never does—drink scotch. So right away I knew something was wrong. I mean really wrong. Turns out that earlier in the day things had taken a turn for the worse with his sister, my aunt. I think I told you about her, in her eighties? She had to go into this nursing home. Now my dad had promised that he would never do that but her Alzheimer's had reached a point where it was beyond his control. He was devastated— So I come trotting in—and I say to him "You want to hear a funny story? I had this wacky woman come in today."

JOY: What do you mean "wacky?"

GRACE: Not in a bad way. I told him all about you—how you'd said that I had a spirit, a guardian angel. Now my father, who was in no mood for this sighed—the way he does when he just hates what I have to say. *(Demonstrates.)* like that. I knew he didn't want to hear it but I went ahead and told him anyway, what you told me, about the G and the R; and what I told you—that I have only one aunt and she's definitely not ten.

JOY: She is more like twelve or thirteen.

GRACE: And then Joy, his eyes opened up wide like saucers—I did have an aunt, I never knew of—who died when she was twelve, of TB. Her name was Gertrude.

JOY and MITCH: Gertrude.

(Music sting.)

GRACE: With a G and an R.

(GRACE finishes up the sonogram; she puts the paddle down on the table and looks over a printout.)

GRACE: We used to have to wait to see the results but now—Joy, I'm afraid that your calcium, is the kind of deposit that is often associated with cancer.

JOY: I have it? I have cancer?

GRACE: This doesn't mean a thing Joy.

JOY: Oh Goddess, Goddess no. I knew it, I knew it—cancer.

GRACE: Plenty of people have a calcium accumulation just like this and it turns out to be nada.

JOY: Everything in my being is shouting "cancer."

GRACE: It just means we do some further testing,

JOY: I can feel it—I can see it, I have cancer.

GRACE: We don't know, we don't—but it could be—it could be Joy. We have to look beneath the skin.

JOY: So now what?

GRACE: There are two options. Choice one: we do a biopsy.

JOY: Which is?

GRACE: With a biopsy—we insert a small wire tracing the path to the spot, and then go to a special clinic in the hospital where they put you under and remove it. The spot and what's behind it.

JOY: Been there, done that; that's what they did last time—the anesthesia made me sick for weeks. What's the other option?

GRACE: Option B is Mammotome—the advantage is we can do it right here, and there's no need for anesthesia.

JOY: What does that involve?

GRACE: You lay down on a table—we clean your breast—then create a vacuum. I insert a needle; it's a little larger than a regular needle—two and a half millimeters. We'd go in and remove the calcium and pull out the surrounding cells. Then we send it out for pathology—hopefully there's nothing there.

JOY: And you would do it? You would be the one?

GRACE: I could do it—if you wanted.

JOY: Okay then—I've decided Mammotome it is.

GERTRUDE: *(With a music sting.)* Ask him about the bear.

JOY: What?

GRACE: I didn't say anything.

GERTRUDE: *(With a music sting.)* Tell her to ask him about the bear.

JOY: It's Gertrude.

GRACE: She's here?

GERTRUDE: The bear. The bear—

JOY: The bear.

GRACE: What about a bear?

GERTRUDE: Ask your father about the bear.

JOY: She wants you to ask your father about a bear—I see a black bear.

(The telephone rings again.)

JOY: Up? Guess who?

MITCH: Robby?

JOY: What do you want to bet?

(Phone rings.)

JOY: They're getting further apart, that's a good sign.

MITCH: You want I should answer it?

JOY: Be my guest.

MITCH: *(Answers the phone.)* Hey Robby—it's Mitchie.

ROBBY: What are you doing out at Mom's—time for your once-yearly visit?

MITCH: I'm helping Mom with her garden—it's Mother's Day.

ROBBY: Mitch, I got problems.

MITCH: Your doctor is a psycho?

ROBBY: Mom tell you?

MITCH: No—you did.

ROBBY: When.

MITCH: Just before when you called.

ROBBY: You were listening in?

MITCH: You were on speaker phone.

ROBBY: Speaker phone?

MITCH: Look—we're eating lunch, can I call you back?

JOY: *(Quietly, so ROBBY doesn't hear.)* Good one.

ROBBY: I don't like being on speaker phone—anyone can hear you.

JOY: Don't worry Robby, nobody's listening.

MITCH: *(To JOY only.)* Especially not us.

JOY: *(To MITCH.)* Oh—you're bad.

ROBBY: What do you mean you're not listening?

MITCH: I'm just kidding.

ROBBY: No you're not—you never listen to me.

MITCH: I'm listening to you right now.

ROBBY: Out here for your once-yearly visit—full of advice, but where are you the rest of the year, when the shit hits the fan?

JOY: Hey—your brother's a very busy boy.

ROBBY: I'm just saying—he's never here when something needs to be done.

MITCH: As opposed to you—who's here all the time and does nothing.

ROBBY: Oh you think so?

MITCH: Yeah I think…

ROBBY: You think so.

MITCH: Yeah I think…

ROBBY: Is that what you think Mitch?

(JOY puts her hand on MITCH—stopping the argument.)

MITCH: Look, I want to eat my lunch.

ROBBY: No one's stopping you.

MITCH: Can we go now?

ROBBY: You want to go? So—go. *(Hangs up.)*

JOY: Oooh—you got him to hang up on you—he never does that with me.

MITCH: Sorry.

JOY: Don't worry, he'll call back—he always does. So—one week later I'm back there.

(Music returns: "The Bear, Part 3.")

JOY: The first thing I want to know about is the bear but when I ask Grace, she just puts up her finger to her lips—I got the feeling she just didn't want to talk about it front of her coworkers, but we were never alone from the time I entered the clinic to until the time I was on the table for the Mammotome.

COUSIN LOUIE: SOMETIMES YOU'RE ON SKID ROW, SOMETIMES YOU'RE WAY UPTOWN. SOMETIMES IT'S LACE AND FURS, SOMETIMES AN OPEN-BACK HOSPITAL GOWN.
(THAT IS SO NOT YOUR COLOR.)

JOY: Finally her assistant left the room.

GRACE: You'll feel a little pinch, a sharp sensation.

JOY: Aow.

GRACE: Then a warming sensation as it spreads.

JOY: You got to tell me what happened. Did you tell your father?

GRACE: I asked my father about the bear—and I have to tell you Joy—he just broke down and cried.

JOY: I'm sorry.

GRACE: Don't be—they were tears of joy. Okay, now exhale slowly, I know it's difficult in this position but try to relax. You shouldn't feel a thing—just discomfort.

JOY: What did he say?

GRACE: Let me tell you a story…

(*GRACE begins the procedure. Music, as GERTRUDE appears.*)

GERTRUDE: When your father was a little boy—he was the youngest of our family. And just after he was born our mother died—it was cancer. He was next younger than me—but I was seven years older. When this happened he was just a little thing. I would tend to him often. I called him Toddy, that was my nickname

for him, and he was my baby—he was my little baby boy.

We didn't live in the woods per se—we had a large acre of property—really more of a suburb but in those days it was not uncommon to see a wild animal roaming about the streets. When I left Toddy he was playing in his sandbox out behind the house—I had just turned and headed up the stairs of the porch when I heard this giggle, this squeal of laughter coming from behind me in the sandbox—what could be so delightful? Then I turned around and I saw Toddy; he was playing with a baby bear—a black baby bear cub. He must have wandered into our yard.

Now Toddy had no idea what kind of danger he was in. Blissfully unaware he kept hitting the cub like this; like this. At first I did nothing. I couldn't—I froze; I stood perfectly still. But the more Toddy hit him—the more I knew I had to do something. So slowly I got closer and closer to the sandbox, but with each step it seemed further and further away. Toddy hit the bear again, again, again he laughed—this time it howled back at him "Rar!" "Danger, Danger—Toddy get away from the bear" I shouted but he just laughed. He couldn't be happier playing with his newfound friend. Maybe nothing would happen? I started to run. "Toddy" I shouted "Toddy—come to me now!" And that's when I saw it—There wasn't just a baby bear in our yard, mama bear was there too. The bushes rustled and there she is. As I ran toward Toddy she must of thought I was headed for her cub—because she started to charge at us too. The bear between us, Toddy was on the other side of the cub. I never moved so fast in my life. I swooped in and grabbed him by the back of his shirt and pulled, just seconds before…and I ran. I sprinted to the porch and up the steps, my heart pounding. The bear still coming at us—I hit the top step and slid, tripping over the door jam I landed on my knee, scraping off the skin, there was blood everywhere but still I had Toddy by the collar. I managed to slam the door. I'll never forget the thump as the black bear slammed into it, the window above our heads shattered. It knocked Toddy and me down to the ground. Then she roared and swung at the door with her large paws.

Then silence…I didn't know what to do. I could hear the bear breathing on the other side of the door. I wanted to peek but I just didn't dare. It was best not to move, not make a sound but Toddy started crying and I just had to know. So I pulled myself up to the window, I had to push up on my tippy toes to see over the broken glass. She sure was still there—staring me right in the eyes. Before I could scream, before I could do anything—thank Gxd—the baby bear let out this wail, it made a noise like a cry. Mama was gone in an instant; she scrambled over grabbed her cub and was gone.

(GERTRUDE now guides GRACE's hand as she works. Music, as GERTRUDE finishes her story.)

GRACE: When I went outside I saw the deep scratches the bear had left in the door—that's how close we were.

GRACE: That scratch is still there today. My family never repaired it, it's the house my dad lives in now. He showed me the worn wood beneath the paint—I never knew. There's no way you could have known that story.

JOY: I didn't. How's your dad?

GRACE: Better. Now he knows his big sister who used to look after him is keeping her eye on me.

(GRACE removes the needle from JOY's breast and places a small Steri-Strip on the spot.)

GRACE: Well that's it. I'll call you as soon as the lab results are back.

(Exit GRACE and GERTRUDE.)

JOY: It only took a couple of hours—Grace called by the time I was home. Tubular cancer. I think I drank a whole box of wine, and then I called you.

MITCH: That's a phone call I'll never forget.

JOY: Me neither—And then of course we had the real surgery.

MITCH: The lumpectomy.

JOY: They would've taken the whole breast if they found cancer in my lymph nodes.

MITCH: If they found any cancer.

JOY: That's true; they didn't find any cancer anywhere. It's awful that this happened but really it couldn't have gone any better. You took great care of me during that period. You were great—are you going to write about this?

MITCH: *(Joking.)* No. I think so.

JOY: It seems terribly uninteresting if you ask me.

MITCH: You would say that. It's extraordinary.

JOY: I know but if you are writing portraits.

MITCH: Stories, snapshots. Capturing moments, like fireflies in a jar.

JOY: Whatever, I mean I just don't see that as an extraordinary life-defining moment.

MITCH: Oh? What story would you tell?

JOY: Simple. When Dad went he died in my arms, with Grandma yelling at him because he pissed his pants. "For Gxd's sake Larry, get your ass to the toilet!"

MITCH: She was distressed.

JOY: You know what he did?

MITCH: What?

JOY: He went like this.

MITCH: He gave her the finger.

JOY: And he died like that—they couldn't get it to go down. Rigor mortis set in. Like this. At the funeral, we had to use a rubber band around his wrist to hold it down.

MITCH: That's great but I'm going to stick with Gertrude. What I find interesting about the story is how when you went in for the full-out surgery, they removed the lump, and the area around the lump, exactly where they took the cancer out of you with that needle—they found nothing. I mean—no cancer. So the only possible scenario is if Grace removed all the cancer—caught every little bit of it when it was so small it could fit through the head of a needle.

JOY: Two and a half millimeters.

MITCH: What are the odds?

JOY: Spooky right?

MITCH: Spooky.

JOY: Thank you Goddess.

(COUSIN LOUIE sings "The Bear, Part 4.")

COUSIN LOUIE: ALWAYS GOTTA LEARN WHICH WAY THE ROAD'LL TURN. AREN'T YOU GLAD YOU TOOK THE TEST? I MEAN, THINGS WORK OUT FOR THE BEST. AND YOU GOTTA BELIEVE YOU'RE BLESSED.

(Lights change. MITCH on the express bus.)

MITCH: On the express bus going home I think about what she said...maybe this isn't a good defining moment to use? I want to distill her essence, create a living portrait. Well? This certainly is a story to tell. *(Steps up to a microphone, as he does in his shows.)*

There is another story— We had stopped at a diner on the West Side Chester, Joy, and me. We had just come from visiting Robby in some hospital, another psycho ward. Once again he had tried to off himself; he survived—only this time his methods were particularly effective. You'd think I'd be over it by now, having grown up with him, all the threats, the couple of times he had already taken action. How many nights had we slept in the visitors' lounge outside the ICU thinking he wouldn't live to see morning?

No, this isn't about him, once again he stole the story, it's about her: Über Mom. I never felt what I was feeling, never knew what I would now know forever. I sat in that diner, a cheeseburger in my hand, a plate full of French fries in front of me, struck dumb with loss. Realizing—it doesn't matter what hospital he goes to, what doctors he sees, what specialists who treat him, or the meds they put him on. It just is what it is and it is what it will be, always—Robby will never be normal.

And as I heard the pop of my optimism shattering, like a Christmas ornament landing on a marble floor, a million pieces never to assemble again—I couldn't speak, I couldn't breathe, I could barely find the strength to lift my head to see her. All I could do was utter "Ma–ah–ah–ah–ah–ah–ah–ah." But she knew... Across the diner's Formica table, this ethereal glow coming off of her, her eyes' slate green beam. I don't have to tell her what I would say if I could ever find the words to say it—she understands me. This woman, who spends her life so selflessly helping so many people—generously putting herself between their pain and suffering. Doctor Joy knows just what to do.

(COUSIN LOUIE sings "The Bear, Part 5.")

COUSIN LOUIE: SOMETIMES YOU KNOW IT ALL,
SOMETIMES YOU'RE UNAWARE.
SOMETIMES YOU GOT NOTHIN',
SOMETIMES YOU GET THE BEAR.

MITCH: She reached out. She took my hand...and said...

JOY: It's going to be all right.

MITCH: And I believe her.

MODERN LIVING (REPRISE)

CHESTER: We tell stories of our triumphs.

GRACE: We tell stories when we lose.

JOY, ROBBY: We tell stories to console ourselves
and stories to amuse.

ALL FOUR: They may not be long on morals
and their meanings aren't clear.
Though they change in every telling,
stories tell us we're still here.

MITCH: There is noise,
but I hear music!

COUSIN LOUIE, GERRIE: There are words,
and we may lose some in translation,

MITCH, COUSIN LOUIE, GERRIE: But we're here for the duration,
and it's cause for celebration.

ALL: I can hear you!
I'm not sure what you are saying,
but you hear me;
I can tell because you're staying.
Though we're fraying at the edges
we're surveying what will be.

We call it modern living,
and we're proud of what's convenient,
but it's just as unforgiving,
and it's not a bit more lenient.
Through the fractured conversation
and the missing information
and the techno-aggravation,
there is one thing that I know.
You weren't here a thousand years ago.

It's hard, this modern living,
but to be with you
is the only life for me.

(End of play.)

G.I. JOE JARED, BASED ON ONE REALLY BAD DATE

Amy E. Witting

AMY E. WITTING was born on June 30, 1979, in Perth Amboy, New Jersey, and grew up in nearby Maplewood. She holds a BS in television/radio from Ithaca College, where she minored in writing and acting. Amy went on to study acting with John Gould Rubin at LAByrinth Theatre Company, and privately with Bruce Ornstein and Zina Jasper. She is the author of *Create Me Pegasus* (Finalist, Strawberry One-Act Festival, 2011), *Classic Eight* (Cherry Pit Theatre, 2010), *Sperm Babies* (semifinalist, The Network, 2009), *His Name is Edgar* (Wild Project, 2008), W*akefield,* (Samuel French Festival, 2007), *The Goldfish Diaries* (Gene Frankel Theatre, 2007), *American Spirits* (The Complex Theatre, Los Angeles, 2007), and *Beautiful Night* (Gene Frankel Theatre, 2006). Amy currently serves as Artistic Director for aWe Creative Group, a NoHo–based theatre company. She is also the producer of PlayFUN!, a twenty-four-hour theatre festival that brings together students and emerging and professional artists for a weekend of pure creativity. A member of the Dramatists Guild, Amy lives in Sunnyside Queens (off the Bliss stop. You can't get any happier than that).

G.I. Joe Jared, Based on One Really Bad Date was first presented by Manhattan Repertory Theatre (Ken Wolf, Artistic Director), in association with aWe Creative Group (Amy E. Witting, Artistic Director) on January 20, 2010, at Manhattan Repertory Theatre, New York City, with the following cast and credits:

Julie .... Kerry Fitzgibbons
Susan .... Salomé M. Krell
Jared .... Billy Weimer

Director: Amy E. Witting
Stage Manager: Kim Braun

Special thanks to all the amazing artists I have ever had the opportunity to work with: my aWe Creative Group family, Billy Weimer, Kerry Fitzgibbons, and Tiffany May McRae—without you I would sometimes not know which end is up; Ken Wolf and Jennifer Pierro at Manhattan Repertory Theatre; Jenn Green for her lovely postcard designs; Martin and Rochelle Denton and the entire New York Theatre Experience Family for this publication and endless support of the Indie Theatre Community; my adorable parents who have never missed a show since my starring role as The Fat Cat in preschool; David, Michael, Bjarni, Laurel, Owen, and Tait for your unconditional support; Kristin Evanoka for witnessing it all; the Brennans—without your couch this play would never have happened; and lastly…The Real Jared, wherever he may be, for providing inspiration.

For Charlie and Grandma Dot.

CHARACTERS

SUSAN CONNER: Late twenties. A very successful business woman who dresses in designer clothes and cares about her appearance.

JULIE ROBINSON: Late twenties. Recently started Internet dating after dealing with a great loss. Has a strong exterior but is ready to crumble at any moment.

G.I. JOE JARED: Recently moved to the big city from small-town U.S.A. He's very passionate about his unique talent, and socially awkward.

SETTING

Irish pub in Manhattan.

TIME

Present day.

A light comes up on SUSAN CONNER, who is dressed in sharp business attire mouthing words to Neil Diamond's "Forever in Blue Jeans." Two drinks sit in front of her untouched. It's clear she has been waiting for an extended period of time. She sits listening to the music and scrolling through her BlackBerry. Minutes pass, and in enters JULIE ROBINSON texting on her phone. She takes a moment to look up and sees SUSAN waiting. She composes herself and enters with confidence. SUSAN immediately puts her phone in her purse and gives JULIE a warm hug.

JULIE: I'm so sorry I'm late.

SUSAN: Hi. That's okay.

JULIE: The train was stuck between stations, I would have called, but I was underground.

SUSAN: That's okay. Here, I got you a Blue Moon.

JULIE: I'm actually not drinking beer anymore.

SUSAN: Oh, I thought you liked wheat beer.

JULIE: No, I did. I loved Blue Moon until last summer when I felt I was having a Blue Moon baby.

SUSAN: Okay. I'll just drink it. Can I get you something else?

JULIE: Vodka soda?

SUSAN: Here, I hardly touched it.

JULIE: Thanks.

(SUSAN gives JULIE her drink and drinks the beer. A moment passes.)

JULIE: How are you?

SUSAN: Great. I've been working on this case that has me tied up at the office, but I actually like working sometimes.

JULIE: You love working.

SUSAN: How's your work?

JULIE: Great. I have a love affair with my computer Monday through Friday.

SUSAN: I wish you didn't have to work from home.

JULIE: I like working from home. I set up the second bedroom as my office, you should come see it.

SUSAN: I will.

JULIE: You won't.

SUSAN: Julie, I'd love to come over.

JULIE: I know, but the truth is you probably will just be too busy, and feel guilty for not spending enough time with Phil, and won't make it.

SUSAN: I'm glad you set up your office. I will come over. Maybe next week?

JULIE: Maybe. *(Looks at her phone as she gets a text, and takes a moment to respond.)* Sorry.

SUSAN: No, go ahead.

(JULIE finishes the text and puts her phone on the table.)

SUSAN: Who are you texting?

JULIE: No one, really.

SUSAN: If you've noticed, I've kept my phone tucked away in my purse because I want to be here and hang out with you.

JULIE: You're the one who's always been attached to your BlackBerry.

SUSAN: I know, and I know it bothers you, so I kept it in my purse.

JULIE: But I can see it's killing you.

SUSAN: It's not.

JULIE: All the emails you're missing, phone calls, what if a client is trying to get in touch with you right now?

SUSAN: I told them I had a very important meeting tonight.

JULIE: Oh, so I'm a meeting. I'm still trying to figure out why you forced me to come to Annie Moore's on a Wednesday night.

SUSAN: I wanted to hang out with my best friend, is that a strange request?

JULIE: No, it's just we haven't been to this bar since we first moved to the City.

SUSAN: I'm feeling nostalgic.

JULIE: That's what makes me nervous. You're never nostalgic. *(Gets another text.)*

SUSAN: Oh, just shut up, and put your phone away.

JULIE: I know, I'm sorry, it's just, this guy keeps texting me.

SUSAN: A guy? Julie are you telling me you are texting someone of the opposite sex?

JULIE: Yes.

SUSAN: Bartender give me another!

JULIE: Shut up.

SUSAN: You're over your vow of celibacy?

JULIE: Did I take a vow of celibacy?

SUSAN: After Michael you said you were gonna be celibate for a year, and that included second base.

JULIE: I don't remember saying that.

SUSAN: Well under the circumstances it was understandable.

JULIE: I guess I did.

SUSAN: So, tell me, who is this guy you're sexting?

JULIE: Sexting?

SUSAN: I heard Phil's seventeen-year-old cousin ask his other cousin at Thanksgiving who she was sexting. Sexting! And to say it at the Thanksgiving table!

JULIE: Is that really a word?

SUSAN: It is now. I wonder what word made our parents feel really old?

JULIE: We're not old enough to be parents.

SUSAN: Julie, I hate to break the news to you, but if we lived in Middle America we would have had four children and be pregnant with our fifth.

JULIE: That's cruel to think about.

SUSAN: It's true. Women are most fertile between the ages of twenty and twenty-four.

JULIE: The middle of America is so fucked up.

SUSAN: So…who are you sexting?

JULIE: I'm not sexting!

SUSAN: Who is he?

JULIE: Who?

SUSAN: This guy that's making you smile.

JULIE: I think the vodka soda is making me smile.

SUSAN: You've had three sips.

JULIE: I haven't been drinking lately.

SUSAN: You?

JULIE: Yes, me!

(JULIE gets another text and SUSAN really takes her in.)

SUSAN: I know this look. This is your I-think-he-likes-me look.

JULIE: No it's not.

SUSAN: You're right, I'm not really sure what your I-think-he-likes-me is, since you haven't given a man a chance in almost two years.

JULIE: I give men a chance, it's just hard for me.

SUSAN: I know. So this is good! This is really good. A guy is making you smile.

JULIE: Maybe.

SUSAN: Phil will be so excited. He keeps wanting to set you up, and I keep saying that we should wait. But he's been dying for a male companion to all those shows we drag him to. Sorry, that came out wrong.

JULIE: It's fine. You know that was my first priority when I thought about possibly putting up a profile, just biting the bullet. I wrote, my best friend's boyfriend needs a new friend.

SUSAN: You didn't!

JULIE: I did.

SUSAN: Why didn't you tell me?

JULIE: It's embarrassing.

SUSAN: I could have written your profile for you.

JULIE: I wasn't really sure if I was going to actually do it but I did.

SUSAN: Which site?

JULIE: I wanted one where I didn't have to do any work so I went with eHarmony.

SUSAN: Isn't that a Christian site?

JULIE: No. But I am Christian so it doesn't really matter. Not that I'm religious but I was brought up Christian.

SUSAN: No I think it's *Christian* Christian. I think it's run by some evangelical Christian guy, and they don't even match same-sex couples. I read a whole article about the fact that, since they believe in marriage as the ultimate goal and gay marriages are illegal, they refuse to include them on their site. I think my brother actually started a petition against them. He would flip out to know that you are on their site. We shouldn't tell him, okay? Because you know how sensitive Pauli is, and if he knew, or thought that you could potentially be siding with them, he would stop talking to me.

JULIE: I'm sorry, I didn't know, that's really awful.

SUSAN: I know, you should deactivate your profile immediately.

JULIE: I just chose them because they match you, you don't have to float through cyberspace looking for someone who is tall, a Pisces, light eyes, dark hair, and good cheekbones.

(Beat.)

SUSAN: You're not going to find him again.

JULIE: No, I guess I'm not. That's why I chose the site that would do the matching for me.

SUSAN: I'm still going to get you that article. You might want to reconsider.

JULIE: Can't. I already put it on my credit card.

SUSAN: So you're invested.

JULIE: I'm invested. But I will sign Pauli's petition to throw him off.

SUSAN: Wow, this is huge! I can't believe you didn't tell me.

JULIE: I'm telling you now.

SUSAN: I always wanted to secretly put up a profile on one of those sites just to see what kind of people I attract, but I wouldn't want to pay for it.

JULIE: I think Phil might have a problem with that.

SUSAN: I asked him if we could do it together as a little experiment, but I don't think that went over so well, so I told him he could move in instead.

JULIE: You two are nuts.

SUSAN: Whatever, he's great, I know it, end of story. Back to you. So, you met this guy online?

JULIE: Yes.

SUSAN: On eHarmony? *(Starts to laugh.)*

JULIE: Susan, stop it. It's not that funny. It's not that strange. It seemed easier. Everyone's meeting people on different sites. My friend from high school is married with a baby from some guy she met online. And he's hot. I've seen pictures, and they look very happy. Also, Clarissa and Alex met on Match. Don't you remember we went to their wedding and they had tiny chocolate computers as wedding favors? As I recall you stole a bunch from other tables because you liked them so much.

SUSAN: It was Lindt chocolate. I love Lindt chocolate.

JULIE: They are so in love. You see the way they act around each other.

SUSAN: Yeah, it's totally nauseating.

JULIE: Come on, you've met Alex and he's totally normal.

SUSAN: That depends on your definition of normal.

JULIE: They're really happy.

SUSAN: You're not Clarissa. She's boring and mousy.

JULIE: She's not boring!

SUSAN: She's boring.

JULIE: I thought you liked her.

SUSAN: Tolerate her.

JULIE: I just thought that since it's been almost two years since Michael, it was time for me to really put a good effort into this whole dating scene.

SUSAN: If you're really ready I could set you up with someone.

JULIE: All your single guy friends are chauvinistic male pigs or closeted gays.

SUSAN: That's not true. What about Ryan?

JULIE: Ryan is forty-three, a partner at your law firm, divorced with three kids.

SUSAN: He's really nice.

JULIE: He's a mess. He's your happy-hour buddy when he should be at home raising his kids.

SUSAN: He's nice.

JULIE: I'm sure he's nice, just not my type. I don't even know why you're friends with him anyway.

SUSAN: I work with him.

JULIE: You've slept with him!

SUSAN: So?

JULIE: My point is I don't want to go to bars with you picking up men who are so drunk they can't even see straight. I thought I would try it out. I have nothing to lose.

SUSAN: Except your dignity. Admitting defeat.

JULIE: I'm not admitting defeat!

SUSAN: I'm not sure if that came out right.

JULIE: No, it didn't.

SUSAN: I just think you should go on a few real dates before sinking into a sulking depression of your newfound dependency on your computer.

JULIE: It's one blind date, Susan.

SUSAN: Are you strictly cyberbuddies or do you talk to him on the phone?

JULIE: Well, we talk on the computer, and text almost every night.

SUSAN: Every night? I don't even communicate with Phil every night and we live together.

JULIE: I like talking to him.

SUSAN: But you haven't actually heard his voice?

JULIE: No. Well, he actually left me a message, but I was nervous, so I didn't call him back.

SUSAN: But you like this guy?

JULIE: I think so.

(JULIE gets another text and responds quickly, half-listening to SUSAN's line of questioning.)

SUSAN: Why?

JULIE: He makes me laugh.

SUSAN: Have you guys had, you know?

JULIE: What?

SUSAN: You know.

JULIE: Spit it out.

SUSAN: Cybersex?

JULIE: God, no! Susan! It's not like that, we're taking it slow.

SUSAN: So he's asked you.

JULIE: No.

SUSAN: He wanted to have cybersex with you.

JULIE: Stop.

SUSAN: Julie, what's become of you?

JULIE: Listen, he just texted and he happens to be around the corner, so I told him to stop by.

SUSAN: Now?

JULIE: Is that okay?

SUSAN: I thought we were having a girls' night.

JULIE: We are, but he just happens to be right around the corner, and you're here, and I thought it would be safe, so I said yes.

SUSAN: Seriously?

JULIE: Seriously. I'm sorry, I just thought—

SUSAN: But you don't even know him.

JULIE: No. I know a lot about him.

SUSAN: Julie!

JULIE: I feel like I know him.

SUSAN: You feel like you know him?

JULIE: *(Gets another text.)* Yes.

SUSAN: You've totally been sexting!

JULIE: Stop saying sexting. Please. You're too old.

SUSAN: I like the word. I'm going to try to incorporate it as much as possible.

JULIE: I could call him and tell him it isn't a good idea.

SUSAN: Or you could sext him.

JULIE: Enough!

SUSAN: Let me get this straight, he just texted you and happened to be in the neighborhood.

JULIE: Yeah.

SUSAN: He's a stalker!

JULIE: He's not a stalker.

SUSAN: We should tell the bartender that we need some extra protection. He's a big guy, and kind of charming, maybe I should let him know to watch out for us just in case crazy stalker starts flipping out.

JULIE: Stop it.

SUSAN: Julie, you don't meet guys from personals. You use them to boost your ego. You talk to them to get reassurance that freaks really do exist and to open your eyes to the options right in front of you. You don't invite them to meet you at a bar.

JULIE: Well, you're here.

SUSAN: Maybe I should leave. I thought we were going to actually have a fun night, the two of us. Or maybe actually talk.

JULIE: We are talking.

SUSAN: I mean bond.

JULIE: Are you mad?

SUSAN: No.

JULIE: I can tell him it isn't a good idea if you want to...bond.

SUSAN: No, never mind.

JULIE: Are you sure?

SUSAN: It's fine, but maybe I should just leave you and your little cyberhunk alone.

JULIE: I thought it would be safe because you could be my buffer.

SUSAN: Wing woman?

JULIE: Yes. My wing woman. You know I would never date anyone you didn't approve of.

SUSAN: Fine, I'm just saying.

JULIE: I need you.

SUSAN: This is awkward.

JULIE: He's charming. You'll love him!

SUSAN: You don't even know him.

JULIE: We have a lot in common.

SUSAN: Like what?

JULIE: Like he just moved to New York from West Virginia.

SUSAN: You're from Jersey.

JULIE: I know, but Don Knotts was from West Virginia, and I love Don Knotts.

SUSAN: Who the hell is Don Knotts?

JULIE: Mr. Furley. The fish in *The Incredible Mr. Limpet*? Barney Fife?

SUSAN: That old guy?

JULIE: I love him. He's my favorite actor.

SUSAN: He's not your favorite actor, he was Michael's favorite actor. You don't know anything about Don Knotts except you stood in line at Barnes and Noble to have him autograph a book for Michael as a joke. You can't tell me that he's your favorite actor.

JULIE: He is.

SUSAN: You just like to be different.

JULIE: What does that mean?

SUSAN: You like to play outside the box, so saying an old fish is your favorite actor is just to be different.

JULIE: Who is your favorite actor?

SUSAN: Matthew McConaughey.

JULIE: Of course it is.

SUSAN: What is that supposed to mean?

JULIE: Typical, that's all.

SUSAN: He's a good actor.

JULIE: He's a terrible actor.

SUSAN: He's nice to look at.

JULIE: Thank you for admitting that the only reason you like him is his looks.

SUSAN: Isn't that the only reason you like Don Knotts?

JULIE: Shut up.

SUSAN: He's so sexy.

JULIE: The book was called *Barney Fife and Other Characters I Have Known*. I have two autographed copies in my apartment if you would like one.

SUSAN: I'll pass.

JULIE: I'm going to buy you *The Ghost and Mr. Chicken* for your birthday and you're going to like it.

SUSAN: Can't wait. So you're basically hoping to meet a seventy-year-old actor who can turn into an animated fish?

JULIE: Shut up.

SUSAN: Sorry, I would love to have a *Three's Company* marathon if you'll let me.

JULIE: I had one with Phil last year.

SUSAN: I know. I regretted the fact I was stuck at the office.

JULIE: You work too much.

SUSAN: That is the truth.

JULIE: *(Looking at her text.)* He said he'll be here in five minutes. Oh my God! Do I look okay?

SUSAN: You look great.

JULIE: Are you sure?

SUSAN: Yes.

JULIE: I think I'm nervous.

SUSAN: So why did you pick this guy to meet? Really?

JULIE: I like him. He's really nice, and he's tall.

SUSAN: How tall?

JULIE: Six one.

SUSAN: That's a plus.

JULIE: He said he looked like Jared Leto from the old days. *My So-Called Life* style. Jordan Catalano.

SUSAN: That's hot. Have you seen a picture?

JULIE: I saw his profile pictures.

SUSAN: And?

JULIE: And what?

SUSAN: Does he look like Jordan Catalano?

JULIE: You couldn't really tell because they were artistically done, kind of mysteriously blurry.

SUSAN: Blurry?

JULIE: Yeah, blurry, but in an artistic way.

SUSAN: Come on, Julie even I know that's a big red flag. It means he has something to hide. Like an extra limb, or fucked-up teeth. Or maybe he has a third eyeball and really is an alien from outer space that tapped into your computer.

JULIE: They're creative pictures, he's an artist. He paints with charcoals. He does some graphic design too.

SUSAN: How does he pay the bills?

JULIE: He works at Circuit City in Union Square.

SUSAN: Is he twelve?

JULIE: No.

SUSAN: He sounds like a real winner.

JULIE: Give it a chance.

SUSAN: Maybe you can get a discount on a flat screen for your apartment. That could be a real bonus.

JULIE: Artists need day jobs.

SUSAN: But Circuit City?

JULIE: If this goes well, I will get you a discount on the video camera Phil won't buy you.

SUSAN: Okay. Deal! So what we're looking for is a hot six-foot-one Jordan Catalano look-alike Circuit City clerk. Actually, maybe I should leave you two alone. *(Gets up to leave.)*

JULIE: Sit down.

SUSAN: Fine.

JULIE: Please. I need support. I want it to be casual. You're right, he could be a crazy psycho.

SUSAN: Now you're thinking smart.

JULIE: But he's not a crazy psycho. His name is Jared.

SUSAN: Jared. You know, you're right, he could actually be the love of your life. Seriously, how cute would that be? Julie and Jared. You could name all your children with J names. Jack, Jessica, Jaime…

JULIE: I'm not having kids with the guy, he's just meeting us for a drink.

SUSAN: Okay. I'll stay, and if he really is the man of your dreams just hock a big lugie and I'll casually slip out and leave you two lovebirds alone.

JULIE: You don't mind?

SUSAN: I don't mind. How will be spot this cyberhunk?

JULIE: He said he's wearing a green jacket.

SUSAN: Green. That's a cool color.

JULIE: Please, stop it. You're the one telling me I should move on with my life. Can you support this?

SUSAN: Sure.

JULIE: Please don't make fun of him. I think he's sensitive about Internet dating.

(JARED enters wearing a green army jacket, a camouflage hat, and dog tags, and is holding an old tattered box. He stands awkwardly smiling at SUSAN and JULIE. They don't notice at first. He is nowhere near six one and uncomfortable in his own body. He holds onto his tattered box for dear life.)

SUSAN: Of course I'll be supportive, Julie. I'm just saying that if he's a freak I might have to kick him in the balls.

JULIE: He's not a freak! There will be no ball kicking tonight. Just let me have some fun.

(JARED starts to walk toward SUSAN and JULIE, eyes intently on JULIE.)

SUSAN: Okay. *(Beat.)* He's not that short guy over there holding that box in the green army coat, is he?

JULIE: No. I don't think so.

SUSAN: He's looking at you.

JULIE: That can't be him.

SUSAN: I think that's him.

JULIE: That's not him.

SUSAN: Yep. It is. Blurry picture and all, I can spot a hottie when I see one.

JULIE: Oh no.

SUSAN: It's him.

JULIE: Shit. Okay. Be nice.

SUSAN: Jared Leto, huh? Maybe my TV was blurry during my *My So-Called Life* years.

JULIE: So he's not six one.

SUSAN: Not even close.

JULIE: That's okay.

SUSAN: You're the biggest heightest I know.

JULIE: No, I was. Now I'm being open minded.

SUSAN: He's short.

JULIE: Should I wave?

SUSAN: Wave away. This should be fun.

JULIE: Be nice.

SUSAN: I am nice. I think you caught yourself a hunk.

JULIE: Please.

(JULIE waves for JARED to come over. He gets overly excited about the gesture, and is overwhelmed by her beauty.)

JARED: Julie?

JULIE: Jared?

JARED: Hi!

JULIE: Hi.

(He goes in to hug JULIE and freezes, and instead shakes her hand nervously.)

JARED: I'm so glad we finally made this work. It's been so long, I never thought we would actually meet. It's really nice to finally meet you.

JULIE: I know, it's great to meet you too. Jared, this is my friend Susan.

JARED: Hi. Nice to meet you.

SUSAN: Hi. Sorry, we were just hanging out. I can leave.

(SUSAN puts her scarf on and gets ready to exit; JULIE pushes her back into her seat.)

JULIE: No, stay.

SUSAN: Really, it's not a problem. I could just slip out and leave you...

JULIE: Susan, I don't think Jared would mind if you stayed for another drink.

JARED: Yeah. Please stay. It would be great to get to know one of Julie's friends.

(JARED grabs a chair from another table and puts it between JULIE and SUSAN.)

SUSAN: This is like speed dating. I love it. Already moving on to the friend stage. Well done. I really need to get my computer fixed.

JARED: I'm really good at fixing computers. I could help you.

JULIE: She was kidding. Would you like something to drink?

JARED: No. I'll pass.

JULIE: Are you sure?

JARED: Well, I actually don't have any money on me. I don't get paid until next Friday.

JULIE: That's okay. I'll get them.

SUSAN: Please, let me get them. It would be my pleasure. What do you want?

JARED: Are you sure?

SUSAN: Yeah.

JARED: Okay. I'll have a vodka cranberry.

SUSAN: Cranberry? Good for the urinary tract.

JARED: I'm sorry?

SUSAN: Never mind. Julie honey, do you want a vodka soda?

JULIE: Double?

SUSAN: I'll be right back. *(Exits.)*

JARED: Thanks. *(Beat.)* She's really nice.

JULIE: Yeah. I've known her for years. She was my neighbor freshman year of college.

JARED: Where did you go again?

JULIE: Villanova.

JARED: Oh. Right. You're pretty smart.

JULIE: Maybe a little. Where did you go?

JARED: I went to West Virginia State.

JULIE: What year did you graduate? I think we went over this, but I can't remember.

JARED: I didn't actually graduate. I have my associate's.

JULIE: Right. So, what were you doing tonight?

JARED: I was out with a few people from work. They're crazy over there.

JULIE: At Circuit City?

JARED: Yeah. It's so busy. Sometimes it's really draining. But we like to kick back and watch the dogs run in Union Square after work some nights.

JULIE: Why?

JARED: It's funny to watch them in heat.

JULIE: Oh.

JARED: My friend Brad gets three forties for the two of us, although sometimes James comes, but he's only seventeen so we have to be careful.

JULIE: You sit in Union Square drinking forties and watching dogs have sex?

JARED: Sometimes we go to Washington Square Park, but that's kind of a walk. It's so funny. If you want to come tomorrow night you're welcome. Depending on how this goes and all, but sometimes James brings his girlfriend. Not that I'm saying you're my girlfriend, I meant that girls were okay. Although James has to buy Zimas and a pack of Skittles. His girlfriend likes to put the purple Skittles in the Zimas and watch them change color.

JULIE: I used to do that in high school. Almost like a trendy wine cooler.

JARED: Yeah. I guess. I've never tried it.

JULIE: You should sometime.

JARED: Maybe I should. You're gorgeous.

JULIE: Thanks.

JARED: More than I expected.

JULIE: Thanks.

JARED: Well, I'm glad you texted me back. I'm glad we're finally here. The big meeting. The first date. An important milestone.

JULIE: I never thought of it that way.

JARED: I always look at these first dates as really good stories to tell my kids. I could always tell them that I met their mom at a bar where her friend Suzie Q was trying to get me to tell crazy stories.

JULIE: What stories?

JARED: I don't know. I just always wished there were crazy stories involved.

JULIE: Yeah. I guess that would be funny. So, how do you like New York?

JARED: It's good. Real good. I miss my mother's cooking, and the lake, and nature, but it's nice.

JULIE: You grew up on a lake?

JARED: Close to Beech Fork Lake. Beautiful. Miss it every day.

JULIE: Right. So, tell me again, where do you live now?

JARED: I live in Williamsburg in a big loft.

JULIE: Do you have roommates?

JARED: Five. Really cuts down on the cost.

JULIE: One big frat party.

JARED: I guess. You have great eyes.

JULIE: Thanks.

(SUSAN enters carrying three drinks.)

SUSAN: Here you go. I hope I'm not interrupting.

JULIE: No, not at all.

(The three of them sit in silence for a moment sipping their drinks.)

SUSAN: So, Jared. Julie tells me you're from West Virginia.

JARED: Yep, born and raised.

SUSAN: Which part?

JARED: Huntington.

SUSAN: Nice.

JARED: You can walk to Ohio.

SUSAN: Really? That's a wonderful little fact.

JARED: There are a lot of wonderful little facts about Huntington, and one real tragedy. In 1970 there was a plane crash that killed the entire Marshall football team from Huntington. I wasn't born yet, but my parents remember it like it happened yesterday.

JULIE: Wasn't there a movie made about that?

SUSAN: *We Are Marshall*, starring Matthew McConaughey. I own it actually. Matthew is brilliant in it, just brilliant.

JARED: I don't think they should have made money off of that tragedy. I refused to watch that movie.

JULIE: Matthew is Susan's favorite actor.

SUSAN: I never miss a movie.

JARED: I do enjoy him in *The Return of the Texas Chainsaw Massacre*.

SUSAN: He's great in that!

JULIE: Seriously?

SUSAN: Yes. *(Beat.)* Do you get home much?

JARED: I try to get back every other month. I'm sure I'll end up settling there one day.

SUSAN: Oh Julie, have you ever been to West Virginia?

JULIE: I've driven through it. It's nice.

JARED: I love it.

SUSAN: Do you have any brothers and sisters?

JARED: One younger sister. She lives with my parents.

SUSAN: In West Virginia?

JARED: Yep.

SUSAN: Must be nice.

JARED: It's really great that they get to be so close, but I really had to come here to pursue my talents.

JULIE: New York is a hard step for many.

SUSAN: You just stepped across the Hudson.

JULIE: I know, but it takes guts to get up and move to New York City and just leave your family.

JARED: I really do miss them.

(Beat.)

SUSAN: Jared, what are you carrying in this box of yours? It seems like something you're very protective about. I noticed you holding onto it when you walked in.

JARED: I sometimes like to carry it around. It's my masterpiece.

JULIE: A painting?

JARED: No, not exactly.

SUSAN: Can I look?

(SUSAN goes to open the box, and JARED pushes her hand away.)

JARED: Please don't touch!

SUSAN: Is it alive?

JARED: No.

JULIE: So what is it?

JARED: My G.I. Joe tarot cards.

SUSAN: Excuse me?

JULIE: What's in it?

JARED: G.I. Joe tarot cards.

SUSAN: G.I. Joe tarot cards?

JARED: I told you about them, Julie.

JULIE: Oh. I thought that was a joke. I guess.

JARED: I've been collecting the backs of G.I. Joe figures for years. I came up with this idea about ten years ago, to make tarot cards out of them.

SUSAN: So you're a fortune teller?

JARED: I guess. Kind of. I mean people tell me I'm right on target with my readings. They really do work.

JULIE: Tarot cards. That's cool.

SUSAN: Why do you carry the box around with you?

JARED: Well, I told Julie about them, and I thought she might like to see them.

JULIE: But you didn't know we were going to be meeting up.

SUSAN: *(Quietly to JULIE.)* Do you want me to get the bartender?

JULIE: No.

JARED: I had a feeling when I left my house this morning that this meeting might happen.

SUSAN: A feeling? So you're clairvoyant?

JULIE: Oh.

SUSAN: You didn't tell me about this! Jules, this is a huge deal! Can you read our fortunes?

JULIE: That's okay, Jared, you don't have to.

JARED: I would love to!

JULIE: What are they exactly?

JARED: Each G.I. Joe figure comes with a trading card, they are usually found on the back of the packaging. I've been carefully cutting them out, laminating them, and preserving them for moments like these. I now have five complete decks.

JULIE: Wow, that's a lot of G.I. Joe cards.

SUSAN: I bet Cobra Commander equals death.

JARED: He is more of a negative card. It brings negative energy, which makes sense because it is Cobra Commander.

JULIE: I thought the Cobra Commander was a good guy?

JARED: Not really.

SUSAN: Not really? Not really at all! Julie, where have you been? Didn't you ever play G.I. Joes?

JULIE: Only child.

JARED: Some of my friends think I really should market this. They said it could really catch on so I like to carry them with me. This is the original set. I have a copy at home, but I thought you might like to see the original set.

(JARED unpacks the deck of cards and opens up a folded piece of paper.)

SUSAN: Is that a cheat sheet?

(SUSAN goes to touch the cards, but JARED quickly moves them away.)

JARED: Don't touch them!

SUSAN: I'm sorry. Why?

JARED: Only the owner of the cards can touch them, or they won't work.

SUSAN: Crazy.

JULIE: Thanks for bringing them, that's really nice of you to share.

SUSAN: How long did it take you to make them?

JARED: I've spent years perfecting each card. This is not a cheat sheet because I don't know what card will come up. That is up to fate. And than I just read accordingly and it's very accurate.

JULIE: You've done this before?

JARED: All the time. Most girls can't get over how right I am.

SUSAN: I bet you're a real ladies' man.

JULIE: Susan!

JARED: Julie, I would love to take this opportunity to read your fortune. I've wanted to do it so many times.

SUSAN: I'm sure you have.

JARED: *(To JULIE.)* But you don't get an accurate read unless you're sitting across from the person you are reading.

JULIE: I don't know.

SUSAN: Read mine! Please?

JULIE: Jared, you really don't have to. Do you want something to eat? Are you hungry?

SUSAN: We could order chicken fingers!

JARED: I think it's better if we hold off on ordering food, because the grease from the chicken fingers could potentially damage the cards.

SUSAN: Of course.

JULIE: Or we could skip the readings altogether.

JARED: No, I need the experience. That's part of the reason I came to New York, for my art.

JULIE: You said you were a painter, a designer.

JARED: I am. I designed these.

JULIE: You didn't say you were a fortune teller.

JARED: Well, it's more than being a fortune teller, it's an art in itself. I think once I make a little money at Circuit City I might start a little booth. I picked the Union Square store because they have all those wonderful booths set up on the park. My dream is to have my own little booth around the holidays.

SUSAN: I think that's great. It could really catch on. I can see it now. G.I. Joe Jared tells your fortune. Beware of the Cobra Commander.

JULIE: Right.

JARED: The Cobra Commander isn't necessarily a bad card, it's more of a transformative card.

JULIE: Susan could use a little transforming right now!

JARED: Do you really want me to read your fortune?

SUSAN: Totally!

JULIE: I don't want you to go to the trouble.

JARED: I love it. This is my passion. For you, Julie, it's nature walks and gardening. For me it's my G.I. Joe tarot cards.

SUSAN: Gardening? You like to garden? We live in New York.

JULIE: I have a garden on my fire escape.

SUSAN: You grow tomatoes. Actually you have grown *a* tomato.

JULIE: I have a great fire escape garden.

JARED: It's her passion.

JULIE: My passion.

SUSAN: Your passion? Well, I would love to hear my fortune.

JARED: Julie, I really would love to read yours.

JULIE: Just read Susan's. I'll watch.

JARED: Are you sure?

JULIE: Yeah, it's okay. I like to be surprised by my future.

SUSAN: I don't. Read away.

JARED: Okay, but first I need to gather a little information about you, and look at your palm. Please give me your hand, and make sure you have no oils leaking from the center of your palm.

(SUSAN gives her hand to JARED, and he studies the lines on the inside of her palms. JULIE is not amused.)

JULIE: Is it Tuesday night?

SUSAN: No, Wednesday, why?

JULIE: Shit! Susan! I totally forgot we have to go to Katie's house tonight for her birthday party.

SUSAN: It's not Katie's birthday. Her birthday was last weekend—don't you remember, we were at O'Reilly's and we…

JULIE: *(Cutting her off.)* Yeah, I know, but she was going to throw a party for Roger at her house and we both promised we would be there, and would you look at that, I have three missed calls from her.

JARED: Oh, maybe you should go.

JULIE: Maybe we should. I'm so sorry.

SUSAN: No, we shouldn't! Jared was just about to tell my future.

JULIE: Well your future isn't going to change your past, so I think you're pretty screwed.

SUSAN: Julie, I want to hear my fortune and then I will go to Jersey or Long Island of Brooklyn or wherever you said that we were supposed to be probably a long time ago. Just listen to my fortune first.

JULIE: You know how Katie is. She's probably devastated.

SUSAN: Devastated.

JARED: I feel so bad. Your friend is waiting for you?

JULIE: Yeah. I totally forgot. I really am sorry, Jared.

JARED: That's okay.

SUSAN: But Jared came all the way over here to hang out. I think the least we can do is let him read a fortune.

JARED: I could do the three-card outlook, that's quick!

SUSAN: He could do the three-card outlook!

JULIE: What's that?

JARED: It's just a three-card draw. Past, present, and future. It's a great simple one.

SUSAN: It's probably your most requested.

JARED: Actually, it is!

JULIE: We really should go to Katie's soon.

JARED: *(Slowly starts to pack up his cards.)* Okay. I'm sorry you have to go.

This is my fault for meeting up so last minute.

JULIE: Oh no, don't worry about it. It's fine. I'll just text her real quick and tell her we'll be there soon.

JARED: Okay. I'll try to be fast. *(He places the cards on the floor, wipes the table with determination, making sure no condensation is left. He places the cards on the table in a G-formation and looks at them like a proud father.)* Susan. Point to three cards. Remember, you can't touch them. When and if I do market them, I will have all the instructions included.

JULIE: How do you know all of this?

SUSAN: Julie, please, it's a gift! Isn't it, Jared?

(SUSAN dramatically points to three cards, making a point not to touch them. JARED gingerly places the rest of the deck back into the box.)

JARED: Some people say it is. I think it chooses you, you don't choose it.

SUSAN: Of course!

JARED: *(Places the three cards face down in front of SUSAN.)* So, this card represents your past.

SUSAN: *(Pointing at the cards without touching them.)* Present, and future.

JARED: Exactly. *(He flips over the first card.)* Oh, Alpine.

JULIE: Who is Alpine?

JARED: Alpine is the mountain trooper, who usually hangs out with Bazooka and makes wisecracks.

JULIE: Sounds just like you, Susan.

SUSAN: I guess that makes you Bazooka. So what does it mean?

JARED: *(Reading from the paper.)* You've been hurt in your past.

JULIE: Haven't we all?

SUSAN: Julie, shut up!

JARED: You've been trying to climb a large mountain containing your health but can't reach the top. As a child you had a serious health condition. This has built strength and endurance to you in your adulthood. You've been really close to death, and have almost tasted it when you were young. This illness has influenced your determination to continue to try to reach the top of the mountain.

SUSAN: Holy shit! That's right on.

JULIE: You weren't close to death.

SUSAN: You didn't know me when I was little.

JULIE: You tell me everything.

SUSAN: Well, I was.

JULIE: When?

SUSAN: In my childhood.

JULIE: Really?

SUSAN: Yes, really.

JULIE: How come I didn't know about this?

SUSAN: I don't talk about my childhood often. Moving on to the present.

JARED: Maybe I should stop.

SUSAN: No, go ahead.

JARED: Sometimes the reading hits too close to home.

JULIE: She's lying.

SUSAN: I'm not lying, but this isn't exactly the time to discuss it.

JULIE: What was wrong with you when you were little?

SUSAN: Nothing, Julie.

JULIE: If you're telling the truth, I want to know.

SUSAN: Okay, G.I. Joe Jared, give me my present.

JULIE: Katie's waiting.

SUSAN: I think you're afraid of the fortune teller.

JULIE: I give up. Go ahead, Jared.

JARED: I'm sorry Julie, if you would like me to stop…

JULIE: No, it's okay.

JARED: Okay? The present. Oh, Chuckles. I don't pull Chuckles that often.

JULIE: There's a character named Chuckles?

JARED: Yep, he's the silent undercover agent.

SUSAN: How mysterious.

JARED: *(Reads from his cheat sheet.)* Chuckles is a very productive and protecting card. It means that in your present life you have been protecting someone from pain and hurt. You have a secret that you are dealing with from your past that you are unable to unleash to the one person that cares about you the most. Perhaps a roommate or significant other. You have strength that took a long time to achieve and are afraid if you allow this secret to surface you are weak. This is not the case. In fact, this is the time to have confidence in yourself.

SUSAN: Wow.

JULIE: Do you just make this stuff up?

JARED: No, it is a gift.

SUSAN: I think it's pretty right on. Don't you, Julie?

JULIE: Well, since you had this mysterious disease as a child that you just admitted to, and I sat here yelling at you because you've kept this fake mysterious disease from me, and I told Jared that we were neighbors freshman year of college, it's a pretty good on-the-spot assumption that in your present, which is now, this very moment, you are keeping a secret from someone you care about, which would be me! You know what, I need to have a cigarette.

SUSAN: Are you okay, Jules?

(JULIE pulls out a pack of cigarettes and starts to head out for a smoke.)

JARED: You smoke?

JULIE: Yes, I do. I know it's disgusting, and I'm sorry. *(Beat.)* Are you sick?

SUSAN: No.

JULIE: Are you lying to me?

SUSAN: Go have your smoke, and come back. You'll feel much better.

(JULIE exits.)

JARED: You shouldn't encourage your friends to smoke, it's not good, it's not healthy at all. Although Brad my friend from Circuit City he smokes when we sit and watch the dogs at the park. Sometimes I like to inhale the secondhand smoke, so I guess that makes me a bit of a smoker too. *(Beat.)* I like her.

SUSAN: You just met.

JARED: We've had approximately ninety-two email exchanges, and seventeen important conversations over Gchat.

SUSAN: Oh, approximately?

JARED: Did I upset her?

SUSAN: No, I think I did.

JARED: I wouldn't want her to be upset. Maybe I should go out there.

SUSAN: No, I think it's best to leave her alone. A cigarette to a smoker is like a timeout to a two-year-old. A punishment and necessity at the same time.

JARED: Got it.

SUSAN: I think she just wants to live in a perfect world, and that world doesn't exist.

JARED: It's what you make of it, right?

SUSAN: Or what the cards make of it.

JARED: They don't lie.

SUSAN: Oh, I know.

JARED: I'm serious, they really don't.

SUSAN: I wish it was as simple as believing in a pack of cards.

JARED: What's the secret you're keeping from her?

SUSAN: We all have secrets we're keeping from someone, right?

JARED: I know, I've been keeping something from Brad, my manager at the City. I stole Tiffany's new CD from Circuit City, but I really didn't mean to. I thought it was a promotional CD, and when I took it out of my bag when I got home, I realized that I just hadn't put the packaging on it yet, so technically I stole it. I was going to tell Brad, but he blamed this other guy Glenn, and I just let it go. Glenn has been stealing more than CDs since I started, so I thought it was okay.

SUSAN: I won't turn you in.

JARED: Thanks. It's not a bad CD.

SUSAN: Tiffany?

JARED: Yeah, it's pretty decent.

SUSAN: I'll have to take your word on that.

JARED: She seems great to me. She's really involved with the documentary she's working on.

SUSAN: And teaching. You're right, she's great. I think she gets frustrated with me sometimes.

JARED: Maybe I should go.

SUSAN: No, don't, we haven't even gotten to my future. The future is the most fun. *(Pulling out a notebook.)* Although I think I should take notes, that way I can figure out if your tarot cards are right or not.

JARED: Do you have a boyfriend?

SUSAN: Are you hitting on me, G.I. Joe Jared?

JARED: I don't think so.

SUSAN: Yes, I live with a guy named Phil. A very nice guy named Phil.

JARED: Julie told me she hasn't been on a date in almost two years.

SUSAN: A vow of celibacy.

JARED: Really?

SUSAN: I'm not sure.

JARED: I like her.

SUSAN: She's a complicated bird, that one.

JARED: I would like to read her fortune. Do you think she'll let me?

SUSAN: Why not.

JARED: She doesn't seem to like the cards.

SUSAN: Do you know Don Knotts?

JARED: Oh, the actor! Yes, he's from West Virginia. I forgot what town, but he lived there his whole life.

SUSAN: You should tell her you know him.

JARED: Why?

SUSAN: She loves him. It could get you an in.

JARED: Oh, okay. Thanks.

SUSAN: No problem. She just doesn't like when she finds out new things about me. That's all. She'll be fine.

JARED: About your illness?

SUSAN: Wasn't really a life-threatening illness, but when I was going through it I felt like I was dying, but it was before I ever met her, so it's not like I didn't tell her, but you had to go and bring it up. *(Laughs to herself.)*

JARED: I wasn't guessing. I already had that written down. I just read what I have already written for each card. I didn't mean to upset her. How sick were you?

SUSAN: I had mono when I was in high school. Not life threatening.

JARED: But like you said it felt that way when you had it.

SUSAN: Yeah, I was so fucking bored. It was the skinniest I've ever been. That was one major benefit.

JARED: You're pretty skinny now.

SUSAN: Again, are you hitting on me?

JARED: No, I like your friend, but I kind of think you're pretty special also.

SUSAN: Thanks, Jared. I just want the absolute best for her.

JARED: Are you sure I shouldn't leave?

SUSAN: No. She's fine.

(They sit in silence for a moment and JULIE comes back in.)

JULIE: Sorry. I had to call Katie and tell her we were running really late.

JARED: That's okay.

SUSAN: Are you ready for my future?

JULIE: I'm ready.

SUSAN: I'm a little scared, Jared!

JARED: Most people are.

JULIE: I'm not scared for the future, can't be any worse than the past.

SUSAN: It could be actually. The world is supposed to end in 2012 according to the Mayans, so we could just all die.

JULIE: And if I knew that information was true I would just go to a private island with all the people I cared about and have a huge party for the next two years.

JARED: It's a cyclical calendar. The world isn't ending.

SUSAN: Why do I feel a bit disappointed by that news?

JULIE: Because you'll have to marry Phil after all.

SUSAN: I guess.

JARED: *(Flips over SUSAN's last card.)* The Destro card. This is an interesting read. Destro supplies Cobra with arms and military hardware. This is the family card. When drawn upside down like so, it represents family and home. You want a family, although others don't see you as a family type. You have a burning desire to raise children and be close to your family home. Your childhood home may have been broken, or a parent perhaps was away often on business. Either way you had a void growing up that you desperately want to fill as an adult, and you will. You will devote yourself to your family. Perhaps being a stay-at-home mother. Very involved in your child's life. It seems that you will meet a man who will be very supportive of this if you have not met him as of yet. He will be very unconventional and it will be a quick romance. *(Looks at SUSAN lovingly.)*

JULIE: Well now I know you're not dying, because Susan and Phil would never have kids.

SUSAN: Why not?

JULIE: Phil hates children.

SUSAN: He doesn't hate children.

JULIE: Loathes children.

SUSAN: Well he says I haven't met him yet.

JULIE: Right. But you love Phillip, and you two are perfect for each other.

SUSAN: I don't know, Julie. It's in the cards.

JULIE: You really think this reading was very accurate?

SUSAN: More than you know.

JULIE: Are you going to tell me what it is I don't know?

SUSAN: Yes, but I think he should read your fortune and we could compare notes.

JARED: I would really love to.

JULIE: We should probably get going.

SUSAN: Come on, Jules. We can meet up with Katie and Roger another night. It's fun, and if you do it I will tell you all my deep dark childhood secrets. Promise.

JULIE: Fine. But just the three-card outlook because it's getting late.

SUSAN: Look at you, already knowing the lingo. The three-card outlook!

JULIE: Shut up!

JARED: Perfect. *(Picks up the deck and shuffles it, and carefully places it on the table.)*

SUSAN: That's his most requested.

JULIE: Of course.

JARED: Okay? *(Places the cards in G-formation on the table.)* Now, point to three cards, and remember don't touch them.

JULIE: I can't believe I'm doing this. *(Slowly and carefully picks her cards.)*

SUSAN: He's right on. I'm gonna ditch Phil and marry the coffee cart man on our street. I know he wants babies, and I'm pretty sure he's fertile because he has like six from at least four different women.

JULIE: How do you know this?

SUSAN: I'm Carlos's therapist. I love it.

JULIE: Carlos?

SUSAN: Carlos Ramanos. Hot. There is something sexy about a man stuck inside a coffee cart.

JULIE: He's not stuck, he can choose to leave.

SUSAN: Hey, this is my fantasy.

JULIE: Okay. I've picked three.

JARED: Great. *(Places the rest of the deck carefully back into the box.)* So, let's start. Past. *(Flips over first card.)* Breaker. He is the communications officer. You are a listener, you are the friend that others come to for advice. In your childhood, you were rich with friends and admirers. There is one person in your childhood you have unresolved feelings for, and you need to force yourself to communicate better in order to maintain this relationship. But this relationship will surprise you in your future.

SUSAN: I thought this was the past.

JARED: The past always influences the future.

SUSAN: Fair enough.

JARED: You have one event that has happened in your recent past that has shaped you as a person. Although the loss was great, without this loss you would not fully be the person you are today.

JULIE: That's a little general.

SUSAN: Did you just not hear what he said, Jules?

JULIE: I heard him, and it's general. Who hasn't been hurt in their past?

JARED: Okay? Moving on to the present day. This is interesting. Very interesting. I don't see this too often.

JULIE: What?

JARED: The Carl W. Greer card.

SUSAN: Who the hell is Carl W. Greer?

JARED: He also goes by Doc because he was G.I. Joe's doctor. Carl W. Greer. When this card is pulled as the present card, it means you are in need of focusing solely on your mental health. You have been dealing with a lot of stresses and change that haven't made living very easy. You often contemplate hurting yourself as a revenge for the one who hurt you the most. This person may or may not still be living but the hurt was one that will take a decade to get over. In the meantime you need to focus on the emotions you are feeling today, and how you can nurture yourself to be healthier for the future.

JULIE: Okay.

SUSAN: He's good.

JARED: Is this making sense?

SUSAN: Total.

JULIE: Sure. Future?

JARED: Are you sure you want to hear your future? The Carl W. Greer card is pretty intense.

JULIE: It's nothing I don't know already.

JARED: Okay. Ahh. An interesting follow-up card. Dr. Mindbender.

SUSAN: I never liked Dr. Mindbender.

JULIE: Did you really watch G.I. Joe?

SUSAN: Yes, I have three older brothers.

JULIE: Okay, give it to me. What is Dr. Mindbender?

JARED: Dr. Mindbender is the genius behind many of Cobra's evil creations, including Serpentor.

JULIE: This can't be good.

JARED: No, it's okay. You will make a drastic change in your current living situation. Although you have maintained a lifestyle that has always been comfortable, you desire change. You will move across the world, perhaps to Sydney if you live in New York, or Ireland if you live in Los Angeles. You will create a new life for yourself due to the toxic relationships you have formed in your past. Clearing yourself of these toxins and getting over that one great love will be your main priority in the years to come. You are changing, and with that so will your environment.

SUSAN: I don't want her to move! Am I the toxic friend? I don't want to be the toxic friend. Seriously, Julie, please don't move.

JULIE: I'm not moving. I swear. I'm not moving.

SUSAN: Okay. I am clearly ready for another round of drinks, Jared?

JARED: Actually, I think I have to get going. *(Starts to carefully pack away his cards.)*

JULIE: Really?

JARED: Well, I have to be honest. I never pursue a relationship with anyone that pulls the Carl W. Greer card. I just can't. It's not a healthy card.

JULIE: Are you serious?

SUSAN: Wait, really?

JARED: I don't want to hurt you, Julie, and I have enjoyed our conversations, but I'm looking for a serious relationship. I need someone a little more stable. The truth is I'm most compatible with Destro, and it's a rare find for me to actually give a beautiful woman a reading where she pulls Destro but since you live with your boyfriend, I'm afraid I should take my cards and leave.

SUSAN: Are you kidding?

JARED: As I have said before, the cards don't lie. I wish I could make up the answers, because I really have enjoyed the time we have spent together, Julie. I think that you need to unleash your demons, and I'm afraid I'm not a strong enough human being to help you through them. You will also be relocating, and I want to have my family in West Virginia.

JULIE: So, no second date?

JARED: I'm afraid not. I thank you both for the drink, and the readings.

(He puts his box under his arm and hands SUSAN his business card.)

JARED: If you ever break up with Phil, please give me a call. You are a special special gifted soul.

(He takes her hand and kisses it. The girls are both in shock.)

JARED: It was wonderful to meet you both, and I think you have a strong friendship. I don't think you should keep secrets from each other. I will remember you both fondly. If you know of any other single women, give them my card. I know one day I will find another woman who will pull Destro. One that doesn't live with her nice boyfriend Phil. I have not given up hope. *(He exits.)*

SUSAN: Oh my God! Did that just happen?

JULIE: You are a special special gifted soul. *(Beat.)* That really did just happen.

SUSAN: I think it did.

JULIE: I'm so sorry for inviting him here.

SUSAN: Stop it, I loved it! *(Beat.)* So that was your first blind date!

JULIE: Oh my God, that was my first blind date! I will never date again, how can anyone ever top that?

SUSAN: They can't.

JULIE: I think I should start talking about him more, and maybe go on a date with one of your random drunk friends.

SUSAN: They are good for a random screw.

JULIE: That's always good for the ego.

SUSAN: Worked for me for years!

(Beat.)

SUSAN: Phil and I are always here for you, whenever. Whatever you need. I'll even make you your own set of Care Bear tarot cards.

JULIE: Care Bears? Grumpy would be the death card.

SUSAN: Sleepy would be the addicted to drugs card.

JULIE: No, I think Cheer Bear would be the addicted to coke card. Actually, that's the first thing he ever gave me. We were in fifth grade and he handed this pink bear to me with a note that just said, I'm glad we're friends, Michael Morris. He always signed his first and last names. Michael Morris. In fifth grade I never imagined knowing him his whole life.

SUSAN: I'm sorry.

JULIE: I don't want you to have to worry about what you say around me anymore. I feel like you're constantly on eggshells when we're together.

SUSAN: Maybe.

JULIE: Don't be, okay?

SUSAN: Okay. *(Beat.)* Two weeks before his diagnosis, Michael called me and asked me if I could spend the day with him. You were at your mother's, I think. We went to five different stores, but he settled for Tiffany's. He said you loved the color blue of their boxes, and so he wanted to go there. It was between two rings, and one was a lot more expensive than the other. He pretended he couldn't decide, but I knew which one he wanted to get you. It was perfect. It wasn't pretentious, it was simple, elegant, and showed just the right amount of love. That's what Michael said when he first saw it. Just the right amount of love. We had a great day, the two of us. I think it was the first time we spent a day without you or Phil. We went to Barneys and ate at Fred's, overindulged on dessert, and talked about how much we loved you. He was planning on giving it to you on New Year's at Washington Square Park, right under the arch, next to the tree. He asked me to keep it, because knowing you, you would find it in the apartment. It wasn't even two weeks when he collapsed at work, and everything happened so fast, we both forgot about the ring. Well, I didn't forget, but I didn't know what to do.

(She hands a blue Tiffany's box to JULIE.)

JULIE: Susan. *(Beat.)* It was quick. He lost so much weight. I got used to his bald head, I actually thought it was really sexy, but he was all bones at the end. I was afraid to touch him, and all I wanted to do was touch him. The last couple of weeks, his mother never left his side. I understood, but I wish I had a few more alone moments with him. You know? Just to tell him what I really felt.

SUSAN: He knew how you felt.

JULIE: I loved him so much. I just wish that when I closed my eyes I could see the healthy Michael, you know? The one who would cook extravagant meals out of ingredients he just found lying around. I loved watching him cook. He never measured anything, and I didn't understand how he could do that. A pinch of this, a pinch of that. It was always the perfect amount of everything. He could be cooking meatballs while preparing a gourmet Gorgonzola and pear salad with a casserole baking in the oven. I never understood how he could figure out how to get everything to finish at the same time. *(Beat.)* How can you replicate that? How can you possibly find someone who can cook perfectly with two hands while always affectionately keeping their eyes on you? *(Puts on the ring.)* It's a little big. *(Beat.)* How could he afford this?

SUSAN: He was on a payment plan, I think.

JULIE: But I don't get any bills from Tiffany's.

SUSAN: That was a wonderful day. *(Beat.)* You know what I think?

JULIE: I always want to know what you think.

SUSAN: It won't always hurt this bad.

JULIE: I miss sex, and I feel really guilty about saying that.

SUSAN: Don't feel guilty.

JULIE: I'm sorry about inviting Jared.

SUSAN: I think Michael invited Jared.

JULIE: He would totally do that, wouldn't he?

SUSAN: I don't think you can even make up shit as good as what happened here tonight.

JULIE: I'm so glad you were here because if I told someone this story they would never believe me, but now they have to believe me because I have a witness, and you took notes.

SUSAN: I took notes! *(Beat.)* Do you want to stay over tonight?

JULIE: I love your couch.

SUSAN: I think G.I. Joe Jared is right.

JULIE: You are going to be a stay-at-home mom?

SUSAN: Well, maybe. But I think you should move.

JULIE: I know.

SUSAN: Just out of that apartment, not to Sydney.

JULIE: *(Picks up the business card that was lying on the table. Looks at it and starts to laugh.)* I will never forget you, G.I. Joe Jared!

SUSAN: I'm sure we know someone who is good for him.

JULIE: I think you like G.I. Joe Jared.

SUSAN: For a moment I thought he was my Cobra in shining armor.

JULIE: Don't ever say that again.

SUSAN: I won't. I promise.

(The girls burst out laughing and continue to talk as the lights fade.)

(The end.)

LOVE ME

a comedy

Jason S. Grossman

JASON S. GROSSMAN hails from Brooklyn and grew up in Brooklyn, Queens, and Great Neck, Long Island. He holds a JD from Benjamin N. Cardozo School of Law and a BS in business administration from SUNY Albany. Jason considers himself a writer/producer/on-and-off-and-on-again actor, and has worked in theatre, film, and TV. He was the head (or sole) writer for a number of comedy groups over the years including, but not limited to, Crispen Tickle, Tonight's Special, Evil Twin and, for the longest time, Funny...Sheesh. His plays have been performed by Mind the Gap Theatre Company and the Shortened Attention Span One Act Festival, and include the shameless multimedia cautionary extravaganza *You Happy Now? Somebody Just Lost an Eye* (with Julie Perkins) and, most recently, *How to Fold a Map?*. He also was a writer for TV Land's "Ultimate Fan Search" and cowriter of the screenplay *The Guy of 2Z* with Matt Fortnow (executive producer of *Certifiably Jonathan*). Jason wrote and developed a motivational course called "The Art of Socializing and Networking" which incorporates improvised social scenarios, and which he has taught at numerous continuing education programs at Baruch College, Hunter College, Marymount Manhattan College, Pace University, and 92nd Street Y, among others. He's also taught comedy writing and improvisation. Jason is a member of the Manhattan Theatre Source Hall of Fame and the Advisory Board of The New York Theatre Experience, Inc. He resides in Manhattan with Amber Gallery and their cat, Chesapeake.

Love Me was first presented by Funny…Sheesh Productions (Jason S. Grossman, Artistic Director; Amber Gallery, Managing Director) as part of the Planet Connections Theatre Festivity (Glory Kadigan, Executive Director) on June 10, 2010, at the Robert Moss Theatre, New York City, with the following cast and credits:

Charlie's Head	Jeff Wills
Charlie	Aaron Rossini
Wendy/Infomercial Director	Daina Schatz
John	James Cichewicz
Susan/Kate	Kaira Klueber
Carol	Victoria Watson
Tom	Ridley Parson
Sara	Laura Schwenninger

Director: Daryl Boling
Set Designer: Sheila Phalon
Costume Designer: Izzy Fields
Lighting Designer: Lauren Parrish
Production Stage Manager: Laura Schlachtmeyer
Assistant Director: Phillip Chavira
Postcard/Image Designer: Daryl Boling

Love Me was nominated for ten awards and won three, including Outstanding Playwriting for a New Script in the Planet Connections Theatre Festivity.

Special thanks to Amber Gallery; John Hartmann; Karen Christie-Ward; Renée Torrière; Penny Di Marco; Sharon Fogarty; Timothy Joseph Ryan; Rob Blatt; Kenny Davidsen; Jason Hefter; Sam Riegel; Felicia Scarangello; Jamie Melser; Michelle Newman; Kelly-Sue DeConnick; Matt Fortnow; Martin Denton; Rochelle Denton; Charles, Beverly, and Tracy Grossman; Sophia Noyer; Robert and Mary Jayne Gallery; Katie & Chesapeake; Rebecca Weitman; Manhattan Theatre Source; and the Planet Connections Theatre Festivity.

CAST OF CHARACTERS

CHARLIE, a writer/actor in his early thirties
CHARLIE'S HEAD, what goes on in Charlie's head
CAROL, a multitalented artist in her early thirties
JOHN, a self-appointed expert on women, mid-thirties
SUSAN, a self-involved actress, age unknown
TOM, large and loyal friend to Charlie, in his late twenties
SARA, an acerbic attorney and Carol's best friend, early thirties
WENDY, a stage manager and Carol's friend, in her late twenties
DIRECTOR, a director
KATE, a coworker of Sara's
WOMAN ONE
ANNOUNCER VOICEOVER

SETTING

Act I: Early January
Act II: Early June
Act III: Late December

Place: The East Village, New York City
Time: Mid-1990s

DIRECTOR'S NOTE BY DARYL BOLING

One of the wonderful discoveries in the process of rehearsing the original production of *Love Me* was the degree to which the role of Charlie's Head was directly connected to the physical manifestation of the psychological. Essentially: whatever Charlie was thinking—the pure and unedited—was potentially physically realized through Charlie's Head. This creates a critical dependence upon an actor in the role of Charlie's Head, with extensive training in physical comedy—from commedia to slapstick—providing a depth and diversity of physical dialogue between Charlie's Head and Charlie. Do not shortchange yourself: make sure you carve out enough time in rehearsal to properly develop that language of the physical-psychological world between Charlie and Charlie's Head.

ACT I
Scene 1

CHARLIE STYPTIC's apartment in the East Village, New York City. There is a weathered, cat-shredded black couch, an end table with a lamp, a chair with strips of black duct tape over torn upholstery, and a basic coffee table with a telephone answering machine and a phonebook. There is a bookcase containing reference books for writing, anthologies of comic strips, and huge volumes of sports statistics. There is a large poster of former New York Knicks all-star guard Walt "Clyde" Frazier, circa 1970, centered on the upstage wall. CHARLIE, thirty, is alone. He's wearing a shrunken, faded baseball T-shirt, speckled with bleach spots. He is pacing back and forth and holding a copy of the Village Voice *opened to the personals. Every few steps, he stops to look at one particular personal. CHARLIE'S HEAD, his inner voice personified, is wearing exactly the same clothes as CHARLIE.*

CHARLIE'S HEAD: My name is Charlie. This is my story. His story. Our story. Or at least how I remember it... I've changed the names for fear of retaliation. If you think this is about you, it might be.

(CHARLIE sits down and picks up the phone receiver. He looks at the same personal and starts to dial.)

CHARLIE'S HEAD: That's me, too. That's actually the real me. I'm just what's going on in his head. My head. Our head.

CHARLIE: *(Thinks better of calling and hangs up, opting for a couple of dry runs. Holding his hand like a telephone receiver.)* Hello, Donna. This is Charles Styptic...

CHARLIE'S HEAD: Actually Charlie.

CHARLIE: You don't know me...

CHARLIE'S HEAD: How could you?

CHARLIE: But I read your personal ad in the *Village Voice*. Issue dated January 1st. On page ninety-eight...column three...

CHARLIE'S HEAD: Necessary details?

CHARLIE: Right under "SWJM looking for SWJF or SWCF willing to convert to SWJF. Ampersand must have good A/C..."

CHARLIE'S HEAD: Did you have to read the whole thing?

CHARLIE: Let's see... I am an *(Looks at his notes.)* S. W. M. And I'm...

CHARLIE'S HEAD: A bit anal. Compulsive, obsessive...

CHARLIE: Organized. And independent. I'm also good at following directions...

CHARLIE'S HEAD: Like a sheep.

CHARLIE: I'm quite good at prioritizing. I have solid communication skills. I'm a real people person, and I was wondering...

CHARLIE'S HEAD: If you would hire me, because I sound like I'm on a job interview!

(CHARLIE gets up to pace, then settles back to sit.)

CHARLIE'S HEAD: ...Just be honest.

CHARLIE: *(Practices again.)* Hello, Donna, this is Charlie. I saw your ad... I am a part-time motivational speaker, presently unemployed. I'm an actor, semi-unemployed in that, too... I've been working on my screenplay, but I've been having some trouble getting over the hump. Been moping around since my girlfriend dumped me, and I—

CHARLIE'S HEAD: Think that's being way too honest.

CHARLIE: *(Ponders, then uses a deep, blunt voice.)* Yo, Donna, this is Chuck. I am your ultimate erotic male fantasy with a magic wand to service all of your needs. Whether you crave bondage or domination, just call one-nine hundred-PRIME-CHUCK— *(Slams down the imaginary phone.)*

CHARLIE'S HEAD: What the hell is that?!

(CHARLIE starts pacing again.)

CHARLIE'S HEAD: ...Need a completely different approach.

CHARLIE: *(Sits. Imitating a Spanish lover.)* Hello, Donna-mia, this is Chaz, your La Mancha of love. I am simply a one-woman man who loves the finer things in life like poetry, candlelight dining, foreign movies, and long walks on the beach. My dearest darling, I can make all your dreams come true if you'll just return my phone call.

CHARLIE'S HEAD: That's it! She'll dig that.

CHARLIE: *(Picks up the phone confidently and dials Donna's number. The call is connected. He suddenly becomes nervous and begins to stammer.)* ...L-l-love me. *(Hangs up the phone, supremely defeated.)*

SCENE 2

A bare rehearsal studio. DIRECTOR is going over her notes.

CHARLIE'S HEAD: I used to think all the people walking the streets in New York talking to themselves were crazy. They're just actors rehearsing their monologues.

(CHARLIE enters carrying his headshot and approaches DIRECTOR.)

CHARLIE: I'm here for the audition for the infomercial?

DIRECTOR: *(Impatiently.)* Did you fill out the audition card?

CHARLIE: I didn't see a...

DIRECTOR: You are Mike, host of Tremendous Inventions. Read the cue cards. I'll tell you when to enter.

CHARLIE: Uh...Is there...I mean, should I—

DIRECTOR: Enter!

(Taken off guard, CHARLIE quickly exits and almost simultaneously reenters.)

CHARLIE'S HEAD: Speak!

(CHARLIE opens his mouth to speak.)

DIRECTOR: Next!

(CHARLIE is stunned.)

DIRECTOR: Let's keep this moving, people!

(JOHN enters, and DIRECTOR approaches him. CHARLIE lingers.)

DIRECTOR: *(To JOHN.)* You are Mike, host of Tremendous Inventions.

(JOHN exits.)

DIRECTOR: Let's run through it. Enter!

(JOHN reenters.)

JOHN: *(As an enthusiastic host.)* Hey, Mike here on "Tremendous Inventions." Do you find it impossible to lose weight? Are you tired of all those fad diets? Now, there's a revolutionary product that guarantees fantastic results in weeks, days, even seconds. Here's Sandy, the inventor, to tell us more.

(SUSAN enters as Sandy carrying Broken Scale.)

SUSAN: Hello, Mike. After years of researching every weight-loss program on the market, I have perfected this must-win, no-lose method.

JOHN: Incredible. Impossible! It could only be a miracle.

SUSAN: Tell me, Mike, how do people usually determine that they're overweight?

JOHN: Hmmm, Sandy. With some sort of scale of some sort?

SUSAN: Exactly! And here is my invention. *(Revealing Broken Scale.)* Broken Scale!

JOHN: Broken Scale?! Wow! But how?!

SUSAN: *And* how, Mike! Here's my secret: Broken Scale is broken. It shows you your incorrect weight. Your *idea-a-a-l* weight! Just preset the number of pounds you wish to weigh. Set Broken Scale on the floor. Approach Broken Scale. Step on Broken Scale. You weigh that number!

JOHN: But, Sandy, what about food?

SUSAN: You can eat whatever you want, whenever you want to! And by following my easy-to-swallow booklet, *Getting Fat on Weight Loss*, you can develop a program to lose weight as you're *actually gaining!*

JOHN: Thanks, Sandybarge. Now, let's listen to these satisfied losers.

(Enter CAROL as an overweight slob gobbling chips and TOM as an overweight slob with his bare stomach bulging over his pants.)

CAROL: *(Spits chips out and grins.)* For years, I was fat and repulsive. My weight was completely out of control. I tried everything. I even sat through all of those boring exercise shows. Then my life changed forever when I tried Broken Scale. I just turn Broken Scale down to a lower weight once each night before I go to bed. And it's so unnoticeable! Everyone still thinks of me as a big fat tank, but I know better, *(Winks.)* thanks to Broken Scale.

TOM: And you can go to work the very next day.

(CAROL exits; TOM remains.)

SUSAN: And Broken Scale is toxic safe and is perfectly compatible with any juicer, hair removal, or hair extension product.

TOM: And you can go to work the very next day.

JOHN: Thanks, Sandybarge. So go get Broken Scale today!

ANNOUNCER: *(Voiceover.)* Brought to you by Winston Products: The water substitute people.

DIRECTOR: *(Entering.)* Stop. Stop. Cut. Stop. *(Pause.)* Tom, you're supposed to exit with your repulsive spouse—Did you forget you already delivered your line? And the inventor's name is just Sandy, not Sandybarge. And it's an easy-to-*follow* booklet. You obviously can't eat the book...Maybe you can—oh, screw it. Just go home. *(To herself.)* I need Valiums. *(Exits.)*

(JOHN and SUSAN exit. CHARLIE greets TOM while CAROL defrumps.)

CHARLIE: Hey, Tom, you were great.

TOM: Thanks, Charlie. You, too. So what did you think of Carol?

CHARLIE: Was she the one playing your wife-troll-thing there?

TOM: Yeah—Hey, there's nothing going on between us. We were just acting. Let me get her.

CHARLIE: Why? *(Trying to stop him.)* Tom!

CHARLIE'S HEAD: Not now, Tommy! Not ready!

(TOM brings CAROL over to meet him.)

TOM: Carol, this is Charlie.

CHARLIE: Hi. You were very good. Very believable…

CHARLIE'S HEAD: Smooth as silk.

CAROL: Thank you. I feel disgusting.

TOM: Charlie is a writer and a freelance motivational speaker. He actually motivated me to audition today. Although I was going to do it anyway.

(TOM nudges CHARLIE.)

TOM: Go ahead.

CHARLIE: Sorry. He really shouldn't. *(To TOM.)* You really shouldn't.

(SARA enters and stands near the door.)

SARA: *(Shouting.)* Carol!

CAROL: I can't believe people actually buy this stuff.

SARA: Carol!

CAROL: That's my best friend.

SARA: Carol! Let's go!

CAROL: I'm coming! *(To CHARLIE.)* Excuse me. When Sara calls… It was nice meeting you.

CHARLIE: Me, too. Keep eating…

CHARLIE'S HEAD: Where's Broken Scale? I need something to crawl under.

(CAROL and SARA exit.)

TOM: *(Nudging CHARLIE.)* Nice meeting you, huh? And I have her number, too.

CHARLIE: Why would I want her number? Let's get something to eat.

TOM: Good, I'm starving.

CHARLIE: Aren't you going to change or something?

TOM: What for?

(They start walking out.)

TOM: Aren't you curious about Carol's number? It's been forever for you, Charlie.

CHARLIE: Let's talk about something else.

TOM: Okay. Did you call that Donna woman from the *Village Voice* ad?

CHARLIE: That's the wrong something else. Could you at least cover the belly there…

(They exit.)

Scene 3

Oogle's Crevice, a bleak dive bar in the East Village. Three days later. There is a ragged dart board, a pinball machine, and a counter with some stools. There is an indefinable picture of a plate of food on the wall and a small table with chairs. CAROL and CHARLIE are seated. He is wearing his only suit. Her dress is tasteful, but considerably more casual.

CHARLIE'S HEAD: The symptoms of anthrax poisoning are sweating, discomfort, and general unease. I must have had anthrax on every date since 1983.

CHARLIE: ...First dates...

CAROL: ...Such a stigma...

CHARLIE: *(Quietly.)* ...Yeah, stigma.

CAROL: Pardon?

CHARLIE: *(Much louder.)* Yeah stigma!

(They look around self-consciously.)

CHARLIE'S HEAD: Really bad choice of venue, man. You overdid the so-crappy-it's-cool thing. It's just crappy.

CHARLIE: Sorry about the bar.

CAROL: ...Why don't we pretend this is a second date?

CHARLIE: Can we make it the third? I don't have a good history with second dates either.

CHARLIE'S HEAD: They usually wind up being last dates.

CAROL: Then let's make it our fourth.

CHARLIE: Bad history with thirds?

CAROL: Only one, but it was really bad.

CHARLIE: Really?

CAROL: I'm not at liberty to go into it, but it involved a hockey mask and a goalie stick.

CHARLIE: But no hockey?

CAROL: No, but there was a slap shot.

(A lull.)

CAROL: Glad that first date is over.

CHARLIE: Me, too. That was a bitch. *(Winces.)*

CHARLIE'S HEAD: I'd ask for the check, but we haven't ordered anything.

CAROL: It's a great place for a fourth date. Kind of creepy-chic.

CHARLIE: The service was voted worst in the city. I think it's their thing.

CAROL: So did you have a business meeting today or an audition to be a secret service agent?

CHARLIE: No. Why? *(Aware of his attire.)* Oh. No, I just don't have much in the way of in-between clothes. It's either informal or extremely formal. Actually, almost exclusively informal.

CAROL: You look nice.

CHARLIE: Thank you...You know, you can be really repulsive...in front of the camera.

CAROL: Thanks...You could have been in the infomercial. I'm sure you're very good.

CHARLIE: *(Affected, cutesy voice.)* I'm even better when given the chance to speak.

(CAROL laughs politely.)

CHARLIE'S HEAD: Great. She digs the silly voice.

CHARLIE: *(Continuing with the shtick.)* I'm a great talking actor. I'm quite good when speaking...

(CAROL chuckles. He starts to overdo it.)

CHARLIE: ...Never better than when I'm with words. It's all in the vocabulary...

(CAROL smiles.)

CHARLIE: ...Once I get started, I just can't stop.

CHARLIE'S HEAD: I'd better stop.

(There is another lull.)

CAROL: So that was your friend playing my husband...He's very nice.

CHARLIE: So that was my friend playing your husband...He's very nice.

(They pause to let the other speak.)

CAROL and CHARLIE: *(Simultaneously.)* Is he...Go ahead. No, you go ahead. No, you...Just go...Okay, this is getting weird. *Now*, it's weird! Please stop that. Okay, I'll stop. Stop! Stop that now!—

CHARLIE: *(Blurts out.)* I have a cat!—

CAROL: I hate them! I mean...I don't have one.

CHARLIE: Her name is Kitty Poo. My father named her as a joke, and it stuck. She loves everybody. The cat, not my dad. Obviously, the cat...'cause she's a she. My dad's nice, too. He's a dog person.

CAROL: I'm sure both are very nice. Are you close? To your dad.

CHARLIE: Yes. To both.

CAROL: So, is acting your primary vocation?

CHARLIE: No. I mean, I'm focusing on my writing...working on a screenplay.

CAROL: Is there a part for me?

CHARLIE: *(Eager.)* You can play them all.

CAROL and CHARLIE'S HEAD: Down boy.

CHARLIE: So, is acting *your* primary vocation?

CAROL: Well, not financially primary. I'm actually a writer, too. A playwright.

CHARLIE: Yeah, I really like writing. When I do it. Not when I don't do it. Sometimes I don't like it when I'm doing it, either. My screenplay is coming along slowly—I know writers aren't supposed to talk about works in progress— *(Rambling.)* Not that I think my script isn't talkworthy—although I realize I'm not talking about it specifically—but it's really gratifying to create something that might be performed—or filmed—I might produce it myself, unless you have five hundred thousand dollars you don't want—I'm kidding, I'm not really asking you for money...

CHARLIE'S HEAD: Squashing the myth that men love to talk about themselves.

CAROL: I'm pretty lucky. My last play was extended after we got some praise in the *Times*.

CHARLIE'S HEAD: Ego check, please!

CAROL: What's your screenplay about?

CHARLIE'S HEAD: Fifteen and a half pages.

CHARLIE: A comic superhero.

CAROL: Like Batman?

CHARLIE: Not exactly. This guy is really a comic—a comedian—and he quits his day job to battle evil full time by telling jokes to people who really need a laugh—like someone who just lost their job or just got dumped.

CHARLIE'S HEAD: Never say *dumped* on a date! Never say *dumped* on a date!

CAROL: I'm sure it'll be great.

CHARLIE: Thanks. *(Looks around.)* You know, I'm not sure there's a waiter on this shift. Do you want to go someplace else?

CAROL: I'm fine staying here.

CHARLIE: Sure.

CAROL: I like the premise of your script. I wrote this character once who would only speak when she was sure that no one was listening…

CHARLIE'S HEAD: *(While she is talking; in a childish tone.)* I like her. She's pretty.

Scene 4

CHARLIE's apartment. Two months later. The furniture has been pushed aside. CAROL and SARA are standing, bored and agitated.

CHARLIE'S HEAD: Carol and I began dating consistently. Like most new couples, we wanted to spread our joy to our best friends, so we set up a double date.

(Pots and pans are rattling; CHARLIE and TOM cheer from the kitchen offstage.)

SARA: Who's idiotic idea was this?

CAROL: Charlie thought it would be a good way for you and Tom to get to know each other.

(CHARLIE and TOM enter in rowdy fashion. TOM is cradling a football.)

CHARLIE: Nice catch!

CHARLIE'S HEAD: Duuuuuude!

TOM: Charlie's apartment is really great for football, Carol. You probably know that already.

CAROL: I didn't realize. Thank you, Tom.

CHARLIE'S HEAD: This is going so great. I am a brilliant social director.

SARA: Hey, why don't we change the teams around?

CHARLIE: Okay. Carol and me on one team, Tom and Sara on the other. Bathroom and kitchen are touchdowns. The walls are out of bounds.

CAROL: Tom, please watch the cat.

TOM: *(Nods.)* How about we play tackle now?

CHARLIE: Two-hand touch.

SARA: *(Sternly.)* One hand.

(They break into two huddles with CHARLIE and CAROL in one, TOM and SARA the other.)

TOM: Sara, why don't you go down and out?

SARA: I don't *down and out. (Snatching the ball away.)* Hey, why don't I throw and you run?

TOM: Okay, I'm going to slant to the right, fake long, and then do a buttonhook over the middle.

SARA: You do that.

(The teams break huddle and get set on the line of scrimmage.)

SARA: One for the money, two for the money, three—do something!

(TOM and CHARLIE run in anticipation of the pass. CAROL stands at the line of scrimmage.)

SARA: Go, Tom. Go! Further…Further!

(The men exit. The cat SCREECHES. SARA flips the ball to CAROL.)

SARA: Go, Carol, go!

(CAROL runs in the opposite direction and exits into the bathroom. The toilet FLUSHES.)

SARA: Touchdown! We win! We win!

(CAROL reenters and celebrates with SARA. TOM and CHARLIE reenter slowly.)

CHARLIE: *(Dejected.)* You guys aren't on the same team.

TOM: I think that's some kind of cheating.

CHARLIE'S HEAD: Girls stink.

(CHARLIE and TOM move the chairs.)

CAROL: So…Sara…Tom is an actor.

SARA: What kind of parts do you play?

TOM: I usually get cast as an offensive, socially awkward person.

SARA: Well, you have to go with your strengths.

CHARLIE and CAROL: *(To each other.)* Can you excuse us for a minute.

(CHARLIE pulls TOM aside. CAROL pulls SARA aside.)

CHARLIE: *(To TOM.)* Why did you tell her that?

CAROL: *(To SARA.)* What is wrong with you?

SARA and TOM: This totally sucks.

CHARLIE: *(Cheerfully to ALL.)* Hey, how about getting something to eat?

SARA: Good idea. I'm getting something to go. *(Exiting.)*

CAROL: *(Exiting after her.)* Sara?!

CHARLIE: Sorry. I had a feeling it wouldn't work out.

TOM: Yeah. She throws like a girl.

Scene 5

Oogle's. Two months later. CAROL, SARA, and WENDY are seated. SARA is generally obsessed with the lack of décor. WENDY is performing some form of table-based yoga.

SARA: …They spend ninety-five percent of their waking day lusting after women and fantasizing, getting all worked up so that by the time they're actually lucky enough to have sex, they last three minutes—Where the hell are we?!

WENDY: Is three minutes bad?

CAROL: We have to find you another boyfriend.

WENDY: I think Burt is sexy.

CAROL: You think everyone is sexy.

SARA: Burt is a lot of things and sexy isn't any of them—Would you look at this hellhole?

CAROL: Let's face it. They're essentially empty vessels. If it weren't for testosterone, they'd be vegetables.

SARA: Like really stale celery…

WENDY: Or saggy scallions…

CAROL: Shriveled string beans…

SARA: With little grape tomatoes…

WENDY: Tomatoes are fruits.

CAROL: Well, supposedly only ten percent of them.

SARA: You have to find a man who can pretend that he's not completely consumed with sex.

WENDY: Well, Charlie's an actor, right?

CAROL: He broadcasts what he's feeling.

WENDY: That's kind of sexy.

(She catches their look.)

WENDY: It is.

SARA: *(Scanning the place.)* Is he clean at least?

CAROL: He's neat but dirty. And he's bad at doing laundry. All his clothes look injured. His T-shirts have these wounded spots all over them. And I'm pretty sure he doesn't use bleach. When I mentioned it, he didn't know what I was talking about.

WENDY: Just three months, and she loves him.

SARA: Sounds like bliss.

WENDY: I like a man who's not afraid of his masculinity. Someone who says, I'm a crude beast, and I'm proud of it.

CAROL: You mean an orangutan.

WENDY: I think that's sexy—I mean, appealing.

SARA: So is Charlie?

CAROL: The top of his back is a little hairy.

SARA: *(Pointed.)* Is he a cool guy?

CAROL: Define cool.

WENDY: You know, *cool*.

(CAROL contemplates and starts to laugh.)

SARA: Was that a funny question?

(CAROL continues to laugh.)

SARA: I think we struck a nerve.

(CAROL's laughter builds.)

SARA: Take deep breaths, Carol.

(CAROL laughs uncontrollably.)

Scene 6

CHARLIE's *apartment. That night. CAROL has fallen asleep on the couch.*

CHARLIE *is leaning over her, holding a book on hypnosis. He quietly attempts to hypnotize her.*

CHARLIE'S HEAD: The mating ritual of the octopus is furious and passionate, the male and female grappling in a savage mass of jabbing beaks and pulsating colors. After thrusting sperm into the female's mantle cavity, the male promptly weakens, his coloration dulls, he stops eating and dies.

CHARLIE: *(Leans over her.)* You are becoming more tolerant. You will think everything Charlie does is charming. You will love sudden death overtime and Slim Jims…

(CAROL giggles in her sleep, then suddenly wakes up. CHARLIE pretends he's fast asleep and snores loudly. CAROL looks at him suspiciously, then goes back to sleep. He slowly opens his eyes and sits up. Once again asleep, CAROL starts chuckling.)

Scene 7

Seconds later. CAROL's dream of CHARLIE on trial. SARA is the judge, TOM is the bailiff, and CAROL is the prosecuting attorney. The jury includes JOHN and SUSAN. CHARLIE is on the witness stand being questioned by WENDY, his attorney.

WENDY: …And, Mr. Styptic, was this incident hard on you?

CHARLIE: Yes.

WENDY: Was there any embarrassment felt on your part?

CHARLIE: Yes, definitely embarrassment.

WENDY: And did you actually see the pass being completed?

CHARLIE: No, but there was a lot of cheering. And...And...

WENDY: Yes.

CHARLIE: The toilet was flushed.

WENDY: *(Looks dramatically at the jury.)* The toilet. Was. Flushed. *(Turns to SARA.)* No further questions, Your Honor.

SARA: *(To CAROL.)* Counselor, you may begin cross examination.

CAROL: Thank you, Your Honor. *(Buttons her jacket and approaches CHARLIE.)* Mr. Styptic, how would you characterize yourself?

CHARLIE: Well, I'm, I would say, I'm very much a—

CAROL: Would you describe yourself as a cool person?

CHARLIE: I would say fairly to moderately cool by today's standards.

CAROL: Hmmm-huh...Would you say one of the activities of a *cool* person is to, on occasion, make mixed cassette tapes for friends?

CHARLIE: Sure. I guess so.

CAROL: And have you, Mr. Styptic, ever made one of these so-called mixed tapes?

CHARLIE: It's kind of my specialty.

CAROL: I see. And did you, in fact, on one occasion make a mixed tape in which you recorded the song "Whole Lotta Love" by the classic blues/rock 'n' roll band known as Led Zeppelin?

CHARLIE: Yes, and I think that would certainly qualify—

CAROL: And isn't it also true, Mr. Styptic, that immediately following the song "Whole Lotta Love" by Led Zeppelin you recorded on that same mixed tape the song "Mandy"?

CHARLIE: *(Reluctant.)* I don't know?—

CAROL: And isn't it true that the song "Mandy" was written and performed by the artist universally known as Barry Manilow?

(There are gasps from the courtroom.)

WENDY: Objection! Using the words "Manilow" and "artist" in the same sentence.

SARA: Sustained.

CAROL: Your Honor, I would like to introduce into evidence *(Whips it out.)* this cassette tape.

(There are more gasps. SARA bangs gavel.)

CAROL: I will read the song titles if it would please the court.

SARA: It most certainly would not.

CAROL: "Walk This Way" by Aerosmith, "Walk on By" by Dionne Warwick. "You Shook Me All Night Long" by AC/DC, "You Light Up My Life" by Debbie Boone. "The Devil Went Down to Georgia" by the Charlie Daniels Band, "The Night the Lights Went Out in Georgia" by Vicki Lawrence—

SARA: *(Banging gavel.)* That is quite enough!

CAROL: I would now like to play the tape in its entirety.

WENDY: Objection! Its prejudicial value exceeds its probative value.

SARA: What?

WENDY: It'll annoy the shit out of us, Your Honor.

CHARLIE: *(Breaking down.)* Wait! I did it! It's true…

(Murmuring from the courtroom.)

CHARLIE: It was late. I thought I was making a really neat tape, but then I got cocky, and I put in some of my guilty pleasures—

CAROL: *Guilty* pleasures. Sir, you followed "Mr. Tambourine Man" with "Mr. Roboto"!

(There are more gasps from the courtroom.)

SARA: *(Banging gavel.)* What is with all the gasping?!

WENDY: Many of Mr. Styptic's supporters are asthmatic, Your Honor.

SARA: *(Bangs gavel.)* Charles Styptic, I sentence you to buy all your girlfriend's feminine products for a year, clean your bathroom thoroughly, and listen to the entire discography of one Debbie Gibson—

CHARLIE: Actually, it's Deborah now.

SARA: Case dismissed! *(Bangs gavel.)*

Scene 8

CHARLIE's apartment. CAROL and CHARLIE are having dinner. CAROL seems preoccupied.

CHARLIE: You don't like it, do you?

CHARLIE'S HEAD: I have absolutely no instincts when it comes to cooking.

CHARLIE: In college my housemates always made fun of me. I'd either massacre a meal from scratch or ruin one that was premade. One night I poured soy sauce on macaroni and cheese. *Macaroni and cheese.*

CHARLIE'S HEAD: You don't mess with perfection.

CAROL: The food is *(Struggles to swallow.)* fine.

CHARLIE: Did I nuke it too long?

CAROL: You nuked it? Why is it cold on the bottom of the bowl?

CHARLIE: I nuked it, then I put it in the freezer to hasten the cooling process… That way it's totally cooked, but you can eat it right away.

CHARLIE'S HEAD: No one appreciates my insight.

(Sounds of utensils against plates.)

CHARLIE: Did Kitty Poo puke in your shoes?

CAROL: She missed this time.

CHARLIE'S HEAD: Good… Now, leave it alone. Don't pout.

CAROL: You're pouting. What's wrong?

CHARLIE: Nothing… Is there anything wrong with you?

CAROL: No.

CHARLIE: You sure?

CAROL: Actually…

CHARLIE'S HEAD: Here it comes…

CAROL: Promise you won't get upset?

CHARLIE: Of course.

CAROL: Say you promise.

CHARLIE: I promise.

CAROL: Okay… Charlie…

CHARLIE'S HEAD: She's starting with my name. That's not good.

CAROL: Sometimes, I think you're just the tiniest bit on the insensitive side.

CHARLIE: What do you mean insensitive?

CAROL: Forget it.

CHARLIE: I can't believe it.

CAROL: *(Sighs.)* Charlie?

(He doesn't answer.)

CAROL: Charlie?

(No answer.)

CAROL: Why do you have to be so sensitive about everything?

CHARLIE: You just said I was insensitive.

CAROL: Being sensitive doesn't mean you're not insensitive…

CHARLIE'S HEAD: Come again?

CAROL: It just means that I can't say anything without you taking it to heart.

CHARLIE: That's so not true. Call me a name, throw something at me. I'll just shrug it off…

(She shoots him a look.)

CHARLIE: Well, *Carol*…as a matter of fact, I think *you're* very insensitive.

CAROL: What are you talking about?

CHARLIE: Well…just look at your plate.

CAROL: Okay?

CHARLIE: Look.

CAROL: There's nothing there.

CHARLIE: There used to be real turkey there.

CAROL: *(Confounded.)* Yes?

CHARLIE: I distinctly remember just last week you were eating that macrobiotic un-turkey…

(CAROL looks at him stone faced.)

CHARLIE: …I think there's some inconsistency there.

CHARLIE'S HEAD: Oh my, God. You did not just say that.

CHARLIE: Where does it end, Carol? Huh?

CHARLIE'S HEAD: Please stop now.

(CAROL gets up and exits.)

CHARLIE: The truth hurts, doesn't it?!

CHARLIE'S HEAD: I hate you.

Scene 9

Oogle's. CHARLIE is seated with his notebook. TOM is reading from CHARLIE's screenplay. He is wearing a cape and a shirt with a hand-drawn "SC" on the front. He takes a short run, then leaps like he's flying.

TOM: *(Placing hand on hip; reading in superhero voice.)* Ha. Ha, ha, ha! In the name of the Comedy gods Dangerfield, Carlin, and Pryor, I, Supercomic, have come to your aid. Puts his arm out.

CHARLIE: That's an action.

TOM: What?

CHARLIE: Just keep going.

TOM: No need to sour, I'm here to save you from despair with *(Big booming voice.)* CHU-CKLE PO-O-W-W-W-E-R-R-R. *(Points awkwardly.)* You, woman whose cat is sick, ever wonder why psychics never know they're going out of business? They should see that coming. Ha-ha! *(Points to him.)* Hey, Gloomy Gus, ever notice that the word "abbreviation" is too long? *(Breaks character.)* Yeah, why is that?

CHARLIE: Don't lose the rhythm.

TOM: You, man with bipolar disorder, why the heck does Duane Reade give you a receipt when you buy a pack of gum? You can't return gum. Ha-ha!

CHARLIE: Great, Tom. Now, go to the scene where you're battling the Evil Witch Monster. *(Becomes witchlike character.)* Supercomic, why are you always making jokes? Are you too afraid to be intimate?

TOM: *(As if struggling in a force field.)* You think you have trapped me in your emotionally abusive force field? Ha! Why do commercials always make such a big deal about putting raisins in breakfast cereals? Is there a shortage I don't know about? Ha-ha!

CHARLIE: I am too hypercritical to laugh at your insipid observational humor, Supercomic. Now lead me to your male associates.

TOM: Before it was just saving the future of the human race. Now, it's personal. *(Puts hands together extended outward as if generating power.)* Why do audiences always applaud big chorus kick lines? Ha! And would someone tell me why women cannot grasp the concept of a seven-game playoff series? What's the deal with that? And would someone explain Dennis Rodman's hair to me? *(Suddenly stops.)*

CHARLIE: I'm still working on that last one.

CHARLIE'S HEAD: That joke sucks.

TOM: *(Continuing with scene.)* And why do cartoon hands always have only four fingers...

CHARLIE: Stop! Stop! Heh, heh. *(Beginning to cower.)* Stop making me laugh. I can't take it anymore. Ha, ha, ha!... *(Finally defeated.)* You have won again, Supercomic. Haw, haw, haw... I am defeated, but I shall return one day to depress you with my passive aggressive powers. *(Breaks character.)* Okay, Tom, that was really good.

TOM: Charlie, Supercomic's supposed to be a good superhero. He's supposed to win, right?

CHARLIE: Of course. Why?

TOM: It's just that the jokes are... I don't think I get them. Except the one about raisins—That's so true.

(CHARLIE grabs the script from him.)

CHARLIE: You're not a writer.

TOM: I'm sure it's going to be great. You'll probably get Malcolm-Jamal Warner or Richard Dreyfuss to star in it.

CHARLIE: No way. I want you to be in it. I want all my friends to be in it.

(They head for the door.)

TOM: Explain Dennis Rodman's hair— I think I get that...

(As they exit.)

TOM: Don King has funny hair, too...

Scene 10

CHARLIE's apartment. CAROL is sitting on the couch working. CHARLIE is on the other side of the room trying to write.

CHARLIE'S HEAD: Supercomic, Supercomic... He's a comic... He's super... I got nothing.

(CHARLIE can't work; he looks over towards CAROL.)

CAROL: *(Her head in her work.)* I thought you were working on a mixed tape.

CHARLIE: Finished it. *(He goes back to writing. His head pops up. Then again.)*

CAROL: What is it?

(CHARLIE goes back to writing, but only lasts a few seconds. He is about to say something, but she cuts him off.)

CAROL: Charlie, we promised we would get together and get some work done tonight. And please don't be upset because I started a sentence with your name.

CHARLIE'S HEAD: How'd she know about that?

CAROL: Woman's intuition.

CHARLIE: *(Walks over to her.)* You know what I'm thinking right now?

(He starts kissing the back of her neck.)

CAROL: How's the screenplay coming?

CHARLIE: I'm stuck…We could use a break.

CHARLIE'S HEAD: Charlie. Want. Sex.

CHARLIE: We could…play Anchorman. *(Like Ted Baxter from* The Mary Tyler Moore Show.*)* This just in…

CAROL: *(Becoming distracted.)* How I hate that.

(They kiss.)

CAROL: I really need to work.

CHARLIE'S HEAD: You don't really need to work.

CAROL: *(Feeling amorous.)* Maybe the actors can improvise the rest of the play.

CHARLIE: And in our top story, Charlie and Carol go all the way…

Scene 11

CHARLIE's apartment. Fifteen minutes later. CAROL and CHARLIE are having sex in the bedroom offstage.

CHARLIE'S HEAD: Sex began over a billion years ago when single-cell organisms developed pores that released sex cells into the ocean.

CHARLIE: *(Offstage; about to climax.)* …And…that's…tonight's…n-n-n-n-n-e-e-e-e-ws! *(Climaxes.)* Goodnight.

(Moments later, CHARLIE enters wearing boxers.)

CHARLIE'S HEAD: Ooh, an apple.

(CHARLIE grabs an apple from the table, sits down on the couch, takes a bite, and starts writing. CAROL enters, appearing quite annoyed.)

CAROL: What are you doing?

CHARLIE: I got an idea for Supercomic's sidekick, Pun Boy. He only speaks in puns. Want a bite?

CAROL: Did you enjoy doing your news brief in there?

CHARLIE: Very much so. Thank you, honey. *(Puts his head down to write.)*

CAROL: *(Impatiently tapping her foot.)* Aren't you forgetting something, Mr. Cronkite?

CHARLIE: *(Looking around.)* Uh, I don't think so. *(Nodding.)* I signed off. Couldn't you tell?

CAROL: Definitely. Did you, by any chance, notice that I didn't exactly get an opportunity to finish my editorial?

CHARLIE: You didn't enjoy it?

CAROL: Not as much as you.

CHARLIE'S HEAD: She doesn't look happy.

CHARLIE: Oh... I'm sorry.

CAROL: Ever heard of blue balls, Charlie?

CHARLIE: I just thought that since you had a few semis and that big one the other day, that it kind of evened out.

CAROL: Are you sure you thought it that far through?

CHARLIE'S HEAD: Absolutely not.

(CAROL starts rummaging through a box of her things.)

CHARLIE: What's going on?

CAROL: I'm looking for someone who understands me. *(Finds vibrator.)* Ah! There he is.

CHARLIE: *(Stands.)* Wait. I'll go back on the air.

CHARLIE'S HEAD: Might need to show a few commercials first.

CAROL: No, William Wonker will do just fine. He's extremely reliable. And he doesn't snore.

(CHARLIE watches CAROL exit.)

CHARLIE: *(At a loss; calling after her.)* ...When you're finished, I can do the weather forecast.

(William Wonker starts a-humming from offstage.)

CHARLIE: Want to catch a movie later?

(CAROL groans with ecstasy.)

CHARLIE: We'll play it by ear.

Scene 12

Oogle's. WENDY is seated at the table with a bottle of booze and shot glasses. She cries a little, blows her nose, and does a shot. She repeats. SARA and CAROL enter.

WENDY: *(Blows nose.)* Hey, guys.

CAROL: Hi, Wendy.

SARA: Why are we back here?

WENDY: I think Burt and I are breaking up.

CAROL: Again, honey?

SARA: Didn't even know you guys were back together.

WENDY: I was cc'ed on an email he sent.

SARA: You weren't even the primary recipient?

WENDY: I don't think he meant to cc me.

CAROL: Why?

WENDY: He wrote, "I'm going to break up with Wendy. Don't tell her." *(Blows her nose, then downs a shot.)*

SARA: So it wasn't mutual?

(WENDY cries into CAROL's arms.)

CAROL: Next question, Counselor.

WENDY: Can I get a hug?

(Group hug.)

SARA: *(Pouring shots en masse.)* Glad that's taken care of... So how's tricks in the Garden of Eden with Captain Needy?

CAROL: They're... you know... it's... it's fine... okay... good... Yeah. *(Downs a shot.)*

WENDY: That's good. I like Charlie.

SARA: *That's good?* That was the longest nonsentence in recorded history.

CAROL: It's fine. Ish... *(Another shot.)* It's not always going to be, you know...

SARA: You're too nice, Carol. We've been through this before. You never want to hurt anyone's feelings. Sometimes you just gotta.

WENDY: Unless you do something so bad *he* has to break up with you.

CAROL: What about your sex life, Sara?

SARA: Off limits. My therapist doesn't even know about it.

(WENDY starts crying again.)

SARA: I thought we covered you?

WENDY: I love you, guys—

(Opening her arms for another hug, and CAROL obliges.)

SARA: Can I just send you an email?

Scene 13

CHARLIE's apartment. CHARLIE is trying to write. Frustrated, he puts the script down and picks up the remote and turns on the TV. The doorbell rings. CHARLIE answers the door. CAROL, visibly inebriated, fumbles in.

CHARLIE: Hi. Glad you could come over. How was the taping?

CAROL: *(Crossing to the couch.)* Dand-a-rific. We all went out for drink.

CHARLIE: Want something to eat? I made macaroni and cheese.

CAROL: You keep it. *(Gestures for him to meet her on the couch.)* C'mere. We need to talk.

CHARLIE'S HEAD: No one *needs* to talk. Talking's always optional.

CAROL: You know, Charlie, we've been having a few problems.

CHARLIE'S HEAD: Does this count? She's blitzed. Or does it count more?

CHARLIE: Is everything alright?

CAROL: Well, actually, I found Kitty poo on some of my music.

CHARLIE: She was lying on your stuff? She likes you.

CAROL: Kitty *poop*. She kitty *pooed* on it.

CHARLIE: I'm sure it's no reflection on your work.

CAROL: Look, I'm always so busy with my stuff. We don't have enough time for each other.

CHARLIE: We've been making time.

CAROL: You should have a friend. A special friend to hang out with. You need...

(The doorbell rings. CAROL gets up to answer it. JOHN enters, smiling broadly.)

CAROL: This is John!—

JOHN: *(As if speaking to a child.)* Wait, don't tell me. Don't tell me. This must be Charlie. How about I call you Chuck? And you can call me Uncle John.

CHARLIE: Who the hell is this?

JOHN: Do you like candy?

CAROL: He's from the Big Brothers for Boyfriends Foundation!

JOHN: I have a really big day planned for us tomorrow. Would you like to toss the ball around? *(Takes out rubber ball and gently tosses it up in the air from one hand to the other, then pauses and tosses it back to the original hand.)*

CHARLIE: *(Pause.)* Carol, can I talk to you for a second?

(CHARLIE pulls her aside.)

CAROL: Isn't he nice? You two are going to have so much fun together.

CHARLIE: I'm thirty years old!

CAROL: He knows.

(JOHN waves to CHARLIE from across the room.)

CAROL: I told him all about you. Your hobbies, your favorite foods, your sexual habits…

CHARLIE: What?! What do you mean my sexual habits?

CAROL: He's here to help.

CHARLIE'S HEAD: Don't I know him from somewhere?

JOHN: How about we get started right here? Where's the bedroom? *(Exits, wandering into the bedroom.)*

CAROL: Unckie John is going to sleep with us.

CHARLIE and CHARLIE'S HEAD: What?!

JOHN: *(Momentarily popping his head back in.)* Ready for a little sex, Chuck?

CHARLIE and CHARLIE'S HEAD: Not with you!

(CAROL exits into the bedroom.)

JOHN: *(Offstage.)* Now where did I put my lubricant?

CAROL: *(Offstage.)* Have you ever played Anchorman?

CHARLIE and CHARLIE'S HEAD: *(Rushing towards the bedroom.)* Carol! *(Exit.)*

(A hard THUD and groan are heard from offstage.)

ACT II
Scene 1

Oogle's. Later that night. Vintage rhythm and blues is playing. JOHN, CHARLIE, and TOM are seated at the table, having drinks. JOHN is nursing a welt under his eye.

TOM: So why did you become a Big Boyfriend, Uncle John? You wanted to give something back to the community?

CHARLIE: He's not really a Big Boyfriend, Tom. There's no such thing.

JOHN: It's a good idea though. Making a mental note.

TOM: I can't believe after all that, she broke up with you.

JOHN: A bunch of us were just hanging out after the infomercial. We were doing shots of Jaeger. Someone made a comment. Someone else made a joke. Someone else said it would make for a funny improv exercise. Or was it all the same person?

TOM: I love improv. It's so spontaneous.

CHARLIE and CHARLIE'S HEAD: Was *not* funny.

JOHN: We weren't really going to have sex. Truth is I never have sex with another guy's girlfriend unless the guy asks.

TOM: That's a pretty honorable code.

CHARLIE: Sometimes they ask?

JOHN: I'm still waiting. *(Touching his eye.)* I can't believe I walked into a door.

TOM: I can't believe she broke up with you.

JOHN: So you're free now. Feels pretty good, huh?

CHARLIE'S HEAD: Like a brain aneurism.

CHARLIE: I don't know. Maybe I just liked having...I mean, when you weigh everything out...

JOHN: Just fill in the blanks, right, Chuck?

CHARLIE: Charlie.

JOHN: Sometimes when I'm feeling, you know, romantic, I buy a dozen roses, and then I find someone I want to impress and then *whap*.

CHARLIE: You just give them away?

JOHN: Well, not exactly *give* them away.

CHARLIE: They owe you something.

JOHN: We all owe someone something...And I don't discriminate.

CHARLIE: You mean you're not selective.

TOM: I can't believe she broke up with you.

CHARLIE: I know you can't, Tom!

JOHN: *(Surveying the place.)* Man, I would never bring anyone here.

CHARLIE'S HEAD: To season wound, just add salt.

CHARLIE: *(To JOHN.)* In a way I envy you. You have no apologies. Nothing. I'm always...deliberating.

JOHN: Deliberating about what?

CHARLIE: What I'm going to say, how I'm going to say it, how it will be interpreted, global warming, the plight of the Caribbean monk seal...

TOM: It's a wonder he has time to date at all.

JOHN: This was the best thing that could have happened to you, Chuck. I'm glad I humiliated you. With all due respect.

CHARLIE'S HEAD: No respect taken.

CHARLIE: Did you know right before we started dating, both of us broke our refrigerators *independently* of each other. Things like that don't just happen...

JOHN: ...So I heard you were really good at the Broken Scale audition.

CHARLIE: I knew I recognized you.

JOHN: *(To TOM.)* Who were you again?

TOM: Fat Disgusting Slob Number Two. I'm trying to get Charlie to write a TV pilot based on the character. How he goes on adventures, eats, maybe fights crime.

CHARLIE: I'll never look at another woman.

JOHN: It's alright to feel that way now. How long did you guys go out?

CHARLIE: Seven and a half months.

JOHN: Recovery time is a complicated formula. Like the QB rating in football...Five days mourning, and you're back in the hunt.

TOM: Sounds like he knows what he's talking about, Charlie.

JOHN: You can't waste time, Chuck—

CHARLIE: Charles—

JOHN: Chuckie—

CHARLIE: Charlie.

JOHN: You can lick your wounds, or you can fuck your way through it.

TOM: This is just like you giving motivational advice, Charlie. Only more practical.

JOHN: You'll bounce back. You might as well have a little fun during the grieving period.

CHARLIE: That doesn't even... Doesn't matter; I'd get in the way of the fun anyway.

JOHN: Can't shut down the penal colony, Chuck.

TOM: Hey, I remember Charlie was ogling that Sandybarge from the infomercial.

CHARLIE: First of all, her name was just Sandy. Second, I'm reasonably sure that wasn't her real name. Third, I was not ogling. Fourth, I don't ogle—

JOHN: So there's hope. I just happen to have Sandybarge's telephone number.

CHARLIE'S HEAD: He knows her, too?

TOM: So convenient.

CHARLIE: Has everyone forgotten I was unceremoniously dumped not more than three hours ago?

TOM: Yeah, I still can't believe... Sorry.

JOHN: It's not just about you. There are women out there in need of sexual companionship.

(The men take long swigs of their drinks.)

CHARLIE: After many years of field research, I've come to the stark realization that both sexes are deeply flawed.

JOHN: It's all we got, Chuck.

TOM: For the time being.

Scene 2

CAROL's apartment. Brooklyn Heights, Brooklyn. Tasteful creative décor. CAROL is unpacking a box of her belongings with WENDY's help. SARA is outstretched on the couch.

CAROL: ...We were doing shots of Wild Turkey, talking about volunteering for UNICEF. Someone suggested helping people in dysfunctional relationships. We thought it would be a funny practical joke.

WENDY: I love practical jokes. They're so impractical.

SARA: So you didn't actually—

CAROL: No! *(Examining her things.)* All my stuff has cat hair on it. Even my mug.

SARA: *(Musing.)* I should start a chapter of Big Brothers for Boyfriends...

CAROL: I think I just wanted to get Charlie's reaction. I didn't realize how upset he'd get. Or how angry I really was.

SARA: Or how drunk.

CAROL: *(Looking in her bag.)* I think his cat puked in my compact.

WENDY: I feel sorry for Charlie.

CAROL: Me, too.

SARA: *(Makes buzzer sound.)* Wrong answer. Carol, he was too immature and clueless, and you ended it. Game over. Next player.

WENDY: Compassion much, Sara?

SARA: All's fair in war and breakups. You either tell the person what's wrong with them with some farfetched hopes that they'll change, or you don't tell them, because you know damn well that it won't change a thing, and it'll only destroy them, so you break up by saying some lame-ass crap like it's just not working out or some vague bullshit like it's not you, it's me, because nobody really wants to hear the truth, and why the fuck should they have to.

WENDY: Just like Hallmark.

SARA: People are lying when they say they don't like to play games.

CAROL: Even if he forgave me, I don't know if I could ever be with someone who let me do that to them. Is that screwed up?

WENDY: I keep hearing you're supposed to work on yourself first before you can be in a healthy relationship.

CAROL: If I waited until I fixed myself before being in a relationship, I'd be dead before finding someone. That's me in a coffin with a ring, holding hands with some other well-adjusted skeleton.

WENDY: Maybe you and Charlie can reconcile.

SARA: Are you living in the same time zone as the rest of us?

WENDY: I just like to see people together. It makes them happier. It makes the world happier.

CAROL: I think it ran its course, Wendy.

WENDY: Hug time.

(She hugs CAROL.)

SARA: Let's get wasted.

Scene 3

Oogle's. Thirty minutes later. The lights have dimmed slightly. CHARLIE, JOHN, and TOM are drinking beer. There are numerous shots lined up on the counter. JOHN is scanning the bar. CHARLIE and TOM are fixated on someone offstage.

JOHN: *(Flirts/waves to a woman offstage.)* What's up, Chuck?

CHARLIE'S HEAD: She is so pretty.

JOHN: Chuckie's in lust. *(Drinks a shot.)*

CHARLIE: I'm not in her league. *(Drinks a shot.)*

TOM: I'm not even in her farm system. *(Drinks a shot.)*

CHARLIE: I'm going to drink till I get drunk and then stay drunk until I can't remember why I started drinking in the first place.

TOM: Don't worry, I'll remind you.

JOHN: Do you guys know the most important thing to remember when you're in a relationship?

CHARLIE: How you first met?

TOM: The correct spelling of her name?

JOHN: Her eye color. Commit it to memory. Rinse. *(Drinks.)* And memorize again…One day, out of the blue, she'll put her hands over her eyes and ask you what color they are, and you won't know. The beginning of the end. The end of the beginning. I've used it many times to my advantage in reverse. Pretend I don't know.

CHARLIE: *(Goes back to staring at the woman offstage.)* I stare at women all the time. How come they never stare back?

JOHN: It would be awkward for two people to stare at each other all night. *(Downs a shot.)*

CHARLIE'S HEAD: He just described most of my first dates.

CHARLIE: I will never get over this.

TOM: Look, Charlie, most relationships are only meant to last just so long before they're played out. You and Carol went as far as you could. It's no tragedy. It'd be cruel to label every relationship you ever had that ended as a failure. You might do better the next time around.

(He burps. JOHN and CHARLIE stare at him.)

TOM: Do I have a big hair sticking out of my nose?

Scene 4

CAROL's apartment. CAROL, SARA, and WENDY are smoking pot. CAROL is staring at the TV, SARA is lounging on the floor, and WENDY is feverishly cleaning everything.

SARA: …So I'm bored out of my skull at the firm's summer outing—the one that's not mandatory but really *is* mandatory which is bullshit, because they could just make it mandatory… What was I talking about?… So I grab some guy from maintenance, and we go outside for an attitude adjustment via some really skunky Chiba. Next thing I know it's six a.m., and I am in some bar named Oogle's Crevice trying to convince a drug dealer there was a second gunman in Dallas. Holy shit, that was the same hole you dragged us to.

WENDY: *(Suddenly lifts up her head from cleaning.)* Hey, guys, check this out: what if we were all like pills, and we were inside someone's stomach? What would that be like. Wait! What if we were pellets inside a gun?—Or we were microchips inside of a computer?

SARA: Small, smaller, and who the fuck cares? *(Scanning the floor.)* There were just three roaches in rotation. What happened?

(CAROL gives her the roaches; SARA talks to them affectionately.)

SARA: My little antidepressants.

WENDY: *(Stops cleaning momentarily and turns to them.)* Can you repeat that last part? I think I have ADD. Or ADHD. *(Sitting down to join them.)* Hey, Carol, do your Fat Repulsive Slob woman. Come on.

SARA: *(Taking a hit.)* Doing a testimonial for pot.

CAROL: *(Musses her hair and stands. As her character from the scale infomercial.)* Hi. For years, I was thin, healthy, and gorgeous. It was awful. I tried everything. I even consumed Richard Simmons's entire Deal-A-Meal program in a day and a half. Nothing worked. I was still a hottie. Then my life changed forever when I tried Sara's Marijuana Slamma Programa. I just smoke a little upon waking up instead of taking a shower. Then I watch TV all day. Now, I'm too paranoid to leave my apartment, and I weigh over three thousand pounds, all thanks to Sara's… *(Breaks character.)* whatever I said before.

(WENDY and SARA clap. CAROL plops back down.)

WENDY: *(Stops clapping.)* Wait! Was that paranoid remark directed at me?

Scene 5

Oogle's. Thirty minutes later. It is darker than before. CHARLIE, JOHN, and TOM are leaning against the bar, heavily inebriated. They each drink a shot.

CHARLIE'S HEAD: In their never-ending effort to mate, male dolphins will join together to cruise for eligible females and attempt to impress them with an elaborate "belly slaps" ritual in synch with their pals.

(JOHN is staring at a woman offstage.)

WOMAN ONE: *(Offstage.)* Take a picture. It'll last longer.

(JOHN promptly takes out an Instamatic camera and snaps a photo.)

CHARLIE: *(To JOHN.)* So you agree that if another guy sleeps with your girlfriend or pretends he's about to, you have the right to punch him in the face?

JOHN: Absolutely. But the exception to the rule is you can't punch me. *(Drinks a shot.)*

CHARLIE: Why? *(Drinks a shot.)*

TOM: Why? *(Drinks a shot.)*

JOHN: I'm a bleeder. And that would've made you feel guilty.

CHARLIE'S HEAD: Can't argue with that.

TOM: I am so hungry. Where's the waitress?

CHARLIE: *(Picks up another shot.)* Did I just do a shot? *(Shrugs and drinks it.)*

TOM: Yes.

CHARLIE: Yes what?

TOM: The ultimate goal is to convince a nice woman that you are in love with her for the long haul...Maybe the only way to do that is to actually feel that way about her.

JOHN: Noah's Ark was the first real *Love Boat*. That was the perfect romantic cruise.

CHARLIE: No competition within the species, and if your date caught you staring at a shapely ostrich or something, you could be reasonably secure that she wouldn't turn around and hook up with a hippo or a platypus.

JOHN: I think two is platapussi...

CHARLIE: Octopussy...

JOHN: Pussy Galore.

CHARLIE: Eva Gabor.

TOM: Dinah Shore.

JOHN: Diane Lane.

CHARLIE: Lois Lane.

JOHN: Susan Saint James.

TOM: Susan B. Anthony.

CHARLIE: Betty Page.

TOM: Betty Rubble.

JOHN: Pinky Tuscadaro.

ALL: *Leather* Tuscadaro!

(All in agreement, they toast and drink.)

Scene 6

CAROL's apartment. CAROL, SARA, and WENDY are stoned. CAROL and SARA are laughing uncontrollably at WENDY who's maniacally brushing a single spot on her sweater with a lint brush.

WENDY: What?

(They laugh even harder.)

Scene 7

Oogle's. Even darker. CHARLIE, JOHN, and TOM are drunk. WOMAN ONE enters and walks across the room as the men lift up their shirts and start slapping their stomachs.

Scene 8

CAROL's apartment. WENDY is trying to de-lint CAROL and her hair.

CAROL: Thank you, Wendy…I think I'm good.

WENDY: Your hair is so linty.

SARA: We should wrap her in flypaper.

WENDY: Hey, Carol, too bad you didn't find out if he was really a *big* boyfriend.

SARA: *(Agape.)* Wendy Rachel Chesapeake Fontana III. *(Thoughtlessly flinging a burned match offstage.)*

CAROL: *(Watching TV.)* How can they watch this for so long? It's pile on the guy with the ball. They're nuts…bananas…Nice buns…

(There is a brief pause.)

WENDY: *(Urgently.)* Carol, what do you have to eat?

(CAROL gets up and exits quickly to the kitchen.)

SARA: We need something from the eight major food groups. Dark chocolate. Fudge. Chocolate chip…

WENDY: That was only three groups. That's all you said, right? What are the rest?

SARA: Heavenly Hash, Mucho Mocha, Antonio Banana, Good & Plenty, Diet Seven-Up.

CAROL: *(As she enters with a tray of half-foods.)* All I have are some stale Cheetos, cherry Jell-O powder, sauerkraut, a bottle of water, some sand, and vanilla extract.

(They begin devouring everything on the tray.)

WENDY: We have to get more. Much *much* more.

SARA: Sand?

CAROL: I think it's something Charlie made.

(SARA sees rising smoke from offstage.)

SARA: Hey, look at that.

WENDY: *(Trying to swallow.)* Can you be allergic to water?

CAROL: *(Facing the opposite direction; starts laughing.)* Rachel Chesapeake Fontana…

WENDY: *(Looking at the smoke.)* That's so beautiful. It must be so great to have one.

SARA: I never knew you had a fireplace, Carol.

CAROL: *(Not paying attention.)* Yeah…I don't.

(There is a pause as CAROL turns to join their gaze. They scramble offstage.)

WENDY: *(Offstage.)* Where's the sand?!

Scene 9

Oogle's. It's very dark. CHARLIE, JOHN, and TOM are slumped against the bar. TOM is out cold. CHARLIE can barely keep his head up. Somehow all three are holding shots.

CHARLIE: …But the hardest thing is that I can drink and drink s-o-o-o-o much and never get really drunkard. It's my mentalism.

CHARLIE'S HEAD: Alcohol feels fun, we-e-e-e-e…

JOHN: I'm not the clearest of brains right now, but I'd have to say you are, you know, very blurry.

CHARLIE: Would you say you love every single woman in the universe?

JOHN: Never felt a breast I didn't like. Hell, slap some fishnets and high heels on a refrigerator, and I'm interested.

(CHARLIE'S HEAD mumbles something incoherently.)

CHARLIE: Ssshhhh… *(Looks around confused; refocuses.)* I can wake him up. Watch this. Watch. *(Yells at TOM.)* Marco!

(No response.)

CHARLIE: Marco!

(No response.)

CHARLIE: Marco!

TOM: *(Gets up suddenly.)* Can't believe she broke up with you. *(Passes out again.)*

CHARLIE: *(Suddenly emotional.)* I love you, guys. You guys are my messiahs, man.

JOHN: Huh?

(CHARLIE puts his hand up to say something then promptly passes out. TOM lifts his head.)

TOM: Polo! *(He passes out again.)*

Scene 10

CAROL's apartment. The women survey the damage from the fire. WENDY is picking ashes from the lint brush.

WENDY: I'm so sorry, Carol.

CAROL: Who knew that cherry Jell-O powder was so flammable.

SARA: And sauerkraut is an effective extinguisher. *(Gets up and grabs her stuff.)*

CAROL: Where are you going?

SARA: The firehouse.

CAROL: The fire is out.

SARA: Someone has to tell them about sauerkraut.

(WENDY gets up to join SARA.)

CAROL: Where are you going?

WENDY: Firemen. Sexy.

(WENDY and SARA exit.)

Scene 11

CHARLIE's apartment. Two days later. CHARLIE is holding an ice cube tray on his head. TOM is sprawled out on the floor with his head in a garbage pail.

CHARLIE'S HEAD: If I actually learned from my mistakes, I'd be the smartest person on the planet.

(JOHN enters looking perfectly fine. He is carrying a paper bag.)

CHARLIE: Ssshhh. Don't slam the door so hard.

JOHN: It was open. It's still open.

CHARLIE: Too many words…

JOHN: You've had two days to sleep it off.

CHARLIE: Too painful to sleep.

CHARLIE'S HEAD: Must take more analgesics.

(CHARLIE grabs a bottle and shakes it. It's empty. He tosses it. He lifts up a few more bottles and follows suit.)

JOHN: I slept all day today. Want to know why?

CHARLIE: Too near death to ask why.

JOHN: Because I didn't sleep yesterday. Want to know why?

CHARLIE'S HEAD: Stop with…speaking.

JOHN: I hooked up. With the photo girl. We took more photos.

CHARLIE: I crawled home on my stomach. I think I ate some Tender Vittles.

CHARLIE'S HEAD: Beef and Liver.

JOHN: *(Indicating TOM.)* Is he looking for something?

CHARLIE: He's been like that since yesterday. Not sure how he got here. Not even sure if it's Tom.

(A soft groan emanates from inside the pail.)

CHARLIE: Now, I'm definitely not sure.

JOHN: *(As he takes out two soda cans from the paper bag.)* Her name was Laurie. Probably. This will make you feel better.

(He hands cans to CHARLIE and TOM.)

CHARLIE: No alcohol.

JOHN: Promise.

(TOM and CHARLIE open their cans. TOM brings it to his head in the pail and manages to take a long drink. CHARLIE takes a sip.)

JOHN: Christy!

(CHARLIE does a spit take.)

JOHN: That was her name.

CHARLIE: *(Grimacing.)* What the hell soda is this?!

JOHN: Dr. Paprika. It just came out.

CHARLIE'S HEAD: Awful.

TOM: *(Reaches his hand out.)* Can I have another one?

JOHN: *(To TOM.)* Nice to have you back, pal.

(He takes the can from CHARLIE and hands it to TOM.)

CHARLIE: *(Holding his head.)* I have to decapitate myself.

JOHN: No, no, no, no, no. No. No. Tonight's the night, Chuckie-boy.

CHARLIE: I don't like Ch— *(In too much pain.)* ow.

JOHN: Don't worry, Chow. This will take your mind off food. You're calling Sandybarge.

TOM: That's awesome, Charlie.

CHARLIE: What? You said I have two years' mourning time. *(Planting a pillow on his head.)*

JOHN: I said two days. Let's go.

CHARLIE: *(Lifts pillow.)* I can't call Sandybarge out of the blue. I'm not good on the phone. Believe me.

CHARLIE'S HEAD: Just ask Donna from the *Village Voice*.

JOHN: *(Taking out a piece of paper.)* Oh, what do I have here? A little piece of paper with numbers on it. *(Picks up the phone.)* This comes at the perfect time, because I have a hankering for a little phone dialing. Think I'll dial me up a number or two. *(He presses some buttons.)* Six. Seven. Seven. Two…Seven…Seven… One more to go, Chuck. *(Starts using his Uncle John voice.)* What is that last digit? It looks an awful lot like infinity. Wait a second. If I turn it on its side, it looks just like an eight. A big round, voluptuous eight. Such a sexy number just begging for me to press—

CHARLIE: *(Ballistic, grabbing phone from him.)* Give me that! I'll do it! Just to get you to stop... My God... *(Looking at the paper.)* It couldn't possibly make me feel any worse than I feel right now.

JOHN: That's it. Get psyched. Be bold.

TOM: They can smell fear.

CHARLIE'S HEAD: Well, then I must be making a major stench right now!

JOHN: Be witty. She likes funny guys. Maybe.

CHARLIE'S HEAD: What the hell am I doing? I can't do this.

CHARLIE: *(Dials the number and brings phone to his ear.)* I know how to be funny—Oh, it's ringing so loudly... Another ring... Well, there's no answer—Hello... Is this Sandybarge?

CHARLIE'S HEAD: Oh my God.

CHARLIE: I'm looking to purchase a Broken Scale...

(JOHN drops his head into his hands. TOM groans.)

CHARLIE: Broken Scale... I believe you invented it...

CHARLIE'S HEAD: Oh my God.

CHARLIE: No, this isn't a prank call. I'm a friend of John's... *(To JOHN.)* What's your last name?

JOHN: Elliot.

CHARLIE: *(Into phone.)* Elliot. You did an infomercial together... *(Puts hand over mouthpiece; seething.)* She doesn't know who you are.

(JOHN shrugs.)

CHARLIE: *(Into phone.)* It was earlier this year... Winston products? Right, that's it! *(Quietly to himself.)* Ow... I was there, too... This is... uh, *(Gesturing to JOHN for help.)* uh...

JOHN: Chuck—

CHARLIE: Chuck— er, Charlie. Styptic... Styptic... Styptic... S. T.— Please don't hang up. That's my... The reason I'm calling is...

CHARLIE'S HEAD: *(Panicking.)* What's the reason? What's the reason?!

CHARLIE: I was wondering if you'd— Uh-huh... Uh-huh... Would you be interested in—Uh-huh... Uh-huh... Would there be any chance that we could— Uh-huh... Yes, I guess I *was* hovering... *(Closes his eyes.)* Would you like to go out sometime?... Really?—I mean, I mean great.

CHARLIE'S HEAD: Excellent!

CHARLIE: Very good.

CHARLIE'S HEAD: Awesome!

CHARLIE: After your show? Okay... So I'll see you then. Bye. *(Hangs up elated.)*

JOHN: One Mississippi, Two Mississippi, Three—

CHARLIE: Oh! *(Head hurts.)* Ow. *(Redials.)* Hi, it's me again... Charlie... Styptic... S. T.— Right. Sandybarge—I mean Sandy isn't your real name, is it?... Susan Fantell. See you then, Susan. Bye. *(Hangs up.)*

JOHN: Four Mississippi, Five Mississippi—

CHARLIE: What? Stop doing that.

(The telephone rings.)

CHARLIE: *(Answers.)* Hello... Who's this?... *(Realizing.)* Sorry! *(Frantically scrambling for a pen.)* Of course I want to know where your show is...

Scene 12

SUSAN's dressing room. Thirty minutes after her show. SUSAN is sitting at a vanity, putting the final touches on her post-performance appearance. CHARLIE knocks on the door.

SUSAN: I'm not taking visitors yet.

CHARLIE'S HEAD: *(Nervously.)* It's Charlie…

(No response.)

CHARLIE'S HEAD: I don't think that was out loud.

CHARLIE: It's Charlie.

SUSAN: You can come in, Charles.

(CHARLIE enters.)

CHARLIE: Hi. I'm from the other side of the door.

SUSAN: Hello.

CHARLIE: You were great.

CHARLIE'S HEAD: *(Infatuated.)* Wow…

SUSAN: Thank you. I never get tired of hearing that. Can I have my brush, please?

(CHARLIE hands her her brush.)

CHARLIE: Are you sure you don't want me to wait outside?

SUSAN: So you thought I was good?

CHARLIE'S HEAD: Tell her she was good, stupid.

CHARLIE: You were very good, stupid—I mean you were great. You have a beautiful singing voice. I really believed that you were on death row.

SUSAN: So you were there for that audition for the scale info-whatchamathinger?

CHARLIE: I was with my friend Tom. He played Fat Disgusting Slob Number Two in the infomercial. Actually, I used to go out with Fat Disgusting Slob Number One.

SUSAN: I don't think I remember them. When I'm acting, I have to be in my own existence. I have to block out all distractions.

CHARLIE: Makes sense.

CHARLIE'S HEAD: It does?

SUSAN: They also told me not to take my eyes off the cue cards. So do you work out, Charles?

CHARLIE'S HEAD: Bulk up! Bulk up!—

SUSAN: So you can relate to this. The other day I'm in my Hip-Hop Tai Chi class—do you know they wanted me to be an instructor, but I'm sorry, I need some time for myself…

CHARLIE: *(Nodding.)* You teach a lot of classes?

SUSAN: No. So I'm doing my plie-lunges, and there's this obese slobbering man staring at me. He was just glaring at my body and drooling. He was practically on top of me.

CHARLIE'S HEAD: Lucky guy.

CHARLIE: *(Transfixed.)* You were working out and someone was staring—uh, was he ogling…

SUSAN: I finally had to turn around and tell him to leave me alone. He just stood there with his mouth open with this pathetic attempt to look innocent…I just had to get out of there.

CHARLIE: Wow. I'm so sorry that happened to you.

SUSAN: You're sweet. I bounce back pretty quickly though. You know, now that I think about it, I might have met your old girlfriend in a show—what's her name?

CHARLIE'S HEAD: Bitch.

CHARLIE: Carol.

SUSAN: I can't imagine you guys together. She was a little too good at playing that slob part if you ask me.

CHARLIE: Yeah, well, I'm not really into acting so much right now. I'm writing a screenplay—

SUSAN: That's so great. I'm going to be starring in my own musical revue. I think I'm going to film it or make it into a TV show. It's about all the difficult things that have happened in my life…

CHARLIE: Uh-huh…Uh-huh…

SUSAN: Being pursued by men and people, dealing with my whole family…And how I overcame everything to be who I am today…

CHARLIE'S HEAD: Uh-huh…Uh-huh…

SUSAN: It's dedicated to all my fans and family.

(She gives him a promotional postcard.)

SUSAN: It's called "Love, Me."

CHARLIE: Did you come from a broken home?

SUSAN: I wish. That would be such a great subject for a song.

CHARLIE: I'd love to see it.

SUSAN: Want to buy my cassette tape? Only twelve dollars.

CHARLIE: Sure.

(She holds out her hand, taking CHARLIE off guard. He scrambles to give her money.)

CHARLIE'S HEAD: Get the cash! Get the cash!

SUSAN: *(Sounding like a southern belle.)* And as a reward, you can take me to a fancy dinner. And maybe a boat ride.

CHARLIE: Sure. I just might have to hock my friend Tom.

SUSAN: *(Beams.)* You're cute.

CHARLIE'S HEAD: I think I'm in love.

Scene 13

CHARLIE's apartment. Two weeks later. TOM, JOHN, and CHARLIE are passing around a basketball.

JOHN: You think you're in what? You were just supposed to have sex with her.

CHARLIE: We'll have sex…eventually.

JOHN: You haven't had sex?! You've got the process all wrong. You feed the horse, you mount the horse, you dismount the horse, you go right back to the singles stable.

CHARLIE: I'm from Queens. I know absolutely nothing about horses.

TOM and CHARLIE'S HEAD: Or women.

CHARLIE: Look, I'm just looking to find someone.

TOM: Maybe that won't happen until you stop looking.

CHARLIE: Then I'm not looking. Or I'm doing whatever it takes to effectively find someone by accident. Is it at all possible for us to talk about someone else's sex life for a change?

TOM: I'm not sure I'd call it a *sex* life.

JOHN: Alright look...I ask out a lot of women every week. Believe it or not, some turn me down. But my weekends are packed.

TOM: With the women you really want to be with?

JOHN: *(Pause.)* My weekends are packed.

TOM: Don't you ever worry about catching something?

JOHN: I always wear a condom.

CHARLIE: So do I.

JOHN: No, I mean always. You never know.

CHARLIE'S HEAD: *(Pause.)* Aw-kward.

CHARLIE: I just couldn't deal with all those women saying no to me.

JOHN: No is just their first response.

CHARLIE: First response?

JOHN: After a female cat initially rejects the advances from a male cat, he comes right back. Then over a three-hour period, they'll have sex up to sixteen times. Sixteen times! It pays to be persistent. Unless you're at the office. There the law permits you one attempt to ask out the sexy mailroom clerk with hypnotic blue-gray eyes before it's considered sexual harassment. So you have to make that first time count.

TOM: You sure have done a lot of research. Sounds like he knows what he's talking about.

CHARLIE: What if Susan's, you know, the one?

JOHN: Yeah? And what if she makes you tomato sauce?

CHARLIE: I'm sorry, I misplaced my misogynist-to-English dictionary.

JOHN: That's how they always get you. Everything will seem fine and then one day, they'll casually say they want to cook you a "special" dinner. Your last supper. And they make you tomato sauce. With real tomatoes.

CHARLIE'S HEAD: I didn't even know that could be done.

CHARLIE: I don't think Susan would ever...what the hell's wrong with that?!

JOHN: What's wrong?! That's what Del Monte and Progresso are for. She'll be doing it for one reason and one reason only and that's to transform you into a docile, obedient dog. Just a dog. *Woman's* best friend. It's tomato sauce today and a water dish tomorrow. Let me have all your possessions, Chuck, 'cause where you're going all you'll need is a leash.

TOM: *(Looking around the apartment.)* Maybe you won't know the difference, Charlie.

JOHN: You know what your problem is, Chuck?

TOM: He eats too much spaghetti?

JOHN: You are obsessed with physical appearance.

CHARLIE: I'm obsessed? You told me you once proposed to a woman after seeing her ass?

JOHN: So?

CHARLIE: Just her ass.

JOHN: She happened to have a really, really great ass.

TOM: Do you have any photos?

JOHN: Don't be an idiot...Not on me...

CHARLIE'S HEAD: That I would see.

JOHN: Still can't believe she turned me down...

CHARLIE: She apparently had really, really great taste, too.

JOHN: We could've been married, had kids...

TOM: With really great asses.

JOHN: I happen to be wonderful with kids. I've entertained kids at parties.

CHARLIE: What do you do, make balloon animals? *(Demonstrating.)* Hello, little girl, here's a nice red erect penis. Yes it's very long. Make sure you keep it blown up. Oh, and here's a big shiny vagina for you, Billy!

JOHN: *(Pause; then like Uncle John.)* Want to toss the ball around, Chuck?

TOM: That sounds like fun. Let's go.

JOHN: It's good therapy. Chuck needs to relax.

CHARLIE: I do not need therapy. You're the one that needs therapy.

JOHN: I don't need therapy. Tom needs therapy.

TOM: I need therapy?

CHARLIE: I don't know, Tom. Sounds like he knows what he's talking about...

(They exit.)

Scene 14

Cruise ship dance hall. Two months later. CHARLIE and SUSAN are slow dancing to "More Than Words." SUSAN is wearing an elegant gown. CHARLIE is wearing his suit.

SUSAN: You're not such a bad dancer.

CHARLIE: You're so beautiful...

CHARLIE'S HEAD: *(Smitten.)* Yeah.

CHARLIE: I'm just so worn out from all my past relationships.

SUSAN: Me, too.

CHARLIE'S HEAD: Yeah.

CHARLIE: I couldn't help but feel self-conscious around my ex. Can you believe she said that I spoke without thinking sometimes?

SUSAN: I totally know what you mean. I told my Antoine the same thing.

(They stop dancing and gaze into each other's eyes.)

CHARLIE: So you want to move in together?

SUSAN: Okay.

CHARLIE'S HEAD: Yeah!

(They resume dancing.)

ACT III
Scene 1

CHARLIE's apartment. Two weeks later. Two environments are struggling to occupy the same space. SUSAN's possessions are strewn about the apartment. There are decorative cloths and flowers on the table and a quilt that covers the bookcase. The Walt Frazier poster is mostly covered by an impressionist art poster of ballerinas. CHARLIE and SUSAN are in a passionate embrace, practically lip locked.

CHARLIE'S HEAD: When I turned twelve, I thought I was all grown-up. Every drug dosage label I read contained the instructions "For children under twelve, one tablet. For children twelve and over and adults, two tablets." I was finally in the Adult category.

CHARLIE: This is going to be great.

SUSAN: Yeah.

CHARLIE'S HEAD: Tell her.

CHARLIE: I so totally love you.

SUSAN: Me, too...Thanks again for helping me move everything.

CHARLIE: Sorry again about your little box.

SUSAN: It was just some stuff. I still have the memories.

CHARLIE: I can't believe you actually have your skate key.

SUSAN: Well, *had.*

CHARLIE: I just hate myself for doing that.

SUSAN: I'm sure everyone burns something when they're moving.

CHARLIE'S HEAD: Idiot!

SUSAN: You didn't have to throw out your baseball cards to make room for me.

CHARLIE: Who even remembers Mickey Mantle anyway?

SUSAN: I made you special coffee.

(*Still locked in an embrace, they shuffle over to the coffee table, crouch down, and CHARLIE lifts his mug. He brings it up to his face and tilts it when SUSAN sneezes, violently knocking the cup over. The coffee spills all over him.*)

SUSAN: (*In baby talk.*) Did my squeezebox spill his coffee?

CHARLIE: I'm okay.

CHARLIE'S HEAD: (*In pain.*) AH!!

SUSAN: I have to practice my recorder.

CHARLIE'S HEAD: Oh, no.

(*Once again, they bend down together to the coffee table. SUSAN picks up her recorder and brings it up in between them. She brings it to her mouth, spearing him in the face with the other end. She plays some awful noises. The telephone rings.*)

CHARLIE: (*Gratefully.*) Telephone!

(*They waddle over to the phone. CHARLIE grabs the receiver and lifts it over them and dangles it so he can listen, and she can speak into the mouthpiece.*)

SUSAN: Hello? Hello?

CHARLIE: (*Craning his neck to listen to the earpiece.*) ...She says hello.

SUSAN: (*Into mouthpiece.*) How are you?

CHARLIE: (*Listening.*) She says fine...She wants to know how it's going with Charlie—uh, me, how it's going with me.

SUSAN: (*Into mouthpiece.*) Fantastic. He's my little lovable puppy.

CHARLIE'S HEAD: Puppy? Don't puppies grow up to be dogs?

CHARLIE: (*Listening.*) She wants to know how the sex is.

SUSAN: (*Into mouthpiece.*) Like a cross between being with Antoine and Derrick.

CHARLIE: What? Who? (*Listening again.*) ...She wants to know whether or not I...Why don't you take this one by yourself, honey?

(*Hands her the phone, untangles himself, and quietly walks away.*)

SUSAN: (*As CHARLIE exits.*) Hello? Oh, it's you, Maryanne... Yes, it's wonderful...He's so clumsy. He just spilled coffee all over me...

Scene 2

Oogle's. CHARLIE has a towel around his neck. He and JOHN are blindfolded and quibbling.

JOHN: Would you hold still?

CHARLIE: *(Nervously.)* I don't like this, John. What if someone sees us?

JOHN: It'd go a lot easier if you didn't squirm.

CHARLIE: How did I ever let you talk me into this?

JOHN: It will teach you to relax.

(JOHN brings a large knife to CHARLIE's face.)

CHARLIE: Ow! That's it.

(They both take off their blindfolds.)

CHARLIE: You're using a kitchen knife? A serrated kitchen knife?!

JOHN: I could have sworn I was holding a barber's razor.

CHARLIE'S HEAD: Who's the real schmuck here?

(A downtrodden TOM enters. He is wearing a ski mask and a shiny sauna workout suit.)

CHARLIE: Hey, Tom.

JOHN: Someone downpour on your parade, Tommy? Man, you are drenched.

TOM: I went to a class at the gym.

JOHN: What's with the mask?

CHARLIE'S HEAD: I will never get used to that look.

CHARLIE: It helps him sweat.

TOM: *(Pulls off the ski mask.)* I was in an aerobic dance class. My therapist said it was good to change things up... Had no idea it would be so hard...

CHARLIE'S HEAD and JOHN: *(Musing.)* Aerobic dance class.

(TOM speaks as JOHN shaves CHARLIE.)

TOM: So I'm trying to do some lunges and all of a sudden this woman in front of me turns around and starts yelling at me for drooling over her.

JOHN: Did she really?

TOM: *(Nods.)* She was fuming.

JOHN: No, have a body to drool over?

TOM: *(Exhausted.)* I don't know, I was face down trying to breathe.

CHARLIE: His eyes sweat when he works out. He can't see. I have to lead him around.

CHARLIE'S HEAD: The world must look so uncomplicated through blind, sweaty eyes.

TOM: I'm so glad I won't have to deal with her again.

(JOHN hands some pills to CHARLIE and TOM.)

JOHN: You have to go back. You softened her up.

TOM: She's the one not coming back. Yuri the manager asked her to leave. She was screaming, calling everyone losers and yelling, "You don't know what it's like to be me!" Yuri said it wasn't the first time she flipped out on someone.

CHARLIE'S HEAD: Apparently there are lots of people at Crunch Fitness doing hatha yoga in a ski mask.

TOM: Hey, Charlie, how did you convince Susan to move into your place?

(CHARLIE and TOM swallow the pills without thinking.)

JOHN: He probably couldn't convince her to move into her place.

CHARLIE: So she's keeping her old apartment. Big deal. A lot of people keep more than one residence. Nearby. What vitamin did I just swallow?

JOHN: Not vitamins. Cigsules. Went down pretty easy, huh?

TOM: Real easy.

CHARLIE: Cigsules?

JOHN: They're for people who don't like to smoke.

TOM: *(Enthused.)* I hate smoking!

JOHN: You just got all the benefits of a nasty expensive cigar in a cheap, tasteless pill.

TOM: Cigars are very trendy.

JOHN: Next time someone offers you one, you can say, no thanks just had one. Want another?

(TOM takes another from JOHN. CHARLIE slaps it out of TOM's hands.)

CHARLIE: No! There *are* no benefits! *(Coughing it back up.)* Come on. *(Wipes his face.)* I think I need an ashtray pill…

CHARLIE'S HEAD: I am definitely the real schmuck here.

SCENE 3

WENDY is crying. Again. SARA enters. She sees WENDY, looks around, and quietly tries to exit, but—

WENDY: Hi, Sara.

SARA: Oh, hey… Wendy. Where's Carol?

WENDY: Not here yet. *(She cries.)*

SARA: That's too bad.

(WENDY whimpers.)

SARA: Is something wrong?

(WENDY cries louder.)

SARA: That's too bad.

(WENDY bawls.)

SARA: *(Panicked, to nowhere in particular.)* CAROL!

(CAROL enters synchronously.)

SARA: It's about time.

CAROL: Sorry I'm late. Just had the worst date of my life.

SARA: I think I rented this movie already.

WENDY: The saxophone player?

CAROL: He kept apologizing for everything.

SARA: Sounds like he was playing your song.

(WENDY starts crying again.)

CAROL: I'm so sorry, Wendy. What happened?

WENDY: Burt and I are breaking up.

SARA: I definitely rented this movie already. Just keep missing the prequel.

CAROL: *(To SARA, while comforting WENDY.)* Shocking you aren't up to speed.

SARA: Maybe I'm a little tired of hearing the same old lament.

CAROL: Too bad you can't bill for the time you spend immersed in your friends' problems.

SARA: *(Eyeing CAROL.)* How did it happen, Wendy? Did you get him a Big Boyfriend?

CAROL: Is that really necessary?

SARA: I think we struck a nerve.

CAROL: I don't think I need a reminder every time we're together.

SARA: Hey, don't shit on the messenger. It's always the same old refrain. Just his name changes. *(To WENDY).* For some of us. *(To CAROL.)* If you need to make some kind of peace, then do it already. Or don't do it. Just don't do it and whine about not doing it—Oh, what's the point? Nobody ever listens to what anyone tells them to do anyway, even if it's the right thing.

CAROL: That *nobody* being me.

WENDY: Sometimes it's good to vent things out.

SARA: Why don't you stick your head back in the sand? The adults are talking.

CAROL: Always fun shooting down the easy targets, right?

SARA: Just calling them as they are.

WENDY: I'm not an easy target.

CAROL: Is it possible that with all the advances in modern psychiatry two sessions a week aren't quite enough?

SARA: It's enough to realize I don't have to be in a relationship to validate my existence.

CAROL: At least I give people a chance.

WENDY: I am not an easy target.

SARA: Yeah, I'd be much better off going out on pity dates with every Charlie in town.

CAROL: When's the last time you felt anything about anyone?

SARA: *(Furious.)* I'm feeling something right now!

WENDY: I broke up with Burt!

CAROL: Get over it—No one even knew you were back together.

SARA: *(Stunned.)* Carol Bettington Williamsburg IV.

CAROL: You're the easiest target, Wendy—You could probably deal with everything better if you would just face it.

WENDY: Maybe I'm a little more in touch with myself. I don't keep things bottled up and let people take advantage of me.

SARA: She speaks.

WENDY: *(To SARA.)* And I'm not some jaded bitch.

(All quiet on the Oogle's front.)

SARA: ...I have to go.

(They watch SARA exit.)

CAROL: I have to go, too.

WENDY: Already?

CAROL: I have a pity date. *(Exits.)*

Scene 4

CHARLIE's apartment. Two months later. CHARLIE is standing; SUSAN seated.

CHARLIE'S HEAD: After mating, the female black widow spider will normally eat the male, but if the female is well fed, the male can escape so that he may mate and be devoured another day.

SUSAN: Come on, Charles, do it.

CHARLIE: I can't believe you want me to do it again.

SUSAN: *(Clapping her hands.)* Yes. I love it. Oh, please, oh, please, oh, please…

CHARLIE: You're not sick of it? It was just a little throwaway thing I did.

SUSAN: But it's my little throwaway thing. If you love me, you'll do it.

CHARLIE'S HEAD: I finally do something somebody likes, and I'm a prisoner for it.

CHARLIE: Are all the blinds closed? *(Sighs, then poses as a lounge singer. He sings in an affected crooner style.)* You're…the…e-pi-cen-ter of my love-e-e-e-e. I know you-u-u-u are the eye of my storm-m-m. E-pi-cen-ter of my love-e-e-e. Only you put the sigh in cy-clone. E-pi-cen-ter of my love-e-e-e. That's right you, you came without warn.

SUSAN: *(Claps happily.)* Now, do the extended version.

CHARLIE'S HEAD: I have to get out of here.

CHARLIE: I have to meet John. He's going to help me with Supercomic's big battle scene with his archenemy, The Heckler.

SUSAN: Sometimes I think you care more about Supercomic than you do me.

CHARLIE: I sang it at least twenty times today.

(SUSAN gives him a hard look. CHARLIE reluctantly picks up the telephone and dials.)

CHARLIE: …Hey, it's Charlie. Going to be a little late… Have to do something… Yes, *Epicenter*… John?… John?! … John—would you… Those aren't even the words! *(Hangs up the phone and prepares to sing.)*

Scene 5

Oogle's. The next day. The men are seated at their usual table. CHARLIE and JOHN have takeout food. TOM and JOHN are singing to CHARLIE in full mock 'n' roll mode.

JOHN and TOM: *(Singing.)* E-pi-cen-ter of my love-e-e-e-e…

CHARLIE: Okay.

JOHN and TOM: *(Singing.)* I know you-u-u-u are the pie of the storm-m-m…

CHARLIE: Alright!

JOHN and TOM: *(Singing.)* E-pi-cen-ter of my love-e-e-e-e—

CHARLIE: Waitress is coming!

TOM: *(Looking around.)* Where?

CHARLIE: And it's *eye* of the storm. *Pie* of the storm makes no sense.

CHARLIE'S HEAD: What makes no sense is I spent the whole night doing that.

JOHN: What makes no sense is you spent the whole night doing that.

TOM: What makes no sense is that I didn't bring any food here. Where's the waitress?

CHARLIE: I have no idea, Tom!

JOHN: Why so tense?

CHARLIE: I have to go.

JOHN: You just got here.

TOM: Why don't all of us hang out?

CHARLIE'S HEAD: Susan prefers to socialize with couples.

CHARLIE: I have to go to…

CHARLIE'S HEAD: Please don't tell them.

CHARLIE: *(Mumbles.)* Susan's friend's turtle's communion.

TOM: What was that?

CHARLIE: Susan's friend's turtle's first holy communion.

JOHN: You are aware that we're required *by law* to mock you every day for the next two thousand years, right?

(As CHARLIE exits.)

TOM, JOHN, and CHARLIE'S HEAD: *(Singing.)* E-pi-cen-ter of my love-e-e-e…

SCENE 6

CHARLIE's apartment. Minutes later. SUSAN is playing a video game. CHARLIE enters.

SUSAN: I didn't know you were going to be gone so long.

CHARLIE: Just being serenaded by the guys.

SUSAN: You sure spend a lot of time with them.

CHARLIE'S HEAD: Don't touch that.

CHARLIE: *(Looking at his watch.)* So are we leaving in like twenty minutes?

SUSAN: Are you kidding? I need at least an hour and a half.

CHARLIE'S HEAD: Don't touch that either.

SUSAN: You have to talk to me while I make myself beautiful.

CHARLIE: You don't need me for that. You're already beautiful.

CHARLIE'S HEAD: Nicely done.

CHARLIE: *(Sees something on couch.)* What's this?

SUSAN: I got you a nice rope.

CHARLIE: What for?

SUSAN: Whatever you want. Maybe you can use it to walk the cat. Or maybe she can just be an outside kitty.

CHARLIE: We live on the Lower East Side.

SUSAN: It'll build character… So, Charles…please don't flirt with Jenna tonight, okay?

CHARLIE: Where did that come from?

SUSAN: Just don't flirt with her.

CHARLIE: I don't flirt with Jenna. Do I?

CHARLIE'S HEAD: No, I don't.

SUSAN: She flirts with you.

CHARLIE: But if I don't know she's flirting, isn't it meaningless?

SUSAN: That's what she'd like you to think. And you do. You're a man.

CHARLIE and CHARLIE'S HEAD: What?

SUSAN: She flirts with you subconsciously. And then bit by bit, you're slowly smitten with her. Trust me. Women know.

CHARLIE'S HEAD: All women?

CHARLIE: But how can I prevent that? I mean, do we only go out with couples when you're absolutely sure the woman isn't the slightest bit attracted to me? That's—

SUSAN: Yes.

CHARLIE: Yes, what?

SUSAN: Yes, we only go out with couples when the woman isn't interested in you.

CHARLIE: ...Really.

SUSAN: Uh-huh.

CHARLIE'S HEAD: How should I proceed?

CHARLIE: *(Putting away the video game controls.)* Is that healthy?

SUSAN: Is what? *(Turning to him.)* What are you trying to say?

CHARLIE'S HEAD: Danger, Will Robinson!

SUSAN: Charles...

(CHARLIE is silent.)

SUSAN: Are you trying to say I'm crazy?

CHARLIE: No. Not at all. Here, come here. *(Goes to a corner of the room.)* Look. Let's meet over at the Solution Corner. Come on.

SUSAN: Just get dressed, Charles. *(Exits.)*

SCENE 7

Oogle's. A week later. Once again, CHARLIE and JOHN have brought food. TOM is pining for some service.

CHARLIE: I just can't say no to her. She wins every time. Sometimes, when we disagree about something, and I'm finally making, you know, a point, she turns into Hal from 2001. *(Imitates her.)* Is there something wrong, Charles? Why are you so angry?

TOM: I love *2001* when they shut down Hal. *(Sings.)* Charlie, Charlie, give me your answer—

CHARLIE: What do you think it means when two different girlfriends criticize you for the same thing?

JOHN: Time to get a third girlfriend. *(He takes out a small spray can and starts spraying his food.)* You know what your problem is, Chuck?...

CHARLIE'S HEAD: Besides hanging out with you guys?

JOHN: You don't know how to argue. Relationships equal arguments. You have to hit 'em hard. You have to hit 'em early. When she hurls a high hard one at you, you have to shoot back without thinking.

TOM: Without thinking. That makes sense.

CHARLIE: What is that? Salad dressing?

JOHN: It's Beeferall.

CHARLIE: Beeferall?

TOM: The spray-on additive that makes everything taste like beef.

(JOHN keeps spraying.)

CHARLIE: Do you really hate salad that much?

JOHN: No, I just really like Beeferall.

CHARLIE: ...I guess I'm always too concerned to get outwardly angry at Susan.

TOM and CHARLIE'S HEAD: Or Carol. Or Annie, or Brenda...

JOHN: Let me tell you something: One night when I was a little kid watching TV, I saw Hank Aaron hit his 715th home run to break Babe Ruth's all-time record...

TOM: I am so hungry.

CHARLIE: It's a classic.

TOM: Does anyone work here?

JOHN: As Hank Aaron was rounding the bases these two guys came out of nowhere and ran onto the field. They ran right up to him, patted old Hank on the back, and joined him in his victory lap around the bases. Those guys were brilliant. They knew they were taking part in the single most celebrated moment in Major League history and that the film of that event would be forever replayed on the TV sets and in the minds of every sports fan in America…

TOM: So famished…

JOHN: So they were arrested, big deal. They paid a fine, who cares. It must have been the greatest thrill. And now they're part of history. Too *concerned?* If you're angry at someone, let them know. What the hell are you waiting for?

TOM: *(Fuming.)* Can we get some service here or what?!

CHARLIE'S HEAD: I don't get the connection.

JOHN: By the time I'm done with you, you'll be able to argue with your vacuum cleaner.

CHARLIE: What the hell did my vacuum cleaner do?

JOHN: A crappy job.

TOM: Your apartment is filthy.

CHARLIE: Because I haven't taken it out of the closet in weeks.

JOHN: Sitting on its fat ass while the rest of us are working. Good-for-nothing contraption.

TOM: There are no free rides, mister.

CHARLIE: But it's a vacuum cleaner.

JOHN: Not your problem.

TOM: Lazy no-good bottom feeder.

CHARLIE'S HEAD: You're not actually considering—

CHARLIE: Let's do it.

Scene 8

TOM's apartment. Later that night. JOHN and CHARLIE are seated around CHARLIE's answering machine. TOM is gorging himself, surrounded by food takeout cartons.

CHARLIE'S HEAD: Judge not.

CHARLIE: This is hard, John.

JOHN: Be firm. But don't lose your cool.

CHARLIE: I'd rather you shave me blindfolded.

CHARLIE'S HEAD: Keep focused.

(JOHN presses the answering machine save button.)

ANSWERING MACHINE AUTOMATED VOICE: I will save messages.

CHARLIE: Oh, yeah?

JOHN: Again. *(Presses the answering machine save button.)*

ANSWERING MACHINE AUTOMATED VOICE: I will save messages.

CHARLIE: N—no…you won't.

(JOHN presses the answering machine save button.)

ANSWERING MACHINE AUTOMATED VOICE: I will save messages.

CHARLIE: I know you are, but what am I?

JOHN: Let's go back to the blender. Come on, give me five sets of ten. *(He presses blend.)*

CHARLIE: This is so stupid.

JOHN: Stupid, huh? If you can't talk back to a machine, then how the hell are you supposed to talk back to a woman?

TOM: *(Sits next to CHARLIE.)* You can do this, Charlie. Remember what you always tell me about getting motivated.

CHARLIE: What do I say?

TOM: I don't know. Something like, *Go* or *Do*.

CHARLIE'S HEAD: I'd have to be a complete idiot to take advice from me.

CHARLIE: *(Frustrated.)* I can't concentrate. *(Turns back to the answering machine and presses the save button.)*

ANSWERING MACHINE AUTOMATED VOICE: I will save messages.

CHARLIE: Maybe I don't want to hear the messages again. What about that?

JOHN: Not bad.

(CHARLIE presses the answering machine save button.)

ANSWERING MACHINE AUTOMATED VOICE: I will save messages.

CHARLIE: Then the messages will just accumulate and we'll run out of space on the tape.

JOHN: Keep it up.

(CHARLIE presses the answering machine save button.)

ANSWERING MACHINE AUTOMATED VOICE: I will save messages.

CHARLIE: *(Confidently.)* It'll be the first savings you've ever made in your life!

JOHN: By Chaz, got it!

TOM: He's really got it! *(Steps in and presses the erase button.)*

ANSWERING MACHINE AUTOMATED VOICE: I will erase messages.

CHARLIE: *(Suddenly stumped.)* …Can we go back to the blender?

CHARLIE'S HEAD: Good grief!

JOHN: Save yourself some time and just agree with everything she says. I have to get ready. I have to go to some friend's/person's/cousin's wedding…I hate weddings. Man was not meant to be with just one woman his whole life.

TOM: Never know who you might meet…I'd like to get married one day.

JOHN: Just so you can get divorced, Tommy? So all your friends can say, "I can't believe they're not together anymore. They always looked so happy in their photographs." You know why? You know why couples always look happy in their photographs? Because you don't stop and pose for photos when you're in the middle of a fucking argument, that's why!

CHARLIE: I pray you're not making the toast.

JOHN: Practice with the vacuum cleaner. At least you'll get some cleaning done. *(Exits.)*

TOM: Hey, let's work on your script. It's been a long time.

CHARLIE: I'm going to talk to the can opener. *(Exits.)*

Scene 9

Oogle's. WENDY is seated at the bar. CAROL enters.

CAROL: Hi, Wendy.

(She doesn't turn around.)

CAROL: Wendy?

(Nothing.)

CAROL: You can use my lint brush.

(Zilch.)

CAROL: Come on, Wendy, we just spoke on the phone a few minutes ago.

(SARA enters, stops in her tracks.)

SARA: …I needed to get my roadkill fix. This was the first place I thought of.

CAROL: *(To SARA.)* Guess she called you, too.

WENDY: Maybe.

CAROL: Wendy's still pissed.

WENDY: Y'up.

SARA: You, too?

CAROL: Y'up.

SARA: What about me?

CAROL: *(Looking around.)* Is there even a bartender on this shift?

SARA: You have to talk to me…I have this thing.

CAROL: What kind of thing?

WENDY: *(Turning around.)* A growth?

SARA: No. A thing. With people.

CAROL: You have a social engagement?

WENDY: That's what you're worried about?

SARA: See? I can worry about people.

CAROL: *(Bluntly.)* You'll survive.

(Pause.)

SARA: You know I'm a dick. There are lots of us around. Then there are others who have to be held to a higher standard of care. Because they're better people. We require more from them.

CAROL: What?

SARA: You see someone on the street you haven't seen in a long time, an old work acquaintance or friend, and you know that if you stop to say hello it's going to take about an hour to catch up with them, so you pretend you don't see them and hope that they don't see you, and you try not to feel bad about it by telling yourself that you'll stop to talk to them the next time you run into them, even though you know that you probably won't run into them again, or if you do, you'll do exactly the same thing you did this time. Have you ever done that?

CAROL: I don't think so.

SARA: See? Higher standard of care. *(Exits.)*

CAROL: Was that an apology?

WENDY: You don't have to beat yourself up, you know.

CAROL: For saying you should get over your breakup?

WENDY: No.

CAROL: For saying you're an easy target?

WENDY: No.

CAROL: Can you help me out here, Wendy?

WENDY: For breaking up with Charlie.

CAROL: Can *you* let me off the hook?

WENDY: *(Turns to her.)* Only if you do Fat Disgusting Slob.

CAROL: I'm really sorry, Wendy.

(Hug time.)

CAROL: You're not an easy target.

WENDY: Yes, I am.

Scene 10

CHARLIE's apartment. Later that night. CHARLIE is restlessly waiting for SUSAN.

CHARLIE'S HEAD: The dead male praying mantis serves as a source of protein for the female and her young.

(SUSAN enters.)

SUSAN: Hi.

CHARLIE: *(Looking for his opening.)* Hi.

SUSAN: I'm so hungry. How's your little script coming?

CHARLIE'S HEAD: Show no weakness.

CHARLIE: It's getting a little bigger. Where were you?

SUSAN: I was trying to find out what my agent was saying about me in a meeting with this casting director.

CHARLIE: How do you know they were talking about you?

SUSAN: What do you mean? *(Looking at takeout menus.)* What would you like to order for dinner?

CHARLIE: What do you mean what would I like to order?

CHARLIE'S HEAD: That's it. Turn the tables.

SUSAN: *(Flipping through menus.)* Think I want sushi.

CHARLIE: Why do we even have to eat dinner?...Is there a law we always have to eat dinner?

SUSAN: *(Not paying attention.)* Ooh, Mexican sounds good.

CHARLIE: Maybe dinner is just some commercial convention perpetuated by the food lobbyists looking to pillage all the struggling artists who'd do just as well, if not better, by not eating a full meal in the evening.

SUSAN: *(Like Hal from 2001.)* Is there something wrong, Charles? Why are you so angry?

(CHARLIE is stymied. His eyes shift back and forth as he thinks of a retort.)

CHARLIE'S HEAD: You have to shoot back without thinking!

CHARLIE: I will save messages.

CHARLIE'S HEAD and SUSAN: What was that?

CHARLIE: I will save messages.

SUSAN: I'll listen to them later.

CHARLIE: I will erase messages.

SUSAN: *(As she exits.)* I'm getting something to eat.

CHARLIE: I think I won that one.

CHARLIE'S HEAD: You suck.

Scene 11

Some friend's/person's/cousin's wedding reception. That same night. Champagne glasses and flower centerpieces sit on round tables; jackets and handbags are draped over empty chairs. We can hear the sounds of people partying while the song "Celebration" plays. JOHN and SARA, bored and silent, sit alone at the center table.

Scene 12

CHARLIE's apartment. TOM is once again portraying Supercomic. CHARLIE is The Heckler.

TOM: *(As Supercomic.)* ...And why are telephone bills so complicated to figure out? Ha-ha! And who is actually getting the free mega-sized soda refills at movie theatres? Ha-ha-ha!

CHARLIE: *(As a drunken heckler.)* You suck, Supercomic! Get out of here!

TOM: And would someone please explain what you do when you receive a letter opener in the mail? *Ha!*

CHARLIE: You're nothing without a microphone and a two-drink minimum, Supercomic. You're just a hack, because you're too afraid to expose yourself.

TOM: Oh, yeah? How many psycho-therapists does it take to— *(Breaks character.)* Really, Charlie, another light bulb joke?

CHARLIE: It's just a holding place.

TOM: Charlie, this is the third scene in a row where Supercomic has to escape. Is he alright?

CHARLIE'S HEAD: There's a lot of kryptonite in the world, Tommy.

TOM: Maybe he needs to battle and destroy something. You know, blow it up.

Scene 13

Same wedding reception. Thirty minutes later. "Sunrise Sunset" is playing. JOHN and SARA are still seated, appearing irritated and fidgety.

Scene 14

CHARLIE is sitting on the couch as SUSAN drifts into the room and crosses to drop off menus. CHARLIE tries to say something to her, but nothing comes out as she passes and exits.

Scene 15

The wedding reception. An hour later. JOHN and SARA are seated as before. The song "Endless Love" plays. More silence, then finally:

JOHN: So are you friends with the groom?

(No response.)

JOHN: Bride?

(No response.)

JOHN: Caterer?

SARA: *(To herself.)* Perfunctory questions.

JOHN: Traffic sucked. I hate rubber-neckers.

SARA: Inane comments.

JOHN: Want to take a walk?

SARA: *(Turns to him.)* Things you'd say to get laid.

JOHN: I'm sure it's fine; you're obviously alone.

SARA: Things a floundering jerk would say?

JOHN: *(Pointedly.)* The password is *obnoxious*.

SARA: I'll take *Creeps* for a dollar, Alex.

JOHN: Pat, are there any F's or U's?

SARA: He'd like to buy a *clue*, please.

JOHN: I'd rather take whatever's behind curtain number one, two, *or* three.

SARA: Would the real man please stand up?

JOHN: I can name that cold fish in one note!

SARA: Circle gets *this* square!

JOHN: Survey said, *Ding! Loser!*

SARA: Joker! Joker! Joker!

JOHN: Psycho bitch, come on down!

SARA: Hmmm, where's his beef?!

JOHN: He-e-e-e-e-e-e-ere's skanky!

(They pause, look into each other's eyes, and kiss passionately.)

SCENE 16

CHARLIE's apartment. CHARLIE is shifting the ballerina poster so that more of his Walt Frazier poster is exposed. He pauses to look at it. SUSAN enters. She is carrying a book.

CHARLIE'S HEAD: You have to talk to her.

SUSAN: *(Excited.)* I just finished this great book called *The Zen of Self*. In the back there's this Essence Exam on whether you've found your soul mate. Let's do it.

CHARLIE: If that can wait, I actually wanted to talk—

SUSAN: *(Reading.)* Question number one: Having a vivid mental picture of your partner's countenance *(Points to her face.)* is indicative of a strong spiritual center. Does she or *(Points to CHARLIE.)* truly know your face. Oh, that one's too easy. *(She covers her eyes.)* Okay, what color are my eyes? This is fun.

CHARLIE'S HEAD: My life is over.

CHARLIE: You're right, that one's way too easy...What's the second one? Or we can start with the last question and work backwards?

CHARLIE'S HEAD: Why do I only take John's bad advice?

CHARLIE: Oh my God, your shoes are dirty. We gotta go!

SUSAN: What?!...Nice try. You know all my shoes have dirt retardants.

CHARLIE: This is silly. You can't classify your eye color under one category. You have your own color...I like to call it...Susan-n-eye-ri-ses—Hey, let's get some Chinese?

SUSAN: Stop teasing.

CHARLIE: Want to hear how we first met?

CHARLIE'S HEAD: Mayday! Mayday!

CHARLIE: *(Brainstorm; sings.)* You're the epicenter of my—

SUSAN: I hate that song. What color are my eyes?

CHARLIE: Your eyes...are...blue. Just kidding. *(Unsure.)* Right?

SUSAN: *(Sternly.)* Charles.

CHARLIE: They're like a greenish, grayish... *(Looking for an indication.)* Not quite, a hazelish...reddish...whiter shade of...

SUSAN: Charles—

CHARLIE: Rainbow! Kind of. Thing.

SUSAN: *(She pulls her hands away, furious.)* They're mystical brown!

CHARLIE: That's it! Mystical brown. Mix all those colors together and that's what you get. I was leading up to it. Okay, I'm hot. Read me the next question.

SUSAN: Wait, let me get you my headshot so you can study.

CHARLIE: It's in black and white. I'm sorry I couldn't remember. It doesn't mean anything.

SUSAN: It doesn't matter, because you failed the test.

CHARLIE: One question and I fail?

SUSAN: You failed. Again.

CHARLIE'S HEAD: I'm a failure?

CHARLIE: If I failed, then we failed.

SUSAN: I know your eyes are blue!

CHARLIE: I'm not talking about eye color.

SUSAN: I'm not talking to you about anything.

CHARLIE'S HEAD: Maybe this isn't a good time.

CHARLIE: Well, I want to talk, Susan.

SUSAN: *(Like Hal from 2001.)* Is there something wrong, Charles.

CHARLIE: Shut up, Hal. Sorry. Can we just talk for a second?

SUSAN: Why, so you can burn more of my things?

(They sit on the couch.)

SUSAN: This apartment makes my skin crawl. Men shouldn't have cats.

CHARLIE'S HEAD: We should go.

CHARLIE: Susan, I think there's a problem.

SUSAN: I know there's a problem. I know it every second I'm with you.

CHARLIE: Why is everything so absolute?

SUSAN: It most certainly is not! But I'm sure that's what you're telling everyone, isn't it?

CHARLIE: What are you saying?

SUSAN: Don't think I don't know that you're telling everyone what a horrible person I am. How miserable you are with me…

CHARLIE: This is too difficult for me, Susan. I'm afraid we rushed this whole thing.

SUSAN: This is too difficult for *you?!* I'm the one always bending over backwards trying to make things work.

CHARLIE'S HEAD: She's too angry. Leave it alone.

SUSAN: I can't stand your moods. Do you have any idea how hard it is for me?

CHARLIE: Susan, I'm not saying—

SUSAN: *(Fierce.)* You never think of that, do you? You don't have the foggiest idea!

CHARLIE: Susan—

SUSAN: You have no idea! You have no idea what it's like to be me!

CHARLIE: Susan… *(Has a moment of clarity.)* You're right, but I can take a guess. It's like being a spoiled, manic child whose primary goal in life is to have the entire universe cater to her every whim.

CHARLIE'S HEAD: …Did I just say that?

SUSAN: *(Buries her face in her hands.)* How can you say that to me?

CHARLIE: Susan, I'm so sorry. I haven't been entirely honest with—

SUSAN: *(Her face is ugly with rage.)* You pathetic loser!

CHARLIE: Susan. We need to break up.

SUSAN: You can't break up with me, because I'm breaking up with you! *(Grabs *her coat and walks to the door, then turns around dramatically.)* And I'm taking you off my mailing list!

(She exits. There is a long pause. CHARLIE inadvertently leans on the answering machine erase button.)

ANSWERING MACHINE AUTO-MATED VOICE: I will erase messages.

CHARLIE'S HEAD and CHARLIE: Shut up.

SCENE 17

CHARLIE's apartment. Two weeks later. SUSAN's things are gone. CHARLIE is working steadily on his screenplay. The doorbell rings.

JOHN: *(Offstage.)* It's John Winston.

CHARLIE'S HEAD: There's the man!

CHARLIE: *(Letting him in.)* Hey! What's going on, Uncle John? Haven't seen you in a couple of weeks. Where have you been?—Listen, I have something to tell you. You were absolutely right... Hey, you okay?

JOHN: Yeah. 'Course.

CHARLIE: It's been tough, but I think I'm doing a little better. But first, tell me, who's the latest conquest, huh? You've probably been with five or six women since I've seen you last.

JOHN: No, there's no conquest, uh...

CHARLIE: You sure you're okay? Get a little too much winky last night? I wonder if you can get a hangover from too much sex? Hey, let's go out. I'll even try that topless place you're always talking about. Gazumba's?

JOHN: Nah, not, uh...

CHARLIE: Hey, your last name is really Winston? I thought—

JOHN: There's something I need to tell you.

CHARLIE: Wait... This isn't about a threesome is it? I'm not...

JOHN: I'm not really an actor.

CHARLIE: Then why'd you audition for that Broken Scale info-whatcha-mathinger?

JOHN: We held the audition because of union rules.

CHARLIE: I knew it... What do you mean *we* held the audition?

JOHN: It's my company.

CHARLIE: Wait. Your name is John Winston.

CHARLIE'S HEAD: He's John Winston!

CHARLIE: You're Winston Products. You make all those crappy products for easy living.

JOHN: I like to keep a low profile.

CHARLIE'S HEAD: I'm going to get lots of free stuff! I love this guy!

JOHN: Listen, I was wondering... if you'd, uh...

CHARLIE: Wait. Are you... *nervous*? I didn't think it was possible for you to be nervous.

JOHN: *(Tries to smirk it off.)* Nervous? Peeshhhhaw.

CHARLIE: *Peeshhhhaw?*

CHARLIE'S HEAD: *(Chuckling.)* I love this guy.

CHARLIE: What are you about to propose or something?

(CHARLIE laughs. JOHN joins in.)

JOHN: No way. *(Stops laughing.)* Did that already... Will you be my best man?

(CHARLIE starts laughing again. JOHN isn't laughing.)

JOHN: Will you? Charlie?

CHARLIE: *(Chuckles then pauses.)* Charlie?

JOHN: Will you be my best man?

(Dead silence.)

CHARLIE: John.

JOHN: Charlie.

CHARLIE'S HEAD: He said it again.

(Deader silence.)

CHARLIE: You're getting married?!

JOHN: Kind. Of.

CHARLIE: ...*Married?!* You? To who?

JOHN: I met her at the wedding reception.

CHARLIE: *(Glaring at him.)* Have you forgotten who you are?!

CHARLIE'S HEAD: I hate this guy!

JOHN: It just happened.

CHARLIE: *It just happened?* That's what you say when you—when you take someone home—when you get laid—when you do what *you* do! Not when you get engaged!

CHARLIE'S HEAD: Who's going to take me to Gazumba's?

JOHN: Well, the engagement is going to be really short. We're getting married next week.

CHARLIE: *(Losing it.)* Why wait?! Do it right now. *(Lifts up the phone.)* Here, call her up. I'll perform the ceremony right over the phone. Dearly beloved, blah-bitty blah, blah. John Schmuckface, do you take this blah-bitty—what the hell is her name?

JOHN: Sara. Sara Billings.

(Deadest silence.)

CHARLIE: *She's* getting married?!

CHARLIE'S HEAD: *She's* getting married?!

CHARLIE: Sara?!

CHARLIE'S HEAD: Sara?!

CHARLIE: Sara?!

CHARLIE'S HEAD: Sara?!

JOHN: I guess you know her.

CHARLIE'S HEAD and CHARLIE: This is insane!

JOHN: What the hell is wrong with you?

CHARLIE: *With me?* You have been fucking with me since the day we met.

JOHN: Name one time I fucked with you.

CHARLIE: You got me to fight with my appliances—You tricked me into asking out Susan.

JOHN: So you're going out with a beautiful woman. Sue me. And I'm sorry, but sometimes the magic doesn't last forever.

CHARLIE: It's just so easy for you to be a dick. And you always get away with it.

JOHN: It's not easy for me. It's just impossible for you!

CHARLIE'S HEAD: Be careful. He's your friend.

CHARLIE: You know, I tried to do that thing where you just have one-night stands, but I couldn't follow through. I had this fear that I'd meet someone, have sex and fall in love with her, and then I'd be crushed, because she was just in it for the one time. Or she'd fall in love with me, and she'd be crushed. Then I finally realized, it wasn't fear. It's just something I never wanted.

JOHN: You know what your problem is?

CHARLIE: I'm getting pretty sick of you telling me.

JOHN: You have a legitimate, detailed, entirely reasonable excuse for everything you don't do. And you judge me, because I'm putting it out there a hundred times more than you.

CHARLIE: You are such an asshole!

JOHN: Why am I an asshole?

CHARLIE'S HEAD: Don't say it!

CHARLIE: Because I'm the one who's supposed to be getting married!! It should be me! I'm the domesticated, semi-responsible one. You're the crude-sexist-treats-women-like-shit one.

JOHN: People can change! And how about you just go fuck yourself! *(He marches to the door.)*

CHARLIE: Well, fuck yourself, too!

JOHN: I'm out of here!

CHARLIE: Good for you!

JOHN: *(Standing at the door.)* So will you be my best man?!

CHARLIE: I'd be delighted!

JOHN: Great! *(Exits slamming the door.)*

(A moment later a more subdued JOHN reenters.)

JOHN: Didn't you have something to tell me?

CHARLIE: I broke up with Susan.

JOHN: *(Looks around the apartment and realizes.)* Hey, man…I'm sorry.

CHARLIE: It's okay.

Scene 18

SARA and JOHN's wedding reception. One week later. TOM, CHARLIE, CAROL, WENDY, and KATE are milling about the room. Everyone is formally dressed. CHARLIE is in his suit.

CHARLIE'S HEAD: Glynn Scotty Wolfe married twenty-nine times in his lifetime. Some people are just better suited for marriage than others.

TOM: And now, ladies and gentlemen, the moment you've all been waiting for. Here are the happy newlyweds, John Elliot Winston and Sara Billings!

(Everyone applauds as JOHN and SARA enter holding hands. They kiss and split up to greet their friends.)

CHARLIE: Congratulations, John.

TOM: Way to go, Uncle John!

CAROL: Congratulations, Sara.

WENDY: You look beautiful.

JOHN: *(Beaming.)* This is great.

(JOHN is furiously shaking their hands.)

JOHN: Isn't this great? This is terrific. I couldn't have done it without you.

CHARLIE: Yes, you could.

SARA: Am I spontaneous or what?

CAROL: You got me beat on this one.

TOM: Did you see all the food and the bottles of Beeferall?

JOHN: And there's a giant keg of Dr. Paprika with your name on it, Tommy.

(Speechless, TOM gives JOHN a bear hug.)

CHARLIE: His company makes all that stuff.

TOM: He likes to keep a low profile.

SARA: *(To CAROL.)* I know I'm bad at human interactive things...

JOHN: *(To CHARLIE.)* Listen, some of the things I said...I've been feeling, what's the word...

SARA: ...Genuinely sorry. Always.

CAROL: I am, too.

WENDY: Me, too.

SARA: I'm really glad you're here, Wendy.

WENDY: *(Tearing up.)* Me, too.

SARA: Uh-oh, here it comes...

CHARLIE: I have a little surprise. I'm going to be a Big Brother. We are signed up for orientation at Big Brothers Big Sisters.

JOHN: What do you mean *we?*

CHARLIE: Ready to toss the ball around, John?

WENDY: You should tell her now, Carol.

SARA: What is it? This is my big day, and I say we party till we lapse into a coma.

JOHN: Great idea to do a good deed, Charlie! You never know when a hot babe might be watching. Score some serious points.

CHARLIE: Wow, you can really make anything sound sleazy.

CAROL: *(To SARA.)* You remember the Big Brother I got for Charlie...

SARA: You got some putz loser lowlife to humiliate your boyfriend. It happens.

CAROL: *(Indicating JOHN.)* Well, that's your putz loser lowlife.

WENDY: I think you struck a nerve.

SARA: *(Pause.)* So he likes to role-play. Means he's versatile.

(SARA walks over to JOHN, as WENDY greets CHARLIE and TOM.)

WENDY: Nice to see you, Charlie.

CHARLIE: Good to see you, too, Wendy. Have you met Tom?

TOM: Hello.

WENDY: Fat disgusting slob, right?

TOM: *(Nodding.)* I had a lot of fun doing that infomercial.

WENDY: You did an infomercial?

(CHARLIE finds himself face to face with CAROL.)

CHARLIE: Hi.

CAROL: Hi.

CHARLIE: Pretty wild, huh?

CAROL: That's putting it mildly...How's Kitty Poo?

CHARLIE: Very temperamental...I heard about your fire.

CAROL: We tried putting it out with Jell-O powder.

CHARLIE: I read somewhere sauerkraut is good for that.

WENDY: *(Pointing towards offstage.)* Hey, it's a guy with a video camera interviewing people.

TOM: Let's go.

(TOM and WENDY exit together.)

CHARLIE: Seeing anyone?

CAROL: No. There was a sax player. It didn't work out.

CHARLIE: ...I heard your play was extended. Congratulations.

CAROL: Thank you.

CHARLIE: I'd like to see it.

CAROL: That'd be great. You could bring a date.

CHARLIE: Maybe not this time.

(JOHN and SARA are pawing each other.)

SARA: *(Playfully.)* For a hundred points, can you tell what am I thinking?

JOHN: I'll take a last second guess.

SARA: Want to see if you qualify for the bonus round?

JOHN: I'd rather play the home edition.

(TOM reenters and approaches CHARLIE.)

TOM: I need a good character for the wedding video, Charlie.

CHARLIE: It's probably staring you right in the face.

TOM: Of course. *(He exits.)*

CAROL: You and John have gotten really close.

CHARLIE: Thanks for setting us up.

CAROL: You know I'm really sorry about that.

CHARLIE: I know.

CAROL: I heard about you and Susan. Sorry about that, too.

CHARLIE: Thank you.

CHARLIE'S HEAD: She's not a bitch.

SARA: ...You'll have to pay the banker, Mr. Winston.

JOHN: I don't own any property, Ms. Billings.

CAROL: Stay cool, Charlie.

CHARLIE: You, too. Wait—what?

SARA: You shouldn't have stepped on my boardwalk.

JOHN: I just wanted to pass Go.

(TOM reenters.)

TOM: Charlie, I have someone I want you to meet.

CHARLIE: Tom, I don't want to meet anyone. I'm just here to celebrate the union of two people who don't know the first thing about one another.

TOM: Just one second. *(Quickly exits.)*

CHARLIE: Tom, no! *(Turning his back on TOM.)*

CHARLIE'S HEAD: Why does he always do this to me?

(TOM reenters.)

TOM: Charlie—

(CHARLIE turns back towards them and abruptly extends his hand out to KATE who has been standing in his vicinity.)

CHARLIE: Hello, I'm sorry, but I'm really not into the whole set-up-to-meet-and-date-fall-in-love-and-die state right now. It's been a really tough year for me and my answering machine.

KATE: Excuse me?

TOM: I wanted you to meet the video guy, but he's videotaping them cutting the cake. He needs some motivational advice.

(CHARLIE is speechless.)

CHARLIE'S HEAD: Nice going, bonehead. You never grow out of being a complete asshole.

CHARLIE: *(To KATE.)* I'm so sorry...I thought you knew Tom...

TOM: He didn't mean to be a blockhead. Sometimes he just acts that way.

KATE: I understand. Just a knee-jerk reaction.

(JOHN and SARA enter fighting. Their faces are covered with wedding cake.)

JOHN: *(Makes buzzer sound.)* Wrong answer!

SARA: Time's up!

JOHN: Game over, baby!

(SARA abruptly gives him her wedding ring.)

SARA: Here's your parting gift!

(JOHN and SARA exit in opposite directions. CAROL exits after SARA.)

TOM: *(Arms extended; in character.)* Supercomic to the rescue! Hey, Wendy, get the video guy! *(As Supercomic.)* What's the deal with Don King's hair?— Ha-ha!

WENDY: That's so sexy.

(TOM and WENDY exit after JOHN. CHARLIE and KATE are the only people left in the room.)

CHARLIE'S HEAD: My whole life is one great big awkward.

CHARLIE: That's okay. My wedding toast was awful.

KATE: Looks like you'll have some time to work on it...I'm Kate. I work with Sara.

CHARLIE'S HEAD: Never know who you might meet.

CHARLIE: Hi, Kate...I'm sorry, I'm Charlie. *(Extends his hand.)*

(KATE shakes his hand.)

KATE: You shouldn't be sorry about that.

CHARLIE: I'm working on that.

KATE: Shouldn't you go after the groom?

CHARLIE: In a minute. They'll be okay. Things tend to work out for him. He always does exactly what he wants to do.

KATE: Just like her. Only more.

CHARLIE: I'm more of a gradual experiment in progress.

KATE: I planned on being impulsive once. It didn't work out.

CHARLIE: I'm positive I know what you mean.

KATE: Sometimes I'll make it a point to do something I would never do in a million years.

CHARLIE: For example?

KATE: About a year ago I placed a personal ad under an assumed name in the *Village Voice*.

CHARLIE: That's funny. I almost answered one.

KATE: Would you believe a guy responded and left me a message but didn't leave his name.

CHARLIE: That's kind of strange.

CHARLIE'S HEAD: Yeah, what an idiot.

KATE: And all he said was, "Love me?" That was it.

CHARLIE'S HEAD: Oh my God!! She's Donna from the *Village Voice!* Hide!

KATE: He sounded…conflicted. I would've talked to him.

CHARLIE'S HEAD: I wouldn't! How humiliating. This is all I need.

CHARLIE: You're pretty open minded.

CHARLIE'S HEAD: You mean completely reckless. What if the guy who called was a serial killer?

KATE: I see you're friends with Supercomic. Is it alright that I know his alter ego?

CHARLIE: Tom was playing a character from a screenplay I've been writing since the dawn of time.

KATE: It's about superheroes?

CHARLIE: It's about a guy who's been writing a screenplay since the dawn of time.

KATE: I'd go see that.

CHARLIE: I'll get you a comp.

CHARLIE'S HEAD: Don't do it! She's way too much of a free spirit for you.

KATE: Good, I don't have any cash on me.

CHARLIE'S HEAD: If she finds out it was you she'll think you're a complete imbecile.

CHARLIE: Kate, would you like to go to the bar and have a drink? Whiskey sours on demand. No waiting.

KATE: Sure.

CHARLIE'S HEAD: This could be a major mistake. She's irresponsible! What if she laughs in your face!—

CHARLIE: *(Turns directly to CHARLIE'S HEAD.)* Would you please just shut up for once?

KATE: What?

CHARLIE: Please excuse me. Just something I needed to do.

(As they walk.)

CHARLIE: So, *Donna,* have you ever heard of Hank Aaron?

(KATE/DONNA makes the association and smiles broadly. As they exit, the audio of Broadcaster Milo Hamilton's famous call of Hank Aaron passing Babe Ruth as the all-time home run king plays, growing louder: "…Here's the pitch by Downing…swinging…there's a drive into left-center field…that ball is gonna be…Outta here! It's gone! It's 715! There's a new home run champion of all time, and it's Henry Aaron!")

(CURTAIN)

HASSAN AND SYLVIA

A play in one act

Manuel Igrejas

MANUEL IGREJAS is a poet, author, and playwright. He hails from Newark, New Jersey, where he was born in 1949. He worked as an actor on the WBAI radio serial *Our Life Together Among the Works of Art* in the late 1970s, and also wrote three of the episodes. This led him to playwriting (*Phyllis and Kirby*, American Theater of Actors, 1980). After a long hiatus, during which he worked as a theatrical press agent—his clients included Richard Foreman and his Ontologic-Hysteric Theatre Company and Blue Man Group—Manny returned to writing for the theatre in 2004. His produced plays include *Shrinkage* (Manhattan Theatre Source, 2004); *Kitty and Lina* (Manhattan Theater Source, 2008); and *Miss Mary Dugan* (Fresh Fruit Festival, 2009), which won three awards including best play of the festival. Manny's poem "Herois do Mar" is published in the anthology *New Geography of Poets*, and his short story "The Little Trooper" is in the anthology *Men on Men 4*. He resides in Montclair, New Jersey, with his partner, Michael Giunta. Manny can be found on the Web at www.mannyigrejas.com.

Hassan and Sylvia was first presented by Emaginer as part of the Fresh Fruit Festival (Frank Calo, Artistic Director; Louis Lopardi, Executive Director) on July 14, 2010, at the Cherry Lane Studio Theatre, New York City, with the following cast and credits:

Narrator	Erik Kever Ryle
X	John Wernke
Ozzie	Casey Burden
Hassan	Vandit Bhatt
Sylvia	Karin de la Penha
Velma	Marilyn Bernard
Jimmy	Casey Burden

Director: David Hilder
Production Stage Manager: Julie Watson
Photographer: Web Begole

For sheet music and recordings of the song "Let's Make a Deal" (music by Brad Howell Houghton; lyrics by Manuel Igrejas), please email Brad Howell Houghton at nycbhh@gmail.com.

Special thanks to John Martello, The Players, Michael Giunta, Christian Hartwig, Jonathan Alexandratos, Karen Winer, Jennifer Skura, Doug Rossi, Cindy Keiter, Lory Henning, Greg Skura, John Borek, Doug Rice and MUCC in Rochester, Spencer Christiano and the Theatre Rehabilitation Company, Christopher Eaves, Brian Scott, Natalie Ferrier, Afrim Gjonbalaj, and Janet Ward.

Hassan and Sylvia was named Best Play of the 2010 Fresh Fruit Festival, and Marilyn Bernard was honored as Best Actress.

Hassan and Sylvia is dedicated to the memory of the late, great Janet Ward.

For Emily, Angie, and Enrique, now and forever.

CAST OF CHARACTERS

NARRATOR: A man in his forties. He wears a white shirt and black pants.

X (our hero): A good-looking man around thirty-five.

OZZIE: A singer, attractive, late thirties.

JIMMY: Limo driver, late thirties.

HASSAN: An exotic-looking man in his late twenties/early thirties, well-dressed.

SYLVIA: A glamorous woman in her fifties.

VELMA: A disheveled, yet glamorous woman in her late seventies.

(Note: Ozzie and Jimmy are played by the same actor.)

SCENE

A white wall. In front of it are four silver folding chairs. The chairs are lined up facing the audience. Through their artful arrangement, the chairs double for most props and locations in the play.

TIME

Right here. Right now.

At rise: X is lying on the floor centerstage. NARRATOR enters, stands slightly to the right of X and addresses the audience.

NARRATOR: We're thirteen miles from Manhattan in a studio apartment in Cedar Gardens, right on Cedar Boulevard, in beautiful Cedar Chips, New Jersey. There is just a futon, nineteen-inch TV set, a small dresser. The other room is a closet-sized kitchenette with a mini-refrigerator and a small oven that doesn't work. There is a full ashtray, and the room smells of cigarette smoke and a hint of Febreze. He's watching TV, something on Bravo. The sound is turned off during one of those endless commercials for *Real Housewives from Hell*... *(Exits.)*

X: *(Stands, centerstage in spotlight.)* I am nobody from nowhere and I have nothing. Three months ago my lover, Vincent, had a heart attack in the kitchen of his restaurant, Bella Italia, and died on the way to the hospital. He was fifty-five years old. We had been together for fifteen years. I met Vincent when I was eighteen and snuck into Feathers, the Notre Dame of Jersey gay bars. He was the big, handsome bartender. I was pretty much on my own from the time I was fifteen, but Vincent scooped me up in his big arms and took me in. He put me through school and subsidized my haphazard acting career. He also ripped me a new one with his big Italian sausage. *(Big sigh.)* Ah, Vincent, my Vincenzo! He ate, drank, smoked, and talked too much. He could be a bully and he wasn't the most tactful man in the world. The last few years there wasn't a day when I didn't think about leaving him and Lord knows I wasn't faithful to him. But all he had to do was level his big, droopy brown eyes at me and pin me to the wall with the depth of his love. I don't know how to live without him.

Vincent's family, the Azzopardis, sold the restaurant. They sold our little house too. There was no will and my name wasn't on any documents. I got this crappy apartment and a job as a receptionist at a magazine called *Media Blitz* in an ugly tower in Manhattan. I shuffle back and forth across the Hudson from one cubicle to another. I used to read a lot, the classics, poetry. Now I can't open a book. I can't seem to concentrate on anything.

My free time is spent in front of the tube. The *Seinfeld* crew, *Friends*, *Golden Girls*. I know all the episodes by heart and just like having their sounds wash over me. To spice things up I watch *Project Runway* and *Top Chef*. I can't absorb anything more than that now.

The night Vincent died, I was watching *Random Harvest* on TCM. The phone rang and I let the machine pick up. It was Vincent:

VINCENT: *(Voiceover.)* "It's me. You there? Listen, I ran out of the house and grabbed the wrong keys. Leave a key under the back door mat for me. Okay, Punkin?...You there?"

X: Oh, I was soooo annoyed. I hate that "it's me" bullshit. And here I am trying to watch this wonderful movie after a day lazing around the house and you have the nerve to ask me a favor because you made a stupid mistake. Then he throws in the Punkin, which he knows I love...I couldn't get off my ass...I was annoyed. I never did leave the key under the mat and Vincent never came home. *(Pause.)* I kept that message for a long time, then the collection agencies started calling, then the phone was turned off. Then I moved and then that message was nowhere, like me. *(Long pause. Recovering.)* My friend, the cabaret singer, Ozzie Potter, calls me The Widow Azzopardi. I like that handle. It's like a comfy old sweater I can wrap around myself.

Ozzie called and asked me to come hear him sing at a new club called The Hideaway, I said yes.

(X remains standing in the middle of the stage. NARRATOR, wearing a white apron around his waist, sets up four chairs to suggest two separate tables at a nightclub. He brings out a sports jacket and helps X on with it as he speaks. HASSAN and SYLVIA enter and sit at a "table." HASSAN is a young exotic man expensively dressed in a dark suit. He has rings on every finger. SYLVIA is in her fifties, slender, handsome, and glamorous, with an expensive hairdo—a hairpiece. She is wearing a sexy cocktail dress with a deep neckline.)

NARRATOR: *(Steps in front of X.)* Welcome to The Hideaway on West 46th Street, a couple of blocks west and a couple of notches below Don't Tell Mama. *(Quoting.)* "This premier music venue showcases the best singers on the scene today in a plush, old-timey nightclub atmosphere, reminiscent of the glamorous Manhattan of our fantasies. So, sit back, relax, have a cocktail, and let New York's finest song stylists work their magic on you." That's what it says on the postcard. Now, just between you and me, some Russian guy with a lot of money and a lot of secrets leased the place so his no-talent girlfriend would have a place to screech out some numbers. Well, she disappeared and he ain't been seen in a while and in a month this place will be deserted. So, drink up! Wilkommen, bienvenue, welcome! *(He stands stage left.)*

X: Ozzie and I were in a terrible show called *Two Left Feet* at Don't Tell Mama years ago. We had a brief romance that turned into friendship. His lover, Dennis, had financed *Two Left Feet*. Dennis is a furrier. They met at the Town House. Oh, you know the Town House, that venerable East Side institution where Men in Tweed meet Boys in Need.

(X turns and faces the newly constructed set of The Hideaway and the "crowd" there. He does a startled take and turns his head back to the audience.)

X: Crap. I don't want to talk to anybody. *(Starts to leave.)*

(OZZIE POTTER enters. Comes over to X and gives him a big hug.)

OZZIE: Jesus. You feel like a bag of bones!

X: Grief has no carbs.

OZZIE: Well, come and have dinner with us.

X: *(Looking around.)* Us?

OZZIE: Okay, me. Eat me. Look this is a historic night. I finally got you to hang out and not scurry back to your cave in what is it, Juniper Creek? No, Tiny Tits. Tiny Tits, New Jersey.

X: Cedar Chips. I had a sandwich at the office. And, I'm not feeling that sociable right now.

OZZIE: Oh, come on, it's on me. Dennis is paying for this whole night.

X: Where is Papa?

OZZIE: In L.A. He's getting his chins and eyes done.

X: The better to see you with, my dear. *(Points to HASSAN and SYLVIA.)* What's with Osama and his foxy mama? They from your international fan club?

(The woman at the table goes offstage to the ladies' room—really the dressing room.)

OZZIE: Never saw them before though I'm tempted to do my whole set on his lap. I'm a free man tonight. Want to come up and see my etchings?

X: I've seen your lovely etchings.

OZZIE: Maybe Osama would like them.

X: *(Points to empty table.)* I'm going to sit right here. Loving you.

(OZZIE goes offstage to get ready for his set. X takes a seat at the empty table.)

X: *(To audience.)* I'm not *feeling* The Hideaway. If Vincent was with me, we would have left immediately. He could walk into a restaurant and size it up in a few sniffs. Was it well managed, were the servers professional, was there trouble in the kitchen? This place is a dump and I can smell the bug spray from here.

HASSAN: *(With an exotic accent.)* Hello!

(X waves back, gamely.)

HASSAN: Are you alone?

X: Yes.

HASSAN: You look like you have a lot to think.

X: Oh, not really.

HASSAN: Would you care to join us?

(His woman companion returns to the table. SYLVIA smiles regally as she seats herself.)

SYLVIA: What did I miss?

HASSAN: I am asking our serious friend to join us. He looks very interesting, don't you think?

SYLVIA: *(Reaches into her handbag and puts on her eyeglasses. She makes a show of studying X.)* Yes. He does look very interesting. *(Puts her glasses on the table.)*

HASSAN: *(To X.)* It is better to sit with friends, don't you think, than to sit unhappy alone?

X: Yes it is. *(Sits at their table.)*

HASSAN: I am Hassan and this is Sylvia.

(They all shake hands.)

HASSAN: Have dinner with us!

X: Oh, I'm not hungry.

HASSAN: Oh, please? It is much more fun if we are all dining. Try the lamb. It looks very good.

(NARRATOR shakes his head.)

X: I don't like lamb. I wouldn't eat here if I were you. Trust me.

SYLVIA: Oh, we do, we do. I'd rather go to Rocky's later anyway,

HASSAN: Yes. Let us just listen to the singer, this Potsie.

X: Ozzie. Potter. Do you know him?

HASSAN: Who is Ozzie?

X: The singer.

HASSAN: Oh. I do not know him but we did come to see him.

X: Why?

HASSAN: To see if he is good. Then I can use him for my parties.

X: Do you throw a lot of parties?

HASSAN: What does that mean? *Throw* parties? Throw? *(Makes throwing gesture.)* I do not understand. *(To SYLVIA.)* What does this mean?

SYLVIA: Hassan gives the most wonderful parties.

X: Is that what you do? Are you one of those party promoters? What are they called now? Oh, you're an event planner.

SYLVIA: Hassan is the event. Things… coalesce around him.

HASSAN: Yes! How beautiful. That is true. The event is me and things collapse around me.

X: But you *are* one of those event planners, right?

HASSAN: I am not one of *those* anysings! I like to have a beautiful life with beautiful sings. I like to know beautiful people.

X: Ah, the beautiful people.

SYLVIA: *(Raises an eyebrow.)* Oh my!

HASSAN: It is my art to make this beautiful life, to make…to bring everysing…to make all one…

SYLVIA: To combine these elements and create exciting, memorable events.

HASSAN: Yes!

X: Do you get paid to do it?

HASSAN: Yes. I get money, but is not why I do. Is for love. *(He puts his hands over his heart.)* You are very American. Very bourgeois. Always money. How much money.

SYLVIA: Oh dear. Our little trolley has hopped the track. Let's start over.

X: I'm sorry. I know that these parties happen all the time. I see pictures of them and overhear people talking about them but I've never been to that kind of party. My life is very, um, Spartan.

HASSAN: What is umspartan?

SYLVIA: Simple, I think.

HASSAN: Simple is stupid, no?

X: Sparta was a city in ancient Greece.

HASSAN: You are Greek? I love Greeks!

X: No. My parents were Irish and Spanish.

HASSAN: I love España! Do you know Almodóvar? He has been to my parties. He *loves* me. Would you come to one of my parties?

X: Sure.

HASSAN: Sewer. I love Americans. Always with this answer that is no answer. Not yes. Not no.

X: I would love to come to one of your parties.

HASSAN: Good. Next week I am giving a beautiful party at an art gallery. Is a party of light, everywhere will be light. You must come.

X: *(To SYLVIA.)* Do you go to all of Hassan's parties?

HASSAN: Sylvia is always with me. I cannot do without Sylvia.

X: *(To SYLVIA.)* You have magnificent shoulders.

(HASSAN bristles.)

SYLVIA: Thank you. Do you know Ozzie?

HASSAN: I go to the gym every day. I have ten percent body fat.

X: Ozzie is a chum. He's very talented.

HASSAN: We will see. And what do you do when you are not being a chum?

X: I just go to my job.

HASSAN: A job? What is your job?

X: Oh, it's boring. Pays the rent. That's all. How did you two meet?

(HASSAN and SYLVIA look at each other adoringly.)

HASSAN: I am giving this wonderful party at Balthazar and I keep seeing this fascinating woman in the edges of my eyes. I see she is standing alone, so I bring her a glass of champagne.

(He squeezes SYLVIA's hand.)

SYLVIA: I had come with someone, a terrible man, and he deserted me to talk business with some people. I thought everything so beautiful, so thoughtful. I wondered who was responsible for this wonderful party and I kept seeing Hassan at the center of everything, looking very official and displeased—

HASSAN: If I relax for one minute the staff will drink and smoke and put their cigarettes out in the caviar.

SYLVIA: Then Hassan was standing next to me and I knew my life was going to change.

(She runs her hand across HASSAN's cheek and tugs his ear lobe. HASSAN and SYLVIA gaze at each other lovingly, then turn to X.)

SYLVIA: Hassan has taught me so much.

HASSAN: You teach me so much.

(He raises her hand to his lips.)

X: And you've both taught me so much.

HASSAN: Yes?

SYLVIA: Oh, you are wicked.

HASSAN: What is wicked?

SYLVIA: Evil. Bad.

HASSAN: No. Impossible. He is an angel.

(OZZIE enters. He goes to NARRATOR, who is now the waiter. They talk over this slightly hushed exchange between X, SYLVIA, and HASSAN—you know, like Robert Altman.)

SYLVIA: When I saw you walk in I thought—Billy Budd.

X: God Bless Captain Vere!

SYLVIA: Good looking *and* well read.

HASSAN: Enough! I know nossing about this Billy or his butt. But I do know that your lips are like ripe figs.

OZZIE: I need you to introduce me.

NARRATOR: Okay.

OZZIE: And can you warm them up? You know, tell a joke. You know any?

NARRATOR: I know one.

OZZIE: Is it gay?

NARRATOR: Uh, no.

OZZIE: Well, make it gay.

(Pushes NARRATOR forward and indicates he wants him to start now. The lights dim, and NARRATOR stands in a spotlight, centerstage.)

NARRATOR: Um, good evening ladies and gentlemen. In a few moments we will be treated to the talents of Mr. Ozzie Potter. While Ozzie warms up his pipes (and puts on his girdle) I want to tell you about something that happened to me. I just came back from Montana. I was driving around the back country, and I saw a sign in front of a broken-down shanty-style house: "Talking Dog for Sale." Talking dog? So I ring the bell and this farmer appears and tells me the dog is in the backyard. So I go into the backyard and see a nice-looking Labrador retriever sitting there. "You talk?"

OZZIE: *(Stage whispers.)* Gay!

NARRATOR: Huh? Um…Okay…so I ask the dog, "You talk?" "Yep," the Lab replies…And I'm gay. "Me too," I say. "So, what's your story?" The Lab looks up and says, "Well, I discovered that I could talk when I was pretty young. I wanted to help our nation, so I told the CIA…In no time at all they had me jetting from country to country, sitting in rooms with spies and world leaders, because no one figured a dog would be eavesdropping. I was one of their most valuable spies for eight years running. But the jetting around really tired me out, and I knew I wasn't getting any younger so I decided to settle down. I moved to New York, opened a bar, called it Splash and ran it for a while. I lived in Chelsea with a boxer who was a dead ringer for Oscar de La Hoya. I had about ten good years, then we broke up, the club life was wearing me out, so I bought this place and came out here to retire. I keep a low profile so I hired Clem out there to pretend like he owns me. Uh…he's gay too." Wow! So I go back and ask the farmer what he wants for the dog. "Ten dollars," the guy says.

"Ten dollars? This dog is amazing! Why the fuck are you selling him so cheap?"
"Because he's a liar. He never did any of that stuff!!!"

OZZIE: *(Pokes his head out.)* Ready.

NARRATOR: Ladies and gentlemen, The Hideaway is proud to present the sensual, soulful, satiny, sibilant, song stylings of our favorite male chanteuse. Nominated for a Mac Award as most promising newcomer—ten years in a row. Fresh from his sold-out engagement at the Women's Correctional Facility at Monsey—Mr. Ozzie Potter!

OZZIE: *(Bounces onto centerstage.)* Wow! What can I say after an introduction like that? I mean it. What the hell can I say? Yes, I'm going to miss the gals at Monsey. How I wound up there is a long story. All I can say is a bottle of Tequila, two Mexican busboys, and a little too much Maybelline can land a gal in a heap of trouble. But you didn't come out tonight to hear me complain. And who said I was complaining? Ladies and gentleman, as far as I'm concerned, it's all about love.

HASSAN: Yes it is. *(To X.)* You see? Already I like him.

OZZIE: *(Sings "Let's Make a Deal.")*
I CAN'T BE HAD FOR THE PRICE OF A COCKTAIL
A HAND ON MY KNEE DON'T DO NOTHING FOR ME
IF PINCHING MY ASS IS YOUR IDEA OF A PASS,
THEN, YODA, TONIGHT ALL ALONE YOU WILL BE.
I'M NOT HERE TO TAKE IN THE SCENERY.
I'M A BOY WITH A PLAN AND MY PRICE TAG IS HIGH.
IF YOU'RE GONNA LEAN INTO ME, SHOW ME SOME GREENERY
IF YOUR INCOME IS LIGHT, SO'S MY INTEREST. BYE BYE.
HEY, I'M NOT HARD TO GET ALONG WITH BUT IF I'M HARD WE'LL GET ALONG BETTER
DON'T GRAB MY THING UNLESS YOU SHOW ME A RING
AND TOSS IN A CASHMERE SWEATER
I'M JUST A LAD WHO NEEDS SOME SECURITY
MY FAVORITE EMOTION IS LIFELONG DEVOTION
WHICH YOU'LL GET ONCE I GET AN ANNUITY
AND AS LONG AS YOU EXTEND YOUR WARRANTY
FOR NOW, LET'S KEEP THIS SOCIABLE,
ANYTHING MORE IS NEGOTIABLE
BE ASSURED, DADDY, MY LOVE IS REAL
LET'S MAKE A DEAL.
SEE I'M NOT ONE TO GIVE IT EASY
OVER A SMOKE AND A DIRTY MARTINI
IF YOU WANT MY TIME THEN LET'S NOT NICKEL AND DIME
JUST THROW IN A LAMBORGHINI
NOW I DON'T MEAN TO COME OFF ALOOF
JUST KNOW MY LOVE IS RECESSION-PROOF
BE ASSURED, DADDY, MY LOVE IS REAL
AND I GET PAID PLENTY FOR MY APPEAL
SO IF YOU'RE THINKIN' OF COPPIN' A FEEL
LET'S MAKE A DEAL.

(OZZIE takes a bow to faint applause.)

SYLVIA: I'm not blown away.

HASSAN: Boring! *(To X.)* Do you go to bed with him?

X: He's my friend.

(OZZIE comes to the table.)

OZZIE: Now this looks like an interesting party.

SYLVIA: Oh, it is! *(Claps her hands.)*

OZZIE: What did you think?

SYLVIA: Delicious!

HASSAN: *(Frowns.)* Well, I think…

X: …The pipes are in great shape. You look terrific. It's all good.

OZZIE: Aw. *(Kisses X.)* I'm trying something new. The old act was more inner-directed. This one is more outer-directed. You know?

SYLVIA: I don't know what that means. You mean instead of singing to yourself, you're singing to…other people?

X: Oh, it's inside showbiz stuff. *(To OZZIE.)* I understand, Rihanna.

(X and OZZIE laugh.)

OZZIE: I guess I won't be seeing you later. You seem like you're in good hands.

HASSAN: Yes. He is.

OZZIE: *(Rolls his eyes at X as if to say "you go, girl"; whispers.)* I want a full report. *(Exits.)*

HASSAN: I do not like it when you act so… *(Flutters his hands, indicating gay.)*

X: But I am so… *(Flutters his hands, imitating HASSAN.)*

SYLVIA: Gentlemen! Put away your parasols. Let's be friends.

HASSAN: *(To X; reaches across the table with his free hand.)* Give me your hand.

(X complies.)

HASSAN: I sink you are very interesting. I sink you are very desirable. I do not know why I feel this way. I do not want to feel this way. But I feel how sad you are and it hurts my heart. I do not know what it is about you. Just holding your hand, my cock is so big it would knock over this table if I stood up.

SYLVIA: Hassan! Really! Somebody had their couscous today.

X: I…should…go now.

HASSAN: Yes! This place is enough for me. *(To X, smiling.)* What now, my friend?

X: Back to Sparta.

SYLVIA: Come with us.

X: Where?

HASSAN: I have to check on a party. To make sewer my people do not goof out.

SYLVIA: Up. Goof up.

HASSAN: You see why I love Sylvia? Please be our guest.

(NARRATOR hands HASSAN the check. HASSAN, frowning, hands the check to SYLVIA.)

HASSAN: Is outrageous!

SYLVIA: Oh, hush. *(She lays the check on the table without looking at it. She digs into her small black bag and pulls out a hundred-dollar bill and leaves it on the table. To NARRATOR.)* Keep the change.

NARRATOR: Yes, ma'am. Thank you!

X: I regret that I cannot accept your offer. But thank you for a most interesting evening.

HASSAN: *(Takes two business cards out of his wallet. He hands them to X.)* Oh, my darling, we are just beginning. You write your number on one and give it back to me.

X: *(Examining card.)* Oasis?

HASSAN: Is my company. *New York* magazine writes about me. Michael Musto. Now, I want you to call me and don't say sewer.

X: Yes sir.

SYLVIA: We will be in touch. Now that we've found you we can't let you go.

(HASSAN and SYLVIA stand up. They each kiss X goodbye, continental style. HASSAN hangs onto X a little too long for X's comfort. OZZIE enters to say goodbye. The sound system is playing "One Note Samba." There is a clump of people at the door as everyone tries to leave at once. HASSAN and OZZIE come face to face and check each other out. HASSAN hands OZZIE a card. A shabbily dressed older woman, VELMA, enters from the back of the house. She wears a worn coat, and her head is wrapped in a babushka. Her makeup looks like that of a sad clown, and her face is a fake cry for help. She speaks in a whiny, singsong voice and tries her pitch on audience members on her way to the stage.)

VELMA: *(To the audience, then to the people onstage.)* Please help me, I'm hungry. Please help me. Please help me, I'm hungry. Please help me.

SYLVIA: Get her out of here!

(HASSAN drapes a black lace shawl over SYLVIA's shoulders and takes her hand. He leads SYLVIA to the door. VELMA follows them out and grabs SYLVIA's arm.)

VELMA: Give me some money, you whore!

(HASSAN, SYLVIA, OZZIE, and VELMA exit. X comes downstage and addresses the audience. Spotlight is on him. NARRATOR pushes the furniture upstage behind him.)

X: What an exit! I gave Hassan my office number, you know, just to be on the safe side. But they are an intriguing couple, don't you think? Kind of like Hamas meets Haddassah. Imagine if they joined forces. Would the world be a better place? It seemed that I had planted my flag, without intending to, on Hassan's heart. I knew he would call me. And sure enough, first thing Monday morning…

(Sound effect: Phone ring.)

X: Media Blitz. How may I direct your call?

(HASSAN stands upstage left and talks on his mobile.)

HASSAN: Good morning, my darling.

X: *(Startled.)* Excuse me?

HASSAN: It's me. I thought about you all weekend. Why did you give me your work number, you bad boy? Don't you want to know me?

X: Um, my home phone service was stopped. I…I forgot to pay the bill.

HASSAN: How much is it? We will pay it! I must be able to talk to you. Will you come and see me tonight? I would love you to see my apartment.

X: No, not tonight.

HASSAN: I like you very much. Do you like me?

X: I love your accent. Where are you from?

HASSAN: Where do you think I'm from? Do you think I'm from Iraq?

X: I have no idea.

HASSAN: I am not a terrorist, if that is what you are worried about.

X: I'm not worried about anything.

HASSAN: I am from Morocco. Beautiful Morocco. My family is descended from the great kings.

X: How wonderful. *(Shrugs at audience.)*

HASSAN: I am giving a wonderful party on Friday. I will send a messenger with an invitation. Will you come to my party on Friday?

X: *(Cuts HASSAN off in midspeech.)* Yes. I have to go. I have another call. *(To audience.)* Oh brother.

(HASSAN looks at his phone, shrugs, puts it away. A spotlight hits him.)

HASSAN: *(To audience.)* Yes, I am from Morocco. Morocco is beautiful and mysterious. Just like me.

In Morocco a guest is considered a gift from God. You are my guests. You are my gifts. Did you know, my darlings, that Morocco was the first country in the world to recognize the United States, when it was just a baby, in 1777? No, you did not. I come from Tangier, a very famous city. My family used to own a beautiful hotel near the beach. When I was born, King Hassan II sat on the throne and I was named for him. He was not a very nice man and many people suffered. One day a British tourist said the King looked like a monkey and my father nodded. The next day my father was arrested and charged with calling the King a monkey.

The next years were The Years of Lead, when a cloud hung over our beautiful country. The six of us lived in my grandmother's tiny apartment and we were all very sad for a long time. We prayed to Allah for guidance. My father was released and got a job as a waiter at a very nice hotel. Then my beautiful mother went to work there as a housekeeper. Allah's wisdom allowed us to accept this situation. My brothers and my sister soon worked at the hotel too and I, the baby, stayed with my grandmother.

I was a very beautiful child. Sometimes when I was out alone, men would offer me sweets and touch my face but I did not go with them. When I went to work in the hotel men from other countries offered me money and I did go with them. I liked all the naughty things I did with them. A very rich American saw me with my little tray of hors d'oeuvres and he fell in love with me. He was a very honorable man and he asked my father if I could come and live with him. In my country no one says too much but all is understood and an arrangement was made.

My first days in New York were like magic. I felt like a happy baby in a big, dirty playground. With my friend, I went to many wonderful parties. When he asked me what I wanted to do with my life, I said that I wanted to go to a wonderful party every day. He set me up with Oasis. I had enough money to bring my whole family to this country. When my friend departed his body, he left me some money and I have been on my own since that time. I am not so rich like I used to be and I would like to do something else, maybe be a movie actor. I have not practiced my religion in many years but I feel that Allah still watches over me. *(Exits.)*

(Sound effect: Phone ring.)

X: Media Blitz. How may I direct your call?

SYLVIA: *(Upstage left on her mobile.)* You've cast a spell on Hassan, you vixen.

X: Hello!

SYLVIA: Promise me you'll come to the party on Friday.

X: You know your voice is remarkable. It's like a seductive woodwind.

SYLVIA: Oh my. You are very good at this. Are you a poet?

X: Nope but I like to read poetry. I have to get back to work.

SYLVIA: I'm not letting you go until you promise to come to the party.

X: I promise! *(X remains on stage, center-stage. He pats his pockets for cigarettes. He can't find them. He looks at NARRATOR.)* Where are my smokes?

NARRATOR: Don't have them. *(To audience.)* Scene. The exterior of the Wretched Wrefuse Art Gallery on Avenue A.

X: Damn! *(Takes a deep breath.)* I smell Sylvia.

SYLVIA: There you are! I saw you in there and then you disappeared. Why are you so late? Hassan keeps asking for you.

X: I got stuck at work. You look smashing tonight.

SYLVIA: Thank you. You don't look bad yourself.

(HASSAN rushes in from stage right. He is on his cell phone, yessing someone to death.)

HASSAN: Okay, okay, okay okay *(He pulls the move I call "Talking to Mr. Weiner." He holds the phone away from his ear and looks at X and SYLVIA, exasperated—)* Okay, okay, okay, okay *(He holds the phone to his crotch—)* Okay, okay, okay, okay *(He puts the phone to his ear again.)* My darling, my darling, my darling. I must go. Gwyneth is beckoning me. *(He does a big smooch into the phone and puts it away.)* Oh, that Patti LuPone talks so much! *(To X.)* There you are! I have been waiting for you all night. Why are you doing this to me?

SYLVIA: Hassan! Settle!

HASSAN: Oh yes. There you are, my friend. Thank you for coming.

X: How is the party going?

HASSAN: Terrible! The Mayor did not come. Julia Roberts did not come! Susan Sarandon did not come!

SYLVIA: Yes, but Ed Koch is here. Amanda Lepore and Robin Byrd are here.

HASSAN: *(Looking upstage through the "window.")* No! No! No! That stupid bartender he is pouring one half-bottle of champagne into another bottle. What is he doing? This is not a Polish wedding! Stop that, you stupid man! Stop… *(To SYLVIA.)* What is the word for mixing the bottles together?

SYLVIA: *(Shrugs.)* Mixing?

X: Consolidate.

HASSAN: Yes! Yes! You are beautiful and brilliant! *(He shouts to bartender inside.)* Do not consolidate the bottles! *(To X and SYLVIA.)* They are like children, these stupid people. I must go talk to him. When I return we must leave this place. *(Exits.)*

SYLVIA: He's crazy about you. You are all he talks about.

X: He's beautiful and very charismatic but I think he's a little too much for me.

SYLVIA: Isn't that better than not enough? Plenty of that going around. He was very nervous about you coming tonight. Be patient with him. He really is very sweet.

X: Why are you pimping for him?

SYLVIA: I want him to be happy.

X: Are you happy?

SYLVIA: I just revel in the pure joy of being.

X: Oh brother! Whatever you're on, I want some.

SYLVIA: I'm serious. I was in terrible shape a few years ago, as unhappy as anyone can be. I was married to a vile man. I had a gruesome divorce, lost my daughter to him. She is grown up now and doesn't talk to me. I wandered around in a daze doing very stupid things. Honey, I was a mess.

X: You seem like a woman with a secret.

SYLVIA: Many secrets.

X: Hassan said he was from Morocco. What exotic place are you from? Lichtenstein?

SYLVIA: East 93rd Street. You're a saucy one. But, I don't know, you seem very sad.

(HASSAN enters stage left. He is on his cell phone.)

HASSAN: Jimmy is just around the corner, he will pick us up now. I am hungry. We will go to Rocky's.

(HASSAN drapes his arms around X and SYLVIA.)

HASSAN: I just want to be alone with my two favorite people.

SYLVIA: Come with us. Whenever we are done, Jimmy will take you home.

X: Back to New Jersey?

SYLVIA: Of course.

(X, HASSAN, and SYLVIA exit.)

NARRATOR: Ladies and gentleman, now, for the first time ever on a New York stage, we will manufacture a car for you. And not some crappy little four-cylinder Ford Focus, No. Our car is a luxurious Lincoln Town Car, with all the bling.

(NARRATOR sets up a table, slightly upstage and four chairs downstage; one is in front of the other three. The chairs face the audience. It's a car, see? The Lincoln Town Car NARRATOR was just talking about.)

NARRATOR: Sweet ride, huh? Now, let me summon the driver. *(Calls out.)* Oh, James!

(A good-looking man in his thirties enters stage right. He is the limo driver, JIMMY, and played by the same actor who played OZZIE. This time around he has long blond hair. He is wearing his version of a driver's uniform, a too-tight, short-sleeved white shirt with the sleeves rolled up high to show off his biceps. He is wearing shiny, tight black pants and black leather boots. A black leather jacket completes the outfit. He looks like a '70s porn star. He sits in the single chair furthest downstage—you know, the "driver's seat." HASSAN gestures to SYLVIA to get in "the car" first. He rolls his eyes at the audience. X gets in next and is between HASSAN and SYLVIA. HASSAN drapes his arm over the back of X's seat.)

HASSAN: Consolidate! I will always remember that.

SYLVIA: Well, it was all lovely, as usual. *(To JIMMY.)* Both hands on the wheel, James!

JIMMY: Yes, ma'am! *(Shrugs—WHAT wheel? And grabs his crotch.)*

X: I really like your perfume.

SYLVIA: It's my own special concoction.

X: What's it called?

SYLVIA: Sylvia!

(They laugh, but HASSAN is not amused.)

HASSAN: I have something special for you too.

(He takes X's hand and puts it on his upper thigh.)

X: Yikes!

HASSAN: And this is just from sitting next to you. Imagine when I have you naked in my bed.

SYLVIA: Don't mind me, boys. I'll just sit here…being superfluous.

HASSAN: Well, here we are!

(He, X, and SYLVIA exit the car. JIMMY takes three of the chairs and sets them around an imaginary table. He places the fourth chair upstage against the wall and exits. HASSAN, X, and SYLVIA sit at the table.)

HASSAN: I am so, so tired. I work so hard and get nossing for it. Nobody understands me.

SYLVIA: Oh, stop complaining.

X: You're living the kind of life most people dream about.

HASSAN: Is work. With no time for love. I very much need love. Where is the waiter? I'm very hungry. *(Snaps his fingers.)*

(NARRATOR comes to the table.)

SYLVIA: You work here too?

NARRATOR: Well, I'm really an actor. Check this out. *(Puts the apron over his head and makes a sad face.)* Look at me, I'm Mother Teresa.

(X, HASSAN, and SYLVIA look at the audience and grimace.)

X: *(To SYLVIA.)* Do you have some fabulous thing you do during the daylight hours or do you just sit in the refrigerator like an orchid until the sun goes down?

SYLVIA: I'm a physical therapist!

(VELMA enters from the back of the house again and makes her way toward the stage.)

VELMA: *(In her pull-string puppet voice.)* Please help me, I'm hungry. Please help me… *(Takes a seat in the audience and makes her pitch to the people sitting around her.)*

SYLVIA: *(Looking at the audience.)* Goddammit!

VELMA: *(Stands and points at SYLVIA.)* Whore! Whore! Whore! Whore!

HASSAN: She is nightmare. You have to do something.

SYLVIA: If I knew what to do, I would do it!

X: Who is she?

HASSAN: This is not really my problem. You know? *(To VELMA.)* You! Old lady! Be quiet or I will kill you!

VELMA: *(Waddles onstage.)* Fuck you! *(To SYLVIA.)* Tell your Puerto Rican boyfriend I'm not scared of him.

HASSAN: I am from Morocco, you stupid woman. *(To SYLVIA.)* This is not my problem. You should take care of this.

VELMA: *(Points at X.)* Who's your friend? *(To SYLVIA.)* Hey, is that my shawl? I see it all now. I know what you're up to. I know everything!

SYLVIA: Really? What day is today?

VELMA: What?

SYLVIA: Simple question. Is it Monday, Tuesday, Wednesday?

VELMA: Er…It's…

HASSAN: *(To X.)* I am sorry, my darling. We will take care of this.

VELMA: It's judgment day, you whore! Miss High and Mighty. *(To X.)* I'm Velma.

X: Hello.

VELMA: I was the most beautiful woman in New York. I had men eating out of my hand, honey.

X: I'm sure…

VELMA: Don't try to sweet talk me. *(To SYLVIA.)* Give me some money, you tramp.

(SYLVIA takes a twenty-dollar bill out of her purse and hands it to VELMA.)

SYLVIA: Here! Now beat it.

VELMA: Fuck you! *(She examines the bill, sneers, and tucks it into her dress. To SYLVIA.)* I got my eye on you. *(She does the "evil eye" gesture and walks off the stage and up the aisle to the back of the house, grumbling the whole time and making the gesture to audience members.)*

(HASSAN, X, and SYLVIA appear a bit lost. NARRATOR has been standing off to the side, with his apron on.)

X: So…you are a physical therapist, huh?

SYLVIA: …Yes I did…am…was…Have we ordered yet?

(NARRATOR shakes his head.)

HASSAN: I have a taste for champagne. What is your best champagne? Never mind, I will only drink Louis Roederer Cristal 2000. Do you have it?

NARRATOR: *(Sweetly.)* Why yes I do. *(Growls.)* I got it right here. *(Grabs his crotch.)*

(HASSAN, SYLVIA, and X, startled, look at him, look at each other, and look at the audience.)

SYLVIA: We should go.

HASSAN: Yes. *(Calls to NARRATOR.)* Where are we supposed to be next?

NARRATOR: Your apartment.

HASSAN: Good. Take us there, oh Great Genie.

X: Does this mean no dinner?

NARRATOR: And no tip. *(Takes off his apron.)* Do you need the car?

(HASSAN and SYLVIA shake their heads.)

HASSAN: *(To SYLVIA.)* I will call you tomorrow, my darling.

SYLVIA: Oh, but I'm coming with…aren't I?

X: Yes. Please.

HASSAN: *(To SYLVIA.)* You look so tired, my darling. It is not fair for me to take up so much of your time. I do not want you to get sick of me.

SYLVIA: I see.

HASSAN: You are my world. You are my queen.

(He kisses her on each cheek.)

HASSAN: I will talk to you tomorrow.

SYLVIA: I'm not very happy right now.

X: I want Sylvia to come too.

HASSAN: *(To SYLVIA, testily.)* Will you join us?

SYLVIA: Why yes. I think I will.

(X steps downstage to address the audience. HASSAN and SYLVIA stay upstage and stare at each other from either side of the chairs, which NARRATOR has lined up to become HASSAN's couch. NARRATOR makes the muffled sound of birds squawking.)

X: What am I doing in this scene? I don't know. Their flattery is shameless. And, shamelessly, I like it. Without Vincent, I feel lost and shaky. I have been a big whore since I was a pup but now, without my Vincenzo, I have no context. He was my family, my rock. Little Punkin is rolling down a cliff. Oh, I'm all over the place. BUT—a hot man with a big hard cock always gets my attention.

(SYLVIA and HASSAN look up, say something like "I hear that," and snap and look at each other again.)

X: *(Continues.)* I'm afraid to be alone with Hassan and something about Sylvia is getting to me She's like the Mona Lisa in Donna Karan. Between one thing and another, my juices are stirring and I feel, well, *alive! (Pause.)* I've got it. Hassan and I are on our first date and Sylvia is our chaperone. How civilized! She'll keep things from getting too jiggy too fast.

NARRATOR: *(Clears his throat.)* Scene: Hassan's apartment on East 50th Street between 2nd and 3rd.

X: *(To NARRATOR.)* Thank you. *(To SYLVIA.)* Jimmy will take me all the way back to New Jersey, right?

SYLVIA: Yes, my darling. Now come and sit next to me.

(X looks back at stage and sees that the apartment is set up. NARRATOR makes the sound of lovebirds screeching. X and SYLVIA cover their ears while HASSAN goes to the imaginary cage and talks baby talk to the BIRDS, which calm down and squawk more quietly.)

HASSAN: These are my babies. Baby One and Baby Two. *(To BIRDS.)* Love you. Love you.

(NARRATOR/BIRDS squawk back, eh-aw, eh-aw, he tosses in one quick "fuck you.")

HASSAN: Do you hear them? See how they love me? Love you.

X: Sounds like they're saying "fuck you."

SYLVIA: Oh, you are wicked!

HASSAN: *(To X.)* Come closer. Touch my face.

X: Yes, your majesty. Why?

HASSAN: Just do it!

(X stands up and reluctantly touches HASSAN's face. NARRATOR/BIRDS screech.)

HASSAN: See how much they love me? How much they watch out for me? Soon they will learn to love you too.

SYLVIA: Hassan! Stop that! Shut those goddam birds up!

HASSAN: Sylvia does not love my babies. But they love her.

SYLVIA: I hate them and they hate me. All they do is squawk, eat, and shit.

X: Are they parrots?

HASSAN: Like parrots. They are Conures. From South America. Very expensive.

X: Of course.

SYLVIA: Really, Hassan. You shouldn't invite people over when the place is such a mess.

HASSAN: Champagne?

(He snaps his fingers to NARRATOR. NARRATOR goes offstage and returns with three plastic glasses and brings them to the trio.)

SYLVIA: Hassan, really! Plastic?

HASSAN: *(He dismisses her with a wave.)* A toast. May we have everysing that we want!

(They all clink glasses.)

SYLVIA: And we want everything!

(HASSAN takes a picture out of his wallet. He sits next to X and drapes himself over him. He shows him the picture.)

HASSAN: My family. That is my brother Tarek, that is me, my brother Dris and my sister, Suzi. Aren't we beautiful?

SYLVIA: Hassan, you're shameless!

X: Suzi looks familiar.

HASSAN: She lives in New Jersey like you do. She has two babies. Do you know her?

X: I've seen her somewhere.

(HASSAN's cell phone rings. He answers it.)

HASSAN: Pablo, my friend! How are you?

X: Oh well. What's on TV? Ooh, *Top Chef*. This is a sad one. Where Jennifer gets eliminated.

SYLVIA: I never watch television... But I love those Voltaggio Brothers.

X: Me too! I'm waiting for Top Poet. Your challenge is to write a sonnet using the words entropy, bodacious, euthanasia, and gangsta. You have thirteen minutes... So, you were married?

SYLVIA: Oh, right to the point. Yes, I was Mrs. Doctor Milton Milstein, GP. We used to live in your neck of the woods. We had a baby girl. Unfortunately, kindly, concerned Doctor Milton Milstein was Doctor Milton Frankenstein at home, an abusive screamer with flying hands. After three years of that nightmare, I left him. I kissed my daughter goodbye, snuck out into the dark Jersey night, and caught the midnight bus to New York. I went through an ugly, ugly, ugly divorce and came away with nothing except a ruined life... Or so it seemed.

X: Looks like you landed on your feet. And you do physical therapy? You mean you rehabilitate accident victims or massage or...

SYLVIA: Hmmm. After school, I got a job in a nursing home but that wasn't for me. I am not a "caregiver." I don't care enough. Then I did massage. Along the way I learned I got bigger tips for happier endings.

X: My, my...

SYLVIA: How much do you want to know?

X: How much you got? Hit me.

SYLVIA: Don't jump ahead. Okay—fade out, fade in: little Sylvia, the masseuse, morphed into Mistress Samantha, the best thing to happen to bad boys.

X: She morphed, you say?

SYLVIA: She morphed, honey.

X: You bad girl.

SYLVIA: Oh yeah, you bad boy. Now, tell me about you, Mr. Billy Budd from Sparta.

X: I'm not sure what I'm doing here.

SYLVIA: You're having a lovely conversation with me, silly. Just relax. I wish I could read you. I'm sensing a lot of pain in there somewhere. And I know something about men and pain. Usually I'm the one causing it. You okay in there?

X: *(Pause.)* I've been having a rough time. Anyway, I hardly know you.

(SYLVIA pats his hand and her tone indicates she's changing the mood.)

SYLVIA: Well, drink up and let's have some fun.

X: *(To himself.)* When the drums come to your door
Do not try to shut them out. Do not turn away and resist them,
For they have come to tell you what you need to hear, they are your fate.

SYLVIA: Drums? What drums? Now you're scaring me.

X: It's from a poem I like by Edward Field. *(Snaps out of his reverie.)* Soooooo, what's up with the old lady? Who is she?

SYLVIA: We were talking about you.

X: I was just curious.

SYLVIA: That's another story for another day. *(To HASSAN.)* Get off the phone. You have company.

HASSAN: *(Puts his hand over the receiver.)* A millionaire from Argentina. He loves me and wants me to come live with him. He is married and very handsome. He gave me the babies.

X: Of course.

(X gets up and steps downstage. The lights upstage on HASSAN and SYLVIA dim. HASSAN remains on the phone and SYLVIA reads a magazine. X addresses the audience.)

X: Okay. This is getting weird. Big dick and all, Hassan is getting on my nerves and I'm losing momentum. Why am I here? What do they want from me? Sylvia is getting twitchy. Is she waiting to shoot up or something? Was I like that kid in *Trash*, you know, the Paul Morrissey movie with Joe Dallesandro and Holly Woodlawn. Have they lured me here to turn me into a junkie? Or are they twenty-first-century vampires, like a reduced-for-clearance David Bowie and Catherine Deneuve in *The Hunger* and I'm like Sarandon, you know, without the rack, the object of their bloodlust? Or is it just a plain sex thing? He can't get it up unless she watches or she can't squirt unless he's watching her? Are they recruiters for a cult, like the chanting-for-dollars NSA freaks or is it about Amway? Maybe it's all of the above. I have a feeling a move will be made and it won't be one I welcome. What I don't want most of all is for it to end *really* badly, you know with me in little pieces in two Hefty bags at the curb. Is that my fate?

(The upstage lights brighten. X goes back onto the couch.)

SYLVIA: *(Snaps her fingers.)* Where did you go just now? It's like you disappeared. You are a strange boy.

X: I'm a Libra. At this time every day I get messages from the home planet, Venus.

HASSAN: *(Ends the call.)* Oh! I have not even checked my messages. I have so many messages!

(He replays his messages. NARRATOR does the voices.)

NARRATOR: Hey bitch. Meet me at the Clown House at ten. Baby needs a new daddy and a new pair of shoes…BEEP Yo, this is Darnell. Where are you, be-aatch? Call me, ho!…BEEP It's Suzi. Tell my lowlife ex-husband he can see his kids on Sunday between two and six…BEEP Message number four:

(OZZIE pops out.)

OZZIE: Hi, it's Ozzie, thanks for the flowers and the…

(OZZIE pops back out.)

NARRATOR: BEEP

X: *(Stands up. To audience.)* Ozzie? *(To SYLVIA.)* Time to go.

HASSAN: Oh no. Not yet. I want to talk to you.

X: Another time.

HASSAN: *(To SYLVIA.)* He wants to go.

SYLVIA: So do I.

(HASSAN sits next to X and takes both of his hands in his. They are face to face. Though he is taller than X, he slumps so that he can look up at X beseechingly.)

HASSAN: You can stay with me tonight.

X: *(Trying to sound pleasant.)* No thank you.

SYLVIA: Come. Jimmy will drop me off. Then he can take you home.

X: You're sure?

SYLVIA: I promised.

(HASSAN holds X's hands.)

HASSAN: You do not like me. After everysing I do, you do not like me. All I want is for you to like me. I have men all over the world who offer me many sings to be with them, but I think only of you. You, who gives me nossing. Look at the flowers. A very rich man has sent them. He wants me to live with him and I sink only of you.

SYLVIA: Oh shut up!

X: Could you wait for me in the car?

SYLVIA: *(To HASSAN.)* Darling, stop babbling and let the poor man go.

(She kisses HASSAN on both cheeks. NARRATOR does the sound of the BIRDS screeching.)

SYLVIA: *(Covers her ears.)* Shut those damn things up!

(She throws on her shawl and comes offstage, walks up the aisle to the back of the house. VELMA appears at the back of the house. The two women struggle, and VELMA yanks the shawl from SYLVIA. She holds it up triumphantly and exits through the back of the house. SYLVIA follows her.)

VELMA: It's mine! *(Exits.)*

HASSAN: All I want is be alone with you but Sylvia is always wiss us and now you are angry.

(He wraps himself around X.)

X: I like Sylvia.

HASSAN: I love Sylvia but I do not want to fuck her. I want to fuck you. I want you in my bed all night and all morning.

X: I just need to go a little slower…

(HASSAN holds on tighter to X.)

HASSAN: Why? We are here now. I want you now. This is a beautiful shirt, so I will not tear it off you. Varvatos, yes?

X: Yes. It was a gift.

(X untangles himself from HASSAN's embrace.)

X: I need to slow down. Can we?...Why don't we sit for a bit and talk? You're from Morocco?

HASSAN: Yes. Morocco...

X: I've read about it. You know, Paul Bowles and that whole crowd. *The Sheltering Sky*. Janes Bowles is my favorite writer. It must be very beautiful.

HASSAN: Yes, it is very beautiful. I think about it every day. You are beautiful and now I think about you every day. Do you think about me?

X: Um, I'm thinking about you right now.

HASSAN: Yes? Good! I know everything I need to know. Come to my bedroom and lie down with me and I will show you everything I am thinking about. I cannot stand to be in these clothes anymore. I want to see you naked and spread out before me. Come!

X: I can't offer you very much right now. I'm at loose ends. *(Pause.)* I just lost someone and I don't think I'm ready to...

HASSAN: Because you could not hold onto one man has nossing to do with me. If you are a bad lover, I will teach you how to please me. My cock is big and my love is big and I am ready to share them with you. My heart tells me that you are the right one for me.

X: When the drums come to your door...

(HASSAN holds on tighter to X.)

HASSAN: That is not drums, my darling. Hold me. Just hold me. I do many sings for so many people and I cannot get this simple sing. One man to hold me.

(X puts his arms around HASSAN. He has been so lonely that he surprises himself by melting into the embrace. He puts his head on HASSAN's shoulder and tears spring to his eyes.)

X: Yes, Daddy.

HASSAN: I feel like I belong to you.

X: *(Grimly. His body stiffens.)* No one belongs to anyone.

(HASSAN lets go of X and stumbles backwards as if punched. He recovers his composure.)

HASSAN: You are a very stupid man.

X: No, I'm not.

HASSAN: You should not say no to me. I do not like it.

X: Nobody likes it but it happens. I have to go.

HASSAN: Now I see you. I really see you. You are pleasing to look at but you are not young. You are teasing me. You are playing with me because that is all you know how to do. You know nossing about life. There is nossing inside you. I am like a painter trying to paint these beautiful colors on you but there is nossing for them to hold onto, the colors just run off. Your big sad eyes are empty, they only look inside and they see nossing. You are not kind, not *simpatico*...

(Sound effect: HASSAN's cell phone rings. HASSAN stands up and answers the phone. He waves X away.)

HASSAN: *(On phone.)* Hello? Oh it's you...Yes, my darling...Yes, my darling...

X: *(To audience. He shudders.)* What the fuck! Well I did get sliced up and left in a Hefty bag after all. I wonder what would have happened if we had fucked? Is he right? Is it true? I don't know what the truth is. But is he accurate? There is accuracy in there. Something to think about. *(Shakes his head and exits.)*

(HASSAN exits. NARRATOR rearranges the couch into the fake limo configuration again, chairs facing audience, this time two in front and two in back. JIMMY enters and sits in the "driver's seat." SYLVIA enters and sits behind him.)

SYLVIA: I'll kill that bitch!

(X enters stage right and sits beside SYLVIA.)

X: Thanks for waiting. You okay?

SYLVIA: Yes, just a little tired.

X: Where's your shawl?

SYLVIA: Oh, I must have left it upstairs. Home, James! I just love saying that.

X: I won't be seeing Hassan again.

SYLVIA: I'm very sorry about that. I hope you and I can still be friends.

X: Sure.

SYLVIA: That would be lovely. *(Pause.)* Hassan is such a fool!

X: What's in it for you?

(JIMMY smiles.)

SYLVIA: *(Takes a long time to answer. She is either thinking of the right thing to say or distracted.)* You're very sweet.

(She squeezes his hand.)

NARRATOR: Our cruise through the glamorous Upper East Side continues up First Avenue, past the sixties, the seventies, eighties. We make a left turn off First onto 93rd Street. There is a faux luxury tower on the corner, but the car passes it and glides down the shabby block. It stops in front of one of a row of run-down five-story tenements.

SYLVIA: I'll call you. Safe home.

(She kisses X on the cheek. SYLVIA and JIMMY exit the pretend car. VELMA enters from stage left. She is wearing SYLVIA's shawl around her head, over the babushka.)

VELMA: Hurry up. I lost my keys. I gotta pee.

SYLVIA: This time next week you'll be in Bellevue, peeing in a paper cup, old woman.

VELMA: Just open the door, you fucking whore! Hurry up!

(She reaches for SYLVIA's purse.)

VELMA: Give me those keys, you tramp!

SYLVIA: Oh, no you don't!

(She pushes VELMA away. VELMA pushes back and manages to get the keys from SYLVIA.)

VELMA: I'm two for two!

(The stage goes dark except for a pin light on SYLVIA.)

SYLVIA: *(To audience.)* That old bag is my mother and yes, she's crazy. I never knew my father. Mommy hinted that it's either Robert Moses, Nelson Rockefeller, or Burt Lancaster. I've decided it was Burt. Mommy was a looker in her time and I had many generous "uncles." I was the original latchkey kid. I learned to take care of myself while my mother swanned in and out, with her perfume and whichever uncle's cigar smoke lingering in the air. I daydreamed about being a real Mommy, a Betty Crocker Mommy in an apron, baking mountains of chocolate chip cookies for my four kids.

I was such a good little girl. With no religion that I knew of, I begged to go to a Catholic school. Mr. Moses, Mr. Rockefeller, or Mr. Lancaster paid for it. Let's say it was Burt. I wanted the structure and the uniform. Then I became a doctor's wife with a baby girl and I was bored out of my mind. I wasn't much of a housekeeper and I can't cook for shit. And I have no maternal instincts whatsoever. Things were tense. I made a salad one night and Milton picked at it, picked up a tomato, and said, "What the fuck is this? You call this a tomato?" "No, I call it a *tomahto*," I said and Bap! He bitch slapped me. I made a note to myself to leave him or kill him. Then we were driving to his mother's house one day. We got stuck in traffic. I said, "We should have taken the Parkway." Bap! Another slap. I got through the visit with the in-laws and that night after he was asleep, I left. I made a deal to never see my daughter again. I wasn't happy about that at the time but there was cash involved so I kept my trap shut. I heard she got married last year. Good luck, honey. I wish I could say there was an ache in my heart about all that...but there isn't. That's my kind of Hallmark card: I wish I cared but I don't.

Anyway, I'm busy. I keep myself busy. I have all these parties to go to. Hassan can be a pain in the ass and an expensive one but I get to dress up and go out. And if people wonder about us, fuck it. I'm having a good time. I'm riding this train till it stops and then I'll do something else. And if I need a little bump, there's Jimmy. He's already on the payroll. It beats singles night at the temple and it's better than sitting home watching TV with Mommy. Her only gentleman caller these days is Mr. Jack Daniels.

(Spotlight upstage. NARRATOR places a chair centerstage. VELMA waddles out and sits in it. She is wearing the shawl around her shoulders now and no babushka. She looks less shabby. Sound effect: the sound of a moving subway train.)

VELMA: I was the most beautiful woman in New York. I could have any man I wanted. Well, I wanted them...and I had them. I knew some of the big guys, famous names in their time, names I can't mention. I have been compensated for my silence.

NARRATOR: *(As a conductor, a little garbled.)* This is a Brooklyn-bound N train. Next stop 34th Street.

VELMA: I'm a New York girl, born in Corona. One of my neighbors was plain, dumpy Esther Mentzer. She admired my flawless complexion, my thick lustrous hair, my fine coloring. She asked me for all my beauty tips, poor sad creature. After she stole all my ideas, she changed her name to Estée Lauder. Maybe you heard of her.

NARRATOR: *(As the conductor. Garbled.)* This is a broken-down N train. Next stop Dirty Whore Street.

VELMA: What?

NARRATOR: I said, this is a broken-down N train. Next stop Dirty Whore Street!

VELMA: You talking to me?

NARRATOR: Your name Velma?

VELMA: Yeah?

NARRATOR: Then I'm talking to you.

VELMA: You calling me a dirty whore?

NARRATOR: Yeah. This is your stop, you dirty whore. You didn't know Estée Lauder.

VELMA: Maybe I did. Maybe I didn't. Shit. Where am I?

NARRATOR: Thirty-fourth street.

VELMA: Okey dokey. *(She gets up, puts the shawl around her head, starts to say something. She turns to NARRATOR.)* Line!

NARRATOR: Please help me, I'm hungry.

VELMA: Right. *(She turns her face into the sad clown one.)* Please help me, I'm hungry. Please help me. *(To NARRATOR.)* Is this all I say?

NARRATOR: Yep.

VELMA: I don't get a monologue?

NARRATOR: Nope.

VELMA: Shit. Okay. Am I crazy? Tomato/potato. I just like to be naughty sometimes. Shake things up. If I'm a quiet little old lady nobody notices me. You gotta make some noise. I might even get a tambourine. *(Pause.)* Nah. I need two hands free. One for asking *(Does the please help me gesture.)* and one for grabbing. I like to keep Sylvie on her toes. If I'm too quiet I know she'll ship me off somewhere.

(NARRATOR clears his throat.)

VELMA: Okay, okay. Let me leave you with this thought. *(To the audience, warmly, grandmotherly.)* If you see something…kill someone. If you see something…kill someone. *(She exits.)*

SYLVIA: That's my mommy! Well, the rotten apple doesn't fall too far from the dead tree. *(Imitates her.)* Please help me, I'm hungry. Please help me. *(As herself.)* If you see her, ignore her. That cow isn't hungry, believe me. So back to me. Mistress Samantha is semi-retired these days. I have other interests and other means. *(Pause.)* All right. Full disclosure. You see, Mommy owns this building…and the one next to it…and the one next to that. It was a package deal. In her day gentlemen gave their mistresses the gift of real estate. Sometimes she knows that but usually she doesn't. She had a stroke a few years ago and I moved in to take care of her. As a doctor's ex-wife, I keep her medicated enough and she keeps herself lubricated enough so that everything is blurry enough to keep her off balance. I have control of the funds and the keys to the kingdom. I'm just waiting for the day when she shuffles in front of a fleet of speeding garbage trucks. Or just doesn't wake up. There's another Hallmark card: Get hit by a garbage truck, you old bag. I'll wait. I have to put up with being called a whore, but that's a price I can pay. Am I a whore? I don't know. Tomato/to*mah*to.

VELMA: *(Stage left.)* Sylvie! What's keeping you? Come and watch *Letterman* with Mama.

SYLVIA: In a minute.

VELMA: *(Offstage.)* He's got on Denzel Washington! We got any of those cupcakes left, the red velvet ones from Two Little Red Hens?

SYLVIA: I think so. Hang on a second and I'll check.

VELMA: Thanks, doll. Oh, and bring Mama a nice little glass of schnapps. Hurry, Denzel just walked out.

SYLVIA: *(To audience.)* Potato/potahto. *(She pastes on a big fake smile. To VELMA.)* Coming, Mother! *(Exits.)*

(Lights go up on the ersatz car. X is still sitting in the backseat. JIMMY is in the front seat.)

JIMMY: And that's just round one. Nine more to go.

(He turns to X and holds out his hand.)

JIMMY: I'm Jimmy Dempsey. Where to, Chief?

X: I don't know if Sylvia told you, but I'm going to New Jersey.

JIMMY: Whatever, Chief. Just tell me where.

X: Cedar Chips. It's right off Route 46.

JIMMY: I know it well, Chief. Just tell me which street.

X: You've been to Cedar Chips?

JIMMY: This job takes me a lot of places. This is my favorite time to drive in this town. I like it after midnight when things get nice and dicey. You know, I used to live in Jersey. I managed a video store in West Caldwell. But I was married to the bitch from hell. Oh yeah.

X: You're married?

JIMMY: No more, I'm proud to say. The bride got the twins and the house in West Caldwell. That's what happens when you marry into the wrong tribe. Time to refuel. *(He takes an airline-size bottle of vodka out of one pocket, takes the cap off, and half-heartedly offers X a swig.)* You don't mind, do you?

(Before X can respond, he downs it and tosses the bottle.)

X: Um, I don't want to be a narc but, you know, DUI.

JIMMY: Huh? Do I what? Where's my backup? *(Pats his pockets, finds another little bottle.)*

X: Hey, there are cops on every corner.

JIMMY: Fuck it. Hold up. How about a toast? *(Raises the bottle.)* Whoops...that was red.

X: Jesus!

JIMMY: May we have everything we want! *(Drains the bottle, tosses it.)*

X: And we want everything?

JIMMY: Exactly. So, how long you know the Gold Dust Twins?

X: Not long. And you?

JIMMY: Long enough. I used to be married to Hassan's sister, the bitch. And then, I was sitting in Rudy's on Ninth, my hangout, and Hassan and Sylvia breezed in, all in diamonds and furs, and swooped down on me. They bought me drinks and offered me a job. I needed the bucks, so I took it...I don't get paid to think, just to drive and you know, "whatnot." Alls I know is the money's good. I can't say nothing, because now I'm in the soup.

X: The soup?

JIMMY: Let's just say it's loaded with cabbage.

(JIMMY'S cell phone rings. He pulls it off his belt and answers it.)

JIMMY: Jimmy. Uh huh. Uh huh. Uh huh. Uh huh, uh huh, uh huh. I think I can handle that. I'll just put it on my timesheet. Yes, your majesty. No, your majesty. I have not been drinking. Yes, I will drive safely, your majesty. *(Puts the phone in his pocket.)*

X: Who was that?

JIMMY: Queen Elizabeth.

(He tousles X's hair.)

JIMMY: You're a real sweetheart, you know that? Shit, I'm still thirsty. *(Pats the chair next to him.)* Chief, why don't you sit up front with me? It makes me feel less like a stooge.

X: *(Looks at audience and rolls his eyes with pleasure, as if he may get lucky.)* Okay. But shouldn't we pull over first?

JIMMY: Nah, just get your ass up here.

(X sits next to JIMMY.)

NARRATOR: Scene: The Lincoln Tunnel.

JIMMY: No offense, Chief, but I hate going back to Jersey. That bitch is sitting in my house, yanking my chain long distance. Sometimes I want to ram this hearse right into a wall. *(He steps on the fake accelerator.)*

X: But not tonight. Right?

JIMMY: It's not worth it, is it? It would give them too much satisfaction.

X: Exactly.

JIMMY: Alls I wanted was to manage the video store, but it was always jump, jump, jump! Well, I was tired of kissing the old man's ass and I said so. You don't fuck with that tribe. I learned the hard way. They ran me out of the business. The bride turned on me. I had to get out of town. Everybody warned me, but I didn't listen. Respect, that's what it's all about. Know what I mean?

X: I think so.

JIMMY: I thought I was free of that mob, but now I'm in the soup.

X: The cabbage soup?

JIMMY: Right. How tight are you with the Gold Dust Twins?

X: I'm through with them.

JIMMY: Good.

NARRATOR: Scene: We exit the Lincoln Tunnel and go up the helix. Imagine sparkling Manhattan.

X: *(To audience.)* That skyline. I remember this ride so many times with Vincent, coming home from a night in the city in his Cadillac. We always felt solid and connected in the car, had our most intimate conversations within its leather and velour plush. It was the quiet reward for staying together.

JIMMY: You say something?

X: No.

JIMMY: You okay?

(He squeezes X's arm.)

X: Yes. *(To audience.)* I can see Jimmy in his high school yearbook, bright eyed and smiling or in a family portrait, the picture-perfect husband in his good suit, with his arm around Hassan's tough, pretty sister and the two kids, Kevin and Abdul. On Sunday mornings, he washed the car in his driveway, barefoot in cut-off jeans. He still has the twinkle of a horny altar boy.

JIMMY: I just want to build up a stake and start my own business, then I'll dump those two.

X: What do you want to do?

JIMMY: Limos. That's where the bucks are today. And porn. Now my idea is: Sex Limos. See? Everybody remembers getting laid in the backseat of a car, right? Sex and wheels, that's America! So what if there's this fleet of stretch limos with roomy backseats and mirrored windows? And at your fingertips you got champagne, rubbers, lotions, vibrators. And there's a sliding panel, so if you want the driver to watch, he can. And you get your choice of drivers, a hot-looking man or woman. So, this limo is cruising all over town and the customers are getting off in the backseat and that's part of the rush—getting off in front of the Guggenheim or the Empire State Building or in the middle of Times Square. And the driver's watching, if you want. Or joining in, but that's extra. And, the whole thing is being videotaped! At the end of the ride, the driver hands you your DVD and you're the star! What do you think?

X: There's probably a market for it.

JIMMY: You think so?

X: Sure. Why don't you try it out with this hearse when you're not on duty. Put an ad in the *Voice*, get on Craigslist, and see what kind of response you get.

JIMMY: Chief, I like the way you think. Maybe you and me could be partners.

X: It's not for me.

JIMMY: I bet I could talk you into it. You smoke?

X: Yeah, but I don't have any smokes on me. Do you?

JIMMY: Yeah. In my jacket. Can you reach in and grab them?

X: Sure.

(Goes through JIMMY's pockets.)

X: What's this? *(He pulls out a small black revolver.)* Shit! *(He shoves it back into one of the pockets.)*

JIMMY: Job security, Chief. You know, just in case.

X: In case of what?

JIMMY: Don't ask. I told you, I'm in the soup.

X: I don't know what that means.

JIMMY: So, what's your story? Who's waiting for you at home?

X: Nobody.

JIMMY: Nobody? A sweetheart like you? That's hard to believe.

X: You get off at the Grove Street exit.

JIMMY: I know. You're very easy to talk to. You know that?

(He turns to X and smiles. He slips his hand over X's and holds it.)

X: Thanks. Make a right at the light, then it's six blocks up.

JIMMY: Okay. I bet we could have a good time. Is there someplace we can get a drink around here?

X: I've got a bottle of Jameson's upstairs.

JIMMY: Excellent. You're making me hard. Besides, I got to pee.

NARRATOR: Scene: A spare studio apartment in an ugly tower on Cedar Boulevard.

(X and JIMMY exit the fake car. NARRATOR moves the fake car chairs and sets them up upstage, facing stage left. He gives X bottle of Jameson's. X hands the bottle to JIMMY. JIMMY grabs his arm.)

X: *(To NARRATOR.)* Do I have any glasses?

(NARRATOR shrugs.)

JIMMY: Glasses? Glasses? We don't need no stinking glasses. Gimme the fucking bottle.

(He takes a good long swig, then licks his lips. He's feeling the glow. He hands the bottle to X.)

JIMMY: Now you.

(X takes a swig and shudders at the sting.)

JIMMY: You thirsty, baby? (Pause.) Or hungry? Gimme. *(He takes the bottle and takes another long swig.)*

(X has been standing but now he sits next to JIMMY.)

JIMMY: Not so fast. Stand up. Take another belt.

(X complies.)

JIMMY: Yeah. Got that fire in your belly?

(X nods.)

JIMMY: Now turn around for me, baby. Nice and slow.

(X turns slowly, a little buzzed. When he turns toward the audience he mugs, "Oh boy" or "What the fuck" or a combo of both.)

JIMMY: Nice. Very nice. You trust me, baby?

X: Fuck no.

JIMMY: *(Laughs.)* Good boy. Now take your shirt off for me.

(X takes off his shirt, tosses it on the floor.)

JIMMY: Give me another twirl, baby. Oh yeah. Now take off your pants.

X: Um…

(JIMMY hands X the bottle.)

JIMMY: Take another swig. Relax. Slip out of your pants for me, baby.

(X slowly takes his pants off. He is wearing briefs.)

JIMMY: That's nice. Very nice. Turn around for me, nice and slow. Wait. Take off one sock.

X: Just one?

JIMMY: *(Nods.)* Good boy. Now give me a nice, slow twirl.

(X complies. When he turns toward the audience he rolls his eyes.)

JIMMY: Sweet! You wanna take care of me, baby?

X: I might…

JIMMY: You a good boy or a bad boy? *(He gestures for X to give him another twirl.)*

X: *(Turns slowly, faces audience.)* I can go either way. Depends on the personnel.

JIMMY: Nice. Now get down on all fours, poochy boy.

(X gets down on all fours, facing away from JIMMY. He is hesitant but turned on.)

JIMMY: Now that's a pretty sight.

X: Yeah?

JIMMY: Oh yeah. *(He takes off his jacket, takes the gun out of his pocket, and puts it on the adjoining chair. He undoes his belt.)*

(Blackout.)

X: *(In the dark.)* Yikes!

(Lights slowly fade up. We find X on the ground, his head turned away from us. He slowly turns his head toward the audience.)

VELMA, SYLVIA, and HASSAN stand upstage.)

NARRATOR: We're thirteen miles from Manhattan, in a studio apartment in Cedar Gardens, right on Cedar Boulevard, in beautiful Cedar Chips, New Jersey.

X: Helllllllllooooooo. I'm not dead. I'm just a little tired. *(He stands.)* Jimmy was gone in twenty minutes. He took the whiskey and twenty dollars for gas for the way home. I'm not proud of myself but at least it's not another night in front of the TV. *(To NARRATOR.)* How about you? Before I close up shop, you wanna piece of me?

(NARRATOR shakes his head, indicates X should be talking to the audience.)

X: *(Softly.)* Please help me, I'm hungry. Please help me. I've fallen through the cracks of my own life and nobody seems to hear me. Am I even calling for help? Or am I just talking to myself?

(VELMA exits.)

X: I miss my Vincenzo so much. His wake and funeral were like a big, silly opera with his family wailing arias every second. His family ignored me. I was the guy who lived in Vincent's house for eighteen years. I felt all crushed and small. I looked around for Vincent, so I could roll my eyes at him and get back his big, brown gaze. But *(Pause.)* ...and I couldn't go near the casket. That wasn't my Vincent. I stood in front of the funeral home, smoking and smoking. I couldn't stay in there and I couldn't leave. That's when Punkin fell through the cracks. Punkin.

None of our friends, my friends, showed up. They left lame messages and sent lame emails. At least Ozzie sent flowers. It was all a little too real for them and made me wonder, what is a friend anyway? Have I ever really had one? Except for Vincent, I've just *known* people. A sad little door opened and I went through it and sat there all numb and dead inside. Sylvia said when she left her husband she wandered around in a daze, doing very stupid things. *(Holds out his arms.)* Ta da!

(SYLVIA exits.)

X: I want to feel the way I feel until I don't feel that way anymore. It's grief. I'm grieving. It's not a lifestyle choice, a mood to be enhanced. It's a deep black river of feeling that needs to flow where it flows. I will wrap myself in a black shawl and wallow in my deep voluptuous sadness. Wail and wail and wail until I just can't stand it anymore.

"I feel like I belong to you," I'm sorry, baby, but I don't even belong to me right now.

(HASSAN exits.)

X: I just met all these new people and because I didn't talk much, they pasted all kinds of expectations on me. They couldn't stop talking about themselves and telling me who they were.

Well, who the fuck am I? Nobody from Nowhere. In all the excitement nobody ever asked me my name. *(Clears his throat.)* Hello, my name is Carlos Quinn Azzopardi. *(With a sweep of his hands to the whole audience.)* What's yours? *(He singles out someone sitting in the front row.)* Seriously. My name is Carlos. What's yours? (Hopefully the person responds—if they are close enough, CARLOS shakes hands.)* Hello. It's good to meet you. Oh, that was nice.

I'm going to try living moment by moment for a while. Whatever living means. All I know is: we're here and then we're not here. So, right now, I'm here. Some of those moments back there, well they weren't good moments. This moment right now where you're looking at me and I'm looking at you, well, I'm loving this moment. Thank you.

NARRATOR: *(To audience.)* Thank you and good night.

(END OF PLAY.)

FLORIDITA, MY LOVE

Javierantonio González

JAVIERANTONIO GONZÁLEZ was born in Hato Rey, Puerto Rico, on January 28, 1980. He grew up in Vega Baja, on the north shore of Puerto Rico, in a lower-middle class neighborhood facing the ocean. He holds a BA in theatre from the University of Puerto Rico in Río Piedras and an MFA in directing from Columbia University. While at UPR, Javier studied playwriting and directing with Arístides Vargas, founder and artistic director of the group Malayerba (Ecuador). At Columbia, he studied directing with Brian Kulick and Anne Bogart. Javier directs the plays he writes, which have included *Barceloneta, de noche* (Union Theatre, London/Teatro La Tea/IATI, 2008–10), *Las minutas de Martí* (Repertorio Español, 2010), *Un instante en una especie de flash* (Yerbabruja, Puerto Rico, 2008), *Uneventful Deaths for Agathon* (New York International Fringe Festival, 2006), and *Never as Happy—The Oresteia* (Theatre of the Riverside Church, 2006). He is currently a member of the Emerging Writers Group at the Public Theatre and a Van Lier Directing Fellow at Repertorio Español. Javier was selected as one of nytheatre.com's People of the Year in 2010. He teaches and designs the theatre curriculum at DreamYard Preparatory High School in the Bronx. Javier resides in Prospect/Crown Heights, Brooklyn.

FLORIDITA, my Love was first presented by Caborca Theatre (Javierantonio González, Artistic Director) on July 8, 2010, at Teatro IATI, New York City, with the following cast and credits:

Floridita	Veraalba Santa
Death/Sofía/Child 2	Tania Molina
Sor Juana/Milagros/Pregnant Woman	Yaremis Félix
Hoffman/Child 1/Manuel	Jorge Luna
García/Severio/Aguilú	Ricardo Hinoa
Adolfo/Pepo	David Skeist
Perhaps a Dead Man/Liberty Enlightening the World	Marcos Toledo

Direction: Javierantonio González
Set and Costume Design: Jian Jung
Lighting Design: Marlon Hurt
Sound Design: Jorge Luna
Stage Management: Erin Koster
Assistant Stage Manager: Pedro Leopoldo Sánchez-Tormes

FLORIDITA, my Love is the second production of Caborca Theatre. It had its first workshop at INTAR Theater, as part of the New Voices Playwriting Series. It premiered as part of Theatro IATI's Performing Arts Marathon in 2010 and was part of Caborca's repertory, *2 Ways to Die in the Fall* at Teatro LaTEA.

FLORIDITA, my Love was loosely inspired by the play *300 Million* by Roberto Arlt.

CHARACTERS

FLORIDITA

DEATH

SOR JUANA

PREGNANT WOMAN

HOFFMAN

GARCÍA

ADOLFO

PERHAPS A DEAD MAN

SEVERIO

LIBERTY ENLIGHTENING THE WORLD, AKA THE STATUE OF LIBERTY

CHILDREN

Mexican Immigrants: MANUEL, AGUILÚ, SOFÍA, MILAGROS, PEPO

SETTING

Manhattan. Today. The downtown platform on the 1 subway station at 125th Street and Broadway. The play moves freely through many different spaces and times, which can be suggested on and around the platform. The station, however, should always remain present as the primary location of the play.

NOTE

Although divided into twenty-one events, *FLORIDITA, my Love* should be performed without interruptions between scenes. It was written as one long scene in which the divisions are only made to facilitate the rehearsal process.

1

FLORIDITA is sitting, a green suitcase next to her. She has all the reasons in the world to be nervous but she is not; she has all the reasons to cry but she doesn't. When alone, FLORIDITA addresses the audience.

FLORIDITA: Tonight's the night.

(FLORIDITA opens the suitcase. A green light glows inside of it. Walking, or more like floating on high heels, fabulous, dressed in green and pink, DEATH enters. She sits next to FLORIDITA.)

DEATH: Fuck! It's so cold out here. Why did it have to be outdoors? There are so many stations, some even with pretty little sculptures. Look at you. So indifferent. You sure are the cold kind. Not even a hello or a look. If you had at least made me some coffee. Black would've been fine. I don't love dairy. Or water at least. For me, who loves you dearly. Answer me!

FLORIDITA: What time is it?

DEATH: 1:07.

FLORIDITA: The trains are so slow at this time.

DEATH: Desperate? One minute more one minute less…what difference does it make? It doesn't make any difference.

FLORIDITA: A minute can be a long time.

DEATH: Really? For whom?

FLORIDITA: For anyone with this much imagination. For some, a minute could be everything.

DEATH: You're very rude, for a waitress, you know. You bring me to a cold station, you don't have me a cup of coffee, and when I arrive you turn optimistic about life. Luxuriously you look at your future waiting to see if it's got something else for you. Cheap vanity because your future has nothing more for you than this cold. And this silence. You're skinny and you smell so bad. If at least you'd smell good, I'd be happy. But you stink. If you were rich you wouldn't smell so bad. Are you going to look at me or not?

(FLORIDITA looks at her.)

DEATH: Why so shocked? You didn't expect Death to look so hot, did you? Look, I'm even wearing stockings. This is a great occasion. Death should be celebrated, even more than a birthday. It's a shame you don't have any friends left to celebrate with. You know, for a little dancing, some wine, sweat.

FLORIDITA: Why do you talk so much? I don't need you. I can die by myself. You're more like a midwife, so much chatter.

DEATH: But my child, what I do is pretty much the same as giving birth. I help a few to leave so that others can arrive. It's very mathematical. I'm here because you've called me many times and today I've decided to finally listen. It is my duty to entertain you, to speak and ask you: Are you sure?

FLORIDITA: No. I want to live.

DEATH: Then be as you wish. People die really when they want to. Those who want to live, live. They crawl, but live. Why don't you get yourself an old sugar daddy who can protect you? With that body you could get yourself a nice husband. Can I see you naked?

FLORIDITA: You will see me naked, when they take my body off the tracks.

DEATH: Then see you later, gruesome bitch. *(Pause.)* If you hadn't worked so long you could've lived many years. Work eats your soul away. And yet there are worse things.

FLORIDITA: Like what?

DEATH: It's so cold out. Why don't you get yourself an old daddy? Old men are horny and feed well. You just have to let them see you naked and touch you from time to time. If you were rich, this wouldn't be happening to you. *(Exits.)*

2

HOFFMAN enters. He looks like a detective taken out of a film noir. He talks to FLORIDITA as if he was talking to an FBI agent, his therapist, or both.

HOFFMAN: While a student at the School of Journalism at Columbia University a couple of years ago, on a morning of November, I was sent to write an article on the suicide of a Hispanic waitress for my Reality and Counterreality class. She was twenty years old and killed herself jumping on the tracks of the 1 train, at the station on 125th street, in front of Floridita, the restaurant where she used to work, at five in the morning. When I first heard about it, I laughed not because I'm cold, but because the name of the victim, do you call a suicide a victim?, I think so, a suicide victim. Anyway her name was Floridita, the same as the restaurant. That was weird. It sounded like a silly yet dark, dark joke or fairy tale. By the time I got there (I was still laughing), the body, in pieces, was already on its way to the morgue. Perhaps I wouldn't be telling you this if it weren't for the fact that further investigation brought me to two details about her death. One, García, the manager of Floridita, the restaurant, said that Floridita, the waitress, left early the night before, at around seven p.m. He saw her going up the stairs into the train station, around 7:03 p.m. But the waitress didn't jump onto the tracks until the morning after, at exactly 5:02 a.m. The other detail is that she had with her a plane ticket to Bolivia for that same morning. A ticket that was never used. The combination of these two details left a very painful mark on me. I walked for several months with the image of a young immigrant, dressed in her waitress uniform, sitting silently on a bench, plane ticket on her lap, deciding what her future was going to be. A decision that took more than eight hours.

3

FLORIDITA is at the restaurant called Floridita. She serves invisible customers. She brings and takes plates away, brings the checks, cleans tables, brings menus, collects tips, etc. All of this with a pleasant smile. A Mexican soap opera plays on the restaurant's TV. SOR JUANA enters.

SOR JUANA: So you are the little immigrant. I don't know why but I imagined you just like that.

FLORIDITA: Excuse me.

SOR JUANA: Thelittleimmigrant, thegirlwithnoland, theforgottenone.

FLORIDITA: What are you saying? Here we are all immigrants.

SOR JUANA: But you are the one who got here by herself, all alone. You were born on a boat, your mother died at sea, and yet you survived four days on your own. Something like Elián González, but with no family waiting on the other shore. I remember your story. Fifteen days of fame, give or take a day or two, and then what? A waitress. Mmh, not exactly what you would expect after that poignant arrival to the U.S. You like it here? Be honest.

FLORIDITA: It's alright.

SOR JUANA: Humble, like a Mexican, and yet, something's off, isn't it? Something doesn't quite match the equation. Something's missing. Something... something... You possess a heart of gold, you've read many books, more than most people of your kind, and therefore you dare to dream higher than the rest. This isn't exactly what you imagined. Or am I wrong?

FLORIDITA: How do you know all this about me?

SOR JUANA: Because that's what I do. I've devoted my life to defending women in trouble. Like you.

FLORIDITA: Sor Juana? You can't fool me, you don't look like Sor Juana.

SOR JUANA: You mean I don't look like America Ferrera. Which is good, I'm not complaining. Look at me carefully; don't I look like the original, the one you imagined carving all of those subversive poems? The original, the one you imagined signing her name in blood?

FLORIDITA: Oh my god. This can't be. You in person? What brought you here? How did you arrive?

SOR JUANA: You know what I'm like, I don't explain myself.

FLORIDITA: You don't explain yourself. I adore you. I've read all of your poems and essays.

SOR JUANA: Even the *Complete Works* with a prologue by Octavio Paz?

FLORIDITA: Yes.

SOR JUANA: Hard cover?

FLORIDITA: Mm huh.

SOR JUANA: In English?

FLORIDITA: And Spanish. The bilingual version.

SOR JUANA: That's impressive! A waitress who actually spends her time lost in fine literature.

FLORIDITA: I would read them again, if I still had them. They were stolen from me.

SOR JUANA: Of course they were.

FLORIDITA: But that didn't matter because the memory of your *Complete Works* followed me everywhere.

SOR JUANA: *The Complete Works of Sor Juana Inés de la Cruz.* Prologued by Octavio Paz. Have you ever heard of another female writer who's had her *Complete Works* prologued by Octavio Paz?

FLORIDITA: Um—

SOR JUANA: None.

FLORIDITA: None.

SOR JUANA: You know I'm considered the mother of all Mexican poets?

FLORIDITA: Of course.

SOR JUANA: Every day thousands of people are born and another thousand die and no one writes a word about them. But Octavio Paz, the Mexican poet *par excellence*, wrote a prologue about my *Complete Works*.

FLORIDITA: Plus the movie.

SOR JUANA: That movie was trash! Not a single Hollywood director can contain the relentlessness of a liberal nun fighting the Mexican Roman Catholic Church, not one. Damned Hollywood producers who always find a way to take a good, profound story and make it a piece of shit…a piece of shit… *(SOR JUANA cannot speak any longer. She's almost in tears.)*

FLORIDITA: *(Serving her a glass of water.)* At least they made them. That means that not only intellectuals will know about you but also those who cannot read. Hollywood is everywhere. It even makes more money in Asia than it does here. All Asians know about you.

SOR JUANA: But America Ferrera?

FLORIDITA: At least she was funny.

SOR JUANA: You're right. You poor people sure know how to look at the bright side of everything. Anyway, I didn't come here to talk about myself but to bring you great news. You've received an inheritance.

FLORIDITA: What do you mean?

SOR JUANA: Are you deaf? An inheritance. Money. Mucho dinero.

FLORIDITA: That's impossible, I don't have any family…

SOR JUANA: Three hundred thousand!

FLORIDITA: *(Hands to her mouth, screaming.)* Three hundred thousand?!

SOR JUANA: Ahem…excuse me. Did I say three hundred thousand? I meant three hundred million.

(Long silence.)

FLORIDITA: Three hundred million?

SOR JUANA: Uh huh.

FLORIDITA: I don't know what to say, I…I need to sit down.

SOR JUANA: Here. Sit. Join me. You are no longer a waitress at a second-class restaurant. You are the poor little immigrant who's made it, miraculously, but made it.

FLORIDITA: *(Sits down.)* I can't take this.

SOR JUANA: You can't take it? Dear, the Mexican poet *par excellence* prologued my *Complete Works* and I can take it quite well.

FLORIDITA: But a prologue is not three hundred million.

SOR JUANA: Please, can you compare the vulgar quantity of three hundred million with a prologue, even more, a wonderful, poetical prologue by Octavio Paz? Any salesman from New Jersey can collect three hundred million on a Black Friday. Sign the receipt.

FLORIDITA: Where?

SOR JUANA: Here.

(FLORIDITA signs. SOR JUANA gives her a check.)

SOR JUANA: Because you see, fate takes very unusual turns.

4

FLORIDITA is sitting. Frozen. ADOLFO enters.

ADOLFO: Floridita! Floridita! Is there a waitress here known as Floridita?

FLORIDITA: Yes. I am she.

ADOLFO: *(Mocking her pronunciation.)* She?

FLORIDITA: Floridita.

ADOLFO: Am I allowed to tell you that I love you?

FLORIDITA: I'm sorry?

ADOLFO: Don't be sorry. I just can't contain myself, so I will say it again: Am I allowed to tell you that I love you?

FLORIDITA: Who are you and what do you want from me?

ADOLFO: Isn't it obvious? I am a man. A common man who happens to be in love with you and who won't leave this restaurant until he has taken you as his wife.

(She slaps him in the face. He takes it.)

FLORIDITA: Sorry, I was just checking. This is too much like a García Márquez novel or a dream.

ADOLFO: It is. Not a novel. Certainly not *Love in the Time of Cholera*. But a dream. A dream come true.

FLORIDITA: And yet it feels so real.

ADOLFO: Why question it then? If it feels real it's real.

FLORIDITA: Who talks like that?

ADOLFO: Oh, come on, don't pretend you are not used to this. I'm sure you get this sort of proposal every day.

FLORIDITA: No, never.

ADOLFO: Then I'm sorry if I'm not what you expected. Can I have my check?

FLORIDITA: You didn't order anything.

ADOLFO: Oh, can I have a coffee then?

FLORIDITA: Sure.

(She serves him coffee.)

ADOLFO: Can I have my check now?

(She gives him his check. He pays. He's about to exit but turns.)

ADOLFO: I can start all over again if you want me to.

FLORIDITA: You don't have to.

ADOLFO: I want to.

(He exits, comes back in, pretends that he sees her for the first time and that the sight of her makes him faint. FLORIDITA laughs.)

ADOLFO: I'm glad to know you rejoice at the sight of my grief.

FLORIDITA: That's not it. I just don't know how to react. I've never had a man in love standing in front of me before.

ADOLFO: But I'm lying down. Would you prefer me to kneel?

FLORIDITA: Oh, please don't. I couldn't resist it.

ADOLFO: Then let me give you a kiss.

FLORIDITA: But I don't know you, sir. You didn't even say your name.

ADOLFO: Adolfo.

FLORIDITA: What you do—

ADOLFO: Writer. Love jazz. Mother died, raised by grandma, Catholic, made it step by step into college and after that into the world of letters. I've known several women, I won't hide it from you, but not until today have I met a single woman that devours me by only being. You stare at me and say nothing but I can see that a thought wants to come out…

FLORIDITA: Your face is so beautiful.

ADOLFO: Touch it.

FLORIDITA: And soft.

(ADOLFO grabs her hands.)

ADOLFO: Wait until you see what's behind the face.

FLORIDITA: Your hands. I have never touched a pair of hands this soft before.

ADOLFO: Wait until you see what these hands can do. For you.

FLORIDITA: This is impossible. It must be part of a very cruel scenario. It's too much for me. You see, I just inherited three hundred million.

ADOLFO: *(As if he didn't know.)* Three hun…? No!

FLORIDITA: Yes. And now this. Please slap me back. If this is a dream, I'd rather wake up now and forget the whole thing. I'll even laugh at myself. Slap me, please.

(ADOLFO slaps her in the face. FLORIDITA starts to cry.)

ADOLFO: Don't cry. Haven't you cried enough, locked in the bathroom, wishing you were not here, but somewhere else? Haven't you walked infinite times from table to table asking yourself why is it that you serve while others are served?

Not anymore. No more dreams. The Lord is manifest in mysterious ways and he has chosen you, that you should be paid not with one but with two miracles in one day. I stand here, ready to wed you and to give you all I have. Floridita, my love.

(He kisses her. They make love.)

5

HOFFMAN enters.

HOFFMAN: *(Talking into a tape recorder.)* García, the manager of Floridita—the restaurant—is a very strange man.

(GARCÍA enters.)

GARCÍA: What do you want?

HOFFMAN: Hi. My name is Alejandro Hoffman. I go to Columbia. I'm here to talk about Floridita.

GARCÍA: You fucking Columbia people, I've told you a hundred times, I'm not selling.

HOFFMAN: I'm not here to buy, I'm here to talk about Floridita the girl, not the restaurant.

GARCÍA: And who are you?

HOFFMAN: I'm a journalist.

GARCÍA: You look like a student.

HOFFMAN: I'm a journalism student. I was sent to investigate her case.

GARCÍA: That's all?

HOFFMAN: For a class.

GARCÍA: Which class?

HOFFMAN: Realism and Counterrrealism.

GARCÍA: Sounds stupid.

HOFFMAN: It's about how to articulate the extraordinary into the news so it can be accepted by the common man.

GARCÍA: There was nothing extraordinary about Flora's death.

HOFFMAN: It's funny you say that, because I don't know how to explain it…

GARCÍA: Try.

HOFFMAN: I never met this girl and yet, I imagine her so often…

GARCÍA: In your dreams?

HOFFMAN: Not only in my dreams. I see her. Everywhere. I think I've started talking to her. Out loud. Is that crazy? I never met her and yet it's like I take her with me wherever I go.

GARCÍA: *(Sitting down at a table.)* And why do you think that is?

HOFFMAN: I…I don't know.

GARCÍA: Think.

HOFFMAN: *(Sitting down with him.)* The story, just the fable, young waitress, with an amazing past. It destroyed me…you don't hear a lot about suicides on the tracks anymore. They happen we just don't hear about them.

GARCÍA: What fascinates you is that she jumped in front of the train? You Columbia people sure are cruel.

HOFFMAN: No, no, that's not what I mean. Something about her being a waitress…

GARCÍA: Here we go.

HOFFMAN: No offense, but most people think about waitressing while waiting for the next best thing, you know, the real thing. A waitress at twenty must have big dreams, big plans, so much energy. Also, being Latina—

GARCÍA: Here we go.

HOFFMAN: No offense.

GARCÍA: Go on.

HOFFMAN: Suicide isn't a very Latino thing to do. Don't give me that look, it really isn't. Suicide belongs to Europe, where people think so hard they go mental, or Scandinavia, where it's so cold. Or—

GARCÍA: NYU.

HOFFMAN: Well, yes. You see, I'd have to look at the statistics, but it just seems to me that suicide is not common among Hispanics.

GARCÍA: Right.

HOFFMAN: You can't take that the wrong way. I'm Hispanic as well. The warm weather makes us...warmer somehow.

GARCÍA: You're very smart.

HOFFMAN: Thanks.

GARCÍA: What do you want to know?

HOFFMAN: The night of the suicide...

GARCÍA: We don't know that it was...

HOFFMAN: Exactly. Are you suggesting someone killed her? Do you have a suspect?

GARCÍA: Calm down, not too fast. If we'd had a suspect, we would've killed him ourselves.

HOFFMAN: The way you do in Peru?

GARCÍA: Excuse—

HOFFMAN: Just kidding.

GARCÍA: *(Smiling at him for the first time.)* What I'm saying is that it's too hard for us to believe that she jumped by herself. Without someone pushing her on purpose or by accident. Or that perhaps she slipped. It was a little rainy that night. Anyone can slip their way onto the tracks.

HOFFMAN: Was she clumsy? What was she like?

GARCÍA: I need coffee.

HOFFMAN: *(To FLORIDITA.)* Dos cafés con leche por favor.

GARCÍA: What was she like? She never wanted to leave. She would stay over time, for little money, the restaurant is doing well, better now that La Rosita closed, but none of us makes that much. But to be honest it was never about the money. She loved waitressing. I mean, don't get me wrong, I love waiting tables too, but it's my restaurant. A girl so young, so committed to her waitressing job as if she had already decided this was going to be the rest of her life.

HOFFMAN: Amazing.

GARCÍA: It's better when you don't talk.

(FLORIDITA brings the coffee.)

GARCÍA: When we hired her we thought it was hilarious she had the same name as the restaurant. It made so much sense and she was so proud of becoming the symbol of the place. The clients loved her. I mean, really loved her. She would collect little pieces of paper with phone numbers, emails, but she would never respond to any of their notes. One day I remember a man grabbed her ass. She dropped her tray and froze for about fifteen seconds. Then she slowly turned to him and said: "More coffee?"

HOFFMAN: Más café?

GARCÍA: How long did you study Spanish for?

HOFFMAN: Years, but I was in high school. I understand it and can also read it, but can't really speak it. My mother never really wanted me to learn, I don't know why... What happened after she said "more coffee"?

GARCÍA: The man laughed and said: "Wherever you're from, you sure are made for service." And she took it as a compliment. I'm sure all these memories bore you, cold as you are.

HOFFMAN: They don't.

GARCÍA: You just want to get to the part when the waitress dies. Admit it, you can't wait to get home and get done with your little homework.

HOFFMAN: I wish this were just homework. But this article is starting to become my life in a way that I don't care what grade I get or what the teacher says or what my classmates think of it. The real thing, her, you, this place, is so much more important to me than whatever paper I can write about it. School is so stupid.

GARCÍA: Well, I guess since I started I may as well go on. That night I saw her going up the stairs with her green uniform and carrying the same green suitcase she always carried around, at around seven p.m. A little cloud of dust covering—

HOFFMAN: What did she have in that suitcase?

GARCÍA: I have no idea.

HOFFMAN: Did she say anything weird that day? I mean, before leaving. Anything that sounded different?

GARCÍA: Nope. Just her normal besos! Wait. Now that you mention it, yes, I remember now. How had I forgotten that? It was so weird. It was so weird! All of a sudden she started talking about moving, a husband, an inheritance...

(FLORIDITA is carrying her green suitcase. GARCÍA is crying.)

FLORIDITA: Please don't cry, we'll miss you too. I hope you can find a new waitress without any problem. I am so happy. I feel like I've been rescued from a deep empty well. Sorry, I didn't mean to say...

GARCÍA: It's okay.

FLORIDITA: Anyway, we bought an apartment in Tribeca, we didn't want to waste that much money, so we'll be close.

GARCÍA: Not so close.

FLORIDITA: I'm going to call you about the housewarming party. We'll have plenty of waiters so none of us will have to serve. We'll be served. Goodbye, friend. I'll miss you. I'll stop by next week for brunch.

GARCÍA: Brunch? We have no brunch at Floridita. And she left. We never got an invitation to her party, never met her husband, never heard from her.

HOFFMAN: An inheritance? A husband? How come I haven't—Tribeca?

GARCÍA: We had never heard of any of that either. But other than that, she didn't seem weird at all.

6

DEATH enters.

DEATH: We are not in Korea, you know.

FLORIDITA: I know.

DEATH: If you really wanted to, you would've jumped already, you know.

FLORIDITA: I know.

DEATH: Are you planning to cover your head with a plastic bag at least? I have one in my purse. I can give it to you if you want. *(Pause.)* For free. *(Pause.)* We can paint it some other color if you don't like it black. We don't want you to look like you're in Guantánamo. *(Singing.)* Guantanamera. Guajira guantamera. *(Stops singing.)* Do you think they call it the 1 train because it's the most popular train in town? You know, the One train, everyone wants to ride on the One train. *(Pause.)* You sure are boring. Or you can even use my scarf, I don't really care for it that much.

FLORIDITA: I will not cover my face with anything.

DEATH: Selfish little bitch. Suicides only think about their petty little selves. Thank god you don't have a mother, poor thing. Don't you know you can traumatize the driver? Poor bastards. Just trying to do their job until suddenly a crazy someone decides to ruin their day. I am certainly not giving you my scarf, you selfish little bitch. Here, a black bag. Simple. Like you.

FLORIDITA: Thanks.

DEATH: You're welcome. If you lived in Korea, Beethoven would stop you. But of course, you wouldn't know who Beethoven was…

FLORIDITA: How could he stop me if he died in 1827? Ten thousand people attended his funeral and at first nobody would say a word because they knew that any sound would be redundant at Ludwig's funeral and that had he been good of hearing he would have even disliked the heavy breathing, the sounds of footsteps, the sniffing.

DEATH: Nobody made a sound?

FLORIDITA: Not for a while. Of course then an inconsiderate someone started coughing and the whole service went to hell.

DEATH: Wikipedia?

FLORIDITA: Wikipedia.

DEATH: I don't trust it.

FLORIDITA: It's all right.

DEATH: He could stop you. In Korea they play his music at the stations to soothe the pain of potential suicides. It's called "music therapy." It works on animals.

FLORIDITA: I'm not an animal.

DEATH: They play *Für Elise*, or *Moonlight Sonata*, and then a voice says: "Dear passengers, let's think again about the parents and brothers and sisters that we love and the preciousness of our lives." In Korean.

FLORIDITA: Does it work?

DEATH: It does.

FLORIDITA: What's the point of this story? We are not in Korea.

DEATH: There's so much music in the air, my child. Can't you hear it?

FLORIDITA: No.

DEATH: Then jump.

(Pushing her.)

DEATH: Jump. What would they think of you in Korea?

7

ADOLFO enters.

ADOLFO: With money, my dear, the invisible becomes visible. It's like turning the lights on inside a cave. No more shadows, everything is there, at your sight, even the bats.

FLORIDITA: Are we in Korea?

ADOLFO: How did you know?

FLORIDITA: This is exactly how I always imagined it.

ADOLFO: Korea. Everyone's bowing at us. Korea.

FLORIDITA: Korea. Everyone's smiling at us.

ADOLFO: That's right, Koreans love to smile.

FLORIDITA: But why do they cover their mouths when they do?

ADOLFO: It's just one of those apologetic gestures developed over time in the developing world. Like the Mexican mande! How I love Korea.

FLORIDITA: They all wave at us. What's that thing everybody's eating?

ADOLFO: Kimchi, they eat it the way that you eat platanos.

FLORIDITA: It smells so good.

ADOLFO: That's because it *is* good. Anything that's good smells good.

FLORIDITA: It's so exciting to be in such an exotic place.

ADOLFO: I'm sure you look exotic to them.

FLORIDITA: Me? Exotic?

ADOLFO: Here you are.

FLORIDITA: I never thought I'd make it this far.

ADOLFO: I never thought you'd make it this far either.

FLORIDITA: What do you mean?

ADOLFO: Well, not before the three hundred million, I mean, not that I thought you incapable, it's just that traveling is not cheap. Look! *(Bowing.)* Korea.

FLORIDITA: *(Bowing.)* Korea.

ADOLFO: Why are you crying?

FLORIDITA: Because everything is so bright, things make so much sense when you're rich. I can see the world, really see it. Even more, the world sees me. I'm not invisible. For the first time in my life I feel like a person, I walk into a room and people look at me. They actually turn their heads and take a moment, a whole moment, to draw two invisible parallel lines between their eyes and mine.

ADOLFO: We call that eye contact.

FLORIDITA: Do you have any idea of how invisible you are when you're poor? But now it's like turning the lights on inside a cave. No more shadows. I can see everything.

ADOLFO: Even the guano, my love?

FLORIDITA: Sure, why not? Even the guano.

8

HOFFMAN enters.

HOFFMAN: Eight hours in the cold and a plane ticket to Bolivia. Where was she going? Was someone expecting her there? Family? She planned a future only to kill herself. Or maybe she didn't kill herself, maybe she was pushed onto the tracks. Who knows? Who knows what happened during those eight hours? Who was she waiting for? I thought a conversation with the man who ran over her could help clarify things.

(SEVERIO enters.)

SEVERIO: I'm sorry I killed her.

HOFFMAN: You should be.

SEVERIO: I didn't mean to.

HOFFMAN: That's what they all say.

SEVERIO: But I mean it.

HOFFMAN: I thought you didn't mean it.

SEVERIO: What I mean is that I didn't mean to kill her.

HOFFMAN: Strange thing meaning.

SEVERIO: I've never killed anybody.

HOFFMAN: Until now. What makes you think you're going to stop now? Maybe you just discovered your calling, running over people.

SEVERIO: Don't say that, please, it was an accident.

HOFFMAN: Why didn't you stop?

SEVERIO: I tried to, but it all happened too fast.

HOFFMAN: Bullshit! You saw her jumping onto the tracks and you did not stop on purpose!

SEVERIO: I could barely see her, it was dark.

HOFFMAN: Trains have headlights!

SEVERIO: The train was too fast.

HOFFMAN: Trains have brakes!

SEVERIO: I pushed the damn brakes but it was too late.

HOFFMAN: You were supposed to be slowing down but no, you thought, "Oh, would you look at that? I see a little Mexican looking like she lost something on the tracks." And then you went faster!

SEVERIO: I didn't!

HOFFMAN: Faster!

SEVERIO: It was blurry and I was tired and the station seemed empty.

HOFFMAN: Faster!

SEVERIO: It wasn't like that I swear.

HOFFMAN: How was it then?

SEVERIO: I've heard many stories about these suicides. First-hand accounts from colleagues. It happens more often than people think, the exact number I couldn't even tell you. But nothing could've prepared me for this. Most people jump. They simply wait very close to the tracks and when the train is close enough they jump.

HOFFMAN: This wasn't like that?

SEVERIO: No.

HOFFMAN: How was it then?

SEVERIO: Horribly normal. I just saw a random woman waiting for the train to stop. She walked closer to the train as anyone would, one step at a time, her look not quite focused on the train, lost in thought, like everyone else. Had she not been the only person on the platform I wouldn't have even noticed her.

(Silence.)

HOFFMAN: And then?

SEVERIO: Then she looked at me. And I swear a look between two people has never lasted this long. She was smiling.

HOFFMAN: She couldn't have, she was about to kill herself.

SEVERIO: I have no proof but I swear to god she smiled and smiled and time stopped and before I knew it.

HOFFMAN: Before you knew it what?

SEVERIO: Do you need me to spell it out for you?

HOFFMAN: Please. I'm recording.

SEVERIO: You are a creep, you know that.

HOFFMAN: I'm just a journalist. Go on.

SEVERIO: I was saying she smiled and before I knew it I was rolling over her, though the subway doesn't really roll over people, it slides.

HOFFMAN: I thought I was the creep.

SEVERIO: And I tried to scream, I tried to stop, I tried a lot of things but nothing happened. I had lost my mind.

(Silence.)

SEVERIO: Is that good enough for your article?

HOFFMAN: I don't know that I'm writing one, really.

SEVERIO: Even better. This kind of writing is unnecessary, there's nothing to learn from it.

HOFFMAN: I know.

9

ADOLFO enters.

ADOLFO: Hi, my love.

FLORIDITA: Hi, my love.

ADOLFO: I—

FLORIDITA: I—

ADOLFO: You go first.

FLORIDITA: No, you go first.

ADOLFO: Okay, I will. I am exhausted.

FLORIDITA: Why? What did you do all day?

ADOLFO: What do you mean what did I do all day? What could I have possibly done but the same thing I do every day? I wrote. All day.

FLORIDITA: Of course. How's the novel coming along?

ADOLFO: Great. This new chapter, oh my god, you are going to flip. I can't wait for you to read it.

FLORIDITA: And I can't wait to… flip.

ADOLFO: You will.

FLORIDITA: Why? What happens in it?

ADOLFO: It's not so much what happens but what is revealed.

FLORIDITA: What is?

ADOLFO: Everything.

FLORIDITA: Wow.

ADOLFO: It's the penultimate chapter.

FLORIDITA: You're that far along?

ADOLFO: What do you mean that far along? I started this novel last week. I'm good, but I'm not a machine.

FLORIDITA: But you said it was the penultimate chapter.

ADOLFO: It is! You look confused. How was your day?

FLORIDITA: Oh, you know.

ADOLFO: I don't. That's why I'm asking.

FLORIDITA: A little bit of this, a little bit of that. I stopped by Floridita.

ADOLFO: You did what?!

FLORIDITA: I don't even know how it happened.

ADOLFO: How dare you?!

FLORIDITA: You're yelling at me.

ADOLFO: Because, honey, we've talked about this before.

FLORIDITA: I know, but I just found myself feeling a little trapped in here.

ADOLFO: You should've gone out for a stroll.

FLORIDITA: I didn't want to stroll, I wanted to do.

ADOLFO: Do what?

FLORIDITA: Anything, I thought about cleaning but the house was so clean.

ADOLFO: Cleaning?

FLORIDITA: Or cooking and then I realized I'd forgotten how.

ADOLFO: So you went to Floridita to remember how to cook?

FLORIDITA: Maybe.

ADOLFO: Honey, one can't forget how to cook just like one can't forget how to ride a bicycle.

FLORIDITA: Here, touch my hands.

ADOLFO: What about them?

FLORIDITA: Don't you see how soft they've become?

ADOLFO: That's a good thing. Money makes you beautiful.

FLORIDITA: I feel like I can't get anything done with them anymore. Have you ever felt that—

ADOLFO: No.

FLORIDITA: You wish you could do, physically do something, but your own hands resist?

ADOLFO: You've done so much already.

FLORIDITA: You always say that.

ADOLFO: It's true. Not only did you have to work all your life as a servant—

FLORIDITA: Waitress.

ADOLFO: But you also accomplished something that most people can't accomplish.

FLORIDITA: What?

ADOLFO: Survival.

FLORIDITA: I was lucky.

ADOLFO: You were not. You were instinctual. When faced with danger human beings have the option of acting according to instinct or not. You did. You survived. You are a survivor, we both are. I survived life as a struggling artist and you survived immigration. All by yourself.

FLORIDITA: You're right. I forget sometimes.

ADOLFO: It is forbidden to forget. A journey like yours, coming all the way from...which island did you come from again?

FLORIDITA: Uh—

ADOLFO: It's not important. What matters is that you survived. And that's why you are here. With me. Because we both are and always will be survivors.

10

DEATH enters.

DEATH: Still here?

FLORIDITA: Yes.

DEATH: Need me?

FLORIDITA: No.

DEATH: A little?

FLORIDITA: No.

DEATH: I'll be back.

FLORIDITA: I know.

DEATH: What is it like to spend these hours alone in the cold? Dreadful?

FLORIDITA: It's actually quite beautiful.

DEATH: Romantic.

FLORIDITA: Yes, romantic.

11

PERHAPS A DEAD MAN enters and sits very close to her.

PERHAPS A DEAD MAN: Don't come any closer.

FLORIDITA: Huh?

PERHAPS A DEAD MAN: If I were you, I wouldn't come any closer. I'm not here to keep you company. I'm waiting for the train, I have no interest in knowing who you are or in seducing you, okay?

FLORIDITA: Men are funny. They're all a little scared.

PERHAPS A DEAD MAN: Scared of what, bitch? I have nothing to be scared of. You are the one who should be scared, not me. I'm scary. Very.

FLORIDITA: I can tell.

(Silence.)

PERHAPS A DEAD MAN: Listen, I didn't come here to talk, okay? I don't like to talk, so don't talk to me, don't even look at me. I'm a man, you're a woman, that's all, don't expect any sexual tension from my side. Just because you're a female and I'm a male doesn't mean we'll fall for each other, there are many people in the world for you, you're not that ugly.

FLORIDITA: I know.

PERHAPS A DEAD MAN: Stop it right there. I know your kind. Do I look like a man who could love you, make you happy? No, right? So don't waste your time trying so hard.

FLORIDITA: I haven't done anything.

PERHAPS A DEAD MAN: Whore.

FLORIDITA: I know.

PERHAPS A DEAD MAN: Don't talk to me.

FLORIDITA: I talk to myself.

PERHAPS A DEAD MAN: I'm compulsive.

(They start speaking at the same time.)

FLORIDITA: It's nice out. A heavenly night.

PERHAPS A DEAD MAN: I have a big issue with time, miss.

FLORIDITA: The sky, so gorgeous, so black.

PERHAPS A DEAD MAN: I look at my watch two, three, four times a minute. Can you imagine?

FLORIDITA: So sad everything is so dead around here, we could do so many things…

PERHAPS A DEAD MAN: What that's like, to be this sick…

FLORIDITA: A nice cup of coffee, play games. I love games.

PERHAPS A DEAD MAN: Compulsive, they call it. Compulsive…

FLORIDITA: We could fly a kite.

PERHAPS A DEAD MAN: I hate the word compulsive, it sounds like repulsive, like coercive, like obsessive, like corrosive…

FLORIDITA: Adolfo hates kites.

PERHAPS A DEAD MAN: But it's something else, I tell you, it's different with me.

FLORIDITA: I used to hide from him at night, after sex, so I could fly my kite.

PERHAPS A DEAD MAN: It's a race, an infinite race with time and people, with people moving in time.

FLORIDITA: To fly a kite outside your window is so sad, don't you think?

PERHAPS A DEAD MAN: A race without beginning, without end.

FLORIDITA: I bet the two of us together could build a kite.

PERHAPS A DEAD MAN: Overwhelming.

FLORIDITA: But then we'll have to take turns…

PERHAPS A DEAD MAN: The worst is when I look at my watch two, three, four times in a row without even noticing, because you stop looking at the watch, really looking…

FLORIDITA: You'll get mad at me because I'm very good, I was the champion in my neighborhood.

PERHAPS A DEAD MAN: Again and again, I look, automatically. I hate automatons.

FLORIDITA: I could fly a kite for at least six hours.

PERHAPS A DEAD MAN: Overwhelming.

(Silence.)

PERHAPS A DEAD MAN: I'm leaving. Please don't be here when I come back or I'm going to have to kill you.

(Silence.)

FLORIDITA: Are you dead?

PERHAPS A DEAD MAN: Perhaps.

(Silence.)

FLORIDITA: That's hot.

12

SOR JUANA enters.

SOR JUANA: Who did this to you? Cool. You don't have to say anything. I won't insist. But I want you to know that you are very sick. If you don't speak, whoever did this to you is going to stay free. All you have to do is say a name. Whoever did this has destroyed the rest of your life and deserves to die.

FLORIDITA: No one deserves to die.

SOR JUANA: Oh, so you can actually speak. Now tell me: Who did this to you?

FLORIDITA: I don't know...

SOR JUANA: What do you mean you don't know? You must've gotten it somewhere.

FLORIDITA: Aren't germs everywhere?

SOR JUANA: Don't joke with me, Floridita. This was no germ.

FLORIDITA: Then what was it?

SOR JUANA: What you have is a form of herpes that can only be transmitted by sleeping with the dead.

(FLORIDITA laughs.)

SOR JUANA: So you think this is funny? You laugh at the misery of your own body?

FLORIDITA: It's not that. It's just that you're so silly, saying things like that. I haven't slept with any zombie.

SOR JUANA: The worst part is that I've heard this story before and always thought it was only an urban legend. The young girl who one morning wakes up with herpes necrophilia. Obviously you were raped, or forced into doing something terrible. Tell me, who did this to you?

FLORIDITA: Why?

SOR JUANA: I need to know.

FLORIDITA: I don't remember.

SOR JUANA: What do you mean? Were you unconscious? Did someone give you anything to drink?

(FLORIDITA dreams.)

SOR JUANA: You know, Floridita, this world is fucked up because stupid people like you don't dare to speak up when it's their turn to do so. You have to speak, not only for yourself, but for all of those who are in the same unfortunate situation as you are. Now tell me, who did this to you?

FLORIDITA: Has anyone ever told you you look like America Ferrera?

(Pause.)

SOR JUANA: This might come as a surprise to you, Flora, but I was once like you. Humble, meek, coy, but I knew deep down that my modesty was an act, an agreement that I had made with the world after it had convinced me that it was better for a woman to act coy, to act modest. But I broke that agreement, I shattered it into pieces in my letter to the archbishop, I signed my name in blood, I seduced men and women alike. Was my rebellion worth it? True. I was asked to step down from the church I had devoted my life to. But only because I rebelled I can be here to help you now. In those dark Mexican Roman Catholic days, I learned that once a woman in trouble, always a woman in trouble.

13

FLORIDITA seats HOFFMAN at her usual spot (the subway platform) to watch the following scene. She and GARCÍA enact the scene, while other members of the cast do the voices. They speak with unplaceable Latin American accents. It should look like a radio soap opera dubbed over a silent film.

ALEJANDRO'S MOM: Buenos días.

ALEJANDRO'S DAD: Hola.

ALEJANDRO'S MOM: El desayuno está en la estufa.

ALEJANDRO'S DAD: Solo quiero café.

ALEJANDRO'S MOM: Tiene que hacércelo. Alejandro se tomó el que quedaba.

ALEJANDRO'S DAD: ¿Alejandro toma café?

ALEJANDRO'S MOM: Hace tiempo.

ALEJANDRO'S DAD: No lo sabía.

ALEJANDRO'S MOM: ¿Qué va a saber usted si usted nunca está aquí?

ALEJANDRO'S DAD: No empieces.

ALEJANDRO'S MOM: A que no sabía que se pelió en la escuela y que lo suspendieron por tres días.

ALEJANDRO'S DAD: Que no empieces.

ALEJANDRO'S MOM: A que no sabía que lo mandaron a dibujar una casa y me dibujó a mi. No a mí en la casa, no. Sólo a mí, a mí.

ALEJANDRO'S DAD: Que no empieces.

ALEJANDRO'S MOM: ¡Hace rato que empecé! ¿Por qué llegó tan tarde?

ALEJANDRO'S DAD: Estaba con unos panas.

ALEJANDRO'S MOM: ¿Hasta las siete de la mañana?

ALEJANDRO'S DAD: Es mi día libre.

ALEJANDRO'S MOM: ¿Y cuál es mi día libre, ah? ¿Cuándo voy yo a tener un día libre?

ALEJANDRO'S DAD: El que tú quieras, mujer, el que tú quieras.

ALEJANDRO'S MOM: ¡El que yo quiera, tu madre! Con todo el reguero que tú dejas por toda la casa, con todo lo que comes y lo poco que limpias, con la cantidad de pelo que dejas en el lavamanos cada mañana. Un día libre mío sería mandarte a morir a ti.

ALEJANDRO'S DAD: Baja la voz, no me gusta que Alejandro nos escuche discutir.

ALEJANDRO'S MOM: Que nos escuche, que nos escuche y aprenda quien es su verdadero padre.

ALEJANDRO'S DAD: ¡Calla!

ALEJANDRO'S MOM: ¿Te pasaste la noche con rameras, verdad? ¡Con rameras!

ALEJANDRO'S DAD: Cállate o…

ALEJANDRO'S MOM: ¿O qué? ¿O qué? ¿Qué vas a hacer, pegarme? Anda pégame que te llamo a la policía y vas a ver, vas a ver.

(He grabs and shakes her.)

ALEJANDRO'S DAD: No te voy a pegar a menos que me sigas jodiendo la bilis, loca.

ALEJANDRO'S MOM: Pégame, lo veo en tus ojos que me quieres pegar.

ALEJANDRO'S DAD: ¿Para qué demonios te traje a este país si lo que haces es joderme los cojones?

ALEJANDRO'S MOM: País ni país, no hacemos más que pasarnos el día encerrados en este Brooklyn donde lo que no es mierda es vómito.

ALEJANDRO'S DAD: Agradece que te saqué de Cajamarca, loca. Ya quisieras tú haber nacido en Brooklyn.

ALEJANDRO'S MOM: Ah, Brooklyn, Brooklyn, que se vaya a al infierno el maldito Brooklyn donde los que no son puercos son escarabajos.

ALEJANDRO'S DAD: Pues lárgate, bruta, lárgate a que te alimenten los machupichus. Lárgate, malagradecida.

ALEJANDRO'S MOM: No hables así de mi gente, gaucho sucio, gaucho puerco, gaucho macharrán.

(He throws her on the floor and leaves. ALEJANDRO'S MOM cries. ALEJANDRO, who has "entered" the scene, stares at her. When she notices him looking at her, she recovers a little. FLORIDITA will play ALEJANDRO'S MOTHER from now on.)

ALEJANDRO'S MOM: Acaba de tomarte tu leche, mijo.

HOFFMAN: I don't speak Spanish, Mom.

ALEJANDRO'S MOM: Sorry...finish your milk, dear.

HOFFMAN: Why are you crying?

ALEJANDRO'S MOM: Nothing, dear. Everything is fine.

HOFFMAN: But you guys were screaming at each other. What were you screaming about?

ALEJANDRO'S MOM: We were having an adult conversation and those can be quite layered.

HOFFMAN: What's layered?

ALEJANDRO'S MOM: Like a three-flavored cake. One layer is vanilla, the other chocolate and the other one, my least favorite, is...¿cómo se dice? Strawberry! Different layers of different flavors. Adult conversations have that, different layers of flavors, colors, cornstarch. Now finish your coffee, we have a lot to do today.

HOFFMAN: We do?

ALEJANDRO'S MOM: You didn't think you were going to spend your whole suspension watching television, did you? You are going to help me around the house so you learn how to value your education.

HOFFMAN: Okay. *(Pause.)* Mom, why didn't you teach me any Spanish?

ALEJANDRO'S MOM: *(With a big smile.)* I didn't want to confuse you, dear.

14

ADOLFO enters.

ADOLFO: Hi, my love.

FLORIDITA: Hi.

ADOLFO: Why don't you call me "my love" back? I know, don't answer, you're mad at me.

FLORIDITA: Hell has broken lose and all the devils are here, inside my head.

ADOLFO: Why are you not calling me "my love" like you used to? Usually when I say "my love" you would say "my love" back. Where are the children? Are you mad at me? Don't answer. I know you are.

FLORIDITA: This house is so big, and yet so uncomfortable, so angular. Why do we live in a house that feels like a labyrinth? We have so much money. I need air. There's no air inside this house.

ADOLFO: Where are the children? And who was that man you were talking to in front of Tom's restaurant? Is he your lover? Huh? Is he? And why the fuck are you not calling me "my love" today? Wait, don't say anything, I know the answer. He's your lover.

FLORIDITA: Do I have enough money to tear down the house and build a new one? A new house with only four walls and one huge window. And a lot of open space inside the four white walls. Just free space inside the house.

ADOLFO: How long have you been together, you and your lover? Do you fuck him often? I bet he makes you laugh more than I do. Don't tell me. I know he makes you laugh more than I do.

FLORIDITA: To destroy and build a new house with one window that will allow some dust to come in, dust that I could clean with my own hands, or perhaps it's better to leave this one and find a small apartment with no interior walls, to find a studio. To leave some money for the children and leave. No, I would never do that.

ADOLFO: Have you seen them today? I went to look for them in school and they weren't there. Sometimes I feel there's something wrong with our children. Since Jean Paul II died. That day something broke in their innocence. They liked the pope. I used to tell them that strange-looking grandpa was Santa Claus in disguise. Now I feel like they hate us. Do you think they hate us? Our flesh...

FLORIDITA: No.

ADOLFO: and blood. No what?

FLORIDITA: He's not my lover. I don't even know if he's alive.

ADOLFO: Have you seen the children?

FLORIDITA: A very small studio, with no walls.

ADOLFO: Our children hate us, my love.

FLORIDITA: We might have to become better parents from now on.

ADOLFO: We might have to become better parents from now on. If you need more air, just turn the AC on.

FLORIDITA: No, I want it off. This is not my house.

ADOLFO: You know, it's okay if you're in love with someone else. I understand I haven't been around.

FLORIDITA: They hated Jean Paul II. They were plotting to burn down the Church of Saint Gregory the Great on 90th Street. They hate the Church. They tell you they like that stupid story about "grandpa the pope" to laugh at you. I've heard them laughing at you.

ADOLFO: Why do I feel like we can't communicate anymore?

FLORIDITA: Don't touch me, your hands are so soft.

ADOLFO: What do you mean they're soft? They've always been soft. Women like soft hands.

FLORIDITA: No, we don't. Every time you touch me I remember you've never worked a day in your entire life.

ADOLFO: That's not true. I'm a novelist.

FLORIDITA: Exactly.

(The CHILDREN come in.)

ADOLFO and FLORIDITA: Hi, lovelies.

CHILD 1: What's wrong with you two?

CHILD 2: Are you getting a divorce?

CHILD 1: Were you about to have sex and had to stop because the "damned children" are here?

CHILD 2: Do you hate us, Father?

ADOLFO: No, why would you say that? I love you. Both of you. With all my heart. All of it.

CHILD 2: But what about that day when you tried to push me down the stairs?

FLORIDITA: You're imagining things. Your father cares about you wholeheartedly.

CHILD 1: Wholeheartedly? When did you start using words as complicated as "wholeheartedly"? You're an immigrant. You don't know fancy words. You sound stupid.

ADOLFO: Don't talk to your mother like that. She speaks perfect English. I taught her how.

FLORIDITA: No, you didn't. I spoke English very well before I met you.

ADOLFO: You had that weird pronunciation, remember? I taught you how to differentiate between the "d" and "th" sounds. It's nothing to be ashamed of, honey, you came in a boat.

FLORIDITA: I did not.

ADOLFO: What do you mean?

FLORIDITA: I made that up to feel heroic. I was brought here by a pack of immigrants who crossed the El Paso border.

(CHILD 1 hugs CHILD 2.)

CHILD 1: Our mother is Mexican.

ADOLFO: I married a phony Mexican?

FLORIDITA: Enough!

CHILD 1: Are you two fighting in front of us? I thought you loved each other.

FLORIDITA: We do.

ADOLFO: We do.

CHILD 2: But Daddy was about to slap Mommy in the face again.

CHILD 1: That's true.

ADOLFO: I have never slapped your mother.

CHILD 2: Perhaps not in the face. But we've seen you slapping her ass real hard while screwing. You get so violent when you screw.

ADOLFO: I told you not to spy on us…

CHILD 1: Don't yell at my sister. She's only a little girl.

CHILD 2: I'm fragile.

CHILD 1: She's fragile. How dare you yell at my sister?

CHILD 2: *(Crying.)* Why do you yell at me, Daddy? I thought you loved me. And Mommy, why don't you do anything? You just stand there, like an ordinary oppressed woman who cries silently while washing the dishes. Didn't you watch enough television today?

FLORIDITA: Shut the f… *(She controls herself.)*

CHILD 2: Say it, Mommy. Come on. Tell me to shut the fuck up. Come on, say it so I can have a good excuse to kill you.

(She has taken out a gun. FLORIDITA hides behind ADOLFO.)

FLORIDITA: Where did you get that gun?

CHILD 2: Daddy got us one each for our birthday.

FLORIDITA: He did not.

CHILD 1: Ask him.

FLORIDITA: Did you?

ADOLFO: I'm sorry, my love.

FLORIDITA: How dare you? I hate you.

CHILD 1: *(Lyrical.)* Wives, submit to your husbands as to the Lord.

CHILD 2: For the husband is the head of the wife as Christ is the head of the Church.

FLORIDITA: What's wrong with you two?

CHILD 2: Don't they read the Bible in Mexico, you wetback?

CHILD 1: Don't hide behind Daddy. It's stupid. We're planning to kill him too.

ADOLFO: Shut up. Don't speak like that. You can't kill us. You love us.

CHILD 2: No, we don't.

(ADOLFO takes out a gun. A back-and-forth shoot-out ensues.)

15

LIBERTY ENLIGHTENING THE WORLD enters.

LIBERTY ENLIGHTENING THE WORLD: Self-indulgence is sin.

FLORIDITA: No, it isn't.

LIBERTY ENLIGHTENING THE WORLD: Just because it is not listed as one doesn't mean it's not one.

FLORIDITA: You're not making sense.

LIBERTY ENLIGHTENING THE WORLD: It's intrinsic to all sins therefore it is sin. One could even say it's mother to all sins.

FLORIDITA: Are you done?

LIBERTY ENLIGHTENING THE WORLD: Gee, I was told you were nicer than this.

FLORIDITA: You can see for yourself that I'm not.

LIBERTY ENLIGHTENING THE WORLD: It's not me you should be mad at.

FLORIDITA: You don't get to decide that. I could be mad at whoever I wanted.

LIBERTY ENLIGHTENING THE WORLD: I welcomed you with open arms after all.

FLORIDITA: Yeah, right.

LIBERTY ENLIGHTENING THE WORLD: But there's only so much I can do being a statue. I am not really the people, I just represent them. Illustration.

FLORIDITA: Wait a second. How is it that today, the day of my suicide, you're part of this landscape? You are too far, you're not supposed to be visible from here.

LIBERTY ENLIGHTENING THE WORLD: Just when you thought you understood magic realism.

FLORIDITA: Your presence here is meaningless. I didn't even come on a boat. I crossed the border. How come they don't have you over there where you're actually needed?

LIBERTY ENLIGHTENING THE WORLD: You have so many statements in you. Why not stay alive and make something with them? Poems. Or allegories. I hear allegories are coming back.

FLORIDITA: I hate allegories.

LIBERTY ENLIGHTENING THE WORLD: But for a waitress to die so young having said nothing? How horribly redundant.

FLORIDITA: Are you done?

LIBERTY ENLIGHTENING THE WORLD: Almost. *(Pause.)* You shouldn't expect anyone to come see you. We all live and die alone. And yet, there are worse things.

FLORIDITA: Like what?

LIBERTY ENLIGHTENING THE WORLD: How come Mexicans never cross the border in groups of three?

FLORIDITA: I don't know.

LIBERTY ENLIGHTENING THE WORLD: Because of the sign that says "No *Tres*passing."

(FLORIDITA laughs.)

16

The Mexican border. Darkness.

MANUEL: Pepo.

PEPO: Mande.

MANUEL: Aguilú.

AGUILÚ: Mande.

MANUEL: Milagros.

MILAGROS: Mande.

MANUEL: Sofía.

SOFÍA: Mande.

MANUEL: Matches?

SOFÍA: Got 'em.

MANUEL: Bread?

AGUILÚ: Got it.

MANUEL: If they catch us?

SOFÍA: We play stupid.

MANUEL: If we're sick?

ALL: We say nothing.

MANUEL: If we're tired?

ALL: We try harder.

MANUEL: If we're starving?

ALL: We pray.

MANUEL: At all times?

ALL: We make no noise.

MANUEL: Mi gente, we're about to make it, really, finally make it, to the U.S. of A. We're only one fence away.

SOFÍA: It's higher that I thought.

MANUEL: You see, when you get all pessimistic like that I just want to leave you here.

SOFÍA: I'm only saying.

MANUEL: Your attitude doesn't help.

SOFÍA: You said it would be as easy as climbing the neighbor's fence, but these neighbors thought it out really well before building this one.

MANUEL: How high it is is irrelevant. We're going underneath it.

SOFÍA: A fence this high needs deep foundations.

MANUEL: You want to go back? Is that what you want? Then go! Go!

AGUILÚ: Guys, please. We're here already. Let's get this done.

MANUEL: How's the hole doing?

PEPO: Fine. A couple of minutes.

MANUEL: What was I saying?

SOFÍA: We're only one fence away.

MANUEL: Right. We're only one fence away.

SOFÍA: And a desert.

MANUEL: And a desert.

SOFÍA: And helicopters.

MANUEL: And helicopters.

SOFÍA: And guns, and fires, and thirst, and scorpions…

MANUEL: And all of that.

MILAGROS: And a birth.

MANUEL: Not now, Milagros.

MILAGROS: I don't think I fit through that hole.

MANUEL: And is that our fault, is it?

MILAGROS: I'm just saying the hole is too narrow.

MANUEL: Well, if you had kept your own hole a little bit more narrow we wouldn't be having this problem now, would we?

MILAGROS: I was raped.

SOFÍA: She was raped.

MANUEL: Really? By whom?

SOFÍA: By your brother Aguilú.

MANUEL: Aguilú would never. Right, Aguilú?

AGUILÚ: No mames.

MANUEL: You see? So while we wait remember the last thing, the most important one, the deal breaker. All together!

ALL: Not to touch the fence.

MANUEL: If you do?

ALL: The vibration will send electric waves to the control room and we're fucked.

MANUEL: Good.

SOFÍA: What if some of us make it and some of us don't?

MANUEL: Then those who make it will speak for the others, will work for all of us. So many jobs await us in the U.S. of A. And so many paychecks. You can even become a janitor if you're lucky.

AGUILÚ: I always wanted to become a janitor.

MANUEL: But let's not get too excited. How's the hole doing?

PEPO: Done.

MANUEL: Let's get started then.

SOFÍA: Milagros goes first.

MANUEL: But she's so big.

SOFÍA: She goes first!

MANUEL: Okay.

(MILAGROS *goes painfully through the hole. She struggles but makes it.*)

SOFÍA: That wasn't so bad.

MANUEL: You go.

(SOFÍA *goes in.*)

SOFÍA: Manuel?

MANUEL: Yes?

SOFÍA: I think the baby's coming.

MANUEL: Great. Just what we needed.

(Baby *cries are heard.*)

SOFÍA: Come, look. It's beautiful.

(They all start going through the hole.)

SOFÍA: It's a girl. It's a girl. Milagros, it's a girl.

MANUEL: What do we do now?

SOFÍA: Give her a name.

PEPO: Carmen.

AGUILÚ: Laura.

PEPO: Eugenia.

SOFÍA: No, I know. Flora. A piece of Mexican flora born in a U.S. desert. What do you think, Milagros? *(Pause.)* Milagros? Milagros? She's dead.

MANUEL: We can't take it with us.

SOFÍA: Yes, we can.

MANUEL: How are you planning to feed her?

SOFÍA: There's plenty of food in the U.S. of A.

17

HOFFMAN, SOR JUANA, and GARCÍA enter.

HOFFMAN: So if you ask me, I think that what happened during those eight hours was that a decision was made.

SOR JUANA: Oh, baby. Who did this to you?

HOFFMAN: One decision.

SOR JUANA: Why didn't you call the police? Why didn't you scream?

HOFFMAN: And nothing else.

SOR JUANA: You have lots of neighbors who love you and who would've been there to rescue you.

GARCÍA: I saw you, Floridita.

SOR JUANA: There's always someone who can and wants to help the unfortunate like you.

GARCÍA: I saw you going up the stairs, with your green uniform and carrying your green suitcase at around 7:10 p.m.

HOFFMAN: You said 7:00 p.m. before.

GARCÍA: Fine. I said around seven p.m.! 7:10 p.m. counts as "around seven p.m."

HOFFMAN: Don't change the facts now! Ten minutes are crucial for my story!

GARCÍA: You are writing a story about this? You're an animal!

SOR JUANA: Am I in it?

HOFFMAN: Of course you are!

SOR JUANA: Honey, who did this to you?

GARCÍA: I saw you and as you went up the escalator you looked back.

HOFFMAN: You never said anything about a look back!

GARCÍA: Of course she looked back. That's what you do when you know you're leaving forever.

HOFFMAN: Are you suggesting she knew at 7:00 p.m.—

GARCÍA: Or 7:10 p.m.

HOFFMAN: Are you suggesting she knew at 7:10 p.m. what she was doing? What about her plane ticket to Bolivia!

GARCÍA: I saw you, Floridita. And you saw me. For a second we saw each other. The wind was blowing a wave of dust on your face but you didn't seem to notice.

FLORIDITA: I don't mind dust. I never have. It's just dust.

HOFFMAN: Dust soils.

GARCÍA: In excess kills.

SOR JUANA: It soils the faces of the passersby,
It soils the heads of those who walk with no hats.
Their faces, their heads so dirty with dust.

GARCÍA: So dirty with dust.

SOR JUANA: Dust asphyxiates the weak.

GARCÍA: Excuse me?

SOR JUANA: Those who lack pulmonary strength.

HOFFMAN: But she…She's immune to dust.

GARCÍA: The train rattling, the crowd screaming, the wind blowing, but her, smiling, immune to dust. It's friends with the wind.

HOFFMAN: She is?

GARCÍA: No, the dust.

SOR JUANA: Wind lifts the dust from the ground
And takes it places, faces, heads, arms. It takes it places.

GARCÍA: Far.

SOR JUANA: My stomach turns.

HOFFMAN: Your stomach turns?

SOR JUANA: It slaps her face.

GARCÍA: It gets inside her eyes.

HOFFMAN: What does?

SOR JUANA: Dust. All of her body covered in dirty, filthy dust.

GARCÍA: Dusty eyes, dusty eyes make me cry.

HOFFMAN: Is this the moment when we all start to cry?

SOR JUANA: Her teeth are no longer white.

GARCÍA: She can't hear no more. All of her, dusty. But untouched.

HOFFMAN: She picks it up from the ground,
Puts it in her green little suitcase
And smiles.

GARCÍA: She's no squirrel.

SOR JUANA: She picks it up because the dust in Bolivia is different.

HOFFMAN: Cheaper.

SOR JUANA: The dust of the third world smells like blood,
The New York dust smells like a latte.

HOFFMAN: A skinny latte.

SOR JUANA: A skinny decaf venti latte.

FLORIDITA: Wait till I arrive to Bolivia with my little suitcase full of dust. They'll think it's Golden Powder. I'll become rich selling dust to the Bolivians.

GARCÍA: In Bolivian, polvo means both powder and dust.

HOFFMAN: It does? Romance languages are so beautiful.

FLORIDITA: In Bolivia I'll be the first one to create a Dust Clock. More subtle, not as pretentious as the Sand Clock, more…human.

HOFFMAN: That suitcase is too pretty to be filled with dust.
They'll stop her at the airport,
They'll think she's crazy.

FLORIDITA: I found it on the street dusting our beautiful city. By taking it with me, I do a big favor to the city of Manhattan. It'll be a sensation in Bolivia. The first time I landed on the dusty pavement it didn't hurt a bit, because the dust in New York is so harmless. Only my knees and my elbows got a little dirty. Just a little. But after the first time came the second, the third, the tenth time. It crawled into my pores, it covered my ears, it glued my pupils, and I started to cry dust, to pee dust, to shit dust, to sweat dust. I became so dusty that with every fall I was the one soiling the dust and not the other way around. The other day I was making love to Adolfo, or he was making love to me rather, actually, I wouldn't call that lovemaking, anyway, we were doing it, having sex, intercourse, coitus, doing the nasty, fucking, screwing, smashing and his dick got so dusty that it started bleeding. It was horrible, but also quite beautiful.

HOFFMAN: I never met you, Floridita. But I think I love you.

FLORIDITA: Punch me in the face.

HOFFMAN: I don't want to.

FLORIDITA: Splash me with a bucket of icy water.

GARCÍA: I don't want to.

FLORIDITA: Burn me with a cigarette butt.

HOFFMAN: I don't want to.

FLORIDITA: Tie my ankles and my wrists. Throw me into the Hudson River. If you love me, kill me. Then fuck me until you get sick of fucking a dead body and then fuck me again so I get sick with your disease.

SOR JUANA: Who did this to you?

FLORIDITA: No one. I did it myself.

18

PREGNANT WOMAN enters and sits next to her.

PREGNANT WOMAN: There are no trains coming. Not today.

FLORIDITA: Then why are you here if the train is not coming?

PREGNANT WOMAN: I have to. I can't afford a cab.

FLORIDITA: Of course.

PREGNANT WOMAN: What do you mean by of course?

FLORIDITA: I...sorry. I just assumed.

PREGNANT WOMAN: You think because I'm fat and ugly...

FLORIDITA: You're not fat. Just pregnant. And you're not ugly. Actually, I find you very attractive. Those red lips really make you stand out.

PREGNANT WOMAN: Sephora.

FLORIDITA: It doesn't matter that the lipstick is from Sephora. What matters is that it looks great on you.

PREGNANT WOMAN: You find me beautiful and yet you assumed that I'm poor.

FLORIDITA: I can't deny that. But you're poor only because you choose to be. You could get so much money if you used your belly and your red lips to manipulate people's sensitivity.

PREGNANT WOMAN: I have dignity, miss.

FLORIDITA: Dignity? What if I ask you to rub your belly like a sick gorilla for some cash? I have a lot in my case.

PREGNANT WOMAN: I don't know who you take me for, Missy, but I won't sit here…

FLORIDITA: Here, take my case with all the money inside.

PREGNANT WOMAN: I am not a beggar or a bitch. Do you think I'm stupid? You obviously have no money in that suitcase, or else you wouldn't be waiting for the train at two thirty a.m. You'd be in one of those yellow cabs on your way home.

(FLORIDITA opens the green suitcase. A splash of green light comes out of it, painting the PREGNANT WOMAN's face and forcing her to stop talking.)

FLORIDITA: Rub your belly like a sick gorilla, cry and say "Ayúdame, necesito alimentar a mi nene, mi nene tiene hambre, quiero ser una madre feliz."

PREGNANT WOMAN: *(With the actions.)* Ayúdame, por favor, necesito alimentar a mi nene…

FLORIDITA: Keep on going.

PREGNANT WOMAN: Mi nene, se me muere, se me muere, mi nene, necesita comer, ayúdame…

FLORIDITA: Say more, use your imagination.

PREGNANT WOMAN: Señoras y señores—

FLORIDITA: Don't overdo it.

PREGNANT WOMAN: Ayúdame, mi nene necesita comida y un sepulcro propio soy una buena madre, una buena madre… *(She stops because by now she's crying for real. She takes the suitcase and exits.)*

19

ADOLFO enters.

ADOLFO: Here you are. Of course, where else?

FLORIDITA: I thought you were dead.

ADOLFO: I'm a survivor.

FLORIDITA: Sure you are.

ADOLFO: Was that sarcasm? How dare you be sarcastic when you don't even speak English that well?

FLORIDITA: Qué?

ADOLFO: Let me finish! You know if there's something that kills me it's when you, the most boring, inarticulate person I have ever met, interrupt my thoughts. How dare you be sarcastic with your husband? I want you back. Don't you miss me? Don't you miss our children?

FLORIDITA: No.

ADOLFO: But they want you back.

FLORIDITA: They do?

ADOLFO: All they talk about is you.

FLORIDITA: Really? What do they say?

ADOLFO: "Daddy, where's Mom? We miss her."

FLORIDITA: Our children don't talk like that. You don't even know who they are.

ADOLFO: Who cares, they're dead.

FLORIDITA: You killed them?

ADOLFO: They started it.

FLORIDITA: How could you?

ADOLFO: I did it for you. Come back.

FLORIDITA: But I hate you.

ADOLFO: Come back.

FLORIDITA: But I really hate you.

ADOLFO: It's okay, I can cope with anything, I'm the penultimate survivor.

(FLORIDITA *laughs like never before.*)

ADOLFO: Why are you laughing?

FLORIDITA: For years you have made fun of my English, Adolfo. Years, oh god, and yet your words are so empty. Who are you? Penultimate means second to last, not the most amazing or anything of the sort.

ADOLFO: I'm leaving, I can't stand you laughing at me. But please come back.

FLORIDITA: No. Tonight is the night that I die.

ADOLFO: I'll die with you.

FLORIDITA: No, you won't. And I'm okay with that.

ADOLFO: (*Taking out a gun.*) Bitch, I'll teach you.

(*Gunshots. The action freezes.*)

20

DEATH enters.

FLORIDITA: No one has called you.

DEATH: I just can't stand to see you like this.

FLORIDITA: Then leave.

DEATH: Flora, love stories are for the weak, they won't help you now.

FLORIDITA: There's only one way to find out. Let me go on.

DEATH: Look at you. You are all messed up.

FLORIDITA: It's a hard day when you realize your love life happens only in your head.

DEATH: (*Grabbing her arm.*) Come with me.

(*FLORIDITA spits in her face.*)

DEATH: Fool. You've watched too much television. Love stories won't help you now. It makes no difference if it's me or a man who helps you, you will see my face again.

21

ADOLFO falls to the ground, perhaps dead. PERHAPS A DEAD MAN appears, gun in hand.

FLORIDITA: Throw that gun away, the cops will be here soon.

PERHAPS A DEAD MAN: We could sell it. Make a couple of bucks.

FLORIDITA: What do you mean "we could sell it"? We are not partners.

PERHAPS A DEAD MAN: Well, I meant...uh, I don't know...What if...how about I sell it and you keep the profit?

FLORIDITA: That's stupid, why would you want to do that?

PERHAPS A DEAD MAN: It'll be the beginning of something. We could...start...a...corporation.

FLORIDITA: Why would you want to start a corporation with me, we only met half an hour ago.

PERHAPS A DEAD MAN: Because...

FLORIDITA: Wait. Why did you rescue me? I thought you didn't want to see me again. "You better not be here when I get back, if I see you again, I'll kill you," you said.

PERHAPS A DEAD MAN: Well, that was the plan. I went home looking for my gun. I came back expecting to see you here and to kill you for trying to seduce me so violently. But then, I saw you with that man and I saw you for what you really are. A woman in trouble. A man who puts a woman in trouble doesn't deserve to live. So I killed him and not you. I think I love you.

ADOLFO: That's sweet.

FLORIDITA: He's not dead.

ADOLFO: Of course I'm not, I'm the penultimate survivor.

PERHAPS A DEAD MAN: Let's run.

FLORIDITA: No, we can't leave him on the floor like that.

PERHAPS A DEAD MAN: I'm going to call an ambulance.

FLORIDITA: No, finish him off.

PERHAPS A DEAD MAN: But you're no longer in trouble, why would I kill him?

ADOLFO: Floridita, who is this, your lover?

FLORIDITA: No, my colleague.

PERHAPS A DEAD MAN: Nice to meet you.

ADOLFO: The same. Are you fucking my wife?

PERHAPS A DEAD MAN: No, we're starting a corporation.

ADOLFO: So are you going to kill me or what?

PERHAPS A DEAD MAN: Do you want an ambulance instead?

FLORIDITA: No, kill him. Use your gun.

PERHAPS A DEAD MAN: I don't want to.

(He gives her the gun.)

PERHAPS A DEAD MAN: Here, you kill him.

ADOLFO: You guys look so cute when you fight. You should make sweet love after you're done with me.

PERHAPS A DEAD MAN: That's a good idea.

FLORIDITA: *(Pointing at him.)* You're a dead man.

ADOLFO: Oh, please, Floridita. You can't shoot a gun. It takes so much courage to shoot a gun.

FLORIDITA: Shut up.

ADOLFO: Your hands are shaking. Why is it so hard to make a decision? Just do it.

FLORIDITA: Adolfo, please.

ADOLFO: Come on, my love. I only married you for the money anyway.

FLORIDITA: No. You deserve to live a very long life. *(She lowers the gun.)* We're leaving.

ADOLFO: You're leaving with him?

(Long silence.)

FLORIDITA: Yes.

PERHAPS A DEAD MAN: Which way do you want to walk?

FLORIDITA: Forward. Let's walk forward.

(FLORIDITA and PERHAPS A DEAD MAN walk forward, into the tracks.)

DIRECTOR'S NOTE

Whenever I direct a play I like to imagine that the playwright has died. This mental exercise works on two different levels: on the one hand I feel free to interpret, cut, or change. I believe a director should always have the final word on which words are spoken and which are not; on the other, I feel an almost religious sense of duty towards the dead playwright. Only I have access to this precious object that is his writing and I must (religiously) make the best of it. I feel both responsible and reckless.

This experience is most accentuated when I direct a text of mine, and even more in the case of *FLORIDITA*. The play—part dream-play, part soap, part detective novel—is constructed as a series of unsolved questions: does Floridita kill herself? Does she actually receive an inheritance and marry Adolfo? How much, if anything, is real?

Instead of rewriting, I approach the play like a puzzle waiting (and wanting) to be solved. In the case of *FLORIDITA*, it begins with the creation of a space concrete enough to make us believe that she is about to jump onto the tracks, yet poetic enough to transform itself into a ballroom in Korea, the border between Mexico and the United States, a restaurant. By playing collaboratively in such a space, every word, prop, set piece, and gesture becomes an attempt at solving the unsolved while creating a physical language invisible on the page. This made-up language allows for miracles to occur: coffee makers appear from trash cans, Beethoven's music is danced through a wiggle of the hips, while the Statue of Liberty hovers over Harlem. And yet some plays refuse to be solved.

APPENDIX—ENGLISH TRANSLATION OF SCENE 13

ALEJANDRO'S MOM: Good morning.

ALEJANDRO'S DAD: Good morning.

ALEJANDRO'S MOM: Breakfast is on the table.

ALEJANDRO'S DAD: I only want coffee.

ALEJANDRO'S MOM: You'll have to make it yourself. Alejandro had the last cup.

ALEJANDRO'S DAD: Alejandro drinks coffee?

ALEJANDRO'S MOM: Since forever…

ALEJANDRO'S DAD: I didn't know.

ALEJANDRO'S MOM: How could you, if you are never here?

ALEJANDRO'S DAD: Don't start.

ALEJANDRO'S MOM: Did you know that he got into a fight in school and was suspended for three days?

ALEJANDRO'S DAD: Don't start.

ALEJANDRO'S MOM: Did you know they asked him to draw a house and he drew me. Not me in the house, no. Just me, me.

ALEJANDRO'S DAD: I said, don't start!

ALEJANDRO'S MOM: I started already!!! Why did you get in so late last night?

ALEJANDRO'S DAD: I went out with some friends…

ALEJANDRO'S MOM: Till seven in the morning?!

ALEJANDRO'S DAD: It was my day off.

ALEJANDRO'S MOM: And which day is my day off? When am I going to get a day off?

ALEJANDRO'S DAD: Whichever day you want, woman, whichever.

ALEJANDRO'S MOM: Whichever my ass! With all you eat and the little you clean, with the mess you have in this house, with all the hair you leave in the sink, my day off would be like putting a hit on you.

ALEJANDRO'S DAD: Lower your voice! I don't like when Alejandro hears us fighting.

ALEJANDRO'S MOM: Let him! Let him! He needs to know who his real father is.

ALEJANDRO'S DAD: Shut up.

ALEJANDRO'S MOM: You spent the night with whores, didn't you. With whores!!

ALEJANDRO'S DAD: Shut up, or I'll…

ALEJANDRO'S MOM: Or what?! Or what?! What will you do, hit me? Come on, hit me so I can call the police and then you will see. You will see.

(He grabs and shakes her.)

ALEJANDRO'S DAD: I'm not going to hit you unless you keep fucking with me, bitch.

ALEJANDRO'S MOM: Hit me! I can see it in your eyes that you want to hit me…

ALEJANDRO'S DAD: Why the hell did I bring you to this country if all you do is break my balls?!

ALEJANDRO'S MOM: This country? All we do is stay in fucking Brooklyn, where what's not shit is vomit.

ALEJANDRO'S DAD: You should thank me for taking you away from Cajamarca, you crazy. You wish you had been born in Brooklyn.

ALEJANDRO'S MOM: Ah, Brooklyn, Brooklyn. Brooklyn can go to hell! Where people are either beetles or pigs.

ALEJANDRO'S DAD: So leave! Leave!! Go be fed by the Matchupitchus. Leave, you ungrateful bitch!

ALEJANDRO'S MOM: Don't talk about my people like that you dirty gaucho, you disgusting gaucho, you chauvinistic gaucho.

WEST LETHARGY

Stephen Kaliski

STEPHEN KALISKI was born June 9, 1984, in Montclair, New Jersey. He spent most of his life in Charlotte, North Carolina, arriving in New York City in 2007. He graduated from Davidson College with a BA in English and a minor in theatre, and holds an MFA in directing from Brooklyn College. Steve is a director, playwright, actor, and acting teacher. He is artistic director and cofounder of Page 121 Productions, and worked as artistic assistant at Classic Stage Company from 2007–09. As an assistant director, he worked with Austin Pendleton at Classic Stage Company and with Roxana Silbert at the Royal Shakespeare Company. *West Lethargy* is his first produced play. His play *His Minute Hand* was seen at the Hollywood Fringe Festival and at 45 Bleecker Theatre in New York. Steve lives in Park Slope, Brooklyn.

West Lethargy was presented by Page 121 Productions (Stephen Kaliski and Jeffrey Feola, co-founders) as part of the New York International Fringe Festival (Elena K. Holy, Producing Artistic Director) on August 14, 2010, at the Kraine Theatre, with the following cast and credits:

Ellie .... Suzanne Lenz
Turner .... Graham Halstead
Ringle .... Joie Bauer
Nugget .... Mikaela Feely-Lehmann
Postman .... Jeffrey Feola

Director: Stephen Kaliski
Producer: Jeffrey Feola
Stage Manager: Dahee Kim
Production Designer: Aaron Switzer
Assistant Stage Manager: Rekima Cummins

West Lethargy was previously produced by Page 121 Productions at the 2009 Edinburgh Festival Fringe and at the East to Edinburgh Festival at 59E59 Theaters in New York City.

www.page121productions.org

AUTHOR'S NOTE

My first impulse for *West Lethargy* came to me while looking at a porcelain figurine of a candle-lit pioneer boy and girl praying across from one another. The image was adorable in the Hummel sense of the term yet also strangely wistful. These cute little icons were sharing an intimate moment, but with their heads bowed and their eyes closed, they were also disconnected from each other, deeply alone, wishing for private and unspeakable things even while they could feel each other's breath. And since they were decked out in pioneer garb, I could also assume they were on a journey. In this moment, were they praying for a destination? And if so, did their prayers call out to the same place? What would happen if, per chance, the girl looked up in the middle of the prayer and saw a changed boy across from her, a boy wishing for an unseen land?

The theatre is the perfect venue for telling stories about people who can't seem to get quite where they want to go. Like the four siblings of *Three Sisters* and the talking heads of Beckett, the two couples of *West Lethargy* can richly imagine their destinations, but when it comes to actually moving their feet, they're left looking out the window, confined by that pervasive longing that so defines this theatre of the stuck. These stories remind us that planning an endpoint is not the easiest step of the journey. In fact, it can be the most suffocating.

The world of *West Lethargy* is obviously full of whimsy, but if you produce this play, remember that its characters are very real. The whimsy merely comes out of the full visualization of their longings. For Ellie, the man on the table is true. For Ringle, the seventy-third floor is where the good stuff really happens. For Nugget, a picture is worth a thousand comic books. For Turner, even the chickens need a lullaby. *West Lethargy* is a play about prayer, about closing your eyes and willing the world to move even when your feet cannot.

CHARACTERS

ELLIE
NUGGET
POSTMAN

TURNER
RINGLE

PLACE

Somewhere on the journey West.

NOTES

Breaks within lines can be used as quick beats, momentary thoughts, or they can be ignored. Other than those that are scripted, don't allow too many pauses to creep in. The pace should be lively.

For the story game sequence in scene 6, the actors step out of character while playing, as if hypnotized. Movement should be stylized.

PROLOGUE

Low light. TURNER sits on the floor, writing a note on a greeting card. He finishes the card, smiles, and stuffs it in a red envelope, which he then seals, addresses, and stamps. He puts the card on the floor. A POSTMAN with a satchel enters, picks up the card, and stows it away, exiting.

1.

Lights up on a wood cabin. A simple living area. Stools, table. Two small piles of personal effects, one his, one hers. A picture of him on the table. ELLIE and TURNER, twenties, wear old-fashioned clothes. ELLIE does chores. TURNER sits on the floor, tossing marbles into a tin. When he runs out, he gathers the marbles from the tin and starts tossing again. ELLIE stops her chores and watches.

ELLIE: Stop sulking. You're like a leak when you sulk. A bunch of noises going drip drop drip drop drip drop. And I'm just the bucket to catch them all.

(He tosses another marble.)

ELLIE: TURNER!

TURNER: I don't understand.

ELLIE: What?

TURNER: We're not settlers, we're pioneers.

ELLIE: If you say so.

TURNER: We didn't need to build this house.

ELLIE: It was time to stop. We needed to rest.

TURNER: Alright. Good. We've rested. Now let's get out of here.

ELLIE: You're dreaming. You're just dreaming. In a dream, nothing gets left behind. In real life, we'd be wasting a perfectly good house.

TURNER: People waste houses all the time. That's how moving works. Besides…there's no mail here.

ELLIE: Mail?!

TURNER: No mail. We're not home till we get mail.

ELLIE: You dreamer.

TURNER: Pioneer. You are too.

ELLIE: Sulk sulk sulk. I'm wrong and you're right. Now get up and help me with the chicken.

TURNER: How are we preparing it this evening?

ELLIE: Maple glazed. Get up.

TURNER: The lives we lead.

ELLIE: Hungry lives if you don't get up and help.

TURNER: Pray with me first.

(Pause.)

ELLIE: Turner...

TURNER: Come on. Come over here and pray with me. Then I'll help you with your chicken.

ELLIE: I don't think so. Not now.

TURNER: Why not?

ELLIE: Why not? It's not a why not question. I don't want to.

TURNER: Why?

ELLIE: Why? I don't have to give you a reason why.

TURNER: Why not?

ELLIE: Be quiet.

TURNER: Wherefore? Wherethither? Hitherwhence?

ELLIE: Please be quiet.

TURNER: It will only take a second.

ELLIE: I don't think it's appropriate.

TURNER: *(Slinking toward her.)* It's just between you and me. No one will see us. We haven't had a passerby since Easter. He was blind and we gave him soup. Then we pointed him in the right direction. It's easy, we told him, it's all downhill from here. Then he went on his blind, merry, hopefully stumpless way and we were left here all by our lonesome. Let us pray for more guests like him.

ELLIE: Turner. It's not... the right time.

TURNER: Why not?

ELLIE: You know... you've been sulking!

TURNER: Oh, please. The door's locked. And the squirrels aren't tall enough to see through the window.

ELLIE: Later.

TURNER: There is no later in our house. There's only chicken, and I determine that.

(Pause.)

ELLIE: Fine.

TURNER: What's that?

ELLIE: I said FINE. But quickly.

TURNER: You won't regret it.

(They kneel across from each other. Praying position. Pause.)

TURNER: You first.

ELLIE: No, it was your idea.

TURNER: I have another idea. You first.

ELLIE: *(She sighs. She thinks long and hard. She prays.)* A beautiful dress. A lifetime supply of cinnamon sugar. A microscope with a built-in compass. A knack for legal documents. A horsie. A decent map of the surrounding counties. Belle of the ball honors. House calls from the doctor. A town named after us. A country formed because of us. Fresh bread. Firm thighs forever and ever. The end.

(Pause.)

ELLIE: Your turn now.

TURNER: *(He prays.)* California. The end.

ELLIE: No fair. You can't just pray for California.

TURNER: It's my prayer.

ELLIE: You're supposed to pray for everything. That's the rule. You pray for everything. Stop sulking and dreaming and forcing me to pray if you're not going to pray for everything.

TURNER: Maybe I did.

(She turns away.)

TURNER: Oh, Ellie. *(Pause.)* I am a dreamer, you're right. You were in my dream last night. It's a recurring dream. It starts with me running through a field then tripping over you like you were a stump or a picnic basket. I ask if I hurt you and all you do is laugh. You laugh till you cry.

(He takes her hands in his and guides them as he talks.)

Then you hold my face and carve lines all up and down with your pinky, and I ask you what you're doing and you say you're showing me where my wrinkles will be. We laugh and pray and repeat each other over and over until we can't remember who began the conversation. Then we run through the field. *(He blows on her hair.)* Wind in our hair.

ELLIE: *(Softly.)* Don't say those things to me.

TURNER: I will if it gets your attention.

ELLIE: You've got it.

TURNER: Then I'll keep saying them. Ellie. What's going on? You can tell me.

ELLIE: Nothing is how I imagined it.

TURNER: California will fix everything. It waits there full of imagined things.

ELLIE: I'm not so sure.

TURNER: Neither am I, but there's only one way to find out.

(Pause.)

ELLIE: Go get the chicken.

TURNER: I thought you had it already.

ELLIE: No.

TURNER: Well where is it?

ELLIE: To the Northeast I think.

TURNER: Fine.

(He touches his nose to ELLIE's forehead and holds it there. She lets him. He stands, grabs a large fork, and leaves to kill the chicken. ELLIE stands by the window and watches him walk away. She goes to his pile of effects and rummages. She pulls out his shirt. She smells it. It intoxicates her. She pulls out his belt. A pair of his pants. His socks. His shoes. She carries them to the table and places them down in the proper order. She puts his picture at the head, forming a man without a body. She lies down on the table next to her creation. She hums. A long time snuggling. Giggling. Staring.)

ELLIE: Do we have to get up? Noooooo. Let's stay in bed. All day long. The chores can wait, everything can wait. My God I love you so much. I want to be next to you the whole day. My God.

(Pause. She holds him close and sings a lullaby.)

Let us pause in life's pleasures and count
    its many tears,
While we all sup sorrow with the poor;
There's a song that will linger forever
    in our ears;
Oh hard times come again no more.

(She sits up, looks around. The cabin actually is drab.)

We could spruce it up, I suppose. Some rugs, maybe. Or bright red chairs. If we had some color around the table, we could…wait!…we could use a big sheet of paper as our tablecloth, and we could get a big box of crayons, and you and I could draw all sorts of pictures while we eat. Perfect. If we run out of things to talk about, we could draw a new topic. Seasonal things. Like Christmas trees. *(Pretending.)* Turner, look what I've drawn, it reminds me that this weekend you need to take an axe out to the woods and chop us down a big beautiful Christmas tree, the one that smells the freshest of them all!

(She's an old lady.)

Whatever you want to make, dear. I'm sure it will be wonderful.

I'm so tired. I will just sit and rest. I will read a book for a while. Only twenty pages to go. I can't possibly stop now.

Ohhhhhhhhh remember when? When I was the belle of the ball?

What is that? It smells delicious. What is it, something with, something with... *(Smelling.)* ...cinnamon? What's a synonym for cinnamon? *(Five times fast.)* Synonym for cinnamon synonym for cinnamon synonym for smonym—

(She laughs.)

It will all be a fairy tale. A bright shimmering kitchen is as infectious as newfallen snow.

(Noise outside. ELLIE quickly gathers up the effects and throws them back into the pile. TURNER enters carrying an enormous model of the Empire State Building. No chicken. ELLIE stares at it. Silence.)

TURNER: No chicken.

(Pause.)

ELLIE: No chicken?

TURNER: They've all gone. Migration season. All the chickens are gone.

I came across two people in the woods, though. They insisted I have this. *(Pause.)* Ellie?

ELLIE: What is it?

TURNER: It's a decoration.

ELLIE: It's...big.

TURNER: Tall.

ELLIE: Yes—

TURNER: As tall as...three chickens. One on top of the other.

ELLIE: Three chickens tall.

TURNER: They all fall down! *(He acts like three chickens falling down.)* Tumble bumble shtumble. KaplowEE!

ELLIE: How much did it cost?

TURNER: It was a gift. What do you think?

ELLIE: I think it's...odd. *(Pause.)* Wait. Who?

TURNER: Who?

ELLIE: The people who gave it to you.

TURNER: Oh. Our new neighbors. Nugget and Ringle.

ELLIE: Liar. New neighbors? I don't believe you.

TURNER: I'm not lying. It's true. I went out for the chicken, headed straight Northeast, like you said. Then I heard a clanging sound, really loud. I followed it. And there she was. Nugget. She was putting pipes in the ground. She said it's for the water. Then she took me inside and introduced me to her husband, Ringle. He had two decorations just like this, and he was doing something to one, working on it.

They're good people. Decent people. I wish we could have talked more. But they were busy of course. Ringle wanted to give me a welcome-to-the-neighborhood gift before I left. So—

ELLIE: He welcomed you? We already live here.

TURNER: The neighborhood's new, though.

ELLIE: So they were welcoming the neighborhood?

TURNER: If you put it that way.

ELLIE: Where are they from?

TURNER: Not sure, but they're heading to California. Like us. They just needed a rest, too. *(He does a happy little dance.)* See? All roads lead to California.

ELLIE: The roads lead everywhere. You're just dead set in your ways.

(He hugs her.)

TURNER: Neighbors, Ellie! We have neighbors. Nugget's coming over tomorrow to install our pipes.

ELLIE: Nugget is—

TURNER: —the girl. Sweet girl.

ELLIE: This is all very exciting.

TURNER: I know. Right? It'll be nice to have some company. You'll like Ringle. He seems like a real jokester.

ELLIE: *(Looks at the Empire State Building.)* What is this thing?

(Pause.)

TURNER: I don't know. It's modern.

I think the dots are all windows. All tiny little windows.

ELLIE: With tiny little people inside?

TURNER: Tiny little people with tiny little lives.

ELLIE: Can you imagine?

TURNER: Can you imagine being in the top window?

ELLIE: And having to get down?

TURNER: Tiny little steps!

(They start to walk down tiny little steps. They laugh.)

ELLIE: Tiny little steps all the way down!

TURNER: To tiny little exits!

ELLIE: Tiny little days of tiny little tasks.

TURNER: Tiny little nights of tiny tired legs.

ELLIE: There's something to it.

TURNER: Tiny little Monday voices saying NO NO NOT AGAIN.

ELLIE: Not again!

TURNER: Not again!!

ELLIE: Give me my tiny little Friday!

TURNER: Give it to me now!!

ELLIE: Everything is so tiny.

TURNER: Tinier than normal, for sure.

ELLIE: But nothing tiny about IT.

TURNER: Right. The pieces all together…

ELLIE: The pieces make a shape. *(Pause.)* Let's dress it up.

TURNER: Why not?

ELLIE: That's what it's for, I think. That must be what it's for.

TURNER: Like a doll. A really strange doll.

ELLIE: Yes. Come on. Let's dress it up.

Like a snowman!

(She runs over to her pile of effects and grabs some articles. Bonnets, scarves, gloves, etc. He does the same. Boots, pants, belt. They decorate the building.)

ELLIE: A snowman named what?

TURNER: A snowman named Joe.

ELLIE: A snowman named Terry.

TURNER: A snowman named Poodleberry.

ELLIE: A snowman named Sophocles.

TURNER: Lorna!

ELLIE: Peter!

TURNER: Merlin!

ELLIE: Arthur!

(They continue with a cascade of improvised names until they've thrown everything on the snowman.)

TURNER: William Eli Tabernacle!

ELLIE: The Fourth!

TURNER: The Fifth.

ELLIE: The Sixth!

TURNER: The Seventh!

(He tears off his shirt, throws it on the snowman. She stares at him. Pause.)

TURNER: It's a nice decoration.

(Lights.)

2.

NUGGET and RINGLE's cabin. Looks the same as TURNER and ELLIE's, but things are arranged differently. The Empire State Building is off to the corner. The two piles of effects are less orderly, and backpacks hang from the wall. The picture remains. RINGLE crouches by the Empire State Building in contemporary clothes. He is intensely focused on one particular story. He occasionally scribbles in a notebook.

RINGLE: When his day's work is done, he takes a moment to look out over his city.

"Janice, come in here! Come and see this! The world is rising up around us! Janice? JANICE?" Janice cannot hear him, though, because Janice is… *(Makes a note.)* …deaf. Totally deaf. Deaf as a doornail. *(Is that right?)* Deaf as a doornail. She writes a hell of a letter, though, that's why he keeps her on. Granted, it's difficult to dictate prose to a deaf assistant—he has to ARTICULATE VERY CLEARLY WITH HIS LIPS—but she makes up for that with her damn fine writing skills. She's a damn fine assistant. *(Makes a note.)* With a damn fine body.

(He moves his focus seven stories higher.)

Nobody knows that better than the boy on seventy-three. He's waiting for her, for her gray…slate…hot…blistering business-suited ass. *(Makes a note.)*

She'll be there soon. It's the end of the day for Janice, but instead of going down to the street she pushes the button heading up. "Forget something up there?" asks Larry the attendant. He has *(Makes a note.)* VERY LARGE LIPS and VERRRY SLOOOWWW DELIVERY—"FORRRGET SOMMMEHING UUUP THEEEERE?"—so she understands him perfectly. "Yes, I left my purse on seventy-three." "And yesterday it was your scarf?" "Yes sir, yesterday it was my scarf." "And the day before it was your Tupperware?" "Yes sir, the day before it was my Tupperware."

Every single day, some object on seventy-three begs for its remembrance. Or so thinks the boy, who sits at his desk with a pencil in hand only so it will look like he's working when Janice walks in, so it will look like she's interrupting him, so it'll feel like what's happening isn't expected, isn't allowed. "You shouldn't be up here," he whispers when she slides in. She can't read his lips, though. His lips are thin, stiff, impatient. *(Makes a note.)* He might as well have said, "Rub-a-dub-dub two pugs in a tub," *(Is that right?)* but whatever. Her purse isn't there, and neither is her scarf, and neither is her Tupperware, and soon neither is anything else as they throw themselves on his desk and the pencil snaps and she pounds the paperweight for dear life.

(He pounds the floor, getting a little too into it.)

Their lovemaking is ferocious, furious. She makes all the noise she wants, because what does she care, she's deaf as a doornail. He tries to silence her at first, but it has the reverse effect and she finds it titillating and cries even louder. *(He makes an absurd orgasmic yawp.)*

(NUGGET enters in rain gear. He acknowledges her but continues his orgasmic yawping unaffected, climaxing in violent spasms. NUGGET takes off her rain gear. She's wearing a T-shirt and jean shorts. RINGLE moves down a story to seventy-two. Postcoital.)

RINGLE: "Sounds like somebody's having fun," the janitor on seventy-two says to himself. What can he do? Nothing, except make sure that the right floor is cleaned at the right time. He'll have to wait awhile for seventy-three.

To pass the time, he walks to the window, looks out over the city. "It's rising up all around us," he thinks. "It's all closing in.

Buildings here, buildings there, buildings here there and everywhere. Soon there won't be room to move. No room to move North, or South, or East, or West. Soon we'll all be...we'll all be..." *(Searching for the word.)*

What's the word?

NUGGET: Stuck?

RINGLE: No. Like that, but less unwilling.

NUGGET: I'm not sure.

RINGLE: Like when you can't move, but it's not necessarily a bad thing?

NUGGET: Lazy?

RINGLE: No.

NUGGET: Asleep?

RINGLE: No. That's not it. What is it? "Soon we'll all be..."

NUGGET: Gleefully immobile. Wildly entrapped. Narcotically lethargic.

RINGLE: Yes, but like all six of those words combined into one.

NUGGET: This is a real word?

RINGLE: Yes, I swear it was in the crossword the other day.

NUGGET: No idea. Just say stuck for now, but in an upbeat tone.

RINGLE: *(As if delivering good news.)* "Soon we'll all be stuck!"

"Soon we'll all be STUCK!"

Yuck.

Oh well.

It will come to me. *(Pause.)* Is he gone?

NUGGET: He is.

(Pause. She glares at him.)

RINGLE: What?

NUGGET: You know what.

RINGLE: We had to give him something.

NUGGET: That wasn't yours to give.

RINGLE: We had two of them. We only need one.

NUGGET: We had two of them because one of them is ours and the other is not theirs.

You know what it means to me.

RINGLE: If your brother had wanted it, he would have taken it to California with him. If he decides he wants it again, he'll come back for it, or at least send a letter. *(Pause.)* Oh, kitten.

(He pats her back.)

RINGLE: You miss him, I know. He'll come back.

NUGGET: No note. No call. No hint of anything. Just one neighbor who said she saw him heading West.

RINGLE: I know. I know. He'll come back.

NUGGET: We'll find him first.

(Pause.)

RINGLE: You know what? I'll say I made a mistake. This weekend when we go to their cabin for dinner, when the meal's over and we're getting ready to leave, I'll say, "Mr. Turner and Miss Ellie, I just realized that this gift has a major structural flaw, and we can't in good conscience leave it with you. So we have ordered a new one that will be here soon. Regards, Ringle and Nugget."

NUGGET: Fine. But don't rehearse it too much.

RINGLE: I want to be prepared.

NUGGET: Everything you say sounds rehearsed. I bet they think we're total nutsos.

RINGLE: Reason being?

NUGGET: You were crouched by your building the whole time he was here. I was in rubber boots and gloves installing a shower. When he asked you where you were born, you said, "Your guess is as good as mine."

RINGLE: I was in the middle of a story. I was distracted.

I'm onto seventy-three now. As you may have heard.

NUGGET: I caught the tail end. Sounds like quite a story.

RINGLE: It's one of the best ones yet.

NUGGET: I can't wait to hear the rest.

RINGLE: It's got lots of elevator action. It involves lots of other floors.

NUGGET: Magnificent.

RINGLE: I agree.

(Pause.)

NUGGET: They probably don't even know what to do with it. You didn't explain it. He probably just thinks it's a decoration. *(Pause.)* He reminds me of him.

There's a resemblance. I don't know.

RINGLE: I thought so, too. A dead ringer, in fact.

NUGGET: Of all the people…

(Pause.)

RINGLE: *(Changing the subject.)* Do you know what I read this morning? Over coffee? I read that as long as you wear close-toed shoes, you're in no danger of being bitten by a coral snake. Their jaws are too small.

(Silence.)

NUGGET: Where'd you read that?

RINGLE: Oh, from some napkin in the pile. Interesting, isn't it? Of course you'd never want to pet a coral snake. They could certainly wrap their fangs around your pinky.

NUGGET: I don't want to pet a coral snake.

RINGLE: Pinkies are dangerous. You forget you even have them. I bet if you counted up all the snakebites over human history, the pinky would be the part of the body that's been bitten most.

(NUGGET kisses him.)

NUGGET: You think more than God himself.

RINGLE: There's so much to consider.

NUGGET: It's good…keeps my mind off things.

RINGLE: Yes…

Ankles, too. I bet they've been bitten a lot, too.

(Pause. She takes the picture from the table. Looks deep into it.)

RINGLE: How's the shower?

NUGGET: It's running.

The pipes connected just fine. Water pressure's great.

RINGLE: Temperature?

NUGGET: Great.

RINGLE: Hot water is important.

NUGGET: It is.

RINGLE: The three criteria to life: clean, safe, and hot water.

NUGGET: Yes. *(Pause.)* You're right. A dead ringer. The spitting image. *(She is near tears.)*

RINGLE: I'm going to try the shower. *(Pause.)* Thanks for hooking up the pipes.

(She cries.)

RINGLE: Oh, kitten…come here.

NUGGET: Go ahead, I'm fine.

RINGLE: Kitten, come here. This is the best plan. I'm sure of it. We'll stay here until we have a concrete reason to keep going. Until we know for sure where he is. Otherwise we may crisscross without knowing it, and then it all would have been for nothing.

NUGGET: We're in the middle of nowhere.

RINGLE: The middle. Exactly. Best place to be.

(She looks at him.)

NUGGET: Go take your shower.

RINGLE: Do I smell?

NUGGET: That's not what I meant.

(She pulls at his waist.)

NUGGET: You should get away from your stories. They must be very draining.

(She spanks him.)

RINGLE: Now I don't want to take a shower.

NUGGET: You have to. All roads lead there. I have deemed it so.

RINGLE: Don't move an inch.

NUGGET: Go.

(He hustles out of the cabin as quickly as possible. She watches him go. Sound of a shower offstage. NUGGET picks up the picture. She crouches by the Empire State Building. She's looking for someone in particular.)

NUGGET: On today's episode of The Astounding Leaps and Bounds of NUGGET and Dollop...

Window washers in peril! A tale of...ultimate danger culminating in...safety!

Weather report: isolated volcanoes with a chance of hurricanes.

And so we rejoin our heroes, Nugget and Dollop, brother and sister extraordinaire, on their sensational quest to elude the gangster, Coral the Snake.

Today, with Coral himself at their very toes, Nugget and Dollop must don the costumes of...window washers! The perfect disguise. Just keep a straight face, wash and repeat, wash and repeat...BUT ZOUNDS! The window carriage is out of order for routine maintenance!

"What are we gonna do, Dollop? We gotta wash. Otherwise Coral will find us and shoot us with his poison arrows!

What's that? What'd you say? Climb up the windows like monkeys?

Great idea! Just don't fall and die, Mom will kill me."

And so our heroes shimmy like apes from floor to floor, their buckets and squeegees dangling from their ankles, imminent death one goof-up away.

Wash and repeat. Wash and repeat.

UNTIL SUDDENLY an unexpected volcano rushes in from the West, all red and hot and gooey! Our heroes know the danger: ninety-nine out of a hundred and two window washers lose their lives via isolated volcanoes.

"It's raining fire, Dollop! What are we gonna do?! The window carriage is out of order!

What?! Pray?

You're right, you're right, it's the best option now.

Which one?

The one where we put ourselves into the grand scheme of things?

Okay Okay! Let's do that one.

But fast!

Hold my hands.

Don't look down.

Look at me.

Don't. Let. Go.

(Pause.)

NOW!

THE UNIVERSE!

The Milky Way.

THE SOLAR SYSTEM!

The Planet Earth.

The atmosphere.

The hemisphere.

The continent.

The island.

The building.

Coral the Snake.

The fifth ledge from the top.

Knock knock knock!

Who's there?

It's me.

It's me.

It's you.

It's you.

Your heart.

Your brain.

My heart.

My brain.

Us.

Us.

Here.

Here.

Hard times come again no more hard times come again no more HARD TIMES COME AGAIN NO MORE THE END!"

(Pause.)

And we're fine.

(Lights.)

3.

Sound of shower offstage continues in scene change. Cabin goes back to ELLIE and TURNER's. TURNER pokes at the Empire State Building. Picks it up. Carries it around. Puts it back. Starts to count the windows. There are too many. He looks at one.

TURNER: Hello?

Is...is anyone in there?

Ellie? Is that you?

Ellie, what if you were in there? Tiny little you in there and big old me out here...I'd always be whispering and you'd always be shouting. *(Pretending.)* THE SALT? yes pass the salt. YOU WANT THE SALT? i want the water. YOU HAVE THE WATER. keep your voice down. WHAT'S NEW TODAY?

I lost track of who's who.

Pssssst. Ellie. Did you check the mail? Ellie!

SORRY sorry, I should keep my voice down. *(Pause.)* Do you want to come out now? *(Pause.)* You're right. Too many stairs.

(Shower stops. NUGGET enters in a bath towel and shower cap. Pause.)

NUGGET: The water pressure's great now. Temperature's just right. You should try it.

TURNER: You amaze me.

NUGGET: It wasn't that difficult. Once I found the pipes, I just had to connect the dots.

TURNER: It seems impossible.

NUGGET: It's not.

(She starts to undo the towel. He watches.)

NUGGET: No peeky.

(He turns around. She slips on a robe.)

NUGGET: An outdoor shower isn't the most current style. But it will serve for the time being. At least you don't need a drain. The water will just drip through the slats and absorb into the soil.

You should really try it.

TURNER: What do I owe you?

NUGGET: Don't worry about it. It's nothing.

(Pause. NUGGET roams around the room.)

NUGGET: When will your lovely lady be back?

TURNER: Who knows.

These walks she takes… they go on and on.

NUGGET: She's just a stroller? A bird-watcher?

TURNER: I don't know.

NUGGET: A naturalist? A devotee of the living world?

TURNER: Maybe.

NUGGET: What does she like to do?

TURNER: She likes…

She likes to walk.

NUGGET: She's beautiful.

(TURNER smiles. Pause.)

NUGGET: You gonna keep her?

(TURNER laughs, looks away, slowly looks back to NUGGET. He knows what she means. Pause.)

TURNER: What does your name mean?

NUGGET: My name is a bastardization of three consecutive tripthongs and a downwardly inflected interrobang that was last seen in a partially extant pottery shard in the Holy Land. The original construction was difficult for native speakers to pronounce. *(Pause.)* Kidding. It just means nugget. I didn't pick it. My brother's name is Dollop, for what it's worth.

TURNER: Nugget.

NUGGET: Like gold and chickens.

TURNER: Which were you named for?

NUGGET: Neither. My mother found it in a crossword puzzle.

TURNER: Tell me about her.

NUGGET: You don't want to know.

TURNER: Tell me about something.

NUGGET: What should I tell you about?

TURNER: The building. Did you make it yourself?

NUGGET: *(Laughs.)* God no. Everyone has one back home. We walk everywhere with them. Take them to the market, take them to the theatre. Tickets are half-price for buildings. That's how the shows stay in business. If theatres charged full price for buildings, no one could afford to be lonely. *(Kidding again.)*

No, we don't make them. We just fill them with all the shit that never came true.

TURNER: You must live in a strange place.

NUGGET: We live in the same place now.

(Pause. NUGGET takes the picture. Looks deep into it.)

NUGGET: This you?

(He nods.)

NUGGET: Handsome man.

(He smiles.)

NUGGET: When are you going to leave her?

(Pause.)

TURNER: It's not my fault.

NUGGET: You're doing the leaving.

If we were in our wagons right now, and we stopped for the night to build camp, and I saw the same thing in her eyes that I see in yours, I'd ask her, "When are you going to remain behind?"

Because she'd be doing the remaining.

But with the new neighborhood and all...you're leaving, buster.

TURNER: I was expecting something, and it's not here.

NUGGET: So you're gonna ride off and find it?

TURNER: I don't know. Maybe.

NUGGET: You boys. So impatient.

TURNER: You're blaming me.

NUGGET: I'm not blaming you.

I can't blame you without blaming myself.

I'm giving you responsibility.

TURNER: Responsibility? So who's responsible in your house?

NUGGET: Your guess is as good as mine.

TURNER: I'm betting it's you.

NUGGET: What am I responsible for?

TURNER: I don't know.

(Silence.)

TURNER: We were heading West to begin with. Then we just stopped. To rest. We're far enough, she said. It's nice right here, she said. Let's just rest. *(Pause.)* It's so weird. I met Ellie in a churchyard back where we used to live. Everyone had gone home for the day, the drought had killed the grass. She was cleaning up the picnic tables, and I was standing on the church step. There was wind...in her hair. "Let's move to California!" I said. That was the first thing I said to her.

Strangers in an open field. That was the closest we got.

Seems backwards to me. Not right.

NUGGET: "They were one before they met, and now ever more the two."

(Pause.)

NUGGET: It does make you wonder... *(Places the picture down, moves face to face with TURNER.)* ...if the best is at the beginning.

(She runs her hands over his arms. He is frozen. She examines his fingers. Listens to his pulse. Like a specimen.)

NUGGET: If that's when you're the closest.

Getting to know you is fun.

Knowing you is such a burden.

TURNER: What are you—

NUGGET: If the best is when we're complete strangers.

(She moves his hands over her face. Pause.)

NUGGET: You remind me of my brother.

TURNER: That's not what I wanted to hear.

NUGGET: But you do.

TURNER: That's weird.

NUGGET: Very weird.

I love him. I worry about him all the time. Then he up and runs away.

Selfish prick.

I told Ringle we had to find him. He went along with the plan until we got here. Then he made me stop.

So who's responsible in our house? It changes.

If we let bygones be bygones, I'll be responsible for the next part.

You really do remind me of him.

Maybe all restless men look alike.

(Pause.)

TURNER: You amaze me.

(TURNER takes her face in his hands. He carves out every detail, shyly at first, then with more confidence.)

NUGGET: That's nice.

What's it called?

TURNER: Showing you where your wrinkles will be.

(They kiss. Lights.)

4.

NUGGET and RINGLE's cabin. ELLIE sits by the building, sobbing. RINGLE stands to the side, not sure how to console her.

RINGLE: Nugget should be back soon. Maybe you'd want to talk to her. I…I'm a sort of goof when it comes to these things.

I'm afraid I'm a terrible comforter.

Of course, if there's anything I can do…

I apologize for not being…

Well.

(He awkwardly pats her on the back.)

RINGLE: You just sit there and get it all out. Get it all out, and you'll feel much much MUCH better. My father used to say that crying is like Chinese food, it never seems to run out of itself, then suddenly, on the third day of leftovers, it's gone.

That is to say, all things of this sort come in a finite amount. Even if it doesn't seem so at first.

There there. There there.

ELLIE: Thank you. Sometimes it's just having someone different to talk to. You're a good listener.

RINGLE: Ah! My first testimonial. I'll put that on my CV and my tombstone, if you don't mind. Quote "a GOOD listener" end quote, the lovely Miss Ellie.

ELLIE: Let's talk about something else.

RINGLE: A fine idea!

ELLIE: *(Gathering herself.)* So, Ringle.

Who are you?

RINGLE: Why, Ringle, of course.

(She laughs. He's a sweetheart.)

ELLIE: I mean, what were you…before you were a pioneer?

RINGLE: I worked in an office.

ELLIE: What did you do there?

RINGLE: I worked for a small unit of an urban planning corporation that oversaw the evaluation of area bridges. When the unit determined that a bridge no longer served its purpose, it was my responsibility to see that the bridge was removed.

It was not a satisfying line of work.

ELLIE: Interesting, though. I love bridges.

RINGLE: I do too, which is why I hated to burn them.

Before I quit, I realized that all jobs either add or remove certain somethings from the world. You need to make sure that your job aligns with your tastes.

Add something you enjoy, or remove something you dislike.

But yes…that's what I did. I worked in an office.

ELLIE: My favorite bridge was a swinging bridge in the mountains. It connected two peaks and overlooked a river a mile below. My father used to take me there the first warm day of every spring. We'd cross to the middle and do our own countdown—"Ten, nine, eight, seven, six, five, four, three, two, one, HAPPY SPRINGTIME!"—I don't know how we started doing that, but it was a tradition and we did it every year.

One spring, my father heard something in the wood, and he told the woodsman. He took a look at the bridge and determined that the wood was completely rotten, one more step from a mouse and that'd be it. He cut it down right away. We were the last people to cross it.

I remember feeling responsible.

Your job must have been difficult. I understand.

RINGLE: It's a job for a certain type of person, to be sure. *(Pause.)* Nugget and I are looking forward to dinner this weekend.

ELLIE: Yes, Turner and I are excited to have you.

RINGLE: I'd be happy to offer the prayer before we eat.

ELLIE: We'd be happy for you to do so.

RINGLE: It's a simple prayer. All I say is, "That our choices have been right, that our roads may be free from traffic. The end."

ELLIE: It's a beautiful prayer.

RINGLE: I'll say it again at dinner.

(Pause.)

ELLIE: Ringle, would you mind…

This may seem like a strange request, but…

Would you mind giving me a hug?

(Pause.)

RINGLE: Not at all.

(ELLIE remains still and lets him awkwardly embrace her. She then clutches him tightly. RINGLE gives her some light pats, wonders when she'll let go.)

RINGLE: I'm sorry, I'm not the best—

ELLIE: No, you are. This is the best. This is all I needed.

(NUGGET enters in her bathrobe, towel and shower cap in hand. ELLIE and RINGLE break their embrace.)

NUGGET: Sorry.

RINGLE: Oh! No worries, kitten. Miss Ellie just needed some comforting, and I was providing—

ELLIE: Ringle—

RINGLE: —just that. She was weeping a little—

ELLIE: I was not—

RINGLE: And I was doing everything in my power to help her reach a sound…conclusion…

NUGGET: Sorry, I—

RINGLE: I explained, kitten, that you were better at this than I, that, so to speak, if we were pitted against one another in a "duel to the death" of sweet nothings, you would beat me handily.

NUGGET: I'm not sure about that.

RINGLE: *(Anxious to get out the door.)* So humble! Ah. Ah yes. Where's Turner? At home? Across the way? How're the pipes?

NUGGET: All fixed.

ELLIE: That's good.

RINGLE: Time for me to check them out myself? To give them a little inspection?

NUGGET: No, they're all done—

RINGLE: But a second opinion is always wise. So the medical profession says. I think it's smart. There's great wisdom in medicine. I shall give the pipes a look-see myself.

NUGGET: Ringle, it's really not—

RINGLE: Miss Ellie, stay as long as you please. Keep the missus company. Girl time! What a valuable commodity. In today's world…

(RINGLE exits. The women look at each other. Long silence. NUGGET moves to her pile of effects. She slips on jean shorts beneath her robe. Uncomfortable.)

ELLIE: What are those called?

NUGGET: Jeans. Jean shorts. They're, um… jean shorts.

ELLIE: Oh. *(Pause.)* Jean shorts.

(NUGGET turns her back to ELLIE and drops her robe. She puts on a loose T-shirt.)

ELLIE: What's that?

NUGGET: Oh. Um… A T-shirt?

ELLIE: Oh.

T-shirt.

It's very nice. *(Pause.)* May I?

(ELLIE walks to NUGGET. She examines the T-shirt. How it fits. How it feels. She pulls at it. She stops. Looks at the floor. Silence.)

NUGGET: We could go shopping sometime. If you want.

ELLIE: Shopping.

NUGGET: Yeah. Shopping.

ELLIE: Huh. Maybe. *(Pause.)* Do you have extras?

NUGGET: Um. Sure.

ELLIE: May I borrow them?

NUGGET: Sure. Let me…

(NUGGET goes to her effects. Finds an extra pair of shorts and a T-shirt and hands them to ELLIE.)

NUGGET: Take these.

ELLIE: Thank you. *(Feels the fabric of the borrowed clothes. Pause.)* How long are you going to stay?

NUGGET: Not long.

(Lights.)

5.

ELLIE and TURNER's cabin. TURNER is frantically packing his effects. Every now and then he peeks out the window to see if ELLIE is coming. He looks at his picture. He brings it to the table and contemplates it. He starts to open the frame. Sound of shower offstage. TURNER jumps. He starts to replace everything he'd packed. Shower stops. RINGLE enters, wet. He's dripping like a savage.

RINGLE: The pipes work!

TURNER: God, Ringle…

RINGLE: I love my lady. She always gets it right. *(Notices the half-packed effects.)* Where to, cowboy?

TURNER: I'm…reorganizing.

RINGLE: Ah right. No time like the present, with running water and beautiful women, to reorganize one's life.

(RINGLE sees TURNER's building.)

Breathtaking, isn't it?

TURNER: Ringle, if you'll excuse me—

RINGLE: Have you been to the fifty-fifth floor yet?

TURNER: Sorry?

RINGLE: Turner my man. Idea. Nugget and Miss Ellie are being girls together. Let us turn the tides and be men!

(RINGLE pounds TURNER on the back, not knowing his own strength.)

TURNER: OW!

(He pushes RINGLE back. RINGLE laughs. In a friendly way, he horse-collars TURNER and slams him to the ground. The two wrestle. RINGLE for enjoyment, TURNER for dear life.)

RINGLE: The fifty-fifth floor! The wrestling floor of the building. Where we men go to wrestle the day away.

(RINGLE straddles TURNER and pushes his face into the ground. He gestures wildly to the building.)

RINGLE: The fifty-fifth floor! Here we may entangle ourselves! Here may the bridges burn and grow and burn and grow again and again! Here we may be MEN!

TURNER: RINGLE dammit get off me now I swear to God—

RINGLE: Glory, glory hallelujah! Glory, glory hallelujah! Glory, glory hallelujah! His truth is marching on.

TURNER: RINGLE!

RINGLE: Gather 'round, ye men of the fifty-fifth floor! Listen to these words long written down! Let your bodies writhe! Let your women swoon! Let your sweat strip them naked!

(RINGLE gets off of TURNER and slides to the building. He hoists it in the air. TURNER crawls to his knees.)

RINGLE: This building is the olive tree of Odysseus's bed! From these roots we men redeem our murders. The bows are strung, the suitors slaughtered. Peace reigns again, deep in the earth. No more war! No more death! To bed! To bed! The fifty-fifth floor to bed!

(RINGLE tackles TURNER once again.)

RINGLE: Victory, Turner!

Victory for us!

VICTORY FOR THE RACE OF MEN!

(Lights.)

6.

ELLIE and TURNER's cabin. ELLIE, TURNER, NUGGET, and RINGLE are all seated around the table. It's the end of dinner. The food has been eaten. They all look for something to say. Forks scrape plates. Silence.

ELLIE: I'm sorry, after food there's really nothing to do here.

RINGLE and NUGGET: Nonsense don't be silly it was delicious really thank you for having us nonsense really.

ELLIE: Oh well, thank you, it was easy really. Turner finds the food, and I just heat it up till it's cooked through.

Where did you find dinner today, Turner?

TURNER: To the Southeast.

ELLIE: Right, well. The Southeast is full of delicious options these days.

RINGLE: How far did you have to go for it?

TURNER: About an hour's walk, I think. I lost track, to be honest.

I stopped by a clearing. I thought about running through it.

You know, how it's fun to run through big clearings...I thought about it for a while.

Wind in my hair.

But nothing happened. I kept walking.

RINGLE: And dinner was right there?

TURNER: Yup. It was crouched right by the road. Just crouching there. It wasn't asleep, but it didn't try to run away. It looked sort of sad. Dry, red eyes. Old and gray. I think it was dying.

RINGLE: Well it sure tasted fresh.

NUGGET: That reminds me...once I saw roadkill and asked my mother, "Why do squirrels go to the road when they're ready to die?"

(Laughter.)

ELLIE: Wouldn't that be something? If it were like an appointment?

TURNER: Wouldn't want to be late.

RINGLE: WOULD want to be late. Would want to be very late. In fact, I might just sleep in.

(Pause.)

NUGGET: I'm sleeping in tomorrow. All this work has taken it out of me.

ELLIE: Me too. I'm just exhausted.

RINGLE: *(To TURNER.)* So it was crouched right there? Right near the road?

TURNER: Yes.

RINGLE: And you did what, snatch it up in your bag?

TURNER: Yes, after I killed it.

RINGLE: Got it. You had to kill it first. I follow. I'm only trying to get things straight because I promised Nugget I'd make dinner this Thursday.

NUGGET: I'm not a good cook. Not like you, Ellie. I only reheat things with instructions on the box.

TURNER: I'll be happy when the chickens come back. *(Pause.)* I miss eating the chickens.

NUGGET: Do they taste better?

ELLIE: So much better. They take less time to cook, and there're so many ways of preparing them. What are some of our favorites, Turner?

TURNER: Chicken nuggets.

(NUGGET laughs. The OTHERS are confused.)

ELLIE: *(Uncertain.)* Yes...those are good. I also make a nice maple glaze that goes quite well with any side dish. I'd be happy to give you the recipe.

NUGGET: I'd appreciate that.

RINGLE: Now the chickens...is there any difference in fetching those?

TURNER: It's complicated. You sort of have to learn as you go.

RINGLE: Ah. So…per chance I were to run into a chicken next Thursday, I should leave it be and fetch something else?

TURNER: God no, you should get the chicken.

RINGLE: I'm confused. *(He stands.)* Turner…would you mind?…maybe if we sort of…acted it out, I'd know what to do?

TURNER: That's really difficult.

RINGLE: Come on, old boy. Show me how it's done.

(He slaps TURNER on the back. TURNER winces.)

TURNER: I'm not sure—

RINGLE: It will be a gas. Ladies, beware.

ELLIE: Oh goodness.

NUGGET: This'll be great.

(TURNER stands, faces RINGLE.)

TURNER: Who should I play?

RINGLE: You, of course. I, as the chicken, will study you carefully to mark how you kill me.

TURNER: Okay. On your mark.

RINGLE: Right! Yes! Here goes…

(RINGLE does an odd characterization of what he imagines a chicken to be. It's only passably chickenlike. He bounces around the room while the others watch. ELLIE giggles. NUGGET is embarrassed. TURNER is unenthused and unconvinced. TURNER doesn't make any violent motions to kill the chicken. Instead, he sings "The Lord Is Good to Me." It is slow, melodic, like he's trying to lure an animal out of its hiding place.)

TURNER: The Lord is good to me
And so I thank the Lord
For giving me the things I need
The sun and the rain and an appleseed
Yes He's been good to me.

(TURNER looks around the cabin. At ELLIE. At NUGGET.)

I wake up every day
As happy as can be
Because I know that with His care
My apple trees will still be there
Oh, the Lord is good to me.

(RINGLE has stopped his dance. Stunned. TURNER points his finger at him like a pistol.)

TURNER: Bang. *(Pause.)* That's one way to kill a chicken.

(Silence.)

RINGLE: *(Recovering.)* Well. Oh…that was so!…oh so! Informative!

Let's play a game!

NUGGET: A game.

TURNER: A game.

RINGLE: Yes a game! The perfect after-dinner activity. I propose a favorite game of Nugget's and mine.

NUGGET: The story game?

RINGLE: Of course. The story game. All we need is the building. It's a fantastic party game. Gets everyone going. C'mon kids, gather round!

(They all sit cross-legged in front of the Empire State Building.)

RINGLE: This is the story game. Now. We are all working on stories for every floor of this building. Sometimes we share these stories with one another, sometimes we don't. Nonetheless, every story is different, and many of them have wonderful actions that can be quite fun to act out at a party!

Here are the rules. We go around the circle, taking turns. When it's your turn, you ask the person to your left for a number between one and a hundred and two. Whichever number you get, you have to tell a story from that floor, and as you narrate it, the other people in the circle must act it out as best they can. Without words, of course. You provide the words, they provide the actions.

The result is laughter so robust you think you might need an exorcism.

Everyone understand?

TURNER: Who wins?

RINGLE: We all do. It's laughter. That's winning enough.

NUGGET: You'll see. You'll learn as you go.

RINGLE: It will be fun. Just play along. Shall we?

(Assent.)

RINGLE: Great. I volunteer to go first.

(He sits. NUGGET is to his left.)

Dearest, my number please.

NUGGET: Twenty-six.

RINGLE: Twenty-six! Good one. Perfect place to start.

I begin. Floor Twenty-Six. The twenty-sixth story. Well, you see children, the twenty-sixth story has a corner window office occupied by a man named Marcus Pontius Aurelius, the world's single most powerful... travel agent.

(TURNER rises.)

This man has booked discount fares and arranged fabulous itineraries for presidents, noted scholars, notorious dictators, you name it. But at night, Aurelius runs a sneaky, shady business that his loyal clients refer to as Discount Code Doldrum. To him, he simply thinks of it as the lethargy business.

He runs it after hours with an exotic, beautiful, tongueless fairy woman from an island somewhere in the calm equatorial seas.

(NUGGET jumps in.)

When his day's work is done, he reaches into his desk and pulls a lever signaling the fairy woman to emerge from her luxurious walk-in closet. She swooshes and sweeps into the office like a silk scarf in the breeze, swooshing in circles until she finally reclines extravagantly on Aurelius's desk, a dead-on sleeping beauty.

Then, his first client comes in, a quiet, suspicious newbie who is not certain that she will get what she paid a premium for.

(ELLIE jumps in.)

"I'm here for Discount Code Doldrum," she says to Marcus Pontius Aurelius. "I know," he says, and he points to the woman on the desk. "You have three hours. Rest yourself and be renewed." The woman nods and he leaves.

Once alone, she examines the exotic fairy with "buyer beware" skepticism. She pokes at her, feels the fabric of her garments, smells her. Fine, she decides. This will do. And then she begins her act of lethargy. She reclines next to the sleeping beauty and closes her eyes. She takes a deep breath and instantly feels relaxed. It's the calm, still, warm touch, motionless skin to skin, that's what relaxes her. And she thinks, here I am, finally, at the center of the world. Here I am at peace. She squeezes the fairy's hand and holds her close, like they're on a raft and the earth is still flat and everyone else is splashing around, trying not to fall off the edge. The East is dead to me, she thinks. The North is too cold, I could never survive there. The South is full of memories, the West an old wives' tale. Here I feel safe. Here I can remain the longest. Right in the middle. The edges burn first. Best to stay put right here. Best to stay in the center. This lethargy isn't bad, it's just good common sense.

(Pause.)

Three hours pass this way, and then Aurelius returns to announce that her time has expired. She refuses to get up. Ultimately, Aurelius must escort her out of the building, so satisfied was she with her purchase, so sad to see it end. On the street, Aurelius points her home. "If you go in that direction, you'll get there eventually." And so she walks…and walks…and walks, not certain what else there is to do.

The end.

(Pause.)

NUGGET: A real gut buster, sweetie.

RINGLE: Well it's not my funniest story! But you said twenty-six and I gave you just that. That's the risk of the game.

So you all get the point now?

(Assent.)

Then kitten, it's your turn. Miss Ellie, give her a number.

ELLIE: Um…ninety-two!

NUGGET: Ninety-two. Good choice. Much better than my prosaic partner over here.

Ready?

Floor Ninety-Two. This floor is the locker room for the entire building. It's where employees change into workout clothes using the gym on ninety-three. Sadly, Floor Ninety-Two is also haunted by the ghost of a Viking Warrior.

(RINGLE rises.)

Of course, as with all Viking Warrior ghosts, you don't want to mess with this guy. He has a very particular way of dealing with things. Unfortunately, our two lovely victims today, one a long-time runner,

(ELLIE.)

the other an accountant whose New Year's resolution was to hit the gym more often,

(TURNER.)

don't know about the Viking Warrior ghost, about the golden rule of the locker room: to make sure that it is never, ever occupied by only two people. One is fine. Crowded is better. But if two people find themselves alone, the Viking Warrior will roar out of his locker, seize control of the victims, and stuff them in the locker from whence he came.

(They are stuck nose to nose.)

The locker is very tight, really only suitable for one scrawny high school freshman. Two people stuck in it for longer than ten minutes can be fatal.

They run out of air. They suffocate. They asphyxiate. And what's worse—oh man, this really sucks—is that our victims today are total strangers. Total. Strangers. And they're stuck there, face to face, awkwardly waiting for mercy, death, or at least a topic for conversation. But they only get breath.

Breath.

"What do we do?" "Wait." "Wait?" "Someone else will come in soon."

Breath.

Breath.

But nothing. *(Thought.)* Well, maybe something happens. Maybe the guy's a perv. Maybe he cops a feel. Maybe she slaps him. Maybe it hurts.

I just don't know... *(Pause.)* But thank God, finally a third gym rat comes along,

(RINGLE, now doubling.)

and like everyone in the building, he knows how to save us all from this claustrophobic bullshit. In his loudest, most frightening voice, he cries to the rafters, "UBI SUNT?" It's a common Viking motif, in Latin meaning "Where are those who were before us?" He calls it three more times. "UBI SUNT, UBI SUNT, UBI SUNT?"

Where are those who were before me? Where have they gone? I know you're in here. I know you're in here. Where can I find you? C'mon and show yourselves, and let's send this ghost back to Nordic hell.

Ubi Sunt?

And the locker door clicks open, and the prisoners are released from their bonds. The Viking Warrior disappears into his locker once more. There are now three people in the locker room, and all are safe.

The moral of the ninety-second floor is...

...that it's considered common building courtesy to check the locker room for those who came before you.

That's it.

(Applause.)

NUGGET: Ellie, you go now. We're on a roll.

ELLIE: I think I'll pass.

RINGLE: Nonsense, dear!

NUGGET: *(To TURNER.)* Give her a number.

TURNER: One.

NUGGET: There it is. One.

RINGLE: One! Miss Ellie, you'll nail it.

ELLIE: Okay...

RINGLE: Just have fun.

ELLIE: One? Okay...

Okay, let me think. One. The first floor. *(She crouches by the building, stares at the first floor.)* The first floor is the building's...day care center?

Because everyone in the building is so focused on their careers, only one person has children, the archivist from forty-seven.

(RINGLE.)

He has a boy

(TURNER.)

and a girl,

(NUGGET.)

neither more than four or five, and he drops them off every morning before he heads upstairs to put history in order.

Today's a very snowy day, and the first floor has the best view of the snow. All the brother and sister want to do is go outside and make snow angels and snowmen and throw snowballs. But the day care supervisor

(RINGLE doubling again.)

is very strict. They are not allowed to…Better to stay inside. Better to be snowed in. Let the snow stay smooth…

So the brother and sister pound their desks and frown their faces and cry their eyes out in protest, but the supervisor merely shakes his finger. So all they can do is kneel by the window and watch the snow fall. The snow falls and falls, accumulations greater than any the building has ever known. It's stunning. The brother and the sister watch all day, and then they hold hands and pray at lunch, "Keep snowing. Keep snowing. Keep snowing. The end."

The supervisor sees this and finds some pity in his hardened heart. "Children, you can make snow angels on the carpet, and you can build snowmen out of blocks, and you can throw snowballs with crumpled notebook paper. Just close your eyes and open your imaginations and it will be just the same, just the—"

(Knock at the door. EVERYONE freezes. Another knock.)

ELLIE: Come in?

(No response.)

ELLIE: Come in!

(The door opens slowly, and a tired man dressed in blue and carrying a large satchel pokes his head in. He's a POSTMAN.)

POSTMAN: Sorry, I…I hope I'm not interrupting anything. I'm…well…you see…I'm on my rounds, and I was told there was a neighborhood here now, so I've come to deliver your mail. I'm sorry for the late hour. My rounds are very long.

TURNER: Mail? You have mail for us?

POSTMAN: Ah yes, well, let me see…yes I believe I do…if your names are… *(He rummages through his bag but can't find what he's looking for.)* What are your names again?

TURNER: Turner and Ellie.

(Doesn't ring a bell.)

POSTMAN: Turner and Ellie Turner and Ellie…I think…yes…just a moment… *(POSTMAN wobbles on his feet.)*

RINGLE: Dear man, you look exhausted. Come on in and have a seat. Take a breather.

POSTMAN: Oh no, thank you. I still have a ways to go.

RINGLE: How far are your rounds?

POSTMAN: They divide us up by latitudes. I'm assigned to your latitude, so my rounds are…all the way around, I guess. East to West.

RINGLE: That seems like a lot to ask.

POSTMAN: It's an odd organizational scheme. I've filed a complaint.

RINGLE: As well you should. Impossible standards just make life difficult. Stay awhile. You need the rest.

In fact! We're playing a party game! You should join us!

POSTMAN: Oh this is too much, really, much too much. I just need to find your mail and be on my—

ELLIE: You are welcome to rest in our home. Turner and I would be happy to have you.

POSTMAN: *(He considers. Sighs.)* You folks are kind, thank you. Yes, maybe I will stay a moment, gather my strength for the walk West. At least it's all downhill from here.

What game are you playing?

RINGLE: The story game! Do you know the rules?

POSTMAN: The story game? I think I know that one. With the stories, right?

RINGLE: Exactly.

POSTMAN: It's a marvelous game. I had two tickets to the championship years ago, but it fell on a Monday, the busiest day for mail. I wasn't even in Brussels by the time match play began. Oh well.

I'd be happy just to rest and watch.

RINGLE: Then you just put your feet up and relax. When we last left our heroes...Ellie was telling us about snow.

ELLIE: Oh no, I had just finished.

NUGGET: No, you were midsentence.

ELLIE: It was just an odd sentence. I'm all done.

RINGLE: Alright dear, if you insist...then Turner, my man! It's your turn!

TURNER: My turn.

RINGLE: And we've come full circle, so it's my turn to give you your number, and the number I give you is...thirty-three!

(TURNER lowers his head, thinks quietly. Silence.)

TURNER: Thirty-three. Thirty-three. Thirty-thirrrrrrd. Thirty-thirrrrrrrrrrrd. What to say about a floor with so many rrrrrrrrrrrrrrrrrs. *(He stands up, starts walking around the room.)* I hope I'm not breaking any rules. Walking gets my mind going. Stories move with our feet.

That's why the trees are so quiet.

Thirty-threeeeeeeeee.

(He looks at ELLIE. At NUGGET. At POSTMAN.)

Why of course. Floor Thirty-Three is the post office.

(POSTMAN starts to rise, wondering if this means he should do something.)

TURNER: No no, sit back down and relax. I'm joining the thirty-third floor halfway through the day, when all the postmen are already on their rounds. Right now there are just three thieves on the floor, and they are all laughing hysterically.

(He gestures to RINGLE, NUGGET, and ELLIE to laugh hysterically.)

They are all laughing hysterically because, you see, the mailing system in the building is kind of chaotic. When an employee wants to mail something, he drops it in a chute by his desk and it comes hurtling out onto the thirty-third floor.

(He looks at POSTMAN.)

May I use your satchel as a prop?

(POSTMAN shrugs. Sure.)

TURNER: At any given moment, one hundred and twenty-five to one hundred and thirty employees are mailing things, so to be present on the thirty-third floor is like being in a blizzard. If you're looking to steal anything, anything at all, this is the easiest possible theft.

(TURNER starts throwing letters at the PLAYERS. He looks at each address briefly before throwing the letter.)

All those letters, right there, flying at you!

So simple. Letters letters letters!

Going all over the world.

All these letters! So much to steal!

(TURNER keeps hurling letters, and the PLAYERS are as if dancing in a rainstorm.)

Here they come!

Flee fly flippity floppety all around, letters everywhere!

Letters letters everywhere, not a word to read.

(He continues to scan each address, but he still doesn't see what he's looking for.)

Eventually the thieves are buried in letters!

(The PLAYERS fall to the floor and rapidly scramble to cover themselves in letters. Mayhem. TURNER dumps the entire satchel on them. Runs his hands through the stack, looking feverishly, while they giggle underneath the pile. It's still not there. He stands up, relieved.)

And their ecstasy over such an easy steal turns out to be their doom, because a kind and gentle postman *(Gestures to POSTMAN.)* has finished his rounds early and caught them.

(POSTMAN runs into the pile and uncovers them.)

POSTMAN: Got you!

TURNER: The end.

(They continue to roll around in the mail. Wild laughter.)

RINGLE: A great story, my friend! Really got us going.

POSTMAN: A joy to watch! And to eventually play a part. You all are very talented.

NUGGET: It was like being in those giant tubs.

RINGLE: With the plastic balls!

NUGGET: And splashing around.

RINGLE: Trying to get unburied.

NUGGET: Don't get buried alive!

POSTMAN: He rises from the dead!

NUGGET: We thought he was gone!

POSTMAN: I'll bury you all!

(He throws more letters on top of the giggling PLAYERS.)

ELLIE: Those tubs must be fun.

POSTMAN: So much fun. When we were younger.

Oh, I think I'm carried away now. Now I want to share a story.

I want to share a story from the pile.

But I shouldn't.

RINGLE: Shouldn't you?

NUGGET: You should.

ELLIE: You should!

POSTMAN: Goodness me.

Oh, well, what the…HELL! I'll open one! Who'll know! *(He picks up an envelope and tears it open.)* Ladies and gentlemen, from across your very latitude comes the following chronicle of intimate correspondence. And so I read…

RINGLE: And so he reads!

POSTMAN: "Dear Nugget,"

(EVERYONE freezes. POSTMAN is perplexed by the letter's contents. Pause.)

POSTMAN: Hm. It starts with a chant of sorts.

"Hard times come again no more hard times come again no more hard times come again no more the end."

I don't get that. I don't get that at all. I don't understand what it means.

And there's so much more.

Too much to read it all. Let me see.

(POSTMAN scans the rest of the letter, trying to make sense of it. NUGGET and RINGLE hold each other.)

POSTMAN: Ah, here we go. At the end. It finishes with, "Please stay where you are and don't come looking for me. It won't help. I'm sorry. I'm fine. The prayer is just a little different now:

Us.

Us.

Here.

There.

The end.

Please stay where you are.

I love you.

Love,

Dollop."

(NUGGET tears the letter away from POSTMAN. RINGLE follows her. POSTMAN realizes which letter he opened.)

RINGLE: We've been looking for him for a long time. You have to understand…

NUGGET: He's hiding something, I know it. He's not well. That tone. We have to keep going.

RINGLE: We have to take his word.

NUGGET: We were just here to rest. Now let's keep going.

RINGLE: He's fine, dear. He must be. It's his handwriting.

NUGGET: It's from months ago. Something could've changed.

RINGLE: Then he'll write another letter.

TURNER: We'll help you look for him.

ELLIE: What?!

RINGLE: Help? We'll be fine.

TURNER: We'll hit the road. There's four of us, we have a better chance—

ELLIE: Turner, it's not our business.

TURNER: We can do something, we can—

RINGLE: Thanks, old boy, but this is our cross to bear.

TURNER: If we all spread out, head West—

ELLIE: Turner, please—

RINGLE: We're on top of it, really.

TURNER: At least let me walk you home.

RINGLE: There's no need.

TURNER: Please? I'd like to come along.

RINGLE: Why?

TURNER: I want…to help.

ELLIE: They just want to go. Let them go.

RINGLE: Again, I appreciate it, but we're fine.

NUGGET: No, it's alright.

Walk with us, Turner.

RINGLE: Kitten…

NUGGET: He can bring the building.

(Pause.)

RINGLE: Oh, right.

I forgot. *(Pause.)* If you wouldn't mind…we'd be grateful. It was his. I was foolish to offer it to begin with. Perhaps we should take it back for a little while.

A new one…we'll order a new one. Be here before you know it.

TURNER: We understand.

RINGLE: Thank you for dinner, Miss Ellie. Sorry for the abrupt exit. We'll return the favor. I promise. When we see you down the road.

ELLIE: We'd like that.

NUGGET: Let's go.

RINGLE: *(Picks up two chairs. To POSTMAN.)* Would you mind guiding us out? Our hands are a bit full.

POSTMAN: Certainly.

TURNER: I'll be right behind you.

NUGGET: Thank you.

(Pause.)

Ellie…thank you. You are…a gracious host.

The belle of the ball.

(RINGLE, NUGGET, and POSTMAN exit. TURNER and ELLIE look at each other. Pause.)

ELLIE: When will you be back?

TURNER: Soon.

ELLIE: It's late. Don't be gone too long.

TURNER: I won't.

ELLIE: Who knows what's out there.

TURNER: I'll be back soon.

ELLIE: I don't want you to go.

TURNER: It's a short walk. I'll be back soon. *(Pause.)* Don't worry about me.

ELLIE: That's not up to you.

(He picks up the building, walks to the door.)

ELLIE: Turner?

Remember the churchyard?

(He stops, turns around.)

ELLIE: What you said? What you called to me?

(ELLIE slowly and shyly starts to unbutton her dress. She lets it drop. Beneath, she is wearing a T-shirt and jean shorts. She stands as if naked. TURNER stares.)

ELLIE: We can go there now. To California.

(He walks to her. Puts his nose on her forehead. She gives him an endless embrace.)

TURNER: You have nothing to worry about.

My Ellie.

(He picks up the building and exits. ELLIE watches him from the window. Silence. POSTMAN enters.)

POSTMAN: Look at you!

ELLIE: I changed.

POSTMAN: You look lovely. Great shirt. May I?

(He checks the label of her shirt.)

POSTMAN: Yes, they make nice things.

ELLIE: Nice T-shirts.

POSTMAN: Yes. Ms. Ellie, Mr. Turner has asked me to stay the night.

ELLIE: Of course. You are welcome in our home.

POSTMAN: I'll be gone at first light.

ELLIE: No hurry.

You must be exhausted.

POSTMAN: I am so very exhausted.

(Pause.)

ELLIE: Can I make a bed for you?

POSTMAN: Oh please, I don't want to put you through too much effort, I'm happy to nod off on a stool.

ELLIE: No no. Here. I'll spread out a blanket on the table. The wood is soft. I insist. *(She turns the table into a bed.)*

POSTMAN: You are so kind.

(Rests his hand on hers.)

POSTMAN: So very kind…and beautiful.

ELLIE: Thank you.

POSTMAN: What a night.

ELLIE: Welcome to the neighborhood.

Can I get you anything?

POSTMAN: No ma'am. A postman needs only the kindness of others, and my cup runneth over.

ELLIE: *(She smiles.)* I'll wish you a good night, then.

POSTMAN: Yes, it's about that time. I'll just get my satchel in order so I'm ready to walk at first light.

ELLIE: I'll help.

(They gather all the remaining letters into a pile. POSTMAN gets his satchel. As they refill the bag, he notices something.)

POSTMAN: Ah. Here it is. *(He pulls a red envelope out of the satchel.)* Your mail. I knew it was here somewhere.

(He hands it to ELLIE.)

ELLIE: "To Ellie. From Turner."

POSTMAN: How charming. How romantic. He sent you a card through the post. It's always more romantic through the post. I think.

ELLIE: The address says, "Our new home."

POSTMAN: Then you should open it, I suppose. Now that you're here.

(Pause.)

ELLIE: Yes. I suppose. *(She places it on a stool.)* Maybe I'll wait till he gets back.

POSTMAN: Good idea. Wait till he gets back. *(Pause.)* You know…the red envelope means it's full of love.

ELLIE: Does it?

POSTMAN: I'm quite the expert at these things. You should greatly look forward to opening it.

ELLIE: I will.

POSTMAN: *(Lies down on the table.)* Red envelopes… *(Yawns.)* You know, I loved a girl on a different latitude…when I worked there…wasn't meant to be. Mondays she put a card with a smooch and a nice note in my satchel…I found it, end of my rounds…who's this for?…and it was for me.

A smooch and a nice note. Stuffed in a red envelope. *(Falling asleep.)* I should work there again…I should…request to move…what are the chances?

It's just one straight line. Of many more.

Goodnight, Miss Ellie.

ELLIE: Goodnight.

(ELLIE looks at the card. She stands at the window for a long time. She moves to TURNER's pile of effects, arranges them on the floor in the shape of a man. She puts the picture where the head would be. She kneels next to the empty man. Prays.)

Two of us in the morning. Two of us in the afternoon. Two of us in the evening. Two of us as I fall asleep.

The end.

(POSTMAN is snoring, dreaming a happy dream. ELLIE snuggles next to the empty man. Sings gently.)

ELLIE: While we seek mirth and beauty,
    and music light and gay
There are frail forms fainting at the door;
Though their voices are silent, their
    pleading looks will say,
"Oh hard times, come again no more…"

(Lights.)

(End of play.)

ENDLESS SUMMER NIGHTS

Tim Errickson

TIM ERRICKSON was born and raised in Vineland, in southern New Jersey, near where *Endless Summer Nights* takes place. He attended Hofstra University's New College, with a semester abroad at the University of London and the King's Head Theatre in Islington. Postgraduate training includes Circle Rep for Directing and Labyrinth Theatre Company for Playwriting. A director-playwright-producer, Tim's probably best known as the artistic director and founder of Boomerang Theatre Company, which since 1999 has produced numerous new and classic plays in repertory, reading series, and outdoor productions. Directing credits with Boomerang include *Burning the Old Man* by Kelly McAllister (included in *Plays and Playwrights 2006*) and *Fenway: Last of the Bohemians* by Kelly McAllister and Lisa Margaret Holub. Other directing work includes *The Wedding Play* by Brian Smallwood, *Unidentified Human Remains and the True Nature of Love* by Brad Fraser (Oberon Theatre Ensemble), and *The Desk Set* by William Marchand (Retro Productions). Boomerang received the 2008 Caffe Cino Fellowship from the New York Innovative Theatre Foundation. Tim is currently coproducer of the Community Dish and a member of the Honorary Awards Committee for the New York Innovative Theatre Awards. He resides in Prospect Heights, Brooklyn. *Endless Summer Nights* is Tim's second play as a playwright and the first to be produced.

Endless Summer Nights was first presented by The Boomerang Theatre Company (Tim Errickson, Artistic Director; Susan Abbott, Managing Director) on September 17, 2010, at The Connelly Theatre, New York City, with the following cast and credits:

Young Tracy/Hostess .... Becky Byers
Young Sam/Waiter .... Bret Richard Hoskins
Sam .... Michael Criscuolo
Scotto .... Joseph Mathers
Tracy .... Synge Maher
Mom .... Nora Hummel

Director: Christopher Thomasson
Assistant Director: Stephanie Caragliano
Stage Manager: Michelle Foster
Assistant Stage Manager: Samantha Steiger
Set Design: Nikki Black
Light Design: Kia Rogers
Sound Design: Jacob Subotnick
Costume Design: Cheryl McCarron
Assistant Costume Design: Kara Burzynski
Props Design: Stephanie Cox-Williams
Press Representation: Joe Trentacosta, Springer Associates PR
Original Artwork: Stefano Imbert

Special thanks to the actors who helped develop this play: Carrie Brewer, Benjamin Ellis Fine, Paula Danielle, Candice Holdorf, Kay Walbye, Deborah Carlson, Vinnie Penna, Philip Emeott, Sara Thigpen, Christopher Yeatts, Karen Sternberg, and Dolores McDougal.

Originally developed with Oracle Theatre Company, New York City.

"Young enough to still see the passionate boy that I used to be, but old enough to say I got a good look at the other side."—B. Joel

CHARACTER LIST

YOUNG TRACY
SAM
TRACY
WAITER

YOUNG SAM
SCOTTO
MOM
HOSTESS

ACT ONE

In half light we see two naked young bodies silhouetted, having sex in a car backseat. Passionate and youthful. After the climax, we see them huddle together, with piles of clothes and a soda bottle and fast food containers on the floor of the car. The surf can be heard in the distance, and maybe some far-off voices, rides, and games.

YOUNG TRACY: What time is it?

YOUNG SAM: Dunno, maybe eleven. Eleven thirty tops.

YOUNG TRACY: *(Begins to gather her stuff.)* We should go.

YOUNG SAM: *(Catching his breath.)* Hey, hold on a minute…

YOUNG TRACY: What? C'mon, if I'm late again, I won't see you for the rest of the summer. You know my dad's like that…

YOUNG SAM: Okay, okay, just hold on a sec. Can't we just lay here for one minute?

(YOUNG TRACY lies against his chest.)

YOUNG SAM: That's better.

(They lie there in the silence for a few seconds.)

YOUNG TRACY: How do you make time stop?

YOUNG SAM: What?

YOUNG TRACY: I want time to stop. So that we don't have to leave this car.

YOUNG SAM: You don't mean that.

YOUNG TRACY: I do. I want to stay right here.

YOUNG SAM: Me too.

(Beat.)

YOUNG TRACY: Can you come with me to Brad's party on Saturday?

YOUNG SAM: Yeah, I think so, I just need to check with my dad. I think he had something planned, some dinner I think with him and his girlfriend. But it should be fine.

YOUNG TRACY: I'm picking up Kathy and we're going to the mall first. She thinks Brian is going to be there, and since it looks like he and Nancy are over…

YOUNG SAM: Interesting, so Nancy is available…!

(YOUNG TRACY pinches him.)

YOUNG SAM: *(Laughing.)* Okay, okay, no Nancy…!

YOUNG TRACY: There better not be. I plan on spending all summer in the back of this car.

(She kisses him.)

YOUNG SAM: There are these things called beds, you know… people seem to really like them.

YOUNG TRACY: Shut up.

(Beat.)

YOUNG SAM: I love you.

(Beat. TRACY lies against his chest; she looks unsure of what to do.)

YOUNG TRACY: You do?

YOUNG SAM: Is that bad?

YOUNG TRACY: No.

(Beat.)

YOUNG TRACY: Say it again.

YOUNG SAM: *(Starts to get uncomfortable. He moves away from her, begins putting on his clothes.)* No, look, it didn't mean anything, it doesn't have to…

YOUNG TRACY: Shut up and say it again. Don't make me hurt you.

YOUNG SAM: *(After a beat, not looking at her.)* I love you.

(Beat, she is looking at him, but silent.)

YOUNG SAM: Look, get dressed, we have to get you back… *(Starts to reach for more clothes.)*

YOUNG TRACY: Stop it.

YOUNG SAM: Stop what? *(Turns to her.)*

YOUNG TRACY: Say it again.

YOUNG SAM: *(Looking at her, a beat.)* I love you. I love you very much.

(She leans back against the seat looking out the window or through the front windshield. He watches her.)

YOUNG TRACY: That is the best thing that ever happened to me.

YOUNG SAM: Really?

YOUNG TRACY: Really. *(Turns to him.)* I love you too.

(They kiss, softly at first, then with more passion until things begin to get going again. On another part of the stage, older SAM appears and watches them.)

YOUNG SAM: We really shouldn't, we should get out of…

(YOUNG TRACY kisses him again, quieting him.)

YOUNG TRACY: *(Between kisses.)* I want to stop time.

(They're making love again. From the corner, SAM watches them, as they slowly drift from his memory and fade to black. SAM is older now, his mid-thirties, and is standing on the boardwalk in Ocean Beach. It is fall, and the sounds of rides and voices have changed to seagulls and surf. After a moment, SCOTTO enters looking for him.)

SCOTTO: Sam? What the hell are you doing down here?

SAM: *(Looking out.)* I didn't know somebody finally bought Sugarman's Pier.

Scott: Yeah, it was in the paper last week.

SAM: Gonna building something cool, or tear it down?

SCOTTO: *(Searching.)* Hey, buddy…

SAM: *(Turns to him.)* I got laid off today.

SCOTTO: I heard. I called you at work, Mario told me. Man, I'm really sorry.

SAM: Yep.

SCOTTO: Well, good. You hated that fucking job anyway. I mean seriously, they treated you like shit, you know it and I know it. Dan always was a cock munch, since high school. So fuck him, man.

SAM: Yeah, right.

SCOTTO: Dude, I'm going to boycott that place. Fuck you Dan!! *(Beat.)* I can't believe they laid you off…I mean, it's SAM'S Club, man. They can't lay off guys named Sam. Who'll ever fucking work there…all the Neds of the world? I don't think so.

SAM: Funny, I tried that logic too, but no go.

SCOTTO: So now what? You looking for something else? *(Thinks.)* My dad might be hiring at the store. Or my pal Calvin works at the bus garage down on Franklin—

SAM: *(Cutting him off.)* I think I'm out.

SCOTTO: *(Searching his face for his meaning.)* What, like, OUT out? Like like really out?

SAM: Yeah, I think so.

SCOTTO: 'Bout fuckin' time. I've been telling you to get out of here for years.

SAM: I know.

SCOTTO: Blow out of here man, never come back. Just leave a forwarding address for your porn and Christmas cards!

SAM: Ha, right.

SCOTTO: Hey, can I come with you? *(Cutting SAM off.)* No no, before you answer, think about it! We'll have this awesome adventure, going road tripping and meeting girls and…

SAM: *(Cutting him off.)* You are not coming. Terri would have my ass when she finally found us. And she would find us. You can't leave your pregnant girlfriend.

SCOTTO: *(Sheepishly.)* I know. *(Beat.)* But, dude, think about it, we'd totally get…

SAM: *(Cutting him off.)* Forget about it. Terri's having your kid, retarded as that kid may be with you as its dad, and so you are staying here. And for Christ sakes, marry that woman already. You want your kid to be retarded, ugly, and a bastard?

SCOTTO: Oh you gotta go and add ugly in there?

SAM: Yeah, I do.

SCOTTO: Well what if it's a girl? Girls can't be bastards.

SAM: Oh yeah, then what are they?

SCOTTO: *(Searching.)* …Bastardas?

(SAM shakes head.)

SCOTTO: …Bastardettes?

SAM: Nope.

SCOTTO: Bastardinas…

SAM: Yeah, keep working on that.

(Beat.)

SCOTTO: So what are you gonna do?

SAM: Well, it's almost the end of the month, I'll start packing and give up my place.

SCOTTO: And go where?

SAM: Dunno yet. I've got a few bucks saved, and I can sell a bunch of my guitars and books and stuff.

SCOTTO: And that's it? You're just going to drive off? How the hell is that going to work? I mean look, I'm all for you getting out of here, but you might need a plan.

SAM: Nah, I've been making plans for a long time, trying it this way or that way to make it through. Fuck that. Nah, I think I'm just going.

(Beat.)

SCOTTO: Wow.

SAM: *(Chuckling.)* Yeah.

(Cross-fade to TRACY walking with HER MOTHER on another part of the boardwalk.)

MOM: Why did you come?

TRACY: Mom, we've been over this.

MOM: *(Overlapping her.)* You didn't have to come…

TRACY: Okay…

MOM: …I'm fine, I can take care of myself.

TRACY: I know.

(Beat, they walk. MOM is getting around gingerly.)

MOM: You should be visiting Shawn instead of me.

TRACY: He's with Ray, he's fine. *(Beat.)* Ray doesn't like me to visit too often.

MOM: He's your son, you should be able to see him when you want.

TRACY: Mom, please, I've fought that battle already. I agreed to this.

MOM: Your father and I would never have agreed to let you or your brother be raised by someone else.

TRACY: It's not someone else, Mom. It's Ray. A boy needs his father. And I'm traveling a lot right now, it's the best thing for Shawn.

MOM: I want to sit down.

(They find a bench and sit.)

TRACY: How are you feeling?

MOM: Tired. And a little sore in my hip.

TRACY: We'll just take it easy. Let's sit here for a bit, then I'll go get the car.

MOM: Why did you come? Just say it.

TRACY: Mom, please.

MOM: *(Overlapping.)* I knew it! I want you to know I can take care of myself, I always have and I always will!

TRACY: I know.

MOM: I just have to be careful where I put things so I don't trip…

TRACY: Mom, you didn't trip…

MOM: …Yes I did!

TRACY: Okay. Okay.

(Beat.)

MOM: You should head back. I don't want to take up too much of your time.

TRACY: I have a trip at the end of the week to Tempe, so I need to be back in Hartford a day or so before.

MOM: Arizona?

TRACY: Yep. A conference on segmentation in disability coverage.

MOM: Sounds thrilling. *(Beat.)* Your father and I were in Arizona once, Phoenix or Scottsdale. He wanted us to retire there, he loved the golf and the sun…

TRACY: I know, you told me.

MOM: *(Softening.)* I miss that man.

TRACY: Me too.

MOM: I know he was hard on you and Chris, but he was so good to me.

TRACY: So then you never should have divorced him.

MOM: *(Back to tough again.)* Oh please, he was a child. A big child in a man's body. He didn't want me, he wanted to run around, chase women, play golf…

TRACY: Mom, listen. I need to talk to you about your house.

MOM: What about my house?

TRACY: Look, I know this is going to be hard, but I think you shouldn't live alone anymore.

MOM: *(Sarcastically.)* Really…Are you getting me a roommate? Or do I start dating at my age?

TRACY: Mom, please.

MOM: Please what?

TRACY: *(Aware they are in public.)* I've talked this over with Dr. Markovic and with Chris. We all think it's time to figure things out in a way that makes sense for you.

MOM: And don't I get a say in this?

TRACY: *(Trying to calm her.)* Yes you do.

MOM: Then I don't want things to change! I can take care of myself just fine. And make sure you relay that message to your brother and to my busybody doctor.

(TRACY's phone rings, she looks at it, but doesn't answer. It stops ringing.)

MOM: You should get that, we're done talking. *(Turns to look at the beach.)*

TRACY: It's work, it'll wait. *(Beat.)* So, this is what I want to talk to you about…I want you to move to Hartford with me. I can look after you and do all the things you need done. I have a big place, especially with Shawn not there now. I think it might be a good fit.

MOM: You just said you're traveling too much to see your own son. Besides, my friends are here, my life is here.

TRACY: Mom, we can…

(TRACY's phone beeps; a voicemail message.)

MOM: You should get that.

TRACY: *(Snaps.)* And you should stop telling me what to do. *(Beat.)* Sorry, sorry. Mom, I just want you to be taken care of. And neither Chris nor I want to think of you in a retirement home or… *(Beat.)*

MOM: …or nursing home. *(Beat.)* You can say it, you're a big girl. And so am I. I know that's coming.

TRACY: No, Mom, it doesn't have to be like that. Please, think about coming up to Hartford with me.

MOM: No. I'm sorry. I can't do that. *(Beat.)* You should move here.

TRACY: What? Uh, no.

MOM: Oh, so it's okay for me to change my life to move in with you, but unreasonable for me to suggest the same thing for you?

TRACY: Mom, you are retired. I have a full-time job, and a ton of travel and a son.

MOM: A son you don't see, and travel that takes you away from your home anyway. I don't see your point…

TRACY: *(Calming her.)* Look, I don't want to argue with you.

MOM: Good, then don't. You should move home, and come back to where your friends are and where your family is. This is where you grew up, where you belong. It'd be about time.

TRACY: You realize this isn't home for me anymore, right? I mean, Ocean Beach never really was, we didn't grow up here.

MOM: You might as well have, you were here enough. With your friends, going to the beach or on the rides. And it's beautiful here even in the winter time, that's why I moved here after your father left.

TRACY: I know Mom, you told me. *(Beat.)* Look, home for me is in Connecticut now. I've lived there for longer than I lived with you and Daddy.

MOM: And you think that makes it your home? You're from here.

TRACY: And I work there, I got married there…

MOM: And divorced there.

(Beat.)

TRACY: *(Stung.)* Look, please don't be vindictive to try and hurt me so I'll give this up. We—you and me and Chris—we need to come up with an answer.

(TRACY's phone rings; she sends it to voicemail.)

MOM: I don't think we do, I don't see a question that needs answering.

TRACY: Mom, please…

MOM: Tracy, I appreciate what you and Chris and Dr. Markovic think you're doing. But I don't want it. And that's final.

TRACY: Mom, I don't think it is final.

(Beat.)

MOM: Good, I will take that to mean you are moving home.

(TRACY's phone beeps to indicate a voicemail. She looks at it, as we cross-fade to YOUNG TRACY and YOUNG SAM in the back of the car, naked and wrapped in a beach towel even though it's hot tonight. YOUNG SAM is eating junk food, trying to tempt YOUNG TRACY with it. YOUNG TRACY stealthily pulls a card out of her jeans which lie next to her, and holds it where YOUNG SAM can't see it. Surf and amusements can be heard in the distance.)

YOUNG SAM: Man it's hot tonight.

YOUNG TRACY: Maybe we should run really fast to the ocean and cool off…

YOUNG SAM: Oh yeah, little skinny dip? I like how you think…

(He gives her a kiss and starts putting junk food down.)

YOUNG TRACY: Okay, easy tiger…but first, tada!

(YOUNG TRACY hands him the card.)

YOUNG SAM: Hey! C'mon, you didn't have to get me anything, you know that.

YOUNG TRACY: Yeah right.

YOUNG SAM: No, seriously.

YOUNG TRACY: Just open it and stop being an ass.

(YOUNG SAM opens the card, reads the inscription, and pulls out a slip of paper and a picture.)

YOUNG SAM: A picture from the fourth of July…that's terrific, where'd you get this?

YOUNG TRACY: My cousin Christine took it, look at how red you were that day! *(She's excited, she points to him in the picture.)*

YOUNG SAM: That was the best day. *(Reads the slip of paper.)* And this is…a "Coupon for one free 'dirty fun time' of your choosing"… *(To her, laughing.)* Well, this might be the greatest gift anyone's ever given me!

YOUNG TRACY: I thought you'd like it. *(Grinning.)* Read the back.

YOUNG SAM: *(Flipping the coupon over, reading.)* "Always remember I love you and believe in you, no matter what." *(To her.)* So you believe in me, huh? Well get in line, cause that makes two of us.

(She hits him playfully and rolls her eyes.)

YOUNG SAM: What?

YOUNG TRACY: *(Pretending to be mad.)* I'm trying to be romantic and you ruin it by being all "guy."

YOUNG SAM: Oh, come on. I'm just saying, I'm going to be rich, you are going to be famous, and we are going to live happily ever after. Forever.

YOUNG TRACY: *(Chuckles to herself.)* Um…happily ever after and forever are the same thing.

YOUNG SAM: See, look how smart you are…

(She's still playfully mad and turns away. He begins to kiss her neck.)

YOUNG SAM: Can I cash my coupon in now?

YOUNG TRACY: *(Smiling.)* Oh, you think that's going to get you out of trouble? *(She playfully pulls away.)*

YOUNG SAM: Tease.

(She playfully gives him her "mad" look, then can't keep a straight face and starts pinching him, laughing.)

YOUNG TRACY: Tease, huh? I'll show you tease!

(SAM enters.)

YOUNG SAM: Whoa, okay, okay not a tease! Not a tease!

(He defends himself and pins her. She laughs. A beat.)

YOUNG SAM: Thank you for this.

YOUNG TRACY: Of course, I mean you only turn eighteen once ya know.

(They begin to make out as we cross-fade to SAM in the sun on the boardwalk. It is again late September/early October, and the air is brisk and cool. SCOTTO enters with a pint bottle in a brown paper bag.)

SCOTTO: So that's it, huh?

SAM: *(Comes out of his memory.)* Hey, yeah…just gave my keys to Mrs. Halberstam, so nothing left to do but gas up and hit the road. What do you have there?

SCOTTO: Little present. I tried to figure out what to get you, then I was like, fuck it. So here.

(Opens the bottle, takes a slug, passes it to SAM.)

SAM: It's moments like this that I'll miss most. *(Takes a small sip.)*

SCOTTO: Which way you heading?

SAM: Figure I'll head south a little, go over the bridge into Delaware and then figure it out from there. Probably not 95 South, but something similar.

(SCOTTO holds his hand out for the bottle.)

SAM: Hey, isn't this my present?

SCOTTO: Why you ungrateful... *(Beat.)* Alright, well I gotta get back... Terri and I had a fight, so I'm apparently apologizing by helping her mother move some furniture down into her basement.

SAM: Gotta love when the in-laws are involved. No work today?

SCOTTO: Nah, season winding down, gettin' kind of slow. Actually, Dad got an offer from the guys who bought Sugarman's. They want to buy the businesses around the pier so they can expand.

SAM: Is he going to take it?

SCOTTO: Dunno, he's a stubborn SOB, who knows. *(Beat.)* So... I guess I'm gonna...

SAM: Right, no. You go.

SCOTTO: What, no homoerotic hug?

SAM: Only if you promise to grab my ass.

SCOTTO: Deal.

(They hug, firm and honest, like men. No ass grab.)

SAM: Say hi to Terri for me.

SCOTTO: Will do.

SAM: Alright, see ya.

SCOTTO: See ya. *(Beat.)* Don't take any wooden nickels. *(Lingers.)*

SAM: Okay. *(Beat.)* Go ahead, I'll be fine dear.

(Cross-fade to another part of the stage, TRACY in a convenience store attached to a gas station. She grabs a Diet Coke from the cooler and heads to the counter to pay. As she finishes her transaction, she turns to the door as SAM walks in.)

SAM: Excuse me...

TRACY: Oh, sorry...

(He sees her and stops. She does the same.)

SAM: Hi...

TRACY: Sam, hi...

(A beat, both stunned.)

TRACY: How are you?

(She hugs him.)

SAM: I'm doing alright... what're you doing here?

TRACY: Oh, just getting a soda.

SAM: No, I mean in town.

TRACY: Oh, right. Visiting my mom.

SAM: How is she?

TRACY: Good, you know... Well, okay, she took a fall so I'm trying to get her to move in with me in Hartford.

SAM: Hartford, wow. How's she taking that?

TRACY: Not well so far.

SAM: *(Smiling.)* Yeah, I bet.

(A beat.)

TRACY: How are you?

SAM: You already asked me *(Smiling.)* I'm okay thanks. Same as two minutes ago.

TRACY: Right. *(Beat.)* You look great, living at the beach obviously agrees with you.

SAM: *(Overlapping.)* Well, I'm about to...

TRACY: *(Overlapping.)* Mom mentioned that you... oh, I'm sorry...

SAM: No, it's okay…

TRACY: No…I was just saying, Mom mentioned that she'd seen you around once or twice.

SAM: Uh, yeah, picking up a pizza one time and uh, at the Shop Rite one time I think.

TRACY: Sure.

SAM: How are you?

TRACY: Me, I'm good, you know. Traveling and working and what have you. Keeps me busy.

SAM: Sure. Good to be busy I guess.

TRACY: Right?

(Beat.)

SAM: Well…

TRACY: Yeah, well…

SAM: It's good to see you.

TRACY: You too. *(Beat.)* Maybe we could get together while I'm in town, I'd love to catch up. I don't know many people around here anymore…

SAM: *(Beat of indecision.)* Uh…Really?

TRACY: I mean, why not…it's great to see you.

SAM: *(Can't believe he's doing this…)* Okay.

TRACY: Really?

SAM: Yeah. How long are you in town?

TRACY: For a few more days, I've got to head home Wednesday or Thursday. How about tomorrow night? Do you want to grab dinner somewhere?

SAM: Yeah, okay…sure.

TRACY: I don't know any good places in town anymore, so I'll meet you wherever you want.

SAM: How about Benjamin's over there *(Points through the window to a restaurant down the street.)* at like six thirty tomorrow. *(Beat.)* Oh, wait, what about your Mom?

TRACY: Actually, Chris will be coming over tomorrow afternoon, I'll see if I can call in a favor.

SAM: Wow, "little Chris."

TRACY: Not so little anymore, he's six two.

SAM: No kidding…that's great.

TRACY: Yep. So he'll be coming up tomorrow.

(Quick beat.)

SAM: Okay, if you're sure. *(A beat.)* Is this weird?

TRACY: Might be. I'm not sure.

SAM: I dunno, maybe.

TRACY: Well, look, if this is a bad idea…

SAM: No, it's a great idea, but it's just…it's great.

TRACY: Okay. Okay, so six thirty. *(Starts to exit.)* My cell number is on my card, if you're running late.

(She hands him a business card from her wallet. Her phone rings. She pulls it out and looks at it.)

TRACY: Speak of the devil. *(Looks at phone.)* I'm sorry Sam, I have to grab this, it's work. See you tomorrow?

SAM: Okay, see you tomorrow.

(Cross-fade to SCOTTO on a different part of the stage, as SAM crosses to him.)

SCOTTO: "See you tomorrow"?

SAM: I dunno, it just happened…

SCOTTO: And you didn't tell her you were leaving town, that you were actually ON YOUR WAY out of town?

SAM: It didn't come up.

SCOTTO: *(To himself.)* Of course, it didn't come up…

SAM: Look, how often do you run into your high school girlfriend on your way out of town?

SCOTTO: Never. Nobody does that.

SAM: Well it happened to me.

SCOTTO: Yeah, and you aren't smart enough to keep moving. I mean, she's why you're leaving, right?

SAM: What?

SCOTTO: Dude…

SAM: Look, not completely.

SCOTTO: Dude… it's me. And believe me, getting together is a bad idea. No good can come of this, you watch.

SAM: Thank you, Asshole-damus.

SCOTTO: *(Beat.)* Ha ha… Fine, do what you want. Stay with us for as long as you like. But just keep your head, okay?

SAM: Deal.

(Cross-fade to TRACY and MOM.)

TRACY: I dunno Mom, I just said let's get together, and so now we are.

MOM: Well, good.

TRACY: This is a bad idea, isn't it?

MOM: Can't hurt for you to see people. You obviously don't see enough people.

TRACY: Mom, I travel all the time, I'm with people all the time.

MOM: But I don't think you are really WITH them.

TRACY: Oh god, please tell me you're not talking about sex, right? Because I'm not sleeping with Sam…

MOM: Oh lord, who said anything about sex?

TRACY: Well…

MOM: No, I mean you need to take time to talk to people, spend time with them. Ever since Albert, I don't think you've given yourself any space to do that.

TRACY: Mom, his name is Ray…

MOM: *(Overlapping.)* Yes, Ray of course.

TRACY: *(Overlapping.)* …Look, I'm just having dinner with an old friend. He's in town, I'm in town, it works out. Nothing more.

MOM: Obviously. I'm not an idiot. I remember what going out to dinner means.

TRACY: I know you do.

MOM: Okay. *(Beat.)* But listen to your mother. Try to relax and enjoy it. And if you sleep with him, you sleep with him. I don't judge.

(Cross-fade to YOUNG TRACY and YOUNG SAM in the car at the shore. There is a tension between them; they are different than we have seen them before. Seagulls and surf again in the background, but further off.)

YOUNG SAM: It's weird, right? Let's not be weird.

YOUNG TRACY: I know, I don't want it to be weird.

YOUNG SAM: Okay.

YOUNG TRACY: Mom's getting me up at eight a.m., she wants to get on the road by nine thirty so they can start heading back before it gets too hot and the traffic gets too bad. She thinks she can get me moved into the dorm and back on the road by three.

YOUNG SAM: Right…

(Beat.)

YOUNG TRACY: It's not going to be that bad. I mean, you'll call me, I'll call you, I'll visit, you'll visit…it's not a big deal, right? We're smarter than that.

YOUNG SAM: No, totally. We're good.

YOUNG TRACY: So what do you want to do? We can walk down to Sugarman's, or go see a movie, or get some food…

YOUNG SAM: Anything, so we're not sitting here thinking about it all night.

(Beat.)

YOUNG TRACY: It's not my fault, you know.

YOUNG SAM: Look, nobody said it was your fault…

YOUNG TRACY: I feel like you're mad at me.

YOUNG SAM: I'm not, I'm really not.

YOUNG TRACY: You could have gone away somewhere too. Then this would have been way worse.

YOUNG SAM: I know. Look, we've been over this.

YOUNG TRACY: It's not too late, you can come with me tomorrow, enroll for classes…

YOUNG SAM: *(Laughs a little.)* Yeah, they're just going to let me enroll, when I didn't even apply to the school?

YOUNG TRACY: And you can live in my dorm room with me.

YOUNG SAM: And how will your roommate feel about that?

YOUNG TRACY: She'll love you just like I do.

YOUNG SAM: Well…maybe living with two hot girls would be all right…

YOUNG TRACY: Alright, maybe you should stay here then *(Laughs a little.)*

(Beat.)

YOUNG SAM: Actually, Dad is excited to have me staying around. I don't think he could take an empty apartment.

YOUNG TRACY: With all his lady friends, I don't think it's ever empty.

YOUNG SAM: Whoa, take it easy there. *(Mock indignation.)*

YOUNG TRACY: Besides, when your classes start, you won't be around that much.

YOUNG SAM: Yeah, I need to figure out my hours at work with my class schedule. Even going part time it's still a lot of money. I hope I can still work three shifts. I can't wait until I don't have to work for anybody. Be my own boss, then I'll come up and see you whenever I want.

YOUNG TRACY: *(Giggling.)* Okay, that doesn't even make any sense…you aren't going to be your own boss before we finish college.

YOUNG SAM: *(Playfully.)* Look, it could totally happen…you don't know!

YOUNG TRACY: Okay big businessman…Look, it'll work out. You'll work it out. 'Cause you are great and you can do anything.

YOUNG SAM: Oh yeah?

YOUNG TRACY: Yeah.

(TRACY enters and sees them. The restaurant begins to reveal behind her.)

YOUNG SAM: So what do we do? Last night of the summer, we're here…and then tomorrow…

YOUNG TRACY: Stop.

YOUNG SAM: Alright, *(Beat.)* let's do something before I go nuts, okay?

YOUNG TRACY: Okay.

(TRACY enters the restaurant scene as we cross-fade to Benjamin's, a nice, clean seafood restaurant but nothing fancy. SAM is there, cleaned up. TRACY looks terrific, in a black dress that is businessy but still sexy. They sit at a small wooden table with two chairs; on the table, a hurricane lamp with a small candle and a bud vase with white flowers. Two glasses of white wine and menus. There is a wine bottle on the table. Sound of a restaurant at dinner time, busy but not nuts.)

SAM: Tracy?

TRACY: Hmm?

SAM: I was asking, how's your mom.

TRACY: She's good, Chris is with her. They're going to rent movies from Blockbuster.

SAM: Good. How is Chris? Other than bigger. I haven't seen him since he was, what, thirteen?

TRACY: Oh, he's good. He and his wife just got a new Shar Pei, so all they talk about is "Alphonse this" or "Alphonse that"…

SAM: *(Laughing.)* Alphonse?

TRACY: Don't ask…I call him "Alf," it pisses them off. *(Smiles.)*

SAM: Nice.

(TRACY and SAM laugh. Beat. They each drink.)

TRACY: You know, I actually never thought I'd see you again.

SAM: Why?

TRACY: I don't know, really. Sort of figured we moved in different circles, lived in different worlds. Maybe I thought it was better that way.

SAM: Huh.

(Beat.)

TRACY: And now I'm glad it didn't end up like that.

SAM: *(Quietly.)* Me too, actually.

(Beat.)

SAM: Trace, I know we haven't seen each other in a while, but there's something I should have mentioned to you…

TRACY: Okay.

SAM: When we ran into each other yesterday…

TRACY: Look, I'm sorry to have put you on the spot, making you meet me like this.

SAM: No, no, it's totally okay, I'm glad—

TRACY: I just thought, I'm never down here, and there you were, and I hardly know anyone here anymore, and so it seemed like...

SAM: No, it's great.

(Beat.)

TRACY: Actually...I might be spending more time around here.

SAM: Oh yeah, that's great. Business down here? I bet your mom would like that.

TRACY: Well, no...I've been laid off from my job, so now it looks like I've got a lot of time on my hands.

SAM: Oh shit, really? Sorry to hear... *(Beat.)* What are you going to do?

TRACY: *(Trying to be upbeat.)* Not really sure yet. I knew the company was having tough times, they all do. Especially nowadays. But I thought I'd survive them. *(Laughs.)* I was supposed to go to Arizona later this week for a conference. Instead, I'll head back next week and sign severance papers.

SAM: Wow. You okay?

TRACY: I'll be fine, it's just a little bit of a shock. But life goes on. I'll find something. Honestly, I didn't love working in insurance anymore. Maybe a career change is in order. Maybe a change of scenery.

SAM: And what, you're thinking of moving here?

TRACY: Well, yeah, thinking about it. Who knows...Mom certainly isn't crazy about moving to Connecticut. And she seems pissed at me all the time. *(Beat.)* I'm worried about her, and so is Chris.

SAM: Can I ask what happened?

TRACY: Well, she's been having a few "moments" lately on the phone where she seemed to forget where she was and who I was. We'd be talking, and suddenly she'd talk for a second like she's having a conversation with my aunt Carol. Then she'll snap out of it and act like I'm crazy when I mention it to her. Then a few weeks back, her neighbor Mr. Kelly calls the police because she left her front door open. Wide open, all night. And then she falls, and bangs up her hip pretty good. I think she forgot where she was, then turned around and never saw the steps. Nothing broken thankfully, but her house has all these stairs inside...yesterday, she told me she didn't know how to work the toaster.

SAM: Wow.

TRACY: Her doctor wants to give her a prescription to clear her head a little, but she won't have it. She just keeps telling me to stop worrying, that's she's fine. Chris tried talking to her too, but no use.

SAM: Does Chris help out?

TRACY: He does the best he can, but he's so far away. Chris is working his way through Georgetown Law, and he and his wife Monica just moved into a small apartment in Silver Spring, barely enough room for them and the dog. Their place is further away than mine.

SAM: Right.

TRACY: So...we're trying to figure it out.

SAM: I'm sure you will. And I'm sorry to hear she's not doing well.

TRACY: How about your dad, how is he?

(Beat.)

SAM: He, uh...

TRACY: Oh no. I'm so sorry, Sam.

SAM: Yeah, well…thank you.

TRACY: He was a great man.

SAM: Thanks. He died about a year ago. Just shy of his sixtieth birthday.

TRACY: My god, that's so young.

SAM: Yeah, well…

TRACY: I'm so sorry.

(Beat.)

SAM: So…what else is new? How do you like Connecticut?

TRACY: It's okay. Mainly what I like right now is being close to my son, so I can…

SAM: You have a son? I didn't know that.

TRACY: Yeah, his name is Shawn, and he's eight. He lives full time with my ex in Norwich.

SAM: And you see him on weekends and stuff?

TRACY: *(Beat.)* As much as I can.

SAM: Oh, I'm sorry.

TRACY: No, it's okay. It's tough, but with my travel schedule, I was never home. Never there for parent-teacher conferences and checking homework. And he started to be a behavioral problem in school, hitting other kids. His teachers thought he was looking for attention, and Ray thought I was being a bad mother, so…

SAM: Ray's your ex?

TRACY: *(Overlapping.)* …My ex-husband, sorry. *(Beat.)* So Ray sued for full custody in our divorce, and he got it.

SAM: Wow, I thought custody always went to the mother…

TRACY: Apparently it's not such a sure thing anymore. And really, I didn't know what was gonna be best for Shawn at that point, and I think I kind of just let it happen. I thought…I dunno. *(She's quiet, not crying but not together either.)*

SAM: Wow, we are a cheery pair, huh? Barrels of laughs, the two of us. Divorce, death, unemployment…the trifecta.

(She smiles. Beat.)

SAM: Look, I'm sorry I brought that up, lets talk about something else…

TRACY: No, it's okay. *(A little lost in thought.)* I love that kid so much.

SAM: So when do you see him?

TRACY: Maybe that'll change now. I go to Norwich when I can. Ray, insensitive prick that he is, thinks I upset Shawn when I visit; upset his routine, make him too emotional. So he tries to steer me away from coming up, saying they're traveling or Shawn has martial arts practice or something. It's funny, I don't even remember now how or why we were married. I can't remember a single moment of kindness in him.

SAM: Sounds like a charming guy.

TRACY: Yeah, well I can pick 'em.

SAM: *(Teasing her.)* Uhh…excuse me.

TRACY: Not you, obviously.

SAM: *(Still teasing her.)* Sweet talker.

(Beat.)

TRACY: Enough about me…how are you?

SAM: I'm doing okay.

(THE WAITER comes over.)

WAITER: Have you decided yet?

TRACY: I think we need a little more time.

SAM: The surf and turf here is excellent, if that helps.

WAITER: No problem, I'll give you a few minutes. Would you like more wine?

TRACY: Yes, please.

(He pours, then exits.)

SAM: Actually, wanna hear a funny story...when you ran into me in the store yesterday, I was loading up to leave town.

TRACY: *(Casually.)* Leave town?

SAM: Yeah.

TRACY: Like for a trip or...

SAM: For good.

(Beat.)

TRACY: How come?

SAM: Ah, I don't know. *(Beat.)* That's a lie, I do know. It's a long story, you ready?

TRACY: Sure, shoot.

SAM: Well, I lost my job too, a little more than a week ago. And...

TRACY: No way.

SAM: No joke.

TRACY: Where were you working?

SAM: Sam's Club.

TRACY: Oh the irony. Sorry, go on.

SAM: *(Smiles.)* So, after that happened, I was going to look for something else, you know...get right back to it. But I know how tough jobs are right now. I mean, hell, Scotto can't get anything better than that liquor store job he's had with his dad for how many years now. Granted, it's Scotto, but still *(Laughs.)*...

TRACY: *(Overlapping.)* Wow, that's a name I haven't heard in a while...

SAM: Anyway, I'm sure it's the same where you live too. And so I thought maybe the thing to do is to make a fresh start, a clean break from this place. I mean, with my dad gone, and no job, I don't really have anything keeping me rooted here. So...I'm going.

TRACY: Wow. This is kind of a shock.

SAM: Is it?

TRACY: Well, yeah, whenever I think of this place...I think of you here.

SAM: I know. But we haven't seen each other in years. The things you are remembering are us as kids.

(Beat.)

TRACY: Maybe. *(Beat. Realizes.)* So wait, when are you leaving?

SAM: Well, I was leaving yesterday.

TRACY: And you let me hold you up?

SAM: No no, it's okay...

TRACY: Where were you heading?

SAM: Not sure. Heading South, figure it might be summer for a little while longer.

TRACY: But no plan...?

SAM: "No plan" is the plan.

(Beat.)

TRACY: Well...I'll say I'm sorry I stopped you, but I'm really not sorry.

SAM: I'm not sorry.

(There is a spark.)

TRACY: So, no girlfriend you're leaving behind broken hearted, no kids, nothing like that?

SAM: Nope, nothing like that.

TRACY: How did that happen?

SAM: Well, I don't know.

TRACY: Another lie?

SAM: Maybe. *(Beat.)* Ah, who knows. Anyway, I thought now would be a good time to go. Summer ending, only people left are the weekenders. Seemed like the right time.

TRACY: Okay. *(Beat.)* I still can't believe you don't have a plan at all. You must have something. I could never do that. But then again, you were always the dreamer.

SAM: Hah, yeah, well…

TRACY: *(Searching.)* What?

SAM: I feel like I've been dreaming for a long time now, and it's time to wise up and move on.

TRACY: What does that mean?

SAM: I've got to get on with my life. I've been stuck in this town for too long, chasing something that was never here. And now I've got to give that up and try something new before it's too late.

TRACY: Wow.

SAM: Sorry. Too much for a "let's catch up" dinner?

TRACY: No, it's alright. We could always be honest with each other.

SAM: Could we?

TRACY: I think so.

(Beat.)

SAM: I'm sorry, this has gotten awkward and heavy and…

TRACY: No, it's okay. *(Beat, she lightens.)* So what was this thing you were chasing? Sounds very mysterious.

SAM: *(Beat.)* Nothing. I'm just kind of stuck in a rut here.

TRACY: *(Picks up glass.)* Okay then…to breaking out of ruts.

(They toast.)

TRACY: So it's not mysterious, but you're not going to tell me, are you?

SAM: Sort of hard to explain…I mean with Dad passing…

TRACY: *(Sensing his difficulty.)* Never mind, we don't need to talk about it. We should change the subject. *(Beat.)* Tell me a joke.

SAM: Really?

TRACY: Yes, before I interrogate you about every move you've made for the last twenty years, including why you never called me or got in touch.

SAM: So, a horse walks into a bar…

(They both laugh. Beat.)

SAM: Look, I'm sorry we didn't stay in touch. That was my fault.

TRACY: True. But I didn't exactly help much.

SAM: I don't know, whenever I talked to Brian or Kathy, it just started seeming like this huge gap opened up between the people who got out of here and those who didn't. So it was easier to hang with Scotto and get drunk than anything else.

TRACY: Sounds like fun.

SAM: Oh it was.

TRACY: What did you do after school?

SAM: I took the long way around, actually. Pete asked me to manage the deli, and I was trying to pay for school and help Dad with bills. And it just seemed easier to take that route at the time. So I quit school. I went back later and finished up, but by then I was already managing Pete's second place out on Route 62. There doesn't seem much need for higher education when you're slicing deli salami and ordering cases of Italian ice. Then eventually, I got sick of working for Pete, and Dan Mackey asked me if I would come work for him at Sam's, so I did. Yep, always the dreamer huh? *(Beat.)* You remember Dan right?

TRACY: Wow, Dan Mackey, he was always sort of a...

SAM: Yeah, still is. And that was good for a little while, and then it wasn't. And so then, he let me go. Claimed times were tight, and that they could get by with more part timers and less full timers because of benefits, insurance...

TRACY: Yep, I know the drill.

SAM: Right, insurance. And so...now I am a free agent.

TRACY: Sexy.

SAM: Oh, of course, it's all the rage. You're a free agent too, ya know. It looks good on you.

TRACY: Why thank you... *(She smiles.)* I would have liked to have talked to you, you know.

SAM: I know. Me too. *(Beat.)* And then so much time had passed, and I just really didn't know how to...

TRACY: Meanwhile, I'm off, marrying, having a son, traveling, divorcing. I kept very busy while waiting for your call. *(Smiles.)*

SAM: Ha ha, very funny.

TRACY: Look the point is, we never should have let this much time go by. And...that was a deft change of subject.

SAM: I'm not changing the subject. You changed the subject.

TRACY: *(Smiles.)* Fine, don't tell me.

SAM: There's nothing to tell. Just time for a change.

TRACY: Okay...But you are still sort of cagey.

SAM: Am I? I don't mean to be.

TRACY: Well you are.

SAM: It's just that I'm looking for something more.

TRACY: A minute ago you said you were here chasing something.

SAM: Yeah, well...

TRACY: So which is it?

SAM: Are you sure you aren't a lawyer, because I think you are badgering the witness...

TRACY: I think I have a hostile witness, so I'll pull whatever stunts I need to. In a second I'll start with guilt trips and twisting your words around.

SAM: How very feminine of you.

TRACY: *(She's quick, and on his every move.)* Watch it, mister. You forget, I'm a mom, I know all the tricks.

SAM: Obviously. Are you always this nice to people you haven't seen in twenty years?

TRACY: You're my first, how am I doing?

SAM: Could use a little work, actually.

TRACY: Duly noted. Gonna tell me your sob story yet?

SAM: Look, it's just…

TRACY: C'mon, what's her name?

SAM: What?

TRACY: I know it must be some cute little beach bunny who broke your heart, right?

SAM: No, it's…

TRACY: Candy? Bambi? Carly? I feel like she had a bimbette/stripper kind of name, I don't know why…

SAM: Look Trace…

TRACY: Sammy? Mandy? Dani with a heart over the "I"…

SAM: *(Maybe a little too loud.)* It's you. *(Beat.)* It's you.

TRACY: Me?

SAM: *(Laughs at how ridiculous that sounds.)* You. Us.

TRACY: Sam, I haven't been here in…forever.

SAM: I'm aware of that.

TRACY: So…?

SAM: The memories of us. I love those days.

TRACY: I do too. *(Beat.)* But I don't understand what this has to do with you leaving.

SAM: Look, we don't have to get into all this.

TRACY: No, maybe we should. It's important enough for you to leave town over. It's obviously bothering you.

SAM: Maybe we should order…

TRACY: *(Beat.)* Wow, okay.

SAM: What?

TRACY: I didn't remember that look on your face when you are scared. Until just now.

(Giggle from the HOSTESS and the WAITER, somewhere behind SAM and TRACY. SAM and TRACY watch as the young WAITER flirts with the HOSTESS, making her blush and laugh. The HOSTESS touches the WAITER, the electricity of some new adventure. The WAITER responds, then is called away. The HOSTESS tries to busy herself, but cannot help watching him walk off.)

SAM: Do you want to get out of here?

TRACY: Sure.

(Cross-fade to YOUNG TRACY and YOUNG SAM, walking on the boardwalk. A little chilly, but not too bad. Sweatshirt weather.)

YOUNG SAM: So you like her?

YOUNG TRACY: She's an okay roommate, I could have much worse. She doesn't seem to be a slob or a slut. Everything else can be overlooked.

YOUNG SAM: Really? Raging bigot…uppity snob…moron, all can be overlooked? Hmm…

YOUNG TRACY: Look, if she's not boning the basketball team every night of the week while I'm studying, and she's cleaning up her crap and doing her dishes, then everything will be fine. *(Beat.)* Alright, maybe lousy taste in music would be a deal breaker too, but we like a lot of the same stuff, so…you'll understand when you live with somebody.

YOUNG SAM: *(A little stung.)* Right.

YOUNG TRACY: No, it's just different, you know…

(Kisses him.)

YOUNG SAM: What's that for?

YOUNG TRACY: Because I missed you and because you are cute. So…when are you coming to visit?

YOUNG SAM: I don't know yet, I need to figure that out…Pete's giving me shit about my hours at the deli. Once I get that straight, I'll be able to plan something.

YOUNG TRACY: Come up! Comeup ComeupComeup!!…I miss you. You'll really like it there.

YOUNG SAM: I know I will. And I miss you too. *(Beat.)* Sooo…it's a nice night…How about you and I go back to the car and replay the highlights of this past summer…

(He begins to make out with her.)

YOUNG TRACY: Sam…Sam…Let's do something. What do you want to do?

YOUNG SAM: I thought we were doing what I wanted to do…I mean, we've got a warm night, a quiet spot, seems perfect…

YOUNG TRACY: No, I mean…I love you, and I love sex with you. But let's do something else.

YOUNG SAM: *(A little stunned.)* Okay.

(SAM and TRACY are on the boardwalk later that night. Sound of surf and kids in the distance.)

TRACY: I've missed this place. It's still such a beautiful place to come home to.

SAM: You know, when I hear people say that I usually think they're trying to convince themselves it still is.

TRACY: I don't know…it still looks pretty great to me. Just like I remember it…a little bit breezy, you can see the spots on the beach where the wind's blown the top smooth…almost warm enough to walk with your feet in the water…I'll always love it here.

SAM: Yeah, well…it's funny, after all this time it still has this rise and fall with summer, and not much more. And someone finally bought Sugarman's.

TRACY: I heard. I was sad to see it closed last time I was here.

SAM: How long ago was that?

TRACY: Wow, I don't know, maybe Christmas two years ago.

SAM: Couldn't drag yourself back to the sticks, huh?

TRACY: Sounds like you don't like it here much anymore.

SAM: No no, just…I see more of it now, you know, all the cracks. But you're right, it's still a beautiful spot, still the same as you left it. Although I think the kids are more obnoxious now.

TRACY: Sounds like you're becoming an old man…"Hey you kids, get off of my lawn!"

SAM: *(Smiling.)* Maybe I am.

TRACY: I see kids now, and they seem so much older than we were at that age.

SAM: Maybe. I kinda think we always wanted to be older, or at least feel like we were.

TRACY: Remember that fourth of July we came here, and you got so sunburned?

SAM: Yeah, well I wasn't the brightest…

TRACY: Yeah, turns out baby oil is not the same as sunscreen.

SAM: Nope. Learned that the hard way. I'm an SPF 30 guy now, so no worries.

TRACY: Well sure, living at the beach…

SAM: That's one of the gains of getting older, picking up a little wisdom along with the gray hairs.

TRACY: So…

(A beat.)

SAM: Look, I'm sorry about…well, you know, at dinner. I shouldn't have said anything.

TRACY: You haven't said anything so far.

(SAM gives her a rueful grin.)

TRACY: Never mind. I mean, I haven't seen you in a long time, and now here we are, on the same boardwalk as when we were kids a hundred years ago.

SAM: See, in my head it was only about seventy-five…

TRACY: *(Playfully.)* Judge's ruling? *(Beat.)* Nope, a full hundred. *(She smiles.)*

SAM: Right. *(Beat.)* You ever wonder if you're just going to become carbon copies of your parents?

TRACY: *(A small laugh.)* Yeah, sometimes.

SAM: I guess it's just one of those things, kind of inevitable, right?

TRACY: Probably.

SAM: Well, I'm trying to keep that from happening.

TRACY: Wait a minute, you loved your dad, everybody did…

SAM: I know that, it's not that he wasn't a good guy…

TRACY: He wasn't a "good guy," Sam. He was a *great* guy, one of the best.

SAM: I know. *(Beat.)*

TRACY: So then what?

SAM: Look, my dad only got up to go to work. His version of a good day was finishing at 5:45 and having a tallboy in his hand by six. And he was great and he was loved, and I adored the guy…But I don't think I can live that kind of life.

TRACY: Okay, so don't.

SAM: So I've gotta get out of here to do that.

TRACY: *(Searching.)* Okay… *(Beat.)* look, what I remember of your dad, he loved you very much too.

SAM: I know. He's also the guy, though, that sat on his porch looking at the bay drinking himself to sleep every night. He never got over Mom.

TRACY: Wait a minute, your dad had all kinds of women throwing themselves at him. I remember…

SAM: Yeah, here's the thing…he's widowed at thirty-five, and so he goes on dates and he plays the part of "interested guy." He does what he's supposed to do, what everyone tells him are supposedly the "next steps," to "get on with things." He goes to support groups, he goes to church events, he's social…he plays by the rules. But all that doesn't do anything for him. The person he's supposed to be going out to dinner with, who he's supposed to be standing here with… *(Beat.)* Mom dies when I'm nine, and my dad is alone for twenty-five years.

TRACY: Hardly alone, he had you and…

SAM: You know what I mean.

TRACY: *(Beat.)* I know.

SAM: I'm not going to let that happen to me.

TRACY: What?

SAM: Not going to turn into him. I love him, I miss him, and I don't want to be like him.

TRACY: You could do a lot worse.

SAM: *(Not cruelly.)* You think I don't know that? I feel like…I could so easily just look at my dad and say, that's cool. He had a job, some friends…I'll take that. But I think I still want more. I want more than just getting to sleep and getting up. But I'm not sure what that is.

TRACY: It's because you don't have children.

SAM: You think so?

TRACY: I know so. *(Beat.)*

SAM: Maybe.

TRACY: I'm telling you, it totally changes your world. Being responsible for another life, making sure they're okay, knowing you'd do even the hardest thing if you thought that's what they needed. That's having a purpose, my friend.

(Beat. SAM is quiet, looking out over the railing toward the ocean.)

TRACY: But…this leads to the weird peeking behind the curtains of your own childhood. The point when you reach some sort of parallel with your parents…

SAM: Yeah?

TRACY: I mean, I'm thirty-six right, Shawn just turned eight in August, and my mom and dad were in their mid-thirties when I was eight. So if you do the math…that means that all the shit I'm going through now…messed-up relationships, money decisions, stress at work…all those things were probably happening for them too, but somehow they hid it from you as a little kid. And so all the times you thought, "Wow, my Mom is such a bitch because we didn't stop and get ice cream today," or "Why didn't Dad get me that Strawberry Short-cake doll I wanted so bad"…it's because your parents were struggling to make it all work. Living paycheck to paycheck, freaking out, tired…Just as screwed up as I am now, but keeping it together…

SAM: For the kids…

TRACY: *(Overlapping a little.)* …For the kids.

SAM: Are you worried about Shawn?

TRACY: Are you kidding? Of course. Every day, all the time. I wonder how he'll deal with growing up with two homes, how he'll deal with me and Ray not being on good terms, with Ray being an asshole…Ray's already remarried, what if I do too?…How does a kid figure all that out? Is it better to have it happen now when he's little…when he might not realize what's going on? Or would it have been better when he's older, when he was better equipped emotionally to handle it? There's so much…

SAM: Okay, it's okay…

(Beat.)

SAM: What about your dad, do you see him much?

TRACY: *(She gathers.)* Not too much. He's got his own life, playing golf and chasing rich widows around the Gulf

Coast. He calls it "bird dogging," if you can believe that.

SAM: Nice...maybe I should go hang out with him for a little while. *(Smiles.)*

TRACY: Somehow I don't see that as your style, but I bet he'd be happy to see you.

(Beat.)

TRACY: Wanna hear another weird thing?

SAM: Wow, you are just full of weird random thoughts, huh?

TRACY: Sometimes...anyway. My BlackBerry is disconnected now, since I lost my job, and I miss it buzzing.

SAM: Do you have a way to get in touch with Shawn if you need to?

TRACY: Yeah, I have my cell, and Ray has the number at my mom's just in case. Although he'll never use it.

SAM: When was the last time your mom saw Shawn?

TRACY: It's kind of embarrassing how long it's been.

SAM: Sorry.

TRACY: *(Beat.)* Ray did a real number on me, he made me feel really bad about myself and the way I was living my life. He told me I was a bad mom, and I was messing Shawn up. I kind of shut the world off for a little while. *(Beat.)* Funny story, after my divorce, I couldn't get used to sleeping alone, so I got one of those full body pillows that you snuggle, and I named it "Brad Pitt." *(She laughs a little.)* I dunno...

SAM: I'm sure you're a great mom.

TRACY: Yeah, I'm not so sure about that one.

SAM: How could you not be? I don't think there's even a chance of that.

TRACY: You never really know, right?...Plus, I work a lot of... *(Catches herself.)* I used to work a lot.

SAM: So then maybe this is a chance to fix things, make a few adjustments.

TRACY: Maybe. *(Beat.)* And is this a second chance too?

(SAM is quiet for a moment.)

TRACY: No, I'm sorry, no, of course it isn't. I'm an idiot. Sorry.

SAM: It's complicated...

TRACY: Right, of course, no... *(Walks away from him, up the boardwalk a little.)*

SAM: Trace, hang on...

TRACY: I'm sorry. I got carried away with being here and seeing you.

SAM: Now you know why I need to go.

TRACY: What?

SAM: I'm living that same thing every day. Every time I'm here, all I see is you. *(Beat.)* This place used to be full of good memories for me...everything from that summer, all of it. And somehow as I got older that all changed.

TRACY: Okay.

SAM: And so now I need to put all that behind me. Hell, any rational person would have done that a long time ago. So I've got some catching up to do.

TRACY: Why do you need to put it all behind you?

SAM: Because I miss those days, and hanging around here trying to bring them back has been...crushing. *(Beat.)*

TRACY: I see. *(Beat.)* I'm not sure what to say to all this.

SAM: Look, you don't have to say anything. You were never going to be a part of all of this. But then I ran into you, on the way out of town no less! And I mixed you up in my psychosis, I'm really sorry. You don't deserve this.

TRACY: Forget that...what if I asked you to stay. What if I said that I want that feeling back too.

SAM: Do you think that's even possible?

TRACY: Why not, people do it all the time, right?

SAM: They do?

TRACY: Sure, right?

SAM: Nobody I know.

TRACY: Well...do you have to leave right away?

SAM: Wait, wait...this is happening too fast.

(TRACY kisses him.)

SAM: Are you sure about this?

TRACY: No, but why not? Let's be kids again...backseat of the car, you remember?

(She kisses him again, he returns it then...)

SAM: Trace, wait... *(He pulls away.)*

(She regains her self-control, beat; they separate.)

TRACY: Man, this place is powerful. Sorry, here I am, throwing myself at you...

SAM: Oh, I was tossing it back to you, don't worry...

(TRACY smiles. Beat. She takes a few steps away, and looks out at the ocean.)

TRACY: You know I can't go with you.

SAM: What?

TRACY: Mom is here, I can't go with you. Wherever is it you're going.

SAM: Trace, I'm not asking you to come with me. *(Beat.)* That came out wrong.

TRACY: *(She turns away.)* No it didn't. It's how you meant it.

SAM: We haven't seen each other in almost twenty years...there's no way I'd expect you to come with me. We probably barely know each other now.

TRACY: Did you think about asking me?

SAM: Wha...no.

TRACY: *(Overlapping.)* Let me try this again...Obviously, I can't go with you, if that was ever part of your thinking. Not that it should have been. But it was part of mine, from the moment you said you were going. And I can't go.

SAM: You thought of going with me?

TRACY: Well, not rationally... *(Beat.)* I just know I love how I felt with you when we were kids, and I want to feel that good again. Things have been kind of down with me for a long time now. So how do I get back to that?

SAM: I dunno. I've been trying to figure that out for a long time.

TRACY: Yeah?

SAM: But can you even stay here, even for your mom? Shawn is in Connecticut somewhere...

TRACY: Well maybe you come to Hartford with me?

SAM: Wait, we aren't actually planning on running away together after one failed dinner twenty years later, are we?

TRACY: I dunno, are we? Are you?

SAM: Me? Why me? You're doing it too.

TRACY: I am, aren't I? *(Smiles.)*

(Beat.)

SAM: Look, this is just a romantic fantasy from being here. We've got to be careful, because we might just be crazy enough to do it.

(Beat, he looks at her.)

TRACY: I feel like I want to go back to being that girl, the girl on the beach with everything in front of her, with all the confidence in the world. When I was seventeen, I could do anything, be anyone.

SAM: And you still can be.

TRACY: I feel like every move I make has to be so perfect so Ray won't use it against me with Shawn. So I get scared to do anything. "Don't come to the house too much," "Don't call too much," "Stop coddling him"…I pretty much hear these in my sleep.

SAM: Right. I'm sure you're fine, kids are really tough, they aren't fazed by every little thing…

TRACY: Oh, and you have so much experience with kids?

SAM: Whoa, I never said I was an expe…

TRACY: Sam, you just don't know how it is.

SAM: Okay.

(Beat. TRACY takes a little walk down the boardwalk.)

SAM: Right.

TRACY: Sam, I'm sorry. I shouldn't have snapped at you.

SAM: No, it's okay. You're right, you are right. I've been here chasing your ghost for two decades. I can tell you all about that, but kids, well I'm a little behind on my reading…

TRACY: Sam…

SAM: Trace, look. I get that you have problems. We all do, I know I do. You're terrific, there's no need for you to be scared of anything or anybody.

TRACY: I'm not though, Sam. I wish I were, but Ray's right, what if I'm doing emotional damage and Shawn pays the price. Or worse, what if I do it Ray's way and then Shawn and I aren't close, I'm this other person who is in the periphery of his life and…

SAM: Look, look…I don't know, okay. You're his mother, you'll be in his life. Take it easy…

TRACY: Real life comes creeping into this little fantasy. I'm not the perfect girl you've probably imagined me to be.

SAM: I'm not perfect either.

TRACY: I know.

SAM: And believe me, you are a hell of a lot better than you think you are. You're terrific. I…

TRACY: Yeah, well… *(Beat.)* Seems the only thing that's still perfect is that summer.

SAM: Yeah.

ACT 2

Cross-fade to YOUNG TRACY and YOUNG SAM in the car, evening. Sounds of surf and wind.

YOUNG SAM: You haven't talked much.

YOUNG TRACY: Haven't I?

YOUNG SAM: Nope, not much.

YOUNG TRACY: Okay. What do you want to talk about?

YOUNG SAM: Seeing everybody while you're home?

YOUNG TRACY: There's almost no time. Mom wants me to hang out with her and Dad a bunch. It's like every time I'm back, I've got to see everybody. It was a struggle to get some time tonight with you.

YOUNG SAM: Well, I'm glad you did.

YOUNG TRACY: Me too.

YOUNG SAM: And sorry I didn't call you back on Tuesday. I was working a double and I had a test the next morning.

YOUNG TRACY: It's okay…I ended up having a study group with my Econ class. It's funny, I think I get Economics and I never thought I would. I mean, markets and unemployment, booms and recessions…it's pretty cool.

YOUNG SAM: Sounds thrilling.

YOUNG TRACY: I know it sounds dull, but seriously it really isn't. And I kind of like how when we were in high school you got to see like ten percent of the world, and now college blows your mind up and you see like so much more.

YOUNG SAM: Right.

YOUNG TRACY: You must have stuff you like…what's your favorite class? *(Beat.)* God, actually I just realized I don't even know what you're taking…I'm so sorry.

(Beat. Cross-fade as SAM enters SCOTTO's place at night. Puts his keys on the table quietly, as SCOTTO enters, smoking a cigarette.)

SCOTTO: *(Mock anger, like a parent.)* And where the hell have you been, young man!?

SAM: Sorry, Mom.

SCOTTO: Beer?

SAM: Yeah.

SCOTTO: Bad?

SAM: Nah, totally fine.

SCOTTO: Really?

SAM: No.

(A wry smile from SAM as SCOTTO hands him the beer.)

SAM: Terri awake?

SCOTTO: *(Takes a drag.)* No, she sleeps like she's in a coma.

SAM: *(Realizing.)* Hey, are you supposed to be smoking around a pregnant woman?

SCOTTO: Probably not, but that's why I'm out here with you, cock knocker. I was gonna play Rock Band, you wanna play? I'm singing first…

SAM: Nah, I'm good.

SCOTTO: So how'd she look?

SAM: She looked good.

SCOTTO: Always did.

SAM: Yeah, you got that right.

(Beat.)

SCOTTO: (Probing, expectantly.) Sooo...you going to take her out again?

SAM: Dude...I, uh...

(Beat.)

SCOTTO: Wait a minute, no...no. You pine after this girl for however many years, and when you finally get a second shot, you're gonna pass?

SAM: I didn't pine. I'm not pining.

SCOTTO: Whatever. Moping, mooning, whatever you want to call it...

SAM: Alright, alright, if those are the choices, let's go with pining.

SCOTTO: Fine. Dick. (Beat.) Anyway, so now what?

(SAM is quiet.)

SAM: I dunno. (Beat.) What would you do if you were me?

SCOTTO: (Beat.) Look man, I know you've got some shit going on, with her and with seeing her here. And with your dad and all...I get that. (Beat.) Look, Terri is sleeping in there, right...and she's having a kid. I love her...but the chance to fix something that I think got royally fucked up, I don't know what I wouldn't give for an opportunity like that. (Beat.) What, you think I don't have things I wouldn't like to do over? Women who got away, times when I would have paid more attention, things I wouldn't try to undo...

SAM: No, I know. But what if it's not a matter of fixing, what if it's something that can't ever come back.

(Beat.)

SCOTTO: Well...then I don't know.

SAM: The thing is, that time with her was perfect. She was perfect.

SCOTTO: And so?

SAM: And so, now it's not. And that sucks. If it goes down in flames now, it takes all of that other stuff down with it. And I can't do that.

SCOTTO: What the fuck?...Are you serious?

SAM: I don't know.

SCOTTO: So you're going to leave a potentially winning hand on the table because you're too chicken shit to place a bet?

SAM: It's not that simple.

SCOTTO: Isn't it? (Beat.) Look, you are an asshole. I love ya, but you are an ASSHOLE...

SAM: Okay okay, your point?

SCOTTO: (Continuous.) I'm willing to overlook this flaw, and I think you should stick around and give this a shot.

SAM: Ya know, a few days ago you wanted to join me on the open road...remember "no good can come of this"?

SCOTTO: Yeah, well, uh... (Changing the subject.) Fuck you, so what?

SAM: I'm just sayin'...why the change of heart?

SCOTTO: Look, Ocean Beach is a great place. We can still tear this place up like we used to. We could have a blast, you and me and maybe Tracy too...

SAM: And Terri and the baby...

SCOTTO: Yeah, sure...

SAM: You really think that's gonna fly with her?

SCOTTO: I dunno, maybe...right?

SAM: Yeah, think again.

SCOTTO: Well, look...how's the kid gonna know his Uncle Sammy if you take off, huh? Think about that! And who's gonna buy the kid beer when he's underage, and get him condoms, and teach him how to hit on girls with low self-esteem?

SAM: I guess he's just gonna have to depend on dear ol' Dad for all that.

SCOTTO: Yeah, maybe... *(Realizing.)* Dear ol' Dad. Fuck.

SAM: You okay?

SCOTTO: Yeah. Just thinking out loud.

(Beat.)

SAM: Why did your dad stay here?

SCOTTO: What?

SAM: I mean, why is it that this town was enough for your dad, my dad, all kinds of people...but not enough for me.

SCOTTO: I dunno. Maybe you're better than us.

SAM: Bullshit.

SCOTTO: Maybe you just think you are. *(Beat.)* No offense, but as the guy sitting here watching this for years now, maybe I've got some perspective. I mean, maybe you think you deserve something better than the rest of us.

SAM: You think that's true?

SCOTTO: I dunno man. It's late, you wouldn't play Rock Band with me...I'm cranky.

SAM: You gonna raise your kid here, ya think?

SCOTTO: I guess so, where else would I go?

SAM: It's a big world, lots of places, right?

SCOTTO: Yeah, but I belong here.

SAM: Do I?

SCOTTO: Probably not.

SAM: Okay...how'd that happen?

SCOTTO: She happened to you. When you were just a kid and couldn't defend yourself. You didn't know any better. So you got this peek that there was always something better.

SAM: So what...You know it too.

SCOTTO: But this was always mine. Totally enough for me...people I grew up with, known my whole life...streets I know by heart. But you, *she* kept you here.

SAM: And my dad was here too...

SCOTTO: Sure, but really...look, you loved your dad, but she could have made you do anything, go anywhere. Maybe you got scared, I dunno.

SAM: So now what?

SCOTTO: What's more important to you, today or twenty years ago?

SAM: We're different, we're not those kids anymore. Hell, I might not even like this person.

SCOTTO: So what?

SAM: So what? Are you serious?

SCOTTO: Well look, you don't want to be that dumbass anymore. And she probably wouldn't like you if you were. Dude…We've "evolved."

SAM: Oh is that what they're calling it these days?

SCOTTO: Look, I don't want to get all *After School Special* on you, but if you don't try…are you going to be fucking bitching to me about it for the next forty years?

SAM: Haha, fuck you. *(Beat.)* She's got a kid, pal, and an ex-husband, and who knows what else. Maybe you never bounce all the way back. *(Beat.)* Remember those nights when we were kids, we'd play baseball down at the school on Valley Avenue?

SCOTTO: Yeah, sure.

SAM: We'd have one cheap baseball for the whole game…The first couple of times it is hit, the ball is fine, but remember how after a few innings of getting smacked around the yard, the ball would always lose its shape. A lump on this side, a split seam on the other side…

SCOTTO: Man, those were fun games.

SAM: No, totally…but my point is, now the ball doesn't travel the same when you throw it or hit it, and it's not going to be the same ever again.

SCOTTO: Fucker, you're not a crappy baseball! And besides, is that so bad? Everybody's got baggage. Stop being a fucking pussy!

SAM: Fuck you.

SCOTTO: Seriously, look at yourself.

SAM: I know.

SCOTTO: Well then maybe if you'd stop crying in your cornflakes for two fuckin' seconds you'd realize this is how life works. Nobody gets the life they planned! You think I did? Did Tracy? Did your dad?

(Beat. He's crossed a line in the heat of the moment. No apology necessary, but they both know it.)

SCOTTO: What's the problem with seeing if you two connect now? So it isn't the same as twenty years ago, so what? I mean really, how perfect could it have been, you were seven fucking teen…you didn't know jackshit about anything. And look, it's not fucking life or death, am I right? So you stay an extra day or two, take her out, maybe fuck her once or twice, see if something could happen.

SAM: But that screws everything up. Don't you get it?

SCOTTO: Alright, don't fuck her, I don't care. *(Beat.)* Although I'd fuck her.

SAM: Hey, did you hear what I just said?

SCOTTO: I'm just sayin'…I mean, you had one dinner with her, right?…

SAM: Not even.

SCOTTO: Whatever…where's the fire? Hang out on the couch for a little while, see what happens…

SAM: First off, I'm not sleeping on your busted couch any longer than I have to…

SCOTTO: Aw, c'mon…now you're just mean.

SAM: *(Continuous.)* …but more to the point…Dude, one minute I think you're telling me to hit the road, get over it…now you're saying stick around again. What gives?

SCOTTO: Nothing. *(Beat.)* Alright, look…I can get you a job somewhere, and if Tracy's here…Mrs. Halberstam is a regular at the store, I can talk to her. She's a bit of a drunk, actually…I'm serious, this town is still great in the summer, you know it is, huh? I mean…I'm going to be playing dad to a kid. Me, I'm going to be a… *(Exhales, gives up. Beat.)* So, what do you wanna do?

SAM: Dunno. She takes her mom to the boardwalk in the morning for walks, I think I'm going to swing by and try to catch her there.

SCOTTO: And do what?

SAM: Beats the hell out of me.

(SCOTTO kills his beer, gets up, and begins to head in.)

SAM: Hey, you never told me, is your dad going to sell to Sugarman's?

SCOTTO: Nope. He found out the plan is to make the pier into a mall complex.

SAM: Wow.

SCOTTO: Yep. He doesn't want any part of it. *(Beat.)* So what, ten or so tomorrow morning on the boardwalk?

SAM: Something like that.

SCOTTO: Alright, I can be a little late for work.

SAM: Whoa, why would you be late? Nobody asked you to come with me.

SCOTTO: See, that's the beauty of me…I don't need to be asked, I just know where I'm needed.

SAM: Really…? I find that hard to believe.

SCOTTO: Oh believe it, my friend. Believe it. *(Starts to exit.)* And look, I really think fucking her can't hurt. Well, maybe a little if you do it right!

(No response.)

SCOTTO: Okaaay, I'm just going to go back in there… *(Exits.)*

(Cross-fade to the boardwalk, the next morning. Enter TRACY and her MOM, who sit on the bench.)

MOM: You don't have to walk me like a dog every morning, you know.

TRACY: Mom, I'm not.

MOM: Good. *(Beat.)* How was your dinner?

TRACY: Um…Nice. It was good to see him. *(Beat.)* I think it was good…Nice.

MOM: Your record is skipping. What happened?

TRACY: Nothing, we just got to catching up and reliving old times…

MOM: Sounds good…nice.

TRACY: *(Realizing.)* You're very funny.

(They sit a moment in silence.)

TRACY: So…is this what grownups do? Fawn over their high school boyfriends?

MOM: Look, there are no rules. If you father was here right now, my heart would skip a beat or two…

TRACY: So if that's true, Mom, why aren't you chasing Dad down?

MOM: Because your father isn't the same man now I fell in love with as a girl. He's older, he's more stubborn, and he's more of a jackass than ever. But the idea of him, the man in his army uniform with a straight back and so trim…that man I would follow to the end the Earth. I still talk to him.

TRACY: What?! On the phone or…?

MOM: Up here. *(Points to her temple.)* And in here. *(Points to her chest.)* He was the most beautiful thing I ever saw.

TRACY: I remember seeing that picture you used to show us… Dad coming back from Vietnam.

MOM: I've lived with that man all my life. I've kept him safe and he's held me through many nights. That's been the love of my life.

TRACY: And you don't feel cheated by that? I mean, no offense Mom, but that's a dream.

MOM: But I haven't lost him. I've held onto him. That's real.

TRACY: But… he's not here, in person. That's a ghost.

MOM: The minute you can do better than what I've had, you let me know.

(Beat.)

TRACY: Mom, I don't think I've been a good daughter lately. I feel like I've let you down, not being around for you.

MOM: Look, I know you have you own life, you have Shawn. I didn't expect you to follow the same course I did. You had to go, so you went.

TRACY: But we lost something, didn't we?

MOM: Yes.

TRACY: Well then I'm sorry for that.

MOM: Don't be sorry, be different! God, I get so angry with you sometimes!

TRACY: Why?

MOM: Because you aren't here!

TRACY: *(Momentarily shocked by the outburst.)* Well then call me, tell me to come down.

MOM: Yeah right.

TRACY: You're my mom, I listen to you.

MOM: I know you and your brother think I need babysitting now, but I don't…

TRACY: I know.

MOM: *(Continuous.)* …And I can't keep straight all the time…

TRACY: *(Overlapping.)* Look, it's okay.

MOM: …whether I'm excited you are here or mad that you haven't been up till now.

TRACY: Mom, what do you want from me?

MOM: I don't want to be alone with this!

TRACY: Oh, Mom…

MOM: Look, stop that right now. *(Beat.)* You don't know what it's like being by yourself when things start to…

TRACY: Okay, Mom, okay… What can I do to help?

MOM: I need you to let me make my own decisions.

TRACY: Mom…

MOM: I know, I know… And I will *try* to let you give me advice.

TRACY: Mom, we can't have you in a situation where you can't take care of yourself, or you might cause an accident or hurt someone…

MOM: I'm not an invalid. I am not a child!

TRACY: I know that, I know. But you have to let me take care of you…

MOM: *(Talking over her.)* I can take care of…

TRACY: Mom! Stop! I don't want to hear this argument anymore. You aren't a child, fine! Stop acting like a stubborn three-year-old. *(Beat.)*

MOM: *(Casually.)* Well if you're going to be like that about it...

TRACY: *(Taken aback, laughs in spite herself.)* Mom...Look, I'm sorry. For not being here more. I think I need to get my bearings again. And part of that is making sure that you're okay.

MOM: Why be sorry? You couldn't have done anything different back then.

TRACY: I don't know...something.

MOM: And what...not have Shawn? Not be successful in your career...

TRACY: Well, the jury's still out on that one...

MOM: *(Sharp.)* Stop that. *(Beat.)* Do something about it now. Be different now. Be here. Be present. *(Beat.)*

TRACY: *(Quietly.)* Okay. I can do that.

(Beat. SAM enters, with SCOTTO in tow.)

SAM: Taking in the sights?

MOM: Well look who it is...

TRACY: Hey...what are you doing here?

SAM: Well you mentioned coming down here in the mornings, so I figured I'd see what all the fuss was about...

TRACY: Oh 'cuz you've never been here before?

SAM: Well me, sure...but Scotto doesn't get out much. *(To MOM.)* Hey Mrs. B., good to see you. You remember Scotto, right?

MOM: Sure, the guy from the liquor store.

SCOTTO: My reputation precedes me.

(TRACY goes to SCOTTO and hugs him.)

TRACY: It's been a long time, sweetheart.

SCOTTO: Yeah, you too. You look good.

TRACY: So do you.

SCOTTO: Well, you know...body by Pilates.

TRACY: Really?

SCOTTO: Oh sure.

(TRACY laughs.)

SAM: So, you wanna get some coffee at Boccelli's?

TRACY: Wow, haven't been there in a while. Mom, would that be okay?

MOM: Large, light, and sweet.

TRACY: I'll take that as a yes. Be back in a few minutes.

(SAM and TRACY walk down the boardwalk. SCOTTO sits with TRACY'S MOM.)

MOM: Liquor store closed this morning?

SCOTTO: Yeah, we don't open till eleven a.m. Anybody who needs booze before that is shit out of luck in this town.

MOM: I'm glad your father's not selling. He's doing the right thing.

SCOTTO: I dunno, he's giving up a lot of money.

MOM: Sometimes there are things bigger than money! They tear up this, they tear up that, and then one day you don't know where you are or how you got here. Your dad is a good man.

SCOTTO: Yeah, maybe. Sometimes when you're his kid it's hard to tell.

(Beat.)

MOM: Seeing Tracy and Sam together again makes me feel old. Where does the time go? *(Beat.)* Is he okay?

SCOTTO: Yeah, sure. *(Beat.)* No, not really. How'd you know?

MOM: I'm a mother, genius.

SCOTTO: Right. How's she doin'?

MOM: Oh, she's fine.

(Beat.)

SCOTTO: Look, why don't we 'fess up…I mean, what do you think…these two? Now?

MOM: Who knows, Albert, she's always done things her own way, just like you. If she's in desperate need of a fling, fine…

SCOTTO: It's Scotto, actually…

MOM: But she certainly doesn't have to stay here for me, I can take care of myself. I keep saying it and saying it…

SCOTTO: Yeah, uh…didn't she come here 'cuz you fell? Sam said something…

MOM: So now it's all over town?

SCOTTO: No no no, just…

MOM: The talk of all the degenerates at the liquor store?

SCOTTO: Whoa, nothing like that…fuck.

MOM: Uh huh. Kiss your mother with that mouth?

SCOTTO: Occasionally yes. When she's not ragging on me.

MOM: Sure, what's not to rag on…working in a liquor store, staring forty in the face…

SCOTTO: Well, my girlfriend is having a baby.

MOM: How nice. Is it yours? *(Beat.)*

SCOTTO: Actually…I don't think so.

MOM: Oh. *(Beat.)* I'm sorry to hear that.

SCOTTO: Yeah, well…what can you do. *(Beat.)* She started having "nights out with the girls" every week, and every time she came home she was defensive and…different. She was acting kind of…Back then we were going through a rough stretch, and we weren't doing it all that much.

MOM: Look…

SCOTTO: And then, she's pregnant. And so I was like, okay.

MOM: That's all you said?

SCOTTO: What else is there? *(Beat. Gets up, looking out toward the water.)* I dunno, maybe I should get out of here too, I mean, what am I staying around for? Fatherhood? I mean…

MOM: Alright look, sit down.

(SCOTTO sits with her again.)

MOM: I used to know a girl who got knocked up one time by accident, tried telling her boyfriend it must be another immaculate conception and that she was carrying Jesus. Said boyfriend, who she had not slept with yet, didn't really buy it. Do you remember that, Albert?

SCOTTO: Albert? What's with Albert?

MOM: She had to go away for a while, missed the whole second term our sophomore year. And then she just came back like nothing had happened. It was quite the scandal. Mom always told us not to say anything about it to her, she said we weren't supposed to draw attention to another person's flaws in polite society. Do you remember?

SCOTTO: Uh...listen, I don't know what to do here... *(He stands up and looks out toward Boccelli's.)*

MOM: *(Coming out of it.)* What are we talking about?

SCOTTO: You were telling me about...

MOM: Oh shit...oh shit, oh shit...

SCOTTO: It's okay...

MOM: *(Frustrated.)* No it's not.

SCOTTO: Look, is there anything I can...

MOM: Stop it! I don't want anyone's pity. *(Beat.)* Now look, you can't leave town, you have a baby on the way.

SCOTTO: Do I?

MOM: *(Looks at him a moment.)* Oh, Jesus Christ, not you too.

SCOTTO: What?

MOM: Another man who thinks he'll be happier somewhere else, when he's got everything in front of him, the world at his feet.

SCOTTO: Look, if you think that "world at your feet" is working at the family liquor store and trying to support this baby...

MOM: You've got a family, you've got a job, you've got friends...not sure what you could be looking for.

SCOTTO: What about adventure? What about freedom? No, maybe Sam's got the right idea.

MOM: What?

SCOTTO: You know, open road, wind in your hair...more open road...world's biggest ball of twine, I dunno, something...

MOM: Sam's thinking of leaving?

SCOTTO: Sure, didn't she tell you? He was gassing up to leave town when he ran into her.

MOM: No, she didn't tell me.

SCOTTO: Yeah. *(Beat.)* Uh...you okay?

MOM: Jesus, yes I'm fine. I wish people would stop asking me! And whatever you think happened here, you take that to your grave with you, you hear me? Not a word of this.

SCOTTO: Do you think that is smart, I mean...

MOM: I didn't ask you if it was smart, did I?

SCOTTO: No, no but I really think...

MOM: Enough, not another word! Understand?

(He seems unsure.)

MOM: Please.

(Cross-fade to SAM and TRACY down the boardwalk a little.)

SAM: So, you staying here a little while longer?

TRACY: I think so. Chris and I still have things to talk over about Mom, what we're gonna do.

SAM: She seems pretty good.

TRACY: She does. She has her good days. But she's still a pain in the ass every day. *(Laughs.)*

SAM: Who isn't? *(Smiles.)* Still thinking about moving her in with you?

TRACY: I don't think she'll go for it.

SAM: So…then are you…?

TRACY: Maybe. We'll see. *(Beat.)* You seem mighty curious about it.

SAM: What can I say, I'm interested. And Shawn?

TRACY: Yeah, I need to solve that somehow… *(Beat.)* At least I know I'll be here for a few more days.

(She looks at him and sees it in his eyes.)

TRACY: But you're not, are you?

SAM: No, I'm not.

TRACY: Sorry to hear that.

SAM: Look, Trace, I've been here a long time. Hell, I've worn tracks in the streets here. I gotta get out of here and figure out what to do with the rest of my life.

TRACY: Right *(Beat.)* Any chance you want to change your mind and stick it out a few more days? *(Beat.)*

SAM: *(He tries to lighten it.)* And stay on Scotto's couch? Yeah, no thank you. I think Terri has started "nesting" with him, and I'm a little in the way.

TRACY: *(She smiles.)* That's funny, I can't imagine Scotto "nesting."

SAM: Then "housebreaking," if you prefer.

TRACY: Right.

(Beat.)

SAM: Look, I'm sorry about last night.

TRACY: Nothing to apologize for, really…I'm sorry too. I said some dumb things.

SAM: No, you were great.

(Beat.)

TRACY: I'm sorry, Sam.

SAM: For what?

TRACY: For ending it, before.

SAM: Twenty years ago?

TRACY: Yeah. Rationally I know it makes no sense, but maybe you need to hear me say I'm sorry.

SAM: *(Small beat.)* Nothing to be sorry for. You didn't need me holding you back. But hell, we were kids, we didn't know what we were doing.

TRACY: Right. You just kind of go by feel, you don't think. It's almost like it's all reaction.

SAM: Funny, now all I do is think. And think. And overthink.

(TRACY smiles.)

SAM: We just had some bad timing. Good stuff at the wrong time.

TRACY: Yeah *(Beat.)* Annnyway…

SAM: Hey, will you do something for me? If you are going to be here a little while, would you go buy a bottle of booze every once in a while? Just check in on him, make sure he's not losing his mind. And plus, the store isn't very busy offseason, so they could use the sales.

TRACY: Sure. With Mom, I have a feeling I'll be needing a drink every once in a while. *(Beat.)* So what's your plan?

SAM: No plan is the…

TRACY: Yeah okay, cut it out…

SAM: Well, I figure I'll see the sights, maybe get a new outlook on life, eat as much Waffle House and Chik-Fil-A as possible…

TRACY: And come back this way?

SAM: Who knows.

TRACY: So just start a new life? Try to forget this whole thing ever existed…

SAM: No no, how could I ever do that?

TRACY: *(Over him.)* So then what?

SAM: I'm looking for a new set of possibilities, Trace. And I think maybe you are too.

TRACY: Maybe. *(Beat.)* I feel like I want to make time stop, just for a minute.

SAM: You always did, as I recall.

TRACY: Always has been my Achilles heel…wanting to stay in the moment longer than I should.

SAM: Right. *(Beat.)* Well look, I'm reachable if your mom needs anything or Scotto loses his shit, or…

TRACY: What about if I need something?

SAM: Well, yeah, sure. *(Beat.)* You understand, right, that I'm not the same guy as when we were together? If I thought us together would be the best thing right now, I'd toss my car keys into the ocean.

TRACY: Right.

(He smiles at her, the smile only SAM could give her, and that only TRACY would accept.)

SAM: Let me give you my email address *(Pulls out his worn little pad and goes for a piece of paper, which has the coupon from earlier in it.)*

TRACY: Is that my writing?

SAM: Oh…uh, yeah.

(TRACY takes it from him.)

TRACY: You kept this? For twenty years? "Always remember I love you and believe in you, no matter what."

SAM: It was a reminder of some very good times. And sometimes I needed that.

(Beat.)

TRACY: Okay.

(She hands it back to him, takes a step down the boardwalk to hide how moved she is. SAM puts it away, watches her.)

TRACY: Part of me would like to remind you that I don't think you ever redeemed the coupon.

SAM: Oh, I know. *(Smiles.)* I'm saving it up, it's aging like a fine wine. 'Cause you know, teenage love notes are binding contracts.

TRACY: *(Comes back, his humor breaks her sadness.)* Is that right?

SAM: Oh, totally. Saw it on *Law and Order*. Sam Waterston got a hummer from a seventy-year-old woman with cataracts…it was a great episode.

TRACY: Okay, stop, enough. My mother's sitting right back there with Scotto…

SAM: Whoa, you aren't suggesting that Scotto and your mother are getting it on?

TRACY: Please for the love of god…

SAM: I'm just saying…your mom is still a looker, so if he's railing her in the car when we get back…I hope her hip is okay is all I'm saying.

TRACY: Will you still be able to drive after I kick your ass?

SAM: Okay, okay, okay…I'm done.

TRACY: Good. *(Deep breath.)* So...you're all packed and everything?

SAM: *(Smiles at her.)* Been packed.

TRACY: *(Smiles.)* Right, of course.

SAM: It's important for me that you know something...I'm not leaving because of you. You didn't do anything wrong here, okay. I just wanted you to hear that. I was leaving before I ran into you. Fresh start.

TRACY: You still believe in those, huh?

SAM: Yeah, maybe. You don't?

TRACY: I wonder if there really ever is a fresh start...And maybe that's why being here, being back...

SAM: I know.

(Beat.)

SAM: I could stand here talking to you all morning, but I've got some places to be.

TRACY: I know.

(She takes his hand.)

TRACY: C'mon, let's get you some coffee for the road.

(YOUNG SAM and YOUNG TRACY enter or come up, sitting in his car. SAM and TRACY know how that scene ends, and cannot look at it very long until finally they exit. YOUNG SAM and YOUNG TRACY remain and begin the scene. They're wearing heavier clothes; it's November and gray.)

YOUNG TRACY: Why are you being like this?

YOUNG SAM: Like what? It's a crime to want to see you?

YOUNG TRACY: No, but you're being so possessive and weird.

YOUNG SAM: Okay. *(Beat.)* Okay.

YOUNG TRACY: You know, it doesn't always have to be about what you want.

YOUNG SAM: What I want? God, how is it ever about what I want?

YOUNG TRACY: Oh don't start the whole "poor Sam" argument again. I can't take it. You stayed here. I get that that sucks a little. But it isn't my fault.

YOUNG SAM: I never said it was your fault. I just want you to need me in your life as much as you seem to need your friends at school and your sorority sisters and all of that.

YOUNG TRACY: And I need you to give me space.

YOUNG SAM: Space? *(A little shocked.)*

YOUNG TRACY: Yes, space. You are familiar with the concept?

YOUNG SAM: Yes, I am familiar with the concept...I'm not an idiot just because I'm not in some big fancy college. I'm not an idiot. *(Beat.)*

YOUNG TRACY: I know you're not an idiot. I never said you...

YOUNG SAM: So how much "space" do you need?

YOUNG TRACY: I don't know, I just...I feel smothered.

YOUNG SAM: You feel smothered...great. How am I smothering you, I'm trying to keep us together.

YOUNG TRACY: I don't know, you just are! *(Beat.)* Are you coming up, ever?

YOUNG SAM: Look, you know it's hard for me to get away...with Pete on my ass at work, my dad, school...

YOUNG TRACY: I know, but I want you to meet my friends. Stop the excuses, you've got to try.

YOUNG SAM: I'm not trying? I have responsibilities. We can't all be like you.

YOUNG TRACY: What?

YOUNG SAM: You know what I mean, I have things here.

YOUNG TRACY: And I have things at school that are important to me too. Do you want to be a part of that?

YOUNG SAM: You know I do.

YOUNG TRACY: Actually, I don't think you do. I think you're threatened by that.

YOUNG SAM: Seriously?!

YOUNG TRACY: What am I supposed to think? You want me, but only on your terms. Here, with you.

YOUNG SAM: That's such crap.

YOUNG TRACY: C'mon Sam, come up to school…you'll see it's a great big awesome world out there, with tons of cool people…

YOUNG SAM: I know, but I like it here. I like you and me right here. There's no need for me to go running around, I've got what I need right here.

YOUNG TRACY: *(Simply.)* But I'm out there.

(Beat.)

YOUNG SAM: Why, why does everything have to be about change, and moving on, and…we're great, this summer was great, we can keep that…

YOUNG TRACY: Who wants to stop time now?

YOUNG SAM: *(Incredulous.)* What? C'mon, look…

(Beat. Beat.)

YOUNG TRACY: This sucks.

YOUNG SAM: I know.

YOUNG TRACY: Can you take me home please.

YOUNG SAM: What?

YOUNG TRACY: *(Beat.)* Can you take me home…please.

(YOUNG SAM looks at her. She can't face him. After a moment…)

YOUNG SAM: Sure.

(Cross-fade to SAM and TRACY entering with MOM and SCOTTO sitting on the bench. They carry cups of coffee for MOM and SCOTTO in a tray.)

TRACY: Who wants coffee?

SCOTTO: You got an extra one there for me?

SAM: Yep. You heading to work?

SCOTTO: Soon. Pop can wait a few minutes for me. *(Beat.)* Trace, can I talk to you a sec?

TRACY: Sure.

(TRACY and SCOTTO pull off stage right and chat, silently. We can see that SCOTTO is filling TRACY in on her MOM's lapse in memory. MOM sees him talking to her.)

SAM: Boccelli's always made the best coffee on the boardwalk.

MOM: You going to miss it when you go, Sam?

SAM: You know about that, huh?

MOM: You can come home again, you know.

SAM: I know.

MOM: There's a lot of good here. There's no need to throw everything over if you can be happy here.

SAM: I know. *(Beat.)* Grass is always greener, right?

MOM: *(Beat. She looks at him.)* Take good care of yourself.

(SCOTTO and TRACY return. We see a look of concern on TRACY's face as she sits next to MOM.)

SCOTTO: Alright, now that I have coffee, I am able to go to work. You leaving right from here?

SAM: Think so.

SCOTTO: So we hugging it out again?

SAM: You know it.

SCOTTO: You going to grab *my* ass this time?

SAM: Well, there are ladies present…

SCOTTO: Right, which makes grabbing my cock inappropriate.

SAM: Thanks for keeping this classy.

(They hug.)

SCOTTO: Alright buddy, last chance to take me with you…going once, going twice…wow, big mistake, but okay. *(Beat.)* Be well. Remember, if you come back this way and you need a place to crash…this town is chock full of motels. *(Beat.)* Bye Trace, Mrs. B.

(MOM doesn't respond to him.)

TRACY: See you.

(SCOTTO exits.)

TRACY: Mom, are you ready?

MOM: I'm going to the car. I'm a little cold.

TRACY: Uh, are you sure? Is your hip bothering you, you want a hand?

MOM: Stop fussing, I'm leaving you alone with him. Take a hint. *(Beat.)* I know I'll see you soon, Sam.

(MOM goes off. TRACY watches her get to the car.)

SAM: Still a piece of work.

TRACY: Yeah. *(Beat.)* I can't believe you're just leaving.

SAM: I know. And you're staying.

(A beat without words, but full.)

SAM: Well, alright…

TRACY: Sam.

SAM: Yeah?

TRACY: You need to go.

SAM: Yeah, I do.

TRACY: I am behind that one hundred percent. This place will always be here.

SAM: Right.

TRACY: And we'll always have all that other stuff. It's not leaving us. Maybe the best thing we can do to keep those days alive is to be happy like that again, at some point.

SAM: You believe that?

TRACY: I think I do.

SAM: When'd you figure this out?

TRACY: See what happens when you buy me coffee? *(Smiles.)*

SAM: Ughh why didn't I know that before, our whole lives would be different. *(Smiles.)*

(Beat.)

TRACY: And thank god for gas stations, huh? I mean, if we had solar power...

SAM: Right, we'd never have...

TRACY: Right.

(Beat.)

SAM: So did I mention a horse walks into a bar...

TRACY: Heard it.

SAM: Right. How about the mushroom who says "I'm a frayed knot."

TRACY: Okay, you are nearly incoherent now.

SAM: Alright, how about "Interrupting Cow"...

TRACY: *(Not looking at him.)* Okay, okay, just stop.

SAM: *(Beat.)* I don't want to stop. *(Beat.)* We got really lucky when we were kids, you know. You, me, at the beach... I mean... I mean, I...

TRACY: Me too.

(She kisses him lightly on the mouth.)

SAM: Bye.

TRACY: Bye.

(SAM exits. TRACY stands for a moment, watching and waving as he drives off. She looks to where MOM is waiting in the car, sees she is fine. She takes a moment to gather herself, looking at the wooden slats and pipe railings. From the side of the stage, YOUNG SAM and YOUNG TRACY enter. TRACY watches them.

SAM enters from the other side, watching YOUNG SAM and YOUNG TRACY. SAM and TRACY don't see each other, only the memory of their younger selves. SAM and TRACY remember various parts of the relationship—a swirl of the beginning, the end. It is a cacophony of sound, as they watch their different memories of this play out together. Lines overlap.)

YOUNG TRACY: Why are you being like this?

YOUNG SAM: Hey, hold on a minute... can't we just lay here for a minute?

YOUNG TRACY: You're being so possessive and weird.

YOUNG SAM: There are these things called beds... people seem to really like them.

YOUNG TRACY: I need you to give me space... I feel smothered.

YOUNG SAM: I love you. I love you.

YOUNG TRACY: I love you too.

YOUNG SAM: It's a crime to want to see you?

YOUNG TRACY: Mmm. Because I missed you and because you are cute.

YOUNG SAM: It's weird, right? Let's not be weird.

YOUNG TRACY: It's not too late, you can come with me tomorrow, enroll for classes...

YOUNG SAM: A picture from the fourth of July... that was the best day.

YOUNG TRACY: I love you too...

YOUNG SAM: I love you. I love you very much.

YOUNG TRACY: I want to stop time.

YOUNG SAM: I miss you too.

YOUNG TRACY: Oh don't start the whole "poor Sam" argument again. I can't take it.

YOUNG SAM: I just want you to need me in your life as much as you seem to need your friends at school.

YOUNG TRACY: This sucks.

YOUNG SAM: Hey, hold on a minute…can't we just lay here for a minute?

YOUNG TRACY: I love you too…

YOUNG SAM: we can't all be like you.

(Beat.)

YOUNG TRACY: This sucks.

YOUNG SAM: I know.

YOUNG TRACY: This sucks.

YOUNG SAM: I know.

YOUNG TRACY: Can you take me home please.

YOUNG SAM: Can you take me home please.

YOUNG TRACY: Can you take me home please.

YOUNG SAM: Sure.

(SAM exits. Lights fade on YOUNG SAM and YOUNG TRACY. TRACY takes out her cell phone.)

TRACY: *(Into the phone.)* Ray, hey it's me. Can you put Shawn on? *(Beat.)* You know, I'm not really interested in your version of things, I'd like to talk to my son please. *(Beat. TRACY's trying to keep her emotions in check, but it's a struggle.)* Ray, I'm very calm and I'm going to ask you one more…Thank you. *(Beat.)* Hey buddy, it's Mom. How are you?

(Blackout.)

ABOUT THE EDITOR

MARTIN DENTON is the founder and Executive Director of The New York Theatre Experience, Inc. (NYTE) and editor and chief theatre reviewer for NYTE's website nytheatre.com. He has edited all the play anthologies published by NYTE Small Press featuring, to date, the work of 165 emerging playwrights. He is also the creator of the nytheatrecast (www.nytheatrecast.com), New York City's first theatre podcast offering original content.

ABOUT THE PUBLISHER

THE NEW YORK THEATRE EXPERIENCE, INC., is a nonprofit New York State corporation. Its mission is to use traditional and new media to foster interest, engagement, and participation in theatre and drama and to provide tangible support to theatre artists and dramatists, especially emerging artists and artists in the nonprofit sector. The principal activity of The New York Theatre Experience is the operation of a free website (www.nytheatre.com) that comprehensively covers the New York theatre scene—on, off-, and off-off-Broadway. An ongoing program is NYTE Small Press, which publishes yearly anthologies of new plays by emerging playwrights. Information about NYTE can be found on the Internet at www.nyte.org. Contact NYTE online at info@nyte.org or by mail at: The New York Theatre Experience, Inc., P.O. Box 1606, Murray Hill Station, New York, NY 10156.

ABOUT THE SERIES

The *Plays and Playwrights* series is a yearly anthology of plays by emerging playwrights whose work received a production in New York City in the previous theatre season. Since 2000, NYTE has published these anthologies, which include complete scripts, biographical sketches, and a detailed introduction by the editor, Martin Denton. In 2004, the Library of Congress designated these anthologies a series. NYTE is a nonprofit corporation that utilizes its small press to promote the works of emerging playwrights so as to reach a wide audience to show the diverse spirit of contemporary theatre, in terms of genre, form, and subject matter. For complete information about these volumes, please visit www.nytesmallpress.com.

ALSO AVAILABLE AS AN EBOOK

This book is available as an ebook in Amazon.com's Kindle Store and Barnes & Noble's Nook Store. Watch for the entire *Plays and Playwrights* series, scheduled for release in 2011 and 2012. This allows a new audience to become acquainted with this popular series and to make use of the plays included for production, readings, monologues, audition material, and much more.

main

FEB 22 2012

WITHDRAWN

PORTLAND PUBLIC LIBRARY SYSTEM
5 MONUMENT SQUARE
PORTLAND, ME 04101

02/10/2012 $19.00